Critical Perspectives on Latino Education in Massachusetts

CRITICAL PERSPECTIVES ON LATINO EDUCATION IN MASSACHUSETTS

EDITED BY
Lorna Rivera AND
Melissa Colón

University of Massachusetts Press
AMHERST AND BOSTON

ISBN 978-1-62534-866-1 (paper); 867-8 (hardcover)

Designed by Deste Relyea
Set in Minion Pro and Monotype Grotesque

Cover design by adam b. bohannon
Cover art by Marcos Casados, *College Corridor.* Adobe Stock #836751122.

Library of Congress Cataloging-in-Publication Data

Names: Rivera, Lorna editor | Colón, Melissa, 1977– editor
Title: Critical perspectives on Latino education in Massachusetts / Lorna
    Rivera and Melissa Colón, Editors.
Description: Amherst : University of Massachusetts Press, [2025] | Includes
    bibliographical references and index. |
Identifiers: LCCN 2024047434 (print) | LCCN 2024047435 (ebook) | ISBN
    9781625348661 paperback | ISBN 9781625348678 hardcover | ISBN
    9781685751463 ebook | ISBN 9781685751470 epub
Subjects: LCSH: Hispanic Americans—Education—Massachusetts |
    Multicultural education—Massachusetts | Public schools—Massachusetts |
    Hispanic Americans—Social conditions—Massachusetts | Emigration and
    immigration—Government policy—United States | Boston (Mass.)—Ethnic
    relations—History
Classification: LCC LC2674.M4 C75 2025 (print) | LCC LC2674.M4 (ebook) |
    DDC 371.829/9680744—dc23/eng/20250528
LC record available at https://lccn.loc.gov/2024047434
LC ebook record available at https://lccn.loc.gov/2024047435

British Library Cataloguing-in-Publication Data
A catalog record for this book is available from the British Library.

We dedicate this book to Kobi, Enrique, and Inez. Their wisdom and joyfulness are constant reminders of the gifts of our ancestors, the preciousness of childhood, and the eternal hope we share for a beautiful world that they and other children will surely help build. A world where we can all be free.

Table of Contents

Part II 85
Reimagining a New Latino Education Policy Praxis

Chapter Five 87
From Culturally Sustaining Classrooms to Culturally Sustaining Campuses
A Call to Action for Hispanic-Serving Institutions
LIYA ESCALERA

Chapter Six 112
The Consequences of Assessing English Learners in a Restrictive and Subtractive Learning Environment
MICHAEL BERARDINO

Chapter Seven 140
A Chance to Compete in Today's America?
Considerations of Academic Performance, Exclusionary Discipline, and Belonging of Latinx Students in Worcester Public Schools
THOMAS E. CONROY, ALEX BRIESACHER, MARY JO MARION, AND TIMOTHY MURPHY

Chapter Eight 165
"You Are One of Us, Miss"
Autobiographical (Re)calling of Critical Cariño Cuentos, Conocimientos, y Consejos in a College Access Program
CARMEN N. VELORIA

Chapter Nine 183
Early Education and Beyond: Centering Latino Children and Families in Policymaking
MARTA ROSA

Part III 197
Culturally Sustaining Student-Centered Practices and Programs

Chapter Ten 199
Student Community-Engaged Policy Research for Transformative Educational Success
ASHLEY TORRES CARRASQUILLO, ESTER R. SHAPIRO, AND LORNA RIVERA

List of Illustrations

Acknowledgments

On the desks and bookshelves of many who care deeply about the future of Latine children and families in Massachusetts is a well-used little blue book with many dog-ears and notes on the margins. Published in 1993, *The Education of Latino Students in Massachusetts: Issues, Research, and Policy Implications* (edited by Ralph Rivera and Sonia Nieto) has been a foundational text that has helped us to contextualize the educational experiences and outcomes of students in the Commonwealth of Massachusetts. To honor its thirtieth anniversary, our goal was to revisit this important book and critically examine the issues, questions, and complexities that shape Latino education in Massachusetts today. We began this project with a call for proposals about Latino education and are grateful that we received many great submissions from well-respected scholars, community leaders, educators, and students who are beginning their research journeys.

It has been hard work and a rewarding experience to put together this volume of so many different authors across the spectrum of education researchers and practitioners. While working on this book, we were contending with ongoing multiple crises impacting our Latine communities, including the devasting impact of COVID-19, so it took *mucha esperanza y comunidad* to produce this book. We are deeply grateful to all the contributing authors who made this project possible and who believed in our vision. We also wish to thank our colleagues and students in the Leadership in Education Department of the College of Education and Human Department, the Gastón Institute, and the Latino Studies Program at the University of Massachusetts Boston for all their support. We are grateful to and inspired by our colleagues from PEAS (In Pursuit of Equity, Accountability, and Success), the Latinx Student Success Initiative at Bunker Hill Community College, Sociedad Latina, and local public school partners who encouraged us each step of the way. Jim O'Brien, Michael Berardino, Gloria Lopez, and Ester Shapiro were instrumental in our editing and revision process. *Muchas gracias!* We also want to convey our deepest gratitude to current and past researchers and scholars of the Gastón Institute, whose work we have learned from and cited in this book, and to Brian Halley, executive editor at UMass Press, who guided us through this process.

Finally, *mil gracias* to our families, friends, mentors, and loved ones who encouraged us to keep going with this project. Lorna has special thanks to Paco, Aida, Lety, Yvette Rivera, and Tara and Nikki Parker. Melissa thanks Herb Polack, Miguel Colón, Celeste Gutiérrez, and the BC crew for their enduring support.

Critical Perspectives on Latino Education in Massachusetts

Introduction

Setting the Context of Latino Education in Massachusetts

MELISSA COLÓN AND LORNA RIVERA

Massachusetts is the home to many Indigenous nations, including the Massachusett, Wampanoag, Pawtucket, Nipmuc, Narragansett, Nauset, Pennacook, and Pocumtuck.[1] For centuries, before the arrival of European settler colonialism and the genocide that proceeded it, Indigenous tribes across what would later be known as the United States developed systems for educating children and youth that included the preservation of ancestral knowledge; practical skills like hunting, healing, architecture, and construction;, the navigation of mountains, forests, rivers, and oceans; and spiritual and moral education.[2] These ways of teaching and learning were the first universal schooling systems in the lands that today we call Massachusetts.

Yet many mark the beginning of public education in these lands, and in the US, writ large, as starting on April 23, 1635, when the Boston Latin School opened its doors, becoming the first public school in the nation. This event would be the first of many milestones steering the Commonwealth of Massachusetts to become a leader in education. In 1837, for example, Horace Mann, who later became known as "The Father of American Education,"[3] was sworn in as the state's first secretary of education. Under his stewardship and with the support of many educators, significant reforms were implemented that ultimately shaped the development of organized public education systems in Massachusetts, and across the United States. Massachusetts was also the first state to establish teacher preparation programs (1839) and the first state to pass compulsory public education laws that required all children to attend school (1852). Private higher education also began in Massachusetts with Harvard University (1636), followed by numerous specialized and well-respected institutions of higher learning to prepare residents for a rapidly changing economy.[4]

More recently, publicly funded transitional bilingual education (1971) and the right to free and appropriate public education for children with disabilities (1972) also began in Massachusetts. Preceding the No Child Left Behind Act of 2002, in 1993, the Massachusetts Legislature passed the Massachusetts Education Reform Act, which aimed to implement rigorous academic and accountability systems, including high-stakes standardized student testing, to track student achievement.[5]

Given its educational history, and long-term public investments in education, it is not surprising that today Massachusetts K-12 public school students consistently have some of the highest achievement rates across many metrics, including literacy, high school graduation, and college enrollment.[6] Further, each year hundreds of thousands of students from across the US and the globe come to Massachusetts to attend some of the world's most prestigious colleges and universities. Consequently, the Commonwealth reaps the benefits of a robust knowledge-based economy and positions itself as an international destination and leader in teaching, learning, research, and innovation. But just beneath the surface of Massachusetts's lauded education prowess, there is another more troubling reality.

The land theft and genocide that preceded European colonialism also included systematic deculturalization strategies, including the dismantling of traditional knowledge systems, and the purposeful exclusion of Indigenous people from colonial public schooling.[7] Enslaved Africans who were trafficked and forced to labor in these lands as well as their descendants also faced inhumane conditions, deculturalization practices, and legalized exclusion. It was not until 1855, 250 years after the first public school opened in Massachusetts, that the legislature passed the Massachusetts General School Act of 1855, which officially banned racial segregation in public schools, a direct result of decades of organizing by Black leaders and Abolitionists.[8] Policies, however, often do not change practices and customs. As such, de facto racial and economic segregation has persisted in Massachusetts public schools. This too is part of the Commonwealth's education history and serves as a backdrop for understanding contemporary patterns of achievement and exclusion. Presently, while Massachusetts has some of the highest educational outcomes in the US, the Commonwealth also has some of the largest educational opportunity gaps, and these gaps are tied to questions of race, citizenship, and exclusion.[9] As a result, schools have often been at the center of struggles for equality.[10]

This book focuses on the educational experiences of one student group that has been at the forefront of those struggles: Latino students. One in four Massachusetts public school students is of Latin American descent,[11] making Latino students the second largest racial-ethnic student group, second only to White students. To many, the large number of Latino students, and Latino communities in general, in Massachusetts is surprising given that New England has historically been one of the least racially diverse areas of the US.[12] Yet, contrary to dominant narratives, the prevalence of Latino students in the Commonwealth is *not* a new phenomenon.

Setting the Context

Massachusetts has been the home of Diasporic Latino communities for more than a century. The first Latino communities in Massachusetts were largely Puerto Rican migrants, who arrived during the early twentieth century seeking economic opportunities and stability; this was a direct result of colonial practices in Puerto Rico following the US assumption of control after the 1898 Spanish-American War. The colonization of Puerto Rico by the US continues to shape migration to and from Puerto Rico to Massachusetts. Massachusetts also has a long history of immigrants from other parts of the Caribbean and Latin America. Cubans began to settle in the Commonwealth between 1963 and 1968 during the Cuban Revolution. By 1970, Cubans were the second largest Latino group in Massachusetts, second only to Puerto Ricans.[13] Significant Dominican migration to the Northeast of the US, including Massachusetts, also began in the 1960s, when changes in US immigration policy paired with economic and political turmoil in the Dominican Republic made it easier and possible for Dominicans to migrate.[14] Today, Dominicans are the second largest Latino origins group in Massachusetts; the state also benefits from having the fourth-largest Dominican community in the US.[15]

Beginning in the late seventies, a substantial number of Central American immigrants, largely from El Salvador, Guatemala, and Honduras, began arriving in Massachusetts. This migration included many refugees who were escaping the civil war, political violence and repression, and difficult socioeconomic conditions in their homelands.[16] Most Central Americans and their descendants, like previous waves of (im)migrants, built thriving communities in the Greater Boston areas, including in the cities of Somerville and Chelsea. Beginning in the 1990s, Brazilian immigrants began to settle in Massachusetts. Differing from other Latin American origin immigrant groups, Brazilians largely reside in suburban communities like Framingham and Cape Cod and the Islands.[17]

Important to note is the varying waves of (im)migration have a relationship with US colonial and imperial political and economic interventions in Latin America and the Caribbean. Further, the diversity of Massachusetts's Latino population expands well beyond national origins. Latinos in Massachusetts also represent a wide range of racialized identities, (im)migration statuses, time in the US, socioeconomic and educational statuses, religious traditions, political affiliations, and languages spoken, just to name a few. For example, Massachusetts is the home to one of the largest and growing Afro-Latino communities in the nation, most of whom are Afro-Boricuas and Afro-Dominicans.[18] These different social locations and identities within and across varying Latino groups have shaped how life in Massachusetts was and is experienced.

By the late 1980s, the Latino community landscape in Massachusetts would soon include people from every corner of Latin America, and by the 1990s, Latinos became the largest minoritized non-White ethnoracial group in the state. This population shift is naturally reflected in the demographics of school districts across the state. By 2023, one in four public school students is Latino. Despite their long history in Massachusetts, however, Latino students in the state have not had access to the educational opportunities for which Massachusetts is famous for. As early as the late 1950s and continuing to the present day, Latino parents, community members, and their allies have raised concerns about the quality of education that their children experience. They have identified systemic barriers that impede their children's education such as low-quality instruction, unsafe schools, inadequate or no bilingual educational opportunities, racial segregation, and discriminatory and hostile learning environments.[19] There is a noteworthy history of Latino parents joining and leading local, statewide, and national movements to reform schools.[20] Despite many successes and some changes in federal and state policies to protect their rights, Latino students and families continue to experience discrimination. As such, *la lucha* to protect the rights and dignity of Latino children, youth, families, and communities, continues.

Thirty years ago, in response to persistent concerns about the experiences and outcomes of Latino students in Massachusetts public schools, the

Gastón Institute for Latino Community Development and Public Policy, a research institute of the University of Massachusetts Boston, published the book, *The Education of Latino Students in Massachusetts: Issues, Research, and Policy Implications*.[21] Edited by Dr. Ralph Rivera and Dr. Sonia Nieto, the book, published in 1993, was the first comprehensive examination of the issues affecting Latino students in the Commonwealth. The contributing authors discussed their research on educational outcomes, bilingual education, graduation trajectories, vocational education, privatization, resilience, and best practices for engaging Latino students and families. Collectively, the authors called for the rejection of deficit-based narratives and recommended swift changes in policies and practices to fully address the magnitude of challenges that Latino students and their families were facing in Massachusetts schools. In the book's conclusion, Nieto wrote, "The challenge for all the citizens and the educational system in Massachusetts is to decide that Latino students are capable and worthy of the best education and to develop approaches and the curricula that are based on that assumption. In the process, a shift in thinking must take place towards possibilities for academic success and away from blaming and academic failure."[22] In this book, we revisit the charge that Nieto and others placed before us and examine how Latino education in Massachusetts has shifted over the last three decades.

Looking at the publicly available data, one could simply conclude that there has been little or no change in the experiences of Latino students because this population continues to "underperform" in almost every metric that the state and federal governments have deemed important. But there is more to this story. As documented by the demographers at the Gastón Institute, Massachusetts has seen dramatic changes in the size, composition, and dispersion of the Latino population. Today, there are close to one million Latinos in Massachusetts, a 400% increase over the last three decades, the largest growth of any of the four major ethnoracial groups in the Commonwealth.[23] In the 1990s, most Latino residents were concentrated in six major urban hubs: Boston, Chelsea, Holyoke, Lawrence, Springfield, and Worcester. Today, while Latinos continue to live in these historic Latino enclaves, there are thriving Latino communities in all regions of the state including the Berkshires, the Cape and Islands, and the suburbs. This is due in part to gentrification, displacement, and the rising costs of urban living. The Latino community is also increasingly more diverse. While Puerto

Ricans continue to be the largest subgroup of Latinos in Massachusetts, a steady increase of Dominicans, Brazilians, Salvadorans, Colombians, Guatemalans, and Hondurans has made the Massachusetts Latino community one of the most diverse in the US.

At the same time that the diversity and size of the Latino population of Massachusetts was increasing, the state's public education witnessed dramatic policy changes. As previously discussed, in 1993, the state passed the Massachusetts Education Reform Act, which was part of a national education reform movement that moved toward standards-based education built around standardized and high-stakes testing. These reforms have had dubious benefits for Latino students. For example, on the Massachusetts Comprehensive Assessment System, a statewide standardized testing program administered in all public schools, school districts with a high concentration of Latino students have the lowest outcomes on the Reading/English Language Arts and Mathematics tests as compared to all other ethnoracial populations.[24] This persistent underperformance is also reflected in Latino students' high school graduation and dropout rates.[25] Compared to other student groups in Massachusetts, Latino students also perform at the lowest levels on the National Assessment of Educational Progress exams (a congressionally mandated large-scale assessment) in reading and math.[26]

The Massachusetts Education Reform Act also established a test-based accountability system that imposed consequences on individual schools and school districts that do not meet adequate yearly progress on the Massachusetts Comprehensive Assessment System (MCAS). Through this accountability system, the Massachusetts Department of Elementary and Secondary Education has the authority to place chronically underperforming school districts into receivership. Through this process, the commissioner of education appoints a new district leader, the "receiver," who is granted the authority and powers of a superintendent and locally elected school committee.[27] The only school districts to have gone under receivership are Latino-majority school districts—Chelsea, Holyoke, Lawrence, and Southbridge.

Amid these standard-based reforms, the state also underwent drastic changes in bilingual education policies. In 2002, fueled by anti-immigrant sentiments, Massachusetts voters dismantled the nation's oldest state-mandated transitional bilingual education programs through a state referendum that mandated English-only instruction. The Gastón Institute's research on the outcomes for English learners (ELs), most of whom are Latino students, suggests that when Massachusetts voters outlawed bilingual education in 2002, the subsequent Sheltered English Immersion programs produced negative academic outcomes for ELs.[28] In sum, despite a myriad of educational reforms and innovations in educational programs and pedagogies for the past thirty years, Latino students are still likely to attend public schools in communities with significant academic achievement and opportunity gaps, poverty, and racial segregation and are less likely to be enrolled in bilingual programs that build on the linguistic strengths of the Latino community.

In this book, we center the complexities of these contexts for Latino students by critically examining the ideologies, policies, programs, and practices that shape educational experiences and outcomes and offer recommendations for advancing Latine education in Massachusetts. By bringing attention to these issues, our goal is to not only raise the visibility of Latine students in the Commonwealth but to also contribute to rigorous scholarship, policy, and practitioner dialogues that will shape the future of education in the nation with Latine students in mind. Across the fifteen chapters presented in this book, central to our inquiry is assessing whether we have moved away from deficit-based thinking toward an asset-based model of education that highlights the strengths that Latine students bring to school. Further, this book features a diverse group of transdisciplinary scholars who offer a comprehensive look at the current Latine educational landscape, covering the spectrum from early childhood to higher education to out-of-school time, and offer recommendations for changing policies and practices. What all the chapters share in common is a strengths-based approach that centers on the cultural wealth of Latine communities.

A NOTE ON TERMINOLOGY

We find it important to discuss and clarify a few terms that are used throughout this book. Given the vast diversity of experiences within and across Latino populations, coupled with entrenched racial-ethnic systems of social stratification reproduced by custom and code,[29] it is no surprise that there are long-standing debates regarding what is the best term to describe people living in the US who have ancestry from what today is referred to as Latin

America. For instance, in this chapter alone we use the terms *Latin American origin, Latino, Latinx, and Latine*, opting to use the terminology used by the authors whose work we are referencing. All of these terms, however, are highly politicized, historically (and geographically) situated, contested, and dynamic because their meaning and acceptance change over time.

In the 1990s, for example, national debates on the appropriate term to describe people of Latin American descent centered around the use of "Hispanic" versus "Latino." Others argued that it was impossible for one term to fully capture the vast cultural, racial, religious, economic, and social diversity of a large group of people that "cannot be defined."[30] However, as first described by sociologist Dr. Felix Padilla (1985), across the vast unique communities of Latin Americans and their descendants in the US, there are shared attributes and social experiences within, across, and between groups that define Latinidad[31] and it is these similarities that speak to the collective and potential social and political power of a pan-Latino identity.[32] This is of particular importance because not only are Latinos the largest minoritized group in the US, but before the even US existed as an independent nation, people from what today is described as Latin America significantly contributed to the culture, history, life, and development of this nation.[33] Further Latino communities in the US have, historically and continuously, been impacted by complex and intersecting systems of power and oppression, including settler colonialism, imperialism, racism, xenophobia, and heteropatriarchy (among others) that have shaped exclusionary and discriminatory policies and practices in the US and its social institutions, including schools.[34]

In the last decade the use of *Latinx*, and more recently *Latine* (or *Latiné*), both gender-neutral terms that "promote inclusivity in language,"[35] have also yielded much debate. While delineating the origins, nuances, and fierce and important differences of opinions regarding these "newer" terms, or more generally "the correct term," is outside the scope of this book,[36] the recent debates continue to amplify long-lasting questions about how we think, study, advocate, and, in our case, write about the vast diversity of identities, beliefs, and experiences of peoples who share deep cultural and ancestral connections to Latin America, present and past. This is further complicated by the fact that people benefit from being members of various social groups, and how individuals choose to best describe themselves and their various social identities and locations (i.e., Garifuna, Negra, Dominicano, Maya

K'iche, Latina) is often in conflict with how governmental and academic institutions define and use these terms, in research, policymaking, and resource allocation.[37] Recognizing the multiplicity of thought regarding these terms, in this book, we have purposefully chosen to not mandate the use of a singular term. Rather we encouraged the contributing authors to interrogate and contextualize these terms and to use the term they prefer. As such, in this book terms like *Latino, Latino, Latinx, Latine,* and even *Hispanic* are used.

ORGANIZATION OF THE BOOK

This book is divided into three parts: "Beyond the Latino Monolithic Myths,"[38] "Reimagining a New Latino Education Policy Praxis," and "Culturally Sustaining Student-Centered Practices and Programs." Each section offers empirical research, theoretical insights, and policy and program analysis, as well as *testimonios*, or first-hand accounts, written by leading educators who are on the ground leading the work to transform schooling in the Commonwealth. Together the research and *testimonios* offer important insights for educators, policymakers, families, and other thought leaders about what is necessary to dramatically improve the future of Latine education in the Commonwealth of Massachusetts.

Part I, "Beyond Latino Monolithic Myths," presents research that deepens our collective understanding of contemporary Latine education in Massachusetts. Specifically, these chapters focus on who are today's Latine students, the diversity of experiences within and across Latine student groups, and factors that impact schooling outcomes and success. We begin with "The State of Latino Education: 2010–2024" by Fabián Torres-Ardila, Nyal Fuentes, and Melissa Colón. This chapter provides a descriptive quantitative analysis of the main trends in Latino educational achievement. The authors offer a profile of Latino students and the school districts they attend, highlighting areas of significant educational progress as well as challenges that remain and/or are growing and how data and research can be used to improve strategic planning that responds to Latino educational outcomes. Their analysis clearly points to the fact that the future success of Massachusetts is tied to the success of its Latine population.

Part I continues with explorations of diversity with a focus on three groups: Brazilian, Puerto Rican, and Latine multilingual students with disabilities. In chapter 2, "Here Is What We Know About Brazilian Students in Massachusetts: Not Much," Cristina Araujo Brinkerhoff amplifies the Brazilian student experience. Massachusetts has the second largest Brazilian population in the US, and Brazilians are the third largest group of Latinos in the Commonwealth.[39] Yet despite their sizeable and growing number, limited research exists about Brazilian students. In this chapter, Araujo Brinkerhoff presents findings from the limited existing research, emphasizes the urgent need for attention and research on understanding this student population, and proposes a research and policy agenda to better understand and support the needs and strengths of Brazilian students and their families. She also discusses how community-based organizing and advocacy efforts led to the passage of the Tuition Equity Legislation (signed into law in 2023), which allows immigrant college students in Massachusetts, including undocumented students, to pay in-state tuition rates and access state financial aid if they attended high school in the Commonwealth.

In chapter 3, "Reflections on the State of Puerto Rican Students in Massachusetts Public Schools," Melissa Colón and Manuel Frau-Ramos present a contextual history of the largest Latino student group in Massachusetts: Puerto Rican students. Focusing on how colonization, migration, racialization, and activism have shaped their educational outcomes, they argue that the future of Latino education in the state is inherently tied to the educational experiences, engagements, and outcomes of Boricua students. The authors offer policy and practice recommendations that can facilitate educational success and equity not only for Puerto Rican students but for all students facing displacement and marginalization.

Part I finishes with a testimonio written by Diana Santiago, an attorney with Massachusetts Advocates for Children, a statewide organization that focuses on improving the lives of children and youth. There she directs Forward!~¡Adelante!~Avante!~展望!~Avanse!~ Tiến về phía trước!~ الدراسة في المقدمة~Horey!: Advancing the Education Rights of Immigrant and Multilingual Children. Entitled "¡Adelante! Avante!; Advancing the Education Rights of Multilingual Children with Disabilities" Santiago's testimonio (chapter 4) brings to light her journey in becoming a fierce advocate for the rights of Latino ELs with disabilities and the work that is yet to be done to support the strengths and needs of this student population.

Part II, "Reimagining a New Latino Education Policy Praxis," focuses on urgent and emergent policy approaches and frameworks that can reshape

Latine education in Massachusetts. chapter 5, "From Culturally Sustaining Classrooms to Culturally Sustaining Campuses: A Call to Action for Hispanic-Serving Institutions" by Liya Escalera, begins with a rich description of Latinx cultural wealth frameworks, which can serve as a basis for the development of culturally sustaining pedagogy and praxis. She then presents an empirical study of a Hispanic-serving institution, exploring how these concepts can be animated by instructors and schools to benefit Latinx student achievement, including in higher education settings. Escalera's research provides clear and compelling examples of how institutions that serve Latinx students can integrate culturally sustaining practices into their everyday work to improve teaching and learning.

In chapter 6, "The Consequences of Assessing English Learners in a Restrictive and Subtractive Learning Environment," Michael Berardino uses a quantitative policy analysis approach to trace the changes in state policies that have guided instruction and assessment of ELs from transitional bilingual education to English-only mandates, noting how these changes have contributed to the reproduction of restrictive and subtractive learning environments. This chapter concludes with a set of recommendations for the promotion of inclusive learning environments for English learning. Berardino's work brings attention to the important policy contexts in which Latino ELs, who comprise one-third of all Latino students in the Commonwealth, contend. Chapter 7, "A Chance to Compete in Today's America?: Considerations of Academic Performance, Exclusionary Discipline, and Belonging of Latinx Students in Worcester Public Schools," by Thomas Conroy, Alex Briesacher, Mary Jo Marion, and Timothy Murphy, examines the impact of racial and economic segregation on the education of Latinx students in New England's second-largest city, Worcester, Massachusetts. Using both qualitative and quantitative data, they present an in-depth historical and social analysis of the ethnoracial and economic challenges and opportunities that Latinx students and their families face in the public school system, highlighting interventions that emphasize belonging, engagement, and representation.

Turning to cocurricular contexts, in chapter 8, "'You Are One of Us, Miss': Autobiographical (Re)calling of Cariño, Cuentos y Consejos in a College Access Program," Carmen Veloria examines the political and ideological frameworks that shaped the development of a college access program for Latina teenagers and unpacks what it means to be positioned as "one of us." Veloria's chapter calls for more "critical caring" in the schooling lives of urban Latino youth and provides compelling examples of how "critical caring" can be operationalized by education to support Latino student success. Veloria's work also suggests we need to pay more attention to race/gender gaps to better understand the differences in schooling outcomes for Latina girls and Latino boys.

Part II ends with a powerful testimonio by Marta Rosa, one of the first Latinas ever elected to public office in Massachusetts and a national leader in educational policies that focus on equity, quality, and access. In "Early Education and Beyond: Centering Latino Children and Families in Policy-making" (chapter 9), Marta Rosa traces her life's work beginning as an early childhood educator and later becoming a leading voice for policy reforms across the educational pipelines. Her testimonio highlights the importance of reimagining a new public education agenda that begins with providing high-quality culturally sustaining early childhood education for all children that is sustained over a lifetime by radical love.

Part III, "Culturally Sustaining Student-Centered Practices and Programs," highlights existing practices and programs for Latine students that are grounded in asset-based and cultural wealth frameworks. Turning our attention to the experiences of Latine college students, in chapter 10, "Student Community-Engaged Policy Research for Transformative Educational Success" Ashley Torres Carrasquillo, Ester Shapiro, and Lorna Rivera discuss the results of a participatory evaluation of the Latino Leadership Opportunity Program (LLOP) at the University of Massachusetts Boston. The LLOP is a thirty-year-old undergraduate research and leadership training program that focuses on action research and policy analysis about issues affecting the Latino community. The authors discuss findings from interviews with LLOP alumni who reflect upon the impact of doing community-based research and the role that their faculty mentors had in their learning, their identities, their leadership experiences, and their future careers.

In chapter 11, "Two Is Better Than One: A Dual-Language Approach for Adult English Learners," Laurie Occhipinti and Melissa Sargent write about adult English learners who participate in a dual-language certificate program in business administration at Mount Wachusett Community College. As academic deans, the authors share valuable insights about how they developed and implemented a dual-language (English and Spanish) program, and they offer recommendations for meeting the needs of Latine community college students who are still acquiring English proficiency. The authors emphasize the importance and connections of community, belonging, and career trajectories of Latine community college students. They argue that while dual-language programs are more common in K-12 settings, it is past time for colleges and universities to adopt dual-language classes in higher education.

Chapter 12, "Seeking Cross-Ethnic and African Diasporic Solidarity Among English Learning High School Youth," by Patricia Krueger-Henney, Judenie Dabel, and Nasteho Ali, discusses the Youth Ubuntu Project, a collaborative Boston-based immigrant teen social justice leadership project guided by Participatory Action Research. Youth Ubuntu leaders built cross-ethnic and African Diasporic solidarity to directly address the racist and xenophobic practices of the English-learning education programs at their schools. This project amplifies the importance of high school students as knowledge producers and the urgency of bringing the voices of ethnically and linguistically diverse English-learning students into discussions and decision-making about their education.

Chapter 13, "Using STEM Learning, STEM Career Development, and Civic Engagement to Support Middle School Latinx Youth to Become Future Ready" focuses on the implementation of a career identity project at Sociedad Latina, one of the oldest Latinx youth-serving organizations in Massachusetts. This chapter describes a community-based research project of Sociedad Latina and Boston University, funded by the National Science Foundation, to help middle-school Latino youth develop STEAM (science, technology, engineering, arts, and math) skills and STEAM-related occupational aspirations. This chapter is cowritten by Sociedad Latina youth and staff and Boston University researchers and highlights the importance of community-based organizations and out-of-school time in the lives of Latino youth, particularly middle schoolers.

Part III closes with a powerful testimonio by Almudena (Almi) Abeyta, who is the first Latina superintendent of Chelsea Public Schools, one of the oldest Latino communities in Massachusetts and a majority Latino school district. Dr. Abeyta began working as the Chelsea superintendent a few months before the onset of the COVID-19 pandemic, and she would become one of the first superintendents in the nation to make the decision to close schools. Dr. Abeyta's testimonio reminds us about the importance of leading with courage and the critical need for leaders to affirm community cultural wealth.

Together these chapters contribute to our collective understanding of the positive impact of asset-based educational policies and practices that position Latine students, their families, and their communities from a strength-based perspective. Further, the authors in this book disrupt popular narratives that treat Latinos as a monolithic group and recognize the differences within and across different Latine communities and contexts. These complex and often contested realities also require a much more nuanced and intentional approach regarding how we think about and make decisions that will impact Latine students, their families, and their communities. As such, this book is also an invitation to educators, community members, students, policymakers, and other thought leaders to continue to raise questions that honor the diversity of experience while recognizing that the future of the Commonwealth of Massachusetts is deeply intertwined with the development, advancement, and success of Latine students. This is especially critical as sweeping changes in federal policy directives have heightened fears and increased uncertainties across our communities. This book also offers a framework and an opportunity to deliberate and act upon the type of research, policies, and practices that are needed to radically transform public education in Massachusetts and beyond, so that all students have the opportunity to benefit from educational opportunities in ways that are transformative and liberatory.

Notes

1   These are just samples of the various tribes that were the original stewards of the land today known as Massachusetts. There are various spellings on the names of these tribes.

2   Joel Spring, *Deculturalization and the Struggle for Equality: A Brief History of the Education of Dominated Cultures in the United States* (Routledge, 2021).

3   Anjanette Hendricks, "Horace Mann," in *The Palgrave Handbook of Educational Thinkers*, ed. Brett A. Geier (Springer International, 2024), 1–17, https://doi.org/10 .1007/978-3-030-81037-5_54-2.

4   Thomas Dee and Brian Jacob, "Do High School Exit Exams Influence Educational Attainment or Labor Market Performance?" (National Bureau of Economic Research, May 2006), https://doi.org/10.3386/w12199.

5   For further historical insights on how Massachusetts became a leader in US public education see, Joel Spring, *Deculturalization*.

6   Massachusetts Department of Elementary and Secondary Education, "Massachusetts Leads States in Fourth and Eighth Grade Reading and Mathematics for the Sixth Consecutive Time," accessed September 18, 2018, http://www.doe.mass.edu /news/news.aspx?id=21276; Laura W. Perna, Joni E. Finney, and Patrick M. Callahan, *The Attainment Agenda: State Policy Leadership in Higher Education* (Johns Hopkins

University Press, 2014); John Bound and Sarah Turner, "Cohort Crowding: How Resources Affect Collegiate Attainment," *Journal of Public Economics* 91, nos. 5–6 (2007): 877–99.

7   For a detailed history of deculturalization and exclusions efforts in US public education systems see, Spring, *Deculturalization*, 2021.

8   Kazuteru Omori, "Race-Neutral Individualism and Resurgence of the Color Line: Massachusetts Civil Rights Legislation, 1855–1895," *Journal of American Ethnic History* (2002): 32–58.

9   Spring, *Deculturalization*.

10 Spring, *Deculturalization*.

11 Massachusetts Department of Elementary and Secondary Education, "2022–23 Enrollment by Race/Gender Statewide Report (District)," accessed February 14, 2023, https://profiles.doe.mass.edu/statereport/enrollmentbyracegender.aspx.

12 Andrés Torres, *Latinos in New England* (Temple University Press, 2006).

13 Phillip Granberry and Krizia Valentino, "Latinos in Massachusetts: Cubans," Gastón Institute Publications 256 (2020), https://scholarworks.umb.edu/gaston_pubs/256.

14 Ramona Hernandez, "The Socioeconomic Status of Dominican New Yorkers," *IUME Briefs* (April 1996), https://eric.ed.gov/?id=ED396034.

15 Phillip Granberry and Krizia Valentino, "Latinos in Massachusetts: Dominicans," Gastón Institute Publications 250 (2020), https://scholarworks.umb.edu/gaston_pubs/250.

16 Lorna Rivera, "Latinos in Greater Boston: Migration, New Communities and the Challenge of Displacement," *Changing Faces of Greater Boston* (Boston Foundation, 2019); Vishakha Agarwal and Phillip Granberry, "Diversity Among Latino Groups in Massachusetts: 1980–2019," Gastón Institute Publications 294 (2023), https://scholarworks.umb.edu/gaston_pubs/294.

17 Phillip Granberry and Krizia Valentino, "Latinos in Massachusetts: Brazilians" Gastón Institute Publications 251 (2020), https://scholarworks.umb.edu/gaston_pubs/251.

18 Trevor Mattos, Phillip Granberry, and Quito Swan, "Latinos in Massachusetts: Afro-Latinos," Gastón Institute Publications 262 (2020), https://scholarworks.umb.edu/gaston_pubs/262.

19 Tatiana MF Cruz, "'We Took 'Em On' The Latino Movement for Educational Justice in Boston, 1965–1980," *Journal of Urban History* 43, no. 2 (2017): 235–55; Melissa Colón, "'We Are Beautiful People:' The Schooling Experiences of Puerto Rican School-Aged Mothers" (PhD thesis, Tufts University, , Child Study and Human Development, 2019).

20 Tatiana MF Cruz, "'We Took 'Em On'"; Sonia Nieto, "A History of the Education of Puerto Rican Students in U.S. Mainland Schools: 'Losers,' "Outsiders," or 'Leaders'?," in *Handbook of Research on Multicultural Education*, ed. James A. Banks and Cherry A. McGee Banks, 388–411 (Macmillan Publishers, 1995); The Taskforce on Children out of School, *The Way We Go to School: The Exclusion of Children in Boston* (Taskforce on Children out of School, 1970), https://files.eric.ed.gov/fulltext/ED046140.pdf.

21 Ralph Rivera and Sonia Nieto, *The Education of Latino Students in Massachusetts: Issues, Research, and Policy Implications* (University of Massachusetts Press, 1993).

22 Rivera and Nieto, *The Education of Latino Students in Massachusetts*.

23 Phillip Granberry and Trevor Mattos, "Massachusetts Latino Population: 2010–2035," Gastón Institute Publications 241 (2019), https://scholarworks.umb.edu/gaston_pubs/241/.

24 Fabián Torres-Ardila and Nyal Fuentes, "The State of Latino Education: 2010–2020," Gastón Institute Publications 292 (2022), https://scholarworks.umb.edu/gaston_pubs /292.

25 Torres-Ardila and Fuentes, "The State of Latino Education," https://scholarworks .umb.edu/gaston_pubs/292.

26 Fabián Torres-Ardila, Nyal Fuentes, and Melissa Colón, in this volume.

27 Massachusetts Department of Elementary and Secondary Education, "Chronically Underperforming Districts: Frequently Asked Questions," *Chronically Underperforming Districts*, June 12, 2023, https://www.doe.mass.edu/level5/districts/faq.html.

28 Miren Uriarte, et al., "Improving Educational Outcomes of English Language Learners in Schools and Programs in Boston Public Schools," Gastón Institute Publications 154 (2011), https://scholarworks.umb.edu/gaston_pubs/154.

29 Sabina E. Vaught, *Compulsory: Education and the Dispossession of Youth in a Prison School* (University of Minnesota Press, 2017).

30 Earl Shorris, "Latino, Si. Hispanic, No," *New York Times*, late ed. (East Coast), October 28, 1992.

31 The term *Latinidad* has transformed into *Latinidades*, to further emphasize the diversity of groups within this framework.

32 Felix M. Padilla, "Latino Ethnic Consciousness: The Case of Mexican Americans and Puerto Ricans in Chicago," 1985, https://cir.nii.ac.jp/crid/1130000794552401280.

33 Vicki L. Ruiz, "Nuestra América: Latino History as United States History," *Journal of American History* 93, no. 3 (2006): 655–72.

34 Kimberle Crenshaw, "Mapping the Margins: Intersectionality, Identity Politics, and Violence Against Women of Color," *Stanford Law Review* (1991): 1241–99; Ruiz, Vicki L. "Nuestra América: Latino History as United States History," *Journal of American History* 93, no. 3 (2006): 655–72; Spring, *Deculturalization*; Mirelsie Velazquez, "Primero Madres: Love and Mothering in the Educational Lives of Latina/Os," *Gender and Education* 29, no. 4 (2017): 508–24.

35 Padilla, Yesenia, "What Does 'Latinx' Mean? A Look at the Term That's Challenging Gender Norms," *The Complex*, accessed July 24, 2024, para 3, https://www.complex .com/life/a/yesenia-padilla/latinx.

36 For a full discussion see Cristobal Salinas and Adele Lozano, "Mapping and Recontextualizing the Evolution of the Term Latinx: An Environmental Scanning in Higher Education," in *Critical Readings on Latinos and Education* (Routledge, 2019), 216–35, https://www.taylorfrancis.com/chapters/edit/10.4324/9780429021206-14/mapping -recontextualizing-evolution-term-latinx-cristobal-salinas-adele-lozano.

37 Salinas and Lozano, "Mapping and Recontextualizing."

38 Many scholars have written about the myths that situate Latinos as monolithic. As it pertains to the focus of this book, the works of Sonia Nieto, in *Affirming Diversity: The Sociopolitical Context of Multicultural Education* (1992), and Juan González, in *Harvest of Empire: A History of Latinos in America* (2000), discuss the complexities and heterogeneity of the Latino communities and how these myths can be harmful.

39 Michelle Borges, et al., "Brazilians in the U.S. and Massachusetts: A Demographic and Economic Profile," Gastón Institute Publications 309 (2023), https://scholarworks .umb.edu/gaston_pubs/309.

PART I

Beyond the
Latino Monolithic
Myths

Chapter One

The State of Latino Education

2010–2024[1]

FABIÁN TORRES-ARDILA, NYAL FUENTES, AND MELISSA COLÓN

There is no dispute that Massachusetts is one of the states leading the nation in student achievement. On the National Assessment of Educational Progress (NAEP) exam, often referred to as the "nation's report card," Massachusetts students have consistently earned at or near the nation's top NAEP scores for decades. For example, on the 2022 NAEP exam, Massachusetts's fourth and eighth graders had among (either first or second) the highest average scores in the entire US in reading and mathematics.[2] However, despite the state's high educational reputation, in 2024, as in 2020 and 2010 (when the Gastón Institute previously published its report, "State of Latinos and Education in Massachusetts")[3] the state continues to leave its Latino[4] students behind. Despite progress shown across various measures over the past generation, particularly in high school graduation rates, Latino students are still experiencing huge gaps in key educational metrics with respect to other student groups.

The Cycle of Inquiry and Why Do These Data Matter?

This chapter provides a demographic profile of educational attainment metrics for Massachusetts Latino students, with a focus on the K-12 student population. Using publicly available data from the Massachusetts Department of Elementary and Secondary Education (MDESE), we describe trends in the demographic profiles and enrollment patterns of Latino students as well as indicators of academic progress through the academic year 2023–24 (referred from here forward as AY2024.[5] To contextualize the educational outcomes of this population and their complex relationships to social factors that contribute to educational attainment, we begin by providing a brief demographic overview of this population, including school enrollment patterns. We then present a series of academic and educational engagement indicators including attendance, graduation, and college attendance rates.

It is important to highlight that the data presented in the chapter offer a "30,000-foot view" of Latino student performance. We share the data in this format as part of our ongoing commitments to contribute to the cycle of inquiry processes that are happening at the local, state, and national levels. The cycle of inquiry process asks school leaders, teachers, students, families, community members, policymakers, and other educational stakeholders to analyze existing data, determine the focus for change, and then develop supports to initiate impact. For this reason, a cycle of inquiry is likely to include the use of quantitative data from the state, paired with local data that may not be in state data sets, as well as what local stakeholders know about their children and communities, to inform policy planning and program implementation. The quantitative data we present in this chapter do not have very specific information about individual students' lives and the communities where they live, nor does it capture broader sociocultural and historical contexts that contribute to these data trends. However, understanding these data can help stakeholders, working in collaboration, to identify inequities, develop questions, deliberate causes, brainstorm solutions, and then develop strategies and supports to address the identified priorities. The cycle of inquiry also provides opportunities to engage in monitoring the efficacy of interventions developed. We argue that these data *are but one* critical component in understanding the achievement and opportunity gaps faced by Latino students in Massachusetts public schools and can be used to inform decision-making as well as the creation and implementation of policies and programming to improve their education.

This inquiry process is critically important, because as the data demonstrate Latino students are facing challenges at all grade levels with a consequent impact on college enrollment and persistence. The cumulative effects of these struggles are seen in the low levels of postsecondary enrollment and completion for the Latino population. As noted in figure 1.1, on average, Latinos have lower levels of educational attainment than other groups in the Commonwealth. For example, 86.6% of Asians[6] ages twenty-five years or older have at least a high school diploma, compared to 73.7% of Latinos. Even starker is the contrast among those with a bachelor's degree or more.

Asian and White residents twenty years or older have the highest rates of bachelor's degree or more, at 63.3% and 48.3%, respectively, whereas for Latinos the rate is only 20.4%. This situation impacts the quality of life of Latinos in Massachusetts, including access to the high-paying jobs for which the state is well-known. This information, along with the subsequent data presented in this chapter, is meant to generate questions and rigorous conversations about the state of Latino education in Massachusetts.

Educational Attainment in MA by Race and Ethnicity

Indicates the highest degree or the highest level of school completed by MA residents. Includes all people age 25+ because not all students earn their degrees in 4 years after high school.

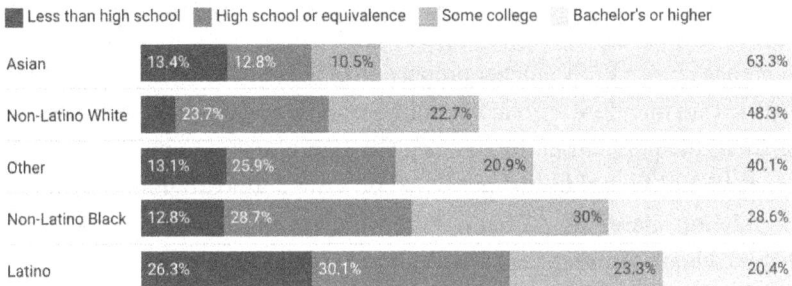

■ Less than high school   ■ High school or equivalence   ▩ Some college   Bachelor's or higher

	Less than high school	High school or equivalence	Some college	Bachelor's or higher
Asian	13.4%	12.8%	10.5%	63.3%
Non-Latino White	23.7%		22.7%	48.3%
Other	13.1%	25.9%	20.9%	40.1%
Non-Latino Black	12.8%	28.7%	30%	28.6%
Latino	26.3%	30.1%	23.3%	20.4%

Source: 2015-2019 American Community Survey, Gastón Institute Analysis • Created with Datawrapper

FIGURE 1.1. Educational Attainment in Massachusetts by Race and Ethnicity.

Latino Public School Enrollment in Massachusetts

Latinos are the second largest (accounting for one-eighth of the population) and second fastest growing racial/ethnic population in the Commonwealth.[7] Latinos call all parts of Massachusetts their home. While established Latino communities such as Chelsea, Lawrence, Worcester, and Springfield continue to grow, many new and "emerging" Latino neighborhoods—and school districts—are growing as Latino families explore opportunities across the Commonwealth. In the last decade there has been substantial growth in areas on the south coast such as New Bedford and Fall River and even in suburban and rural areas of the state such as Cape Cod (e.g., Barnstable, Falmouth, Sandwich, and surrounding areas) where the number of Latinos grew a significant 78% from 2010 to 2020 (from 7,000 to about 12,500).[8]

According to the US 2020 Census, Latinos represent 12.3% of the population of the Commonwealth, the second largest ethnoracial group behind

Whites.[9] While the Commonwealth's overall population grew by a modest 7.4% from 2010 to 2020, its Latino population grew by 41.4% in the same period. This makes Latinos the second fastest growing population in Massachusetts, trailing only Asian and Pacific Islanders (a smaller population group), whose numbers grew by 45.3% over the same period. By 2030, Latinos are projected to account for 15% of the Commonwealth's residents.[10]

The population growth and age of the Latino population have a major impact on the composition of students in public schools in Massachusetts. Relative to other ethnoracial groups, Latinos are a young population. For example, there are approximately equal shares of Latino and White residents that are between the ages of twenty-five and sixty-four years (~63%). According to the US 2020 Census, about 30% of Latinos are between the ages of five and seventeen, compared to about 14% of non-Latinos in the same age range.[11] With a higher proportion of the population under eighteen, Latinos are therefore enrolled in public schools at rates above their overall share of the population. In AY2024, for example, about one-fourth of all students in Massachusetts' public schools are Latino, double the overall population share.[12] In AY2024, there were 914,959 students in the state's public schools. This represents a decline of about 4.4% (or 42,094 students) since AY2010 (2009–10).[13] Massachusetts has 399 operating school districts with more than six students, including seventy-six charter schools. Of its about 1,827 public schools, 60% are elementary schools, 18% are middle/junior high schools, and 20% are high schools.[14] Latinos are the largest ethnoracial minoritized student group in Massachusetts (229,930 students) and the second fastest growing student population behind only non-Hispanic Multi-Race students. From AY2010 to AY2024, the size of the Latino student population increased by 56%, at an average yearly rate of growth of 3.8%.[15] Table 1.1 shows that after the COVID-19 pandemic, Latino students were the student group with the largest increase in enrollment (24,794), defying the trend for all other groups except Multi-Race students.

While Latino students attend schools throughout the state, most Latino students are highly concentrated in just a few school districts. In AY2024, about 60% of Latino students enrolled in just twenty-eight of the state's public school districts (out of 399).[16] In AY2024 there were twelve school districts where Latinos make up more than 50% of the student population (Lawrence, Chelsea, Holyoke, Lynn, Springfield, Everett, Greater Lawrence Technical, Southbridge, Revere, Fitchburg, Marlborough, and Methuen), and these

TABLE 1.1. Change of Enrollment by Race and Ethnicity.

Race/Ethnicity	2010	(%)	2020	(%)	2023	(%)	2024	(%)	Growth Rate 2010–2024
Asian	50,801	(5.3)	67,527	(7.1)	67,010	(7.3)	67,847	(7.4)	2.3%
Black	78,044	(8.2)	87,053	(9.2)	85,662	(9.4)	88,104	(9.6)	0.9%
Latino	**141,933**	**(14.8)**	**205,136**	**(21.6)**	**221,044**	**(24.2)**	**229,930**	**(25.1)**	**3.8%**
Multiracial	21,365	(2.2)	37,244	(3.9)	40,277	(4.4)	41,418	(4.5)	5.2%
Pacific Islander	1,086	(0.1)	781	(0.1)	787	(0.1)	790	(0.1)	-2.4%
White	661,292	(69.1)	549,006	(57.9)	496,800	(54.4)	484,692	(53)	-2.4%
All Students	957,053	(100)	948,828	(100)	913,858	(100)	914,959	(100)	-0.3%

List of Massachusetts school districts where the share of Latino students is at least 40%. In AY2024, these school districts enrolled about 60% of all Latino students in the state.

Since Latinos can be of any race, the racial categories listed in the table are for non-Latinos.

Source: DESE, "Enrollment by race and race/gender," (2024).

districts enroll almost one-third of all the Latino students in the state (31%). Lawrence Public Schools has the highest concentration of Latino students, accounting for 94.5% of the overall student population in the district. When it comes to numbers, Boston Public Schools enrolls about 9% of all students in the state, and 44.7.% of all its students are Latino. Table 1.2 enumerates the number and concentration of Latino students in various communities in AY2024. It also shows enclaves of Latino families in areas outside the traditional urban centers in Massachusetts, including Southbridge and Milford.

As the trends discussed in the chapter will demonstrate, educational policy and reforms at the local, state, and federal levels that have aimed to improve the educational outcomes of all students have struggled to sufficiently improve results for the large and growing Latino student population in the Commonwealth.

TABLE 1.2. Proportion of Latino Students in Selected School Districts.

District	No. Latino Students	Pct. Latino Students	Pct. Total Latino Students in State
Lawrence	12,296	94.5%	5.3%
Chelsea	5,444	88.5%	2.4%
Greater Lawrence Regional Vocational Technical	1,448	81.6%	0.6%
Holyoke	3,980	81.3%	1.7%
Lynn	11,620	72.5%	5.1%
Springfield	16,416	69.3%	7.1%
Everett	4,962	67.6%	2.2%
Southbridge	1,245	66.0%	0.5%
Revere	4,713	64.2%	2.0%
Fitchburg	2,961	57.8%	1.3%
Marlborough	2,700	57.1%	1.2%
Methuen	3,447	52.8%	1.5%
Framingham	4,517	49.5%	2.0%
Waltham	2,709	47.5%	1.2%

Salem	1,793	47.0%	0.8%
Haverhill	3,677	46.7%	1.6%
Worcester	11,191	46.0%	4.9%
Northeast Metropolitan Regional Vocational Technical	614	45.7%	0.3%
New Bedford	5,605	44.9%	2.4%
Boston	20,436	44.7%	8.9%
Chicopee	3,038	44.6%	1.3%
Nantucket	730	43.4%	0.3%
South Middlesex Regional Vocational Technical	364	41.8%	0.2%
Leominster	2,512	41.8%	1.1%
Clinton	820	41.2%	0.4%
Lowell	5,795	40.6%	2.5%
Tisbury	110	40.6%	0.0%
Somerville	1,992	40.4%	0.9%

List of Massachusetts school districts where the share of Latino students is at least 40%. In AY2024, these school districts enrolled about 60% of all Latino students in the state.

Source: DESE, "Enrollment by race and race/gender," (2024).

English Learners (ELs)

Between AY2010 and AY2024 the enrollment of English learners (ELs) in Massachusetts increased by 27%. In AY2010, there were 59,337 ELs in the Commonwealth or 6.2% of the total student population.[17] By AY2024 ELs represented 13.1% of the total student population.[18] Table 1.3 shows that in AY2024, Latino EL students represented about 64% of the state's ELs and accounted for almost one-third (33.3%) of all Latino students.[19] This is a much larger proportion as compared to other ethnoracial groups. As detailed by Berardino (chapter 6), the large representation of Latino ELs speaks to the need for additional resources for educating these students, especially in school districts with large Latino student enrollment.

TABLE 1.3. English Learner (EL) Status by Race and Ethnicity in Massachusetts.

	Not EL	EL	Total	Pct. ELs
Asian	56,720	11,127	67,847	16.4%
Black	72,618	15,486	88,104	17.6%
Hispanic	153,419	76,511	229,930	33.3%
Multiracial	40,022	1,396	41,418	3.4%
Native American	1,689	489	2,178	22.5%
Pacific Islander	648	142	790	18.0%
White	470,094	14,598	484,692	3.0%
All	*795,210*	*119,749*	*914,959*	*13.1%*

In AY2024, Latino EL students represented about 64% of all ELs in the state and 33% of all Latino students enrolled.

Since Latinos can be of any race, the racial categories listed in the table are for non-Latinos.

Source: DESE, "Student Information Management System (SIMS)," (2024).

Educational Outcomes for Latinos in the Commonwealth

There are noteworthy disparities across indicators of Latino academic progress, such as attendance, disciplinary actions, achievement, dropping out, and high school graduation.

ATTENDANCE

Not only is attendance one of the basic measures for student engagement, but high absenteeism rates also influence learning and graduation. Research by the MDESE on its Early Warning Indicator System shows that students who are chronically absent (missing 10% or more of school) in grade 10 have an on-time graduation rate of 69% while those who are not chronically absent have a 96% rate.[20] In addition, research shows that attendance is tied to academic success and high rates of absenteeism have been associated with dropping out of school.[21]

In AY2023, over one-third of Latino students were chronically absent (34.5%) and Latino students were twice as likely to be chronically absent than White students (see table 1.4). In AY2023, Massachusetts students were absent for an average of 13.1 days during the school year. Latino students had the highest rate of absenteeism of any group in the state, averaging 17.1 missed days (roughly two and half weeks). The average in AY2023 was five days more than the Latino attendance data reported in AY2020 (12.6 days).[22]

TABLE 1.4. Attendance by Race and Ethnicity in Massachusetts Schools.

Student Group	Attendance Rate	Average # of Absences	Absent 10 or More Days	Chronically Absent (10% or more)
Asian	94.7%	9.4%	35.2%	13.9%
White	93.4%	11.6%	46.0%	17.0%
Multi-race	92.4%	13.4%	50.2%	23.3%
Black	92.0%	13.9%	48.0%	25.3%
Native Hawaiian or Pacific Islander	92.0%	14.0%	51.9%	28.3%
American Indian or Alaskan Native	90.2%	17.0%	60.3%	33.5%
Latino	**90.1%**	**17.1%**	**61.7%**	**34.5%**
All Students	*92.5%*	*13.1%*	*49.5%*	*22.2%*

In AY2023, Latino students displayed the largest average number of absences across the different racial and ethnic groups. In addition, almost two-thirds of Latino students (61.7%) are absent from school 10 or more days, and about one third are absent at least 10% of all school days.

Since Latinos can be of any race, the racial categories in the table are for non-Latino students.

Source: DESE, "2022–2023 Attendance Report (District)," (2023).

DISCIPLINARY ACTIONS

The achievement gap coincides with what has been called the discipline gap—or the observation that Black and Latino students are more likely to be disciplined in school than their White peers.[23] There is evidence of the discipline gap in Massachusetts especially for Latino and Black students, who are disciplined at rates higher than their shares in the student population. In AY2023, the number of Latino students disciplined (12,330) represented 37.2% of the total number of disciplined students (33,062), more than 10 percentage points higher than the proportion of all students in the state who are Latino (24.9%). Similarly, Black students accounted for 17.5% of all students disciplined, but only 9.4% of all students.[24] As discussed by Conroy and colleagues (chapter 7), variations on disciplinary enforcement and practices vary by school district; however, across the Commonwealth and mirroring national trends, Black and Latino students are disproportionately disciplined by school officials.

A robust body of literature suggests that there is a relationship between racial bias and disciplinary decisions and therefore more direct efforts to address policy and practices are needed to address racial and ethnic disparities in school discipline.[25] In addition to questions of equity, this higher rate of discipline is also a powerful reflection of school culture and climate and may result in negative academic outcomes for students. Research for the MDESE's Early Warning Indicator System, for example, shows that students suspended one or more times in tenth grade have an on-time graduation rate of 74% compared to a 96% rate for those students who were not suspended.[26]

DROPOUT RATES

A high school credential is critical to the future of all our young people as a passport to college and career. Massachusetts measures high school noncompletion in several ways. The most commonly used are the *annual dropout rate* and the *four-year cohort graduation rate*. The annual dropout rate is the percentage of students (in grades 9–12) who did not return to school by the following October 1 of the reporting year and/or have left school before earning a high school diploma.[27] This measure of noncompletion is one of the primary ways that the state monitors students' overall progress and reports to the US Department of Education.

Across all student groups, the rates of students dropping out have been greatly reduced over the past ten years and are now among the lowest rates since dropouts began to be calculated in the 1960s. In AY2023, the Latino student dropout rate for all grades was 4.4%, down from 7.4% in AY2010. However, it is important to note is that in AY2020 the Latino dropout rate was at 3.5%.[28] The dropout rate increase between AY2020 and AY2024 has been hypothesized as an artifact of the COVID-19 pandemic because, in AY2020, it was difficult to accurately track dropouts due to school closures from March to June. Along the same vein, it is also important to emphasize that due to the growth in the Latino student population numbers, the actual number of Latino students who drop out remains high: in AY2010 there were 2,915 dropouts and in AY2024 there were 2,987.[29] There is still a large gap between the dropout rate for the Commonwealth as a whole and Latino students. Specifically, Latino students compose 50.8% of total high school dropouts, while Asian and White students who make up 62.7% of the high school population only account for 30.1% of the dropouts (see table 1.5). Massachusetts has one of the nation's highest costs of living, so a high school diploma is essential currency for future students, family, and community economic viability.

TABLE 1.5. Distribution of High School Dropouts by Race and Ethnicity in AY2023.

	9–12 Enrollment	Share of 9th to 12th Graders	No. of Dropouts	Pct. of All Dropouts
Black	27,597	9.6%	767	13.0%
Asian	20,161	7.0%	123	2.1%
Latino	**68,292**	**23.7%**	**2,987**	**50.8%**
Native American	683	0.2%	28	0.5%
Multiracial	10,678	3.7%	207	3.5%
Pacific Islander	255	0.2%	10	0.2%
White	160,262	55.7%	1,793	30.1%
All	*287,928*	*100%*	*5,915*	*2.1%*

Latino students are disproportionally represented in student dropout data. Latino students' share of enrollment in grades 9–12 is 23.7%, but the share of Latino student dropouts is 50.8%.

Source: DESE, "Statistical reports: dropout rates," (2024).

GRADUATION RATES

Another way of measuring students' academic progress is by examining graduation rates. There are multiple ways of calculating graduation rates, one of them being the four-year cohort graduation rate, which tracks the graduation rate of a cohort of students that start grade 9 in the same year and subsequently graduate together. As seen in table 1.6, between AY2010 and AY2023, the four-year cohort graduation rate in Massachusetts rose from 82.1% to 89.2%.[30] During this time, the four-year cohort graduation rate for Latino students rose more sharply than for all students, increasing from 61.2% in 2010 to 77.2% in 2020 and then to 78.9% in 2023. This general improvement in the Latino four-year cohort graduation rate (and to access to a critical high school credential) has reduced the gap between Latino students and the rest of the Massachusetts student population from about 21 percentage points in 2010 to about 10 points in 2023. The improvement in graduation rates is part of a long-term goal and investments by the Commonwealth to address gaps. Despite the improvements in graduation rates, these figures still mean that barely four out of five Latino students graduate from high school on time, which suggests the need for more targeted policy and programmatic approaches to increase on time graduation.

TABLE 1.6. Four-Year Cohort Graduation Rate by Race and Ethnicity.

	2010	2020	2023
Asian	86.9%	95.0%	95.2%
White	87.7%	93.2%	93.0%
Black	68.7%	83.1%	85.6%
Latino	**61.2%**	**77.2%**	**78.9%**
All	82.1%	89.0%	89.2%

The cohort graduation rate tracks a cohort of students from grade 9 through high school. It represents the percentage of that cohort that graduates in four years.

Source: DESE, "Statistical reports: graduation rates," (2023).

Looking closer at the Latino graduation rates, table 1.7 disaggregates data on Latinos by subcategories. From AY2010 to AY2021, there have been considerable improvements in graduation rates among all Latino subgroups, particularly for non-EL Latino students who experienced almost a 20 percentage point improvement in graduation rates (from 64.6% to 85.4%). Latinas continue completing high school at higher rates than Latino males. The lowest graduation rate is observed for Latino ELs—in AY2021 only 67.3% of these students graduated within four years, about 15 percentage points lower than the rate for Latino non-ELs. This is consistent with the findings of the educational outcomes presented by Berardino (chapter 6 of this volume) and the need to critically address the strengths and needs of this student population. Despite these challenges, however, there has been a substantial increase in graduation rates across the different subcategories of Latino students.

TABLE 1.7. Latino Four-Year Cohort Graduation for Selected Subcategories.

	2010	2020
Latino	61.2%	77.1%
Latino, Male	55.9%	72.8%
Latino, Female	66.7%	81.7%
Latino, ELL	48.9%	62.1%
Latino, Non-ELL	64.6%	84.0%
All Students	82.1%	89.0%

Percentage 9 to 12 graduates of the same cohort that graduate within four years for different Latino student subgroups. Notice that despite the gains, the gap between Latino students and all students is still high, at about 12 percentage points in AY2020.

Source: DESE, "Statistical reports: graduation rates," (2022).

COLLEGE ENROLLMENT OF GRADUATES OF MASSACHUSETTS HIGH SCHOOLS

Many of the careers in Massachusetts with family supporting wages require postsecondary education. Between AY2010 and AY2019, the statewide college enrollment for high school graduates remained steady except for a drop among Latinos. In AY10 the college enrollment rate for Latino high school graduates was 61.6%; in AY2019 it was 55% (see table

1.8). Then in AY2020, the first "pandemic class," there was a precipitous drop in college enrollment, particularly for Latino high school graduates. Postpandemic data from AY2023 indicate that the problem has worsened for Latinos, with the percentage of Latino high school graduates immediately enrolling in college decreasing from 42.3% in 2020 to 38.2%.[31] To put this in context, in AY2020 11,987 Latino students graduated from high school in Massachusetts, and in AY2023, 13,598 Latino students graduated from high school. However, the number of Latino students attending college was similar: 5,073 in AY2020 and 5,193 in AY2023. This means that the additional 1,700 Latino high school graduates in AY2023 did not produce a proportional increase in college going to reflect population growth.

The are many working theories that explain the magnitude of the drop in Latino college enrollment. The drop, for example, may reflect the exacerbated economic hardships that many communities with large Latino high school populations are experiencing because of the effects of the COVID-19 pandemic, coupled with a fairly robust job market that redirects high school graduates away from postsecondary education debt to immediate job opportunities. However, understanding the actual causes of the drop would require additional research.

TABLE 1.8. College Enrollment Massachusetts Public High School Graduates.

	2010	2019	2020	2022	2023
Asian	81.4%	84.2%	78%	78.5%	79.9%
White	76.6%	75.7%	69.6%	69.4%	67.9%
Black	71.5%	69.7%	56.6%	56.6%	55.5%
Latino	**61.6%**	**55%**	**42.3%**	**38.5%**	**38.2%**
All	*74.7%*	*72.2%*	*64%*	*62.4%*	*61.2%*

The table displays the percentage of enrollment in any college by March after the senior year for high school graduates. Note the drop of Latino enrollment in AY2020, presumably because of COVID-19. Data from 2023 shows Latino students' enrollment to be the lowest since 2010, and the lowest of all racial and ethnic groups.

Source: Massachusetts Department of Higher Education.

Latino high school graduates who are enrolled in college attend community colleges at nearly twice the rate of Massachusetts high school graduates overall (about 40% as compared to 20% for all high school graduates). Therefore, community colleges are an essential incubator for higher education for Latino students. According to data from the Massachusetts Department of Higher Education, in the first year of COVID-19, from fall 2019 to fall 2020, the community college enrollment of Latino first-time first-year students dropped by 25.4%.[32] However, in AY2022, enrollment numbers seem to have recovered slightly, from 14,279 in AY2020 to 14,747 in AY2022. In addition, in AY2022, Latino students represent 23.7% of all enrolled students in community colleges, slightly up from 21.5% in AY2020. However, all these gains need to be considered in the context of a reduction of about 15,000 students in total Massachusetts community college enrollment between AY2019 and AY2022.[33]

COLLEGE PERSISTENCE

Beyond college enrollment, there are also sizeable disparities in college persistence, defined as a student continuing from the first to the second year of college. Only about three-quarters (76%) of Latino students that initially enrolled in college persisted into a second year of college, the

Student Academic Progression AY2021

The graph displays the adademic progression of all AY2021 student groups, taking as reference baseline the students who enroll in 9th grade in that year.

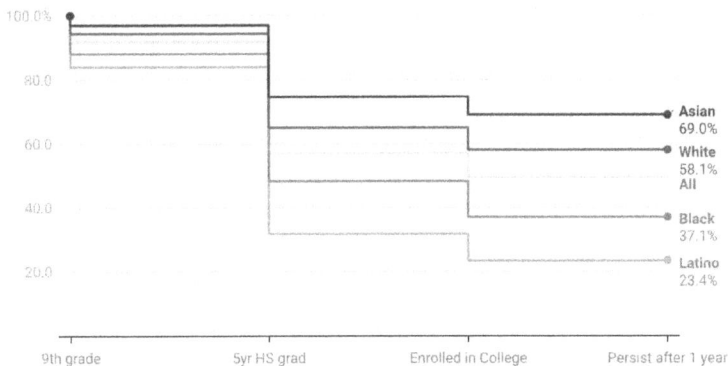

Source: DESE 2024. Analysis by Gastón Institute. • Created with Datawrapper

Figure 1.2. Student Academic Progression of the Graduating Class of AY2021.

lowest rate among all ethnoracial groups and far below the rates for Asian (93.8%) and White (91.2%) college students. To better understand the complete trajectory of students from the beginning of high school into the second year of college, figure 1.2 displays the academic trajectory of the high school class of AY2021, showing the cumulative progression from high school graduation to college enrollment, to persistence in college into a second year. The figure shows that at all stages of the progression, Latino students have the lowest rates falling far behind their peers, with particularly large gaps between Latino students and Asian and White students. In particular, the percentage of Latino students from the class of AY2021 who persist in college after one year was 23.4%, over 45 percentage points below the corresponding percentage for Asian American students (69%).[34]

Conclusion

Educational data clearly illustrate the tremendous opportunity and achievement gaps facing Latino students in Massachusetts in 2024 and beyond. They also illustrate progress in educational achievement over the past thirteen years, particularly in high school graduation rates. However positive these advances have been, we realize that the promise of educational reform that began in the 2000s has not benefited those students that needed them the most: Latino and Black students and ELs. Instead, these reforms appear to have widened the gap between these students and their White and Asian peers, as well as those from higher-income backgrounds and non-EL students. The data presented in this chapter illuminated enormous gaps in opportunity and achievement for one of our fastest-growing populations, Latino students. Closing these achievement gaps is critical for the future of the state and its economy as Latinos become an increasingly larger population in Massachusetts. Efforts to address opportunity and achievement gaps will require additional resources from the federal, state, and local levels to be targeted toward academic and social success for our Latino students. It will also require considerable work on the part of educators, students, their families, policymakers, and other stakeholders to actively work to address historical and systemic challenges that have created these opportunity and achievement gaps.

In alignment with models that promote the cycle of inquiry, our intent in sharing these data is to inform calls to action to center the needs and strengths of Latino students, their families, and communities in order to increase access to high-quality education and improve outcomes. Because the achievement and opportunity gaps for Latino students in the Commonwealth remain high, when reviewing these data, many may feel discouraged about the state of Latino education in Massachusetts. Others may feel that these data serve to pathologize Latino students, their families, and our communities. We stand resolute that neither is the intent of this chapter. Instead, we argue that providing access to this critical information and defining achievement and opportunity gaps are essential to improving outcomes and transforming schooling experiences for all students. By providing a snapshot into current academic conditions that Massachusetts Latino students face, our goal is for educational stakeholders to use these data, in conjunction with other information and research as well as on-the-ground local knowledge, to raise questions, identify priorities, deliberate solutions, and begin to implement policies and practices that significantly improve district, school, classroom, and ultimately student-level outcomes. This work requires that communities across the Commonwealth come together to prioritize the state of Latino education and develop action plans to track implementation and impact. We are hopeful that the data presented in this report will serve as a first step toward the creation of such action plans.

ACKNOWLEDGMENTS

The authors would like to thank the authors of the 2010 "State of Latinos and Education in Massachusetts" report for inspiring this work. Fabián Torres-Ardila would like to thank Dr. Phil Granberry, the senior data analyst at the Gastón Institute, for his support in analyzing census data and Sofia Aravena, communications apprentice at the Gastón Institute, for her help with tables and graphs. We would also like to thank the MDESE for their assistance, mainly former senior associate commissioner Cliff Chuang and associate commissioner Elizabeth Bennett, for the invitation to contribute to this chapter. Finally, we thank Dr. Michael Berardino, whose thorough reading and thoughtful questions greatly contributed to improving the chapter.

Notes

1 This chapter is an update of the descriptive analysis of the main trends in Latino educational achievement presented in the 2022 Gastón Institute report, "The State of Latino Education: 2010–2020." Updates include school enrollment, college

enrollment, and graduation rates data up to academic year 2024, which display some of the effects of the COVID-19 pandemic on Latino students.

2 Commonwealth of Massachusetts, "Massachusetts NAEP Results Lead Nation for 12th Year" https://www.mass.gov/news/massachusetts-naep-results-lead-nation-for-12th-year, accessed March 21, 2022.

3 Billie Gastic, Melissa Colón, and Andrew Flannery Aguilar, "The State of Latinos and Education in Massachusetts: 2010," Gastón Institute Publications 160 (2010), http://scholarworks.umb.edu/gaston_pubs/160.

4 In this chapter we have decided to use the terminology that is currently used to gather the state and school data presented and use Latino or Hispanic interchangeably to refer to this group.

5 If data from AY2024 were not available, we used the latest year available and noted it as such.

6 Racial categories often obscure significant differences in educational experiences and outcomes among ethnic groups within the same racial classification. Numerous calls have been made to disaggregate education data to reveal these disparities. For instance, disaggregated data among Asian American students highlight substantial differences in educational attainment between Southeast Asian groups and other Asian American populations. See Bic Ngo and Stacey J. Lee, "Complicating the Image of Model Minority Success: A Review of Southeast Asian American Education," *Review of Educational Research* 77, no. 4 (2007): 415–53. In this chapter, however, we utilize publicly available data that use racial classification categories.

7 US Census Bureau, "Decennial Census of Population and Housing by Decades," https://www.census.gov/programs-surveys/decennial-census/decade.2020.html.html, accessed March 1, 2022.

8 Explore the census tool created by the Gastón Institute at https://public.tableau.com/views/Census_2020/CensusData?:language=en-US&publish=yes&:display_count=n&:origin=viz_share_link.

9 US Census Bureau, "Decennial Census."

10 US Census Bureau, "Decennial Census."

11 Phillip Granberry, Victor Luis Martins, and Michelle Borges, "The Growing Latino Population of Massachusetts: A Demographic and Economic Portrait," Gastón Institute Publications 307 (2023), https://scholarworks.umb.edu/gaston_pubs/307.

12 MDESE, "Enrollment by Race/Gender Report," 2024, https://profiles.doe.mass.edu/statereport/enrollmentbyracegender.aspx.

13 MDESE, "Statistical Reports: Enrollment Data," 2024, https://www.doe.mass.edu/infoservices/reports/enroll/.

14 MDESE, "Statistical Reports: Enrollment Data."

15 MDESE, "Enrollment by Race/Gender Report."

16 MDESE, "Enrollment by Race/Gender Report."

17 Faye Karp and Miren Uriarte, "Educational Outcomes of English Language Learners in Massachusetts: A Focus on Latino/a Students," Gastón Institute Publications 159 (2010), http://scholarworks.umb.edu/gaston_pubs/159.

18 MDESE, "Student Information Management System (SIMS)," 2021, https://www.doe.mass.edu/infoservices/data/SIMS/.

19 MDESE, "Statistical Reports: Enrollment Data."

20 MDESE, "The ABCs of Success in High School and Beyond," https://abcs.sites.digital
    .mass.gov, accessed March 2022.

21 Nicole Lavan and Miren Uriarte, "Status of Latino Education in Massachusetts: A
    Report," Gastón Institute Publications 133 (2008), https://scholarworks.umb.edu
    /gaston_pubs/133.

22 MDESE, "Attendance Report," 2022, https://profiles.doe.mass.edu/statereport
    /attendance.aspx.

23 Anne Gregory, Russell Skiba, and Pedro A. Noguera, "The Achievement Gap and
    the Discipline Gap: Two Sides of the Same Coin?" *Educational Researcher* 39, no. 1
    (2020): 59–68.

24 MDESE, "2022–23 Student Discipline Days Missed Report—All Offenses—All
    Students," 2022, https://profiles.doe.mass.edu/statereport/ssdr_days_missed.aspx.

25 See, e.g., Russell J. Skiba, Robert H. Horner, Choong-Geun Chung, M. Karega
    Rausch, Seth L. May, and Tary Tobin, "Race Is Not Neutral: A National Investigation
    of African American and Latino Disproportionality in School Discipline." *School
    Psychology Review* 40, no. 1 (2011): 85–107; Kelly Welch and Allison Ann Payne,
    "Latino/a Student Threat and School Disciplinary Policies and Practices," *Sociology of
    Education* 91, no. 2 (2018): 91–110; Gage, Nicholas A., Antonis Katsiyannis, Kelly M.
    Carrero, Rhonda Miller, and Danielle Pico. "Exploring Disproportionate Discipline
    for Latinx Students with and Without Disabilities: A National Analysis." *Behavioral
    Disorders* 47, no. 1 (2021): 3–13.

26 MDESE, "The ABCs of Success in High School and Beyond."

27 MDESE, "Annual Dropout Rate vs. Cohort Graduation Rate," 2007, https://www
    .doe.mass.edu/infoservices/reports/gradrates/dropoutvsgrad.html.

28 MDESE, "Statistical Reports: Dropout Rates," 2022, http://www.doe.mass.edu
    /infoservices/reports/dropout/.

29 MDESE, "Statistical Reports: Dropout Rates."

30 MDESE, "Statistical Reports: Graduation Rates," 2022, https://www.doe.mass.edu
    /infoservices/reports/gradrates/.

31 MDESE, "2021–22 Graduates Attending Institutions of Higher Education," 2022,
    https://profiles.doe.mass.edu/statereport/gradsattendingcollege.aspx.

32 Massachusetts Department of Higher Education, "Equity Spotlight: Pandemic Enroll-
    ment Changes by Population," https://www.mass.edu/datacenter/2020enrollment
    trends.asp, accessed on March 20, 2022.

33 Massachusetts Department of Higher Education, "Community Colleges Total
    Undergraduate Enrollment Fall Term," https://www.mass.edu/datacenter/access
    /CCMinorityHTC.asp, accessed on October 20, 2024.

34 MDESE, "DART Success After High School," 2024, https://www.doe.mass.edu/dart/.

Chapter Two

Here Is What We Know About Brazilian Students in Massachusetts: Not Much

CRISTINA ARAUJO BRINKERHOFF

Well, because I did not have a lot of support in high school. It took me two or three years to go into college and I went into community college . . . , which is where I found professors that actually told me like, look you actually have potential, you can do this, here is how you do it.

—JULIANA, 1.5 GENERATION BRAZILIAN COLLEGE STUDENT[1]

In the Brazilian community, we hear many anecdotes about the ways Brazilian children are succeeding against all odds as well as struggling in the US education system. The stories we hear about Brazilian students in Massachusetts have a strong foundation in what we know about Brazilian immigrants and Brazilian immigration to the US. At the same time, it is a story of unanswered questions, where what we know about this group of students is outweighed by what we do not know.

In this chapter, I provide a demographic profile and a brief history of the migration patterns of Brazilians in Massachusetts. I begin with a discussion about Brazilian communities. Then I discuss why education researchers do not have a lot of data about Brazilian students as well as factors that might influence the educational outcomes of Brazilian children in Massachusetts. Finally, I share what we know about the experience of Brazilian children in

Massachusetts schools and propose some practice and policy recommendations to improve our knowledge and the education outcomes of Brazilian immigrant children and Brazilians by heritage.

My interest and expertise in Brazilian students, families, and communities emerges from personal experiences and my research practice with immigrant communities. I arrive at this work as a first-generation Brazilian immigrant, a Brown woman who lived undocumented in the US for seven years and who today is a naturalized US citizen, a mother, and a doctor of social work with a degree from Boston University. Together, these experiences have not only informed how I have navigated public education systems, but they have also informed the questions, research, and community work to which I am committed. My research explores Brazilian mothers' social networks of support and how these connections contribute to familial mental health and well-being. As a social worker, I am trained to look at health holistically and as such, education is one of the most consequential social determinants of health.

Brazilians in Massachusetts

The terms "Brazilian immigrant" and "foreign-born Brazilian" will be used interchangeably to refer to a person born in Brazil who migrated to the US. "First generation" refers to immigrants who migrated to the US as adults, while "generation 1.5" refers to immigrants who migrated to the US as children or teens. My use of "Brazilians by heritage" or "Brazilians by ancestry" refers to second-generation persons born in the US with at least one Brazilian immigrant parent. "Undocumented" or "unauthorized" applies to any immigrant who does not have legal status in the US. Legal documentation may be in the form of Legal Permanent Residency, or Green Card, and citizenship by naturalization. Temporary Protected Status, Deferred Action for Childhood Arrival (or DACA), and visas are unstable but provide provisional legal documentation. These terms are essential to understanding the complexities of the Brazilian communities in Massachusetts and impact the educational experiences of children who are of Brazilian heritage.

The Brazilian immigrant community in Massachusetts has grown significantly from 2007 to 2024, contributing to the cultural, economic, and social fabric of the state. Massachusetts was an early destination for the Brazilian diaspora in the US, with a large wave spanning the 1980s and 1990s of visa overstayers and transitory migrants who established a pattern of comings and goings that researchers called "yo-yo" migrations.[2] Another large wave of migration was observed in the 2000s, especially around 2007, related to political and economic instability in Brazil. This time, due to changes in immigration procedures, the patterns and profiles of migration changed, with more Brazilians coming through the Mexican border and staying for a longer term.[3] Brazilians established roots throughout the US, forming large communities, notably in Florida and Massachusetts.[4] According to US Census estimates, there are approximately 112,446 Brazilian residents in Massachusetts.[5] However, the Brazilian consulate in Boston claims that there could be as many as 350,000 Brazilians in its jurisdiction, an estimate based on the US Census's undercounting of low-income and undocumented populations.[6] Nevertheless, according to official counts, Brazilians are the third largest Latino[7] community in Massachusetts after Puerto Ricans and Dominicans.[8]

The median age of Brazilians living in Massachusetts was 34.3 in 2021 and 49.7% identified as female.[9] More than half were married (62%), and, according to the US Census Bureau, there were an estimated 16.9 births per 1,000 Brazilian immigrants in the prior twelve months in Massachusetts,[10] as compared to 11.4 births per 1,000 nationally.[11] Over 20% of Brazilian immigrants in Massachusetts are children between the ages of five and seventeen, while young adults between the ages of eighteen and twenty-four represent 9.7% of Brazilians in the Commonwealth.[12] In sum, a great many Brazilians in Massachusetts are in, or are soon likely to enter, public schools or public colleges or universities.

WHY DO WE NOT KNOW MUCH ABOUT BRAZILIAN STUDENTS' EDUCATIONAL OUTCOMES?

There is limited research on the schooling experiences or educational outcomes of Brazilian immigrant students or children in US public education systems. As noted in Torres-Ardila, Fuentes, and Colón's demographic profile of Latino students in Massachusetts public schools (in this volume), the Massachusetts Department of Elementary and Secondary Education (MDESE) does not collect easily reportable data about students' ethnic backgrounds that could identify students as foreign-born Brazilian or

Brazilian by heritage. As a result, we have little empirical knowledge about the educational outcomes of Brazilian immigrant children and Brazilians by ancestry or second-generation Brazilian children. For instance, we do not know the dropout rates, graduation rates, or academic performance of Brazilian students in Massachusetts. Are Brazilian high school students in Massachusetts going into colleges, trade schools, or the job market? How are Brazilian immigrants and heritage students performing on the state-mandated assessments like Massachusetts Comprehensive Assessment System (MCAS)? How many are receiving English learning support? We cannot answer these questions.

Brazilians are often miscategorized in institutional settings because of ambiguity on what it means to be Latine and because the race-ethnicity options available in public education system demographic questionaries are often not a good fit for Brazilians. Brazilians are not considered Hispanic by the federal government's definition of the term, which includes Spanish-speaking people from the Caribbean, Central and South America, and Spain, regardless of race.[13] While the term "Hispanic" is often coupled with the term "Latino" (Hispanic/Latino), the Hispanic definition explicitly excludes Brazilians. Yet Brazil is the largest nation in Latin America and has a similar history of resource extraction, colonization, slavery, oppression, and genocide of Indigenous and African peoples, as well as imposed Catholic faith. Brazil's population is also approximately four times larger than the second most populated country in Latin America, Colombia. The importance of Brazil's place in Latin America is further illustrated by continental size and its economic potential and contributions at a regional and global scale, as well as by its vast cultural and ethnic diversity. This shared history and sociocultural contexts makes a strong argument for including Brazilians as Latines.

Yet researchers have found that some Brazilians are reluctant to self-identify as Hispanic/Latino because they speak Portuguese and not Spanish as the term "Hispanic" suggests.[14] Brazil is the only country in Latin America whose official language is Portuguese and the largest Portuguese-speaking country in the world. A lot of Brazilians' Latine experience in the US revolves around being non-Spanish-speaking Latines. Research also suggests that the stigma of discrimination and undocumented status that Latine populations have in the US further reinforces the reluctance to identify as Latino.[15] As such, Brazilians, who are one of the fastest growing

Latino communities in the Commonwealth and who also have the highest number of undocumented people in Massachusetts, often hide in plain sight to achieve "successful Americanization."[16]

Like many other immigrant groups, many Brazilians are also unclear about racial and ethnic categorizations in the US. Preliminary research suggests that they are likely to adapt US racial categories to their premigration ethnoschemas and identify as White or Black when there is no option to self-identify as Brazilian or other.[17] The lack of clarity regarding their acceptance of a pan-Latine ethnicity and status and the lack of an option of a Brazilian ethnicity choice contribute to the invisibility of Brazilians in institutional spaces and the lack of research data.

To address this invisibility and recognize the growing Brazilian population in Massachusetts, the Mauricio Gastón Institute for Latino Policy Development at the University of Massachusetts Boston has published a series of reports and white papers about Brazilians dating back to 2007.[18] The institute is also home to the Transnational Brazilian Project, which, under the leadership of Dr. Eduardo Siqueira, organized a network of Brazilian college students and faculty to foster collaborations locally and transnationally.[19] These initiatives contribute to the visibility of Brazilians and help bring the Brazilian community and students into programs and policy discussions. However, despite these efforts, the research on Brazilians in Massachusetts, and in particular Brazilian students in the Commonwealth's schools, is extremely limited.

As previously mentioned, this invisibility is further complicated by the fact the MDESE does not report data on the ethnicity or nationality of students. While researchers can process data about official racial and ethnic categories—White, Black, Asian or Pacific Islander, American Indian or Alaskan Native, and/or Hispanic/Latino—educational researchers cannot use publicly available data to report on Brazilian students' educational outcomes in Massachusetts. Similar to other Latine heritage groups, like Puerto Rican students (see Colón and Frau-Ramos in this volume), there are pathways in the data to uncover Brazilian foreign-born students, such as place of birth or Brazilians by heritage with languages spoken at home, but these data points are not easy to report or reliable. For instance, the data about Portuguese-speaking children in Massachusetts would include Portuguese and Cape Verdean communities and would not likely be reliable for households where only one parent is Brazilian. The limits of publicly available data contributed to hiding Brazilian students in plain sight, which can be problematic in the allocation of resources for students and proper support for communities.

Educational Outcomes of Brazilians in Massachusetts

Although there may not be extensive data or research about the education outcomes of Brazilian students in Massachusetts, there is available information about the overall Brazilian population. I will use what we know about Brazilian immigrants in Massachusetts to inform and make inferences about the micro-, meso-, and macrolevel systems of development connected to education outcomes.[20] Academic research and demographic data will provide an ecological view of the current environment for Brazilian immigrants in Massachusetts to discuss factors that may influence Brazilian heritage students' educational trajectories in Massachusetts public school systems. This discussion will highlight community assets that contribute to this population's success as well as factors that pose challenges to Brazilian students in Massachusetts.

Before I begin exploring systems impacting the education of children and what they might look like for Brazilian populations in Massachusetts, I would like to make a disclaimer: the Brazilian immigrants in Massachusetts are diverse communities divided by social class, race, skin color, and immigration status.[21] These layers of intersectional vulnerabilities are responsible for differences in the experiences and possibly the outcomes of sections of the population. Migration path (visa overstaying or border crossing without inspection or legal entry) and premigration experiences and/or traumas are indicative of how certain slices of the community might adapt and thrive. For instance, among the undocumented, visa overstayers have an easier transition into documented status, notably through marriage, than those who cross the border without inspection since the latter triggers a return to their country for legal reentry.[22]

While we do not know exactly the educational outcomes of Brazilian children in Massachusetts, we know the "societal blueprint," the culture and subcultures these children are inserted into that might influence them academically.[23] Previous research has found that families have a great impact on the education of children.[24] Latine values such as family interdependency and parental support have been found to be a strong predictor of Latine students' academic success.[25] Brazilians share with other Latine communities' principles related to familism, in which honor, loyalty, and obligation to family are core cultural beliefs; they are the basis for some findings related to the academic success of some Latine students despite structural and financial disadvantages.[26] Some Brazilian college students share a sense of responsibility and a desire to perform well in school to make the best of the opportunities their parents had to sacrifice for in order to provide for them, which is comparable to previous research on other Latino students.[27] During a cultural conversation with Brazilian 1.5 college students, for the project Transnationalism, Social Network and Culture: Implications for Health and Behavior, also known as Aqui Lá (here there), a strong theme was the realization of the American dream through education.[28] Project Aqui Lá centered on an ecological framework of immigrants' experiences to explore the dynamics between cultural processes and social determinants of health and well-being. As one Brazilian student reflected, "I felt like, often in my Brazilian group of Brazilian friends I was the only one dreaming big. Like all these Brazilian kids were like, yeah, my dad works as a carpenter, my dad works as a painter, I am just going to be a painter, carpenter or work in construction, live paycheck to paycheck. And I was like, well you are in America. Your parents brought you here for an opportunity. Are you going to waste that? Why are you limiting yourself to this?"[29] This quote demonstrates the expectations for future educational aspirations of Brazilian immigrant youth and reflects differences and difficulties within the community. The differences within the community also shape the opportunities Brazilian children might have to attend preschool, after-school programs, and extracurricular activities, as well as their chances to apply and be accepted into college.

Brazilian immigrants in Massachusetts have completed high school or an equivalent at higher rates than the overall Latino population (49.2% and 29.8%, respectively), yet the proportion of persons over twenty-five with a bachelor's degree or higher is almost exactly the same for Brazilians as for the overall Latino population (18.7% and 18.3%, respectively).[30] For comparison, 46.7% of the non-Latino population in Massachusetts have a bachelor's degree or higher. These gaps are important to consider because parental educational background, for example, has been strongly associated with children's academic achievement, number of years attending school, and success later in life.[31] Parents who are better educated are more likely to be able to afford to live in neighborhoods with better school systems and can use their social capital to promote the educational development of their children. They may participate actively in their children's schooling by joining parent-teacher organizations, volunteering, and attending parent-teacher conferences.[32]

There are, of course, other factors that might facilitate or hinder the participation of immigrant parents in schools. A study found that among immigrant parents the ability to speak English and time in the US were positively associated with participation in their children's school.[33] In 2021, more than half of Brazilian immigrants living in Massachusetts, 55%, reported that they speak English "less than very well."[34] Additionally, Brazil is the country of birth for the largest number of undocumented immigrants in Massachusetts, representing 20% of the unauthorized population in the state followed by El Salvador (11%) and Guatemala (9%).[35] Brazilians in Massachusetts are relatively new migrants, with 63.7% of the noncitizen population entering the country between 2010 and 2020.[36] Thus, as opposed to many other Latine communities that have been in the US for a longer time, Brazilian children in Massachusetts are mostly first, 1.5, and second generation, retaining strong ties to the Portuguese language and Brazilian heritage. Brazilian children in families that lack immigration documentation and English proficiency are more vulnerable to challenges in accessing educational support and opportunities.

Brazilians in Massachusetts are largely employed in the construction and service (including domestic work) sectors.[37] Brazilian immigrant parents are likely to be vulnerable to work pressure from employers and hold early and irregular shifts, making it hard to keep educational routines at home or be present at school functions. A study by Dr. Gabrielle Oliveira and colleagues at Harvard University found that, according to elementary school educators, Brazilian immigrant parents' busy work schedules, lack of knowledge about the public school environment, and unstable immigration status are factors influencing Brazilian children's "school readiness."[38] These perceptions of family engagement coupled with lower expectations of Brazilian students from educators may affect these students' opportunities for gifted programs, Advanced Placement courses, and participation in college access and support programs.

Although Brazilians are dispersed throughout Massachusetts, Brazilians are most likely to reside in the towns and cities along the eastern part of the state in cities such as Framingham, Everett, and Somerville.[39] These cities contain approximately 30% of the Brazilian population, with the remainder dispersed.[40] Previous research found that Latino students nationwide and in Massachusetts experience racial and economic segregation in schools.[41] It is probable that Brazilians within these enclaves experience the same type of racial-ethnic and economic segregation as other Latine students. However, the overall distribution of the population in the Commonwealth points to a more diverse experience within schools for Brazilian immigrant children and Brazilian children by heritage.

Brazilian Children's Education Experience in Massachusetts

There is very limited research focusing specifically on the educational experiences of Brazilian students in Massachusetts public schools. Literature searches on academic databases and Google Scholar using keywords "Brazilian students," "Brazilian students Massachusetts," "Brazilian immigrants' education," and "Brazilian Immigrants education Massachusetts" yielded very limited results. Only four articles specifically focused on the schooling experiences of Brazilian students in Massachusetts. One of the few studies available explored how students and education professionals navigate the cultural complexities of culture, immigration, and language in a Portuguese-English dual-language bilingual education program in Massachusetts.[42] This ethnographic study, by Oliveira, Lima Becker, and Chang-Bacon, found that Brazilian children in this dual-language bilingual education program brought value and expertise to the classroom during Portuguese language instruction yet they did not receive appropriate recognition for their contributions or have lessons that further enriched their foundational knowledge.[43] According to the research, the teachers were aware that the Portuguese-speaking Brazilian children were unchallenged by the material but the teachers felt a need to cater to English-dominant students to "keep the program alive."[44]

A follow-up study detailed the perceptions of parents and teachers of the Portuguese-English two-way immersion (TWI) program, which revealed that although there were some contradictions, parents, and teachers had similar concerns.[45] Parents and teachers reported that the TWI program was beneficial to students, independently of background, yet, they worried about school staffing and the program's expansion or discontinuation and lack of communication about the TWI program.[46] Despite the challenges, overall, Brazilian children's parents were grateful for the opportunity to learn Portuguese in school and that a TWI program enabled them to participate in their kids' education. However, it also created an unequal power dynamic where Brazilian parents were in a subject position.[47] The TWI program incited feelings of gratitude for the program and fear of losing it.[48] The fear of losing Portuguese language instruction and speaking abilities must be further contextualized.

According to the American Community Survey, Portuguese is the second most spoken language other than English in Massachusetts.[49] Further, Portuguese is the second home language for English learners (ELs) in Massachusetts public schools, following Spanish. Massachusetts Portuguese-speaking ELs are largely Brazilian, Cape Verdean, and/or of Portuguese heritage. Most ELs in Massachusetts are children born in the US (58%) with the greatest share in grades 2–5 (37%).[50] Yet, as of February 2023, only five schools in Massachusetts offer TWI in Portuguese, two of them in Framingham.[51] There are forty schools offering TWI in Spanish in Massachusetts, including five in Framingham, a city known for having a large Brazilian and Portuguese-speaking population. There are anecdotes of Portuguese-speaking students being placed in Spanish-speaking programs in Massachusetts. Moreover, the experiences of Brazilian students and parents with a Massachusetts Portuguese-English TWI program have been those in which Portuguese-speaking students' experience and language were centered around English-speaking students' needs.[52]

The gap in the literature on the schooling experiences and outcomes of Brazilian students in Massachusetts and overall in the US, paired with the growth of Brazilian communities, suggests the need for more comprehensive examinations of this student population.[53]

Policy: A Love Language We Can Understand

In August 2023, Massachusetts improved access to college for all students with the passing of the Tuition Equity Law, which makes any person who attended high school in the Commonwealth for at least three years or obtained a high school equivalency eligible for in-state tuition as well as state-funded financial assistance at state-funded public and state-approved private independent nonprofit institutions of higher education.[54] The

Tuition Equity Law's passage resulted from the hard work and lobbying of organizations such as Stories Inspiring Movement, formerly the Student Immigrant Movement, the Brazilian Worker Center, and Centro Presente, which formed the Massachusetts Tuition Equity Movement. Before this law, undocumented students, especially the 1.5 generation, had to pay tuition fees as international students despite having lived most of their lives in the state and in many cases having graduated from Massachusetts public schools.[55] The impact of this legislation on the community will be reflected in the state demographics in the following years with an increased number of Brazilians holding a bachelor's degree.

The projection above is optimistic and assumes that Brazilian students may follow a different trajectory than the overall Latine student population, which has a much lower extent of college completion than their White peers.[56] In 2021, only 29% of Latines had completed an associate's degree or higher, in contrast to 58% of White adults over twenty-five years of age.[57] Thus, implementation of the Tuition Equity Law should include outreach and education efforts in immigrant communities and public schools with large enrollments of immigrant children from populations overrepresented in unauthorized legal status, such as Brazilians in Massachusetts. It is important that public school counselors have the knowledge to guide students to a college education. Additionally, policies that address social determinants of education inequalities as well as inclusive and integrative schools and systems are needed to bring parity to Brazilian and other Latine communities.

Massachusetts students are the highest achieving in the nation, yet data from the MDESE show that Latine students are consistently falling through the gaps.[58] However, the data are not clear about the outcomes of Brazilian students. The MDESE should track students by race *and* ethnicity more granularly and report on questions such as birth country and birth country of parents. If we tracked students' backgrounds, we would be able to better identify the trajectory of specific populations through the education system and tailor interventions to support student success. These reports could answer questions like where are Brazilian children enrolled and what are their graduation rates, dropout rates, MCAS and other standardized test scores, and college acceptance rates. These answers would prompt new questions, such as, Who are the Brazilian children that are succeeding (who is going to college and why)? Who is dropping out of high school? Where and why? Are there gender differences in academic outcomes? Until we have actionable, empirical data, all we have is work at the local level and knowledge about the community on average.

Local school districts are a good place to start ensuring that Brazilian children have the best opportunities to complete their education. Massachusetts cities and towns with the largest presence of Brazilian immigrants, such as Malden, Everett, and Framingham, are probably the ones with the largest enrollment of Brazilians by heritage and Brazilian immigrant children. These school districts should assess their communities' barriers to school participation and develop programs and policies to promote and integrate the Brazilian community within the school system and alleviate possible burdens. There are examples of school districts in Massachusetts where changes in policies and practices resulted in greater participation from parents, which translates into better academic outcomes for children. In Chelsea, for example, changes in practices and communication policies through the Chelsea Family Literacy Program increased parental involvement in school activities for children in grades K to 3 in five elementary schools.[59] This was substantial, especially for first-generation Spanish-speaking immigrant parents, and resulted in greater engagement in school from their children.[60]

A barrier to parental participation in school for many Brazilian parents may be related to documentation status. As described above, a large slice of the Brazilian immigrant population is undocumented, with an estimated 42,000 foreign-born Brazilians in Massachusetts representing 20% of the overall unauthorized population.[61] While there is no formal requirement that one be documented in order to attend parent-teacher conferences and school events, parents must fill out a CORI form to take part in PTOs, volunteer in school, or provide any assistance at in-school locations. Undocumented parents, regardless of English language proficiency, are discouraged from participating since they do not have social security numbers. Other options for reference checking should be offered to parents who would like to participate but could not provide a social security number for a CORI check. These types of accommodations would integrate, engage, and welcome parents beyond document translations and English-Portuguese meeting interpreters.

If solutions are at the local level, so is the burden: school officials and teachers have been historically exploited by the education system and expected to do the work without support or resources. Principals, teachers, and other school personnel need the appropriate training and competitive compensation to deliver the solutions our communities expect of them. It is vital that we pay our educators for the value they provide and support their work with material needs and training opportunities and stop cutting vital services like music teachers, drama teachers, arts educators, social workers, and psychologists from school budgets. Education professionals are confronted daily with issues beyond their reach as they try to help generations of children transcend the conditions in which their parents live. Diversity, equity, and inclusion teams need to be a pivotal part of every microsystem, and these professionals should be delegated the responsibility to present and discuss pedagogical strategies to meaningfully build community within the school.

Although these proposed changes are local, investments and resources must be made at the state and federal levels as well. Massachusetts is already ahead by providing free school lunches to every child, independent of need. The policy of free lunches for all cuts the paperwork for new immigrant families and undocumented families, who many times do not know how to navigate school bureaucracies. But this is just policy and there is much more work to be done to ensure that all children have access to the best public education possible.

Brazilian students in Massachusetts are an asset to our communities, but right now, they are our best kept secret. These students are thriving and struggling outside of our purview, and our failure to sing their praises and pinpoint the exact places where they might need assistance is a problem. It is unacceptable that the fastest growing Latine community in Massachusetts does not know whether their children are graduating high school or at what rate Brazilian students are being accepted to college. There are too many questions. Education researchers should be able to develop a Brazilian students' education agenda that reflects the academic progress and educational experiences of this population because without it all we have is anecdotes, inferences, and hypotheses. Data about the state of Brazilian education in Massachusetts will be a first step toward building a brighter future for generations of Brazilian students with the opportunities and support to honor the sacrifices of their parents.

Notes

1 Quote from the cultural conversation with Brazilian students from generation 1.5 from the 2013–16 project Transnationalism, Networks, and Culture: Implications for Health and Behavior, Office of Behavioral and Social Science Research and National Institute of Minority Health and Health Disparities (R24MD00819). Pseudonyms have been used throughout this chapter.

2   Maxine Margolis, "Goodbye, Brazil: Émigrés from the Land of Soccer and Samba," *American Anthropologist* 116, no. 2 (2014): 462–63; Carlos Eduardo Siqueira and Tiago Jansen, "Updating Demographic, Geographic, and Occupational Data on Brazilians in Massachusetts," in *Becoming Brazuca: Brazilian Immigration to the United States*, ed. Clemence Jouet-Pastre and Leticia J. Braga, 105–24 (Harvard University Press, 2008).

3   Margolis, "Goodbye, Brazil"; Siqueira and Tiago Jansen, "Updating Demographic."

4   Michelle Borges, et al., "Brazilians in the US and Massachusetts: A Demographic and Economic Profile," Gastón Institute Publications 309 (2023), https://scholarworks .umb.edu/gaston_pubs/309/.

5   Borges et al., "Brazilians in the US and Massachusetts."

6   Borges et al., "Brazilians in the US and Massachusetts"; Phillip Granberry and Krizia Valentino, "Latinos in Massachusetts: Brazilians," Gastón Institute Publications 251 (2020), https://scholarworks.umb.edu/gaston_pubs/251/.

7   In this chapter I have chosen to use the gender-neutral term "Latine" to describe people who are of Latin American heritage. When citing research, I also use the terms that are used by the referenced authors. As I discuss in this chapter, the terms "Latino" (and its derivatives) and "Hispanic" generate a lot of questions and discussion relative to their application to Brazilian populations.

8   Granberry and Valentino, "Latinos in Massachusetts."

9   US Census Bureau; American Community Survey, 2017–2021 American Community Survey 5-Year Estimates, Table B01002, https://data.census.gov/table?q=median+age &t=519&g=040XX00US25&tid=ACSDT5YSPT2021.B01002.

10 Borges et al., "Brazilians in the US and Massachusetts."

11 USAFacts, "Births per 1,000 people," USAFacts, 2020, https://usafacts.org/data/topics /people-society/health/longevity/birth-rate/.

12 US Census Bureau; American Community Survey, 2021 American Community Survey 1-Year Estimates, Table S0201, https://data.census.gov/table?q=United+States &t=519:Age+and+Sex:Children&g=040XX00US25&tid=ACSSPP1Y2021.S0201.

13 Office of Management and Budget, *Office of Management and Budget (OMB) DIREC-TIVE NO. 15 Race and Ethnic Standards for Federal Statistics and Administrative Reporting*. Office of Management and Budget, 1977, https://wonder.cdc.gov/wonder /help/populations/bridged-race/directive15.html.

14 Helen Marrow, "To Be or Not to Be (Hispanic or Latino) Brazilian Racial and Ethnic Identity in the United States," *Ethnicities* 3, no. 4 (2003): 427–64.

15 Marrow, "To Be or Not to Be."

16 Marrow, "To Be or Not to Be."

17 Marrow, "To Be or Not to Be."

18 A complete list of publications by the Mauricio Gastón Institute for Latino Policy Development about Brazilians in Massachusetts can be found on their website: https://scholarworks.umb.edu/gastoninstitute/.

19 See the Transnational Brazilian Project website, https://www.umb.edu/gaston -institute/core-programs/transnational-brazilian-project/, for more information.

20 Urie Bronfenbrenner, "Ecological Models of Human Development," *International Encyclopedia of Education* 3, no. 2 (1994): 37–43.

21 Natalicia Rocha Tracy, "Transnational Brazilians: Class, Race, Immigration Status and Family Life," (PhD diss., Boston University, Department of Sociology, 2016).

22 Kara Cebulko, "Documented, Undocumented, and Liminally Legal: Legal Status During the Transition to Adulthood for 1.5-Generation Brazilian Immigrants," *Sociological Quarterly* 55, no. 1 (2014): 143–67.

23 Bronfenbrenner, "Ecological Models of Human Development."

24 Anna J. Egalite, "How Family Background Influences Student Achievement," *Education Next* 16, no. 2 (2016): 70–78.

25 Anthony D. Ong, Jean S. Phinney, and Jessica Dennis, "Competence Under Challenge: Exploring the Protective Influence of Parental Support and Ethnic Identity in Latino College Students," *Journal of Adolescence* 29, no. 6 (2006): 961–79.

26 Karina M. Cahill, et al., "Familism Values and Adjustment Among Hispanic/Latino Individuals: A Systematic Review and Meta-Analysis," *Psychological Bulletin* 147, no. 9 (2021): 947; Gustavo Carlo, et al., "Culture-Related Strengths Among Latin American Families: A Case Study of Brazil," *Marriage and Family Review* 41, nos. 3–4 (2007): 335–360; Ong, Phinney, and Dennis, "Competence Under Challenge."

27 Cristina Araujo Brinkerhoff, et al., "'There You Enjoy Life, Here You Work': Brazilian and Dominican Immigrants' Views on Work and Health in the US," *International Journal of Environmental Research and Public Health* 16 no. 20 (2019): 4025; Jean S. Phinney, Jessica Dennis, and Saloniki Osorio, "Reasons to Attend College Among Ethnically Diverse College Students," *Cultural Diversity and Ethnic Minority Psychology* 12, no. 2 (2006): 347–66; Marisa Saunders and Irene Serna, "Making College Happen: The College Experiences of First-Generation Latino Students," *Journal of Hispanic Higher Education* 3, no. 2 (2004): 146–63.

28 Brinkerhoff et al., "There You Enjoy Life, Here You Work."

29 Quote from the cultural conversation with Brazilian students from generation 1.5 from the 2013–16 project "Transnationalism, Networks, and Culture: Implications for Health and Behavior," Office of Behavioral and Social Science Research and National Institute of Minority Health and Health Disparities (R24MD00819).

30 Granberry and Valentino, "Latinos in Massachusetts: Brazilians."

31 Egalite, "Family Background."

32 Egalite, "Family Background."

33 Kristin Turney and Grace Kao, "Barriers to School Involvement: Are Immigrant Parents Disadvantaged?," *Journal of Educational Research* 102, no. 4 (2009): 257–71.

34 US Census Bureau; American Community Survey, Table S0201.

35 Migration Policy Institute, *Profile of the Unauthorized Population, Massachusetts* (Migration Policy Institute, 2019).

36 Borges et al., "Brazilians in the US and Massachusetts."

37 Borges et al., "Brazilians in the US and Massachusetts"; Brinkerhoff et al., "Brazilian and Dominican Immigrants"; DeAnne K. Hilfinger Messias, "Transnational Perspectives on Women's Domestic Work: Experiences of Brazilian Immigrants in the United States," *Women & Health* 33, nos. 1–2 (2001): 1–20; Bindu Panikkar, et al., "'They See Us As Machines': The Experience of Recent Immigrant Women in the Low Wage Informal Labor Sector," *PloS ONE* 10, no. 11 (2015): e0142686; Carlos Eduardo Siqueira and Tiago Jansen, "Working Conditions of Brazilian Immigrants in Massachusetts," *Journal of Immigrant and Minority Health* 14, no. 3 (2011): 481–88.

38 Gabrielle Oliveira, Mariana Lima Becker, and Marisa Segel, "Constructing the (Un) Readiness of Brazilian Immigrant Children in One Elementary School," *Multicultural Perspectives* 23, no. 4 (2021): 206–16.

39 Borges et al., "Brazilians in the US and Massachusetts;" Boston Planning and Development Agency Research Division, *Brazilians in Boston* (Boston Planning and Development Agency, 2017); Granberry and Valentino, "Latinos in Massachusetts."

40 Granberry and Valentino, "Latinos in Massachusetts."

41 Bruce Fuller, et al., "Variation in the Local Segregation of Latino Children—Role of Place, Poverty, and Culture," *American Journal of Education* 128, no. 2 (2022): 245–80, https://www.journals.uchicago.edu/doi/epdf/10.1086/717674.

42 Gabrielle Oliveira, Mariana Lima Becker, and Chris K. Chang-Bacon, "Eu Sei, I Know": Equity and Immigrant Experience in a Portuguese-English Dual Language Bilingual Education Program," *TESOL Quarterly* 54, no. 3 (2020): 572–98.

43 Oliveira, Lima Becker, and Chang-Bacon, "Eu Sei, I Know."

44 Oliveira, Lima Becker, and Chang-Bacon, "Eu Sei, I Know."

45 Gabrielle Oliveira, et al., "Parent and Teacher Perceptions of a Brazilian Portuguese Two-Way Immersion Program," *Bilingual Research Journal* 43, no. 2 (2020): 212–31.

46 Oliveira et al., "Parent and Teacher Perceptions."

47 Oliveira, Gabrielle, Mariana Lima Becker, and Ahrum Jeon, "Gratidão, Gratitude: Brazilian Immigrant Parents' Perspectives on Their Children's Bilingual Education," *Diaspora, Indigenous, and Minority Education* 15, no. 1 (2021): 47–60.

48 Oliveira, Lima Becker, and Jeon. "Gratidão, Gratitude."

49 Massachusetts Office of Public Health Strategy and Communications, *Translation Toolkit—Foreign Language Guide* (Massachusetts Department of Public Health, 2010).

50 MDESE, "Dual Language Education Programs," MDESE, 2023. https://www.doe.mass.edu/ele/programs/dle.html.

51 MDESE, "Dual Language Education Programs."

52 Oliveira, Lima Becker, and Chang-Bacon, "Eu Sei, I Know"; Oliveira, Lima Becker, and Jeon. "Gratidão, Gratitude."

53 Boston Planning and Development Agency Research Division, *Brazilians in Boston* (Boston Planning and Development Agency, 2017), https://www.bostonplans.org/getattachment/ad985146-c34a-4f51-8c6e-b277d4cda498#:~:text=Brazilians percent20settled percent20in percent20cities percent20and percent20towns percent20in percent20eastern,home percent20to percent205 percent20percent percent20 of percent20Massachusetts' percent20Brazilian percent20population.

54 Massachusetts Department of Higher Education, "Celebrating Tuition Equity for Massachusetts Students," Massachusetts Department of Higher Education, 2023, https://www.mass.edu/tuitionequity.

55 Cebulko, "Documented, Undocumented, and Liminally Legal."

56 Excelencia in Education, *Latino College Completion: Massachusetts—2023* (Excelencia in Education, 2023), https://www.edexcelencia.org/research/latino-college-completion/massachusetts.

57 Excelencia in Education, *Latino College Completion: Massachusetts—2023.*

58 Fabián Torres-Ardila and Nyal Fuentes, "The State of Latino Education: 2010–2020," Gastón Institute Publications 292 (2022), https://scholarworks.umb.edu/gaston_pubs/292.

59 Lorna Rivera and Nicole Lavan, "Family Literacy Practices and Parental Involvement of Latin American Immigrant Mothers," *Journal of Latinos and Education* 11, no. 4 (2012): 247–59. https://doi.org/10.1080/15348431.2012.715500.

60 Rivera and Lavan, "Family Literacy Practices."

61 Migration Policy Institute, *Profile of the Unauthorized Population, Massachusetts.*

Chapter Three

Reflections on the State of Puerto Rican Students in Massachusetts Public Schools[1]

MELISSA COLÓN AND MANUEL FRAU-RAMOS

Mirroring national trends, in the last three decades, a robust body of research suggests that (1) Latino students continue to experience persistent gaps in academic outcomes and access to high-quality education and (2) given the population trends and the nature of the state's knowledge-based economy, the future success of Massachusetts is tied to the educational success of its Latino population.[2] While this research has brought much-needed attention to the systemic barriers that Latino students and their families face in schools, most findings as well as policy directives largely treat Latinos as a homogenous group, ignoring the vast diversity of experiences and outcomes that exist within and across different Latino communities.[3] National meta-narratives about Latino students as "newcomers," immigrants, and English learners are ubiquitous and typically at the center of educational policy and practice discussions on how to improve the educational outcomes of this student population. Yet the majority of Latino students in Massachusetts are not newcomers; they are US citizens and English speaking, mostly because the largest Latino origins group within the Latino student population is Puerto Rican.

In this chapter, we argue that to radically improve Latino students' educational experiences and outcomes, a more nuanced understanding of the diverse experiences and outcomes of various Latino students and their communities is necessary. Specifically, we highlight the experiences and outcomes of Puerto Rican students. Because an estimated 40% of Latino students in Massachusetts are Puerto Rican,[4] we propose that to fundamentally address and improve Latino education in Massachusetts, we must consider and understand the schooling lives of Boricua[5] students. Using a Freirean approach and Diasporic frameworks for learning and analysis, we begin by providing a very brief history of Puerto Rican students in the Commonwealth, including an overview of educational attainment trends and salient themes that have shaped the schooling experiences of Puerto Rican students in US schools, with a focus on Massachusetts. Then, drawing from a series of *charlas* with Puerto Rican educators, parents, and activists, we reimagine a public education system that is culturally sustaining, equitable, and academically rigorous for Puerto Rican students.

Framing: Diasporic, Dialogic, Emancipatory

Our analysis and (re)imaginations draw from the work of Puerto Rican education scholars who developed Diasporic frameworks for teaching, learning, and analysis.[6] The concept of Diaspora typically refers to the dispersion of people from their original homelands. Diasporic frameworks, in part, emphasize the importance of migration not as a one-time event but rather as a "fluid and dynamic construct" that shapes identities and communities across time and locations.[7] In the case of Boricuas who have experienced circular migration for more than one hundred years, Diasporic frameworks ask us to consider how social and historical processes and factors, past and present, *aquí* and *allá*, and across generations, shape our lives, including our experiences in school.

Diasporic analytic frames and ways of being have been central to our own educational lives. Manuel was born in Puerto Rico and is a product of Puerto Rico's public school system. He studied at Papa Juan XXIII High School, one of the first bilingual public schools established on the island to host the increasing number of English-speaking Puerto Rican students returning to Borikén. He has a master's degree in bilingual education and an EdD from the University of Massachusetts Amherst. As an educator, he was a long-time advisor to the Hispanic Parent Advisory Council, known as PAC Bilingüe, of the Holyoke Public Schools. Melissa was born in Cambridge, Massachusetts, but like many Puerto Rican children, she experienced circular migration; she spent her childhood in Coamo, Puerto Rico, and attended her local public school. Upon returning to the Boston area, she was placed in a transitional bilingual education program. She has had to (re) and (un)learn Spanish and English several times in her life. As an educator, advocate, and mother she amplifies Puerto Rican language and cultural traditions and resists subtractive schooling[8] in all shapes. Melissa and Manuel became involved in Latino educational research in Massachusetts during their college years. Over time, their shared interest in advocating for Latino educational issues brought them together at community gatherings and professional conferences related to these social justice issues.

Our personal Diasporic experiences are typical of many Boricuas. As such, when we considered the future of Puerto Rican education in Massachusetts, we committed ourselves to not only reviewing the extant literature and available data but also to learning with and from others. Our analysis also benefits from the teachings of renowned Brazilian educational philosopher Paulo Freire, which emphasize the importance of dialogue in critical and emancipatory analysis and learning.[9] Grounded in the principles of faith, trust, love, and hope that change is possible,[10] we engaged in informal *charlas* with each other and with other Puerto Rican educators, parents, and activists to discuss this project and the recommendations we are putting forth. Our conversations were grounded by the notions that:

- learning is an emancipatory process that contributes to consciousness-raising and the creation of a more just world.[11]
- Puerto Rican students, families, and educators are powerfully equipped to reimagine schooling. Their knowledge is essential in the development of educational policies and interventions.
- schools can serve as "radical sanctuaries"[12] and critical partners in all nation-building efforts.

It was through these *charlas* that we clarified our collective learning and thinking regarding the future of Puerto Rican education in Massachusetts.

Puerto Rican Students in the Massachusetts Public Schools: A Brief Historical Background

> *Do not believe them when they tell you that I do not exist.*
> —BILLIE GASTIC [13]

In her book *Puerto Rican Students in U.S. Schools*, Sonia Nieto reminds readers that "Puerto Rican students are no strangers to US schools."[14] Student population records from as early as the 1910s indicate concentrations of Boricua students in US public school districts in what would soon become historic Puerto Rican enclaves.[15] These early Puerto Rican communities developed partly as a response to revolutionary movements and wars in the Caribbean and Latin America, including the Spanish-American War of 1898, at which point Puerto Rico became an "unincorporated territory" of the US. Nineteen years later, the US "extended" citizenship to all Puerto Ricans through the Jones Act of 1917, which eliminated any legal barriers to migration between Borikén and the US.

The largest wave of Puerto Rican migrants to the continental US arrived during the post–World War II period and settled primarily in the northeast corridor of the US.[16] During the 1940s, Puerto Rican laborers started coming in significant numbers to Massachusetts. They were first hired to work as seasonal workers in the agricultural sector, especially in the tobacco fields in the Pioneer Valley (Western Massachusetts), in most cases by the same American companies already operating in Puerto Rico.[17] The workers began to settle and build Puerto Rican communities near their jobs.[18] Among the historical Puerto Rican enclaves that emerged from this migration, the largest are in Holyoke, Springfield, and Westfield. In the eastern and central parts of the state, Puerto Ricans largely came to industrial cities like Boston, Cambridge, Lawrence, and Worcester to work in manufacturing and there too laid the groundwork for what later would become Latino enclaves.[19]

In the last fifty years, the Puerto Rican community in Massachusetts has experienced consistent growth and dispersion. Today, Massachusetts continues to have one of the largest Puerto Rican communities in the US.[20] According to the 2022 American Community Survey,[21] 305,000 Boricuas reside in Massachusetts, making them the largest ethnic group within Massachusetts's Latino population, accounting for one-third of Latinos in Massachusetts.[22] There is a continued concentration of Boricuas in the western part of the state; Springfield has the largest Puerto Rican population and Holyoke has the highest concentration of Puerto Ricans not only in Massachusetts but in the continental US. While there are Puerto Ricans in cities and towns across the state, 50% of all Boricuas in Massachusetts continue to live in the five communities of Springfield, Boston, Worcester, Holyoke, and Lawrence.[23]

These community patterns are also reflected in enrollment patterns in public schools. Given the long histories and the sizeable Puerto Rican population in Massachusetts, conversations about Latino students that perpetually position them as only "newcomers," English learners, or immigrants are both confusing and misleading since Puerto Ricans have resided in the continental US since the nineteenth century and many are raised in multilingual households. We should nevertheless be aware that this student population presents some unique characteristics compared with other Latino students, which we now turn to.

Scholars of the Puerto Rican diaspora have argued that to understand the experiences of Puerto Rican students in Massachusetts public schools it is important to consider four interrelated themes: colonization, migration, racialization, and activism. To begin with, since 1898, Puerto Rican children have experienced an American colonial school system purposefully designed to disrobe the Puerto Rican nation of its history, culture, and power.[24] Understanding that schooling is a mechanism that reproduces imperial power, the first commissioner of education of Puerto Rico, a federally appointed position, vowed to develop a Puerto Rican public school system that focused on deculturalization so that Puerto Rican children could become more American.[25] With the goal of rapid Americanization, colonial-appointed bureaucrats implemented educational policies across the archipelago that included the replacement of local curricula and books with textbooks from the US, attempts to enforce the use of English as the *only* language of instruction, the celebration of American holidays in schools, the replacement of Boricua teachers with American ones, and the expulsion of teachers who were involved in anticolonial efforts, to name a few.[26] Puerto Rican students, families, and teachers resisted these efforts and fought (and continue to do so) for control of their schools and, more importantly, their children's future.

These harsh practices were central not only to the schooling lives of Puerto Rican children living in Borikén but also to children living in the Diaspora as they too contended with schools that were actively committed to deculturalization.[27] Unlike other (im)migrant groups, Puerto Rican families were more likely to come together to the US.[28] This meant that where there were Puerto Rican adults working, there were children, and these children needed to go to school. Schools in the US, like the ones in Borikén, also wanted to assimilate Puerto Rican children as quickly as possible into the "American way of life." These assimilation policies assumed (1) that Boricuas accepted their colonial status and (2) that the US would be their final and preferred destination. Yet for most Puerto Rican families, the goal of migration has not been to permanently leave Puerto Rico, but rather to live transnationally. This cultural phenomenon is colloquially understood and referred to as *el vaivén*.[29] Important to underscore is that these movements are not simply about visiting the homelands but rather represent ongoing commitments to cement substantive and reciprocal relationships with and in Borikén. Circulatory patterns have also been described as an adaptive response to crises in the US or Puerto Rico.[30] For example, the humanitarian and political crisis that ensued after Hurricanes María and Irma in 2017 resulted in an influx of Puerto Rican families moving to the US, including Massachusetts. Between 2010 and 2019, for example, Massachusetts's Puerto Rican population increased by about 30% from 262,804 to 340,893.[31] By 2019, Massachusetts had the fifth largest concentration of Puerto Ricans in the US.

Transnationalism among Puerto Ricans is a salient cultural phenomenon that is often front and center in Boricua cultural expressions. For example, the classic Diasporic anthem from 1943, "En Mi Viejo San Juan," whose lyrics include the chorus "Pero un día volveré," has become a call for action for many Boricuas. Another iconic song, "Boricua en la Luna," is a patriotic anthem based on a 1980 poem by Juan Antonio Corretjer. It was popularized by Roy Brown, a Puerto Rican singer/songwriter born in Florida, who adapted it into a song. The poem emphasizes the idea that Puerto Ricans, no matter where they are born, even if it is on the moon, continue to feel Borincanos. The goal of Boricuas to return to the homeland or to have "dual home bases"[32] requires that children have the intercultural skills necessary to navigate various social contexts. Circulatory migration patterns and the hopes of "dual home bases" have contributed to the maintenance of strong cultural and familial ties and practices between Boricuas in the Diaspora and Puerto Rico, as well as valuing bilingualism and biculturalism. It has also placed Puerto Rican children and their families in conflict with assimilation paradigms implemented by most US schools, which require students to disrobe themselves of their home language and heritages.

Racism and racialization are a third theme that is central to understanding the schooling experiences of Puerto Rican students in the US. As has been the case for other "native minorities," for Puerto Rican students, schools have largely been a place where social and legally sanctioned segregation, exclusion, and marginalization routinely take place.[33] Longitudinal research on residential patterns, school enrollment records, and educational outcomes suggests that Puerto Rican students in the urban centers of the Northeast have experienced extreme levels of school-based racial and economic segregation.[34] This is the case in Massachusetts as well. In the academic year 2024–25, enrollment data from the Massachusetts Department of Elementary and Secondary Education (MDESE) indicates that cities with long-established Puerto Rican enclaves have some of the highest concentrations of Latino students (e.g., Holyoke, 81%; Lawrence, 95%; Springfield, 68%; Southbridge, 66%).[35] Many of the school districts with the highest concentration of Latino students are also the school districts that have been identified as "chronically underperforming" by MDESE and have long-documented histories of civil rights violations and discrimination.[36]

Being made to feel unwelcome, experiencing teacher bias and bigotry, inadequate language support, tracking into nonacademic programs, low expectations, curricula erasure, and disproportionately harsh punishments and expulsions from school have been identified as systemic challenges that have limited Puerto Ricans' educational opportunities.[37] This is not a new phenomenon. In one of the first longitudinal and multisite qualitative studies on the schooling experiences of Boricuas students in US schools, *The Losers*, published in 1968, Richard Margolis concluded that even though Puerto Rican children were US citizens, like African American children, they were burdened by an unjust education system.[38] "The Puerto Rican child and the Negro child," Margolis wrote, "share many humiliations, not the least of which is a system of even-handed injustice."[39]

Unjust and racist educational settings have been well documented in the experiences of Boricua students in Massachusetts public schools. Currently, Puerto Ricans have some of the lowest educational levels of any population in Massachusetts.[40] For example, Puerto Ricans twenty-five years and older in Massachusetts had an especially high share of people "with less than a high school diploma: 31%, compared to 24% for Other Latinos and 7% for Non- Latinos."[41] Low college completion rates have also been observed. Only 10% of Puerto Ricans in Massachusetts have completed at least a bachelor's degree.[42] As a point of reference, 23% of other Latinos and 47% of non-Latinos have completed at least a bachelor's degree in Massachusetts.[43] High dropout rates and low college enrollment among this population are consistent with outcome trends of school districts and the "chronically underperforming schools" they attend.[44]

As previously discussed, a metanarrative that exists about Latino students is that they are English learners, and therefore, their lower educational outcomes can be attributed to not having English mastery. But for Puerto Rican students, this logic is faulty. Based on the state's English proficiency assessment and placements, the majority of Latino students do not qualify for English language services because they are determined to be English proficient. And the level of English fluency is much higher among Puerto Ricans than among other Latino groups. According to the 2022 American Community Survey, more than three-quarters (76%) of Puerto Ricans ages five and older in Massachusetts either spoke only English or spoke it very well. As noted by Granberry and Valentino, this puts Puerto Ricans' English proficiency closer to non-Latinos (94%) than to other Latinos (59%) in the state.[45] Of course, there are many Puerto Rican students who are English learners, and as outlined by Bernardino's analysis (in this volume), Boricua English learners face a host of additional systemic challenges that limit their access to a high-quality education.

The MDESE does not yet report on academic or school engagement outcomes by ethnic/national groups, and therefore it is impossible at this time to identify where in the educational pipeline (grades, schools, or districts) Puerto Ricans are "falling behind" or excelling. Without individual-level data that include information on students' ethnic background, it is also not yet possible to conduct correlational or causational quantitative analysis. What we do know, however, is that educational attainment and school engagement outcomes relative to other racial and ethnic groups are two of the many "social indicators" that have been used to pathologize the Puerto Rican community.[46] Puerto Rican students (and their families) are often discussed as being solely responsible for lower educational outcomes without addressing the structural barriers, including the long-term impact of liminal citizenship, deculturalization, racialization, discrimination, low-quality teaching and instruction, lackluster curricula, inappropriate English-language instruction, chronically underfunded schools, and systemic oppression that have been operationalized by and in schools. These structural barriers are not unique to Puerto Rican students; it is a history that we share with our African American, Indigenous/First Nations, and Pacific Islander siblings and more recently with immigrant communities in Massachusetts and beyond.[47] The argument, therefore, has been made that Puerto Rican students are not "falling behind" but rather they are being systematically "pushed out." In other words, negative schooling experiences play a role in how Puerto Rican students engage and academically perform in school. [48]

While structural barriers present a challenging context, it is essential to amplify that Boricua students, their families, and communities have always resisted colonial control and inequitable schools. As such, resistance and activism are the final theme that is central to understanding Puerto Rican education in Massachusetts. The Puerto Rican community has been purposeful in its rejection of assimilation and deculturalization practices and has sustained participation and leadership in school reform efforts that recognize the humanity and rights of children and families.[49] For example, Puerto Rican students, parents, and community members across the state and in collaboration with other groups, have long served as advocates for bilingual education, culturally responsive education, and desegregation efforts.[50] Inspired by the US civil rights movement and the human rights movements in the Caribbean and Latin America, Puerto Ricans in the Diaspora organized against discriminatory practices, founded education programs and advocacy organizations, ran for elected office, and even founded schools. As noted in CENTRO's special issue *The Education of the Puerto Rican Diaspora: Challenges, Dilemmas, and Possibilities*, Puerto Rican educators, activists, and scholars, many with Massachusetts roots, have emerged as national educational leaders.[51] Today, the Puerto Rican community continues to advocate for education equity so that schools can become "radical sanctuaries" for *all* students.[52]

Yet despite the large number of Puerto Rican students and families in Massachusetts, the challenges previously mentioned, and our ongoing contributions to improving the educational landscape in the Commonwealth and beyond, there is a ubiquitous invisibility and silence regarding the strengths and needs of Boricua students. There is hesitancy to focus on this population even though one in three, possibly more, Latino students in Massachusetts is Boricua. In our own work as teachers, researchers, parents, journalists, and advocates, we have been told we should not focus our work on Puerto Rican students. We have heard "there are not that many Puerto Rican students here" or "that they didn't know or don't know where the Puerto Rican students are" as though we are invisible. But we firmly respond as educational scholar Dr. Billie Gastic has called us to do: "Do not believe them when they tell you that I [we] do not exist."[53]

(Re)imaginations of Educational Policies and Praxis

Our decades-long work with and in Puerto Rican communities has led us to spaces and events where the future of Puerto Rican students, and more specifically Puerto Rican children and families, have been at the center of discussion. Guided by Freirean teachings on the importance of self and communal reflexivity and dialogue as moments "where humans meet to reflect on their reality as they make and remake it,"[54] for over a year we engaged in conversations with one another, as well as with parents, educators, activists, and scholars in our respective communities, discussing the educational experiences and outcomes of Puerto Rican students in Massachusetts public schools and what is most needed to improve their educational conditions. These conversations have affirmed our collective belief in a future in which Puerto Rican children, their families, and communities will have what they need to maximize their potential and experience freedom in ways that we have yet to know.[55] Essential to this vision is an education that values Puerto Rican children, families, and communities and that understands learning as an emancipatory process that contributes to consciousness-raising and the creation of a more just world.[56] In this work, schools—and educators in particular—can serve as critical partners. This requires a (re)commitment, and for some a (re)imagination, of what it will take to drastically improve public education so children, families, and communities have what they need to thrive.

Toward this end, we envision a future in which Puerto Rican children and students will

- Have access to high-quality early education programs and care that are committed to ensuring that children are multilingual, literate, compassionate, and joyful.
- Attend schools that offer free nutritious and culturally appropriate meals to all students, regardless of income.
- Attend schools with teachers who are committed to culturally sustaining pedagogical approaches, including native/heritage language maintenance.
- Attend schools that value and have implemented ethnic studies curricula, including Puerto Rican history and culture, across all grade levels.
- Attend schools where English learners receive an education that is grounded in best practices of multilanguage acquisition, including native language instruction.
- Attend schools where the rights of students with disabilities are honored and central to all planning processes and not merely an afterthought. This includes the right to an inclusive education with educators who are prepared and committed to meeting their needs.

- Attend schools where teachers have the resources and support they need, including fair and equitable pay and working conditions so that they are best equipped to help their students meet their goals.
- Attend schools that have robust, responsive, and transformative mental and physical health services and other supports so that trauma and challenging circumstances are not further pathologized and criminalized in schools.
- Attend schools that prepare them to read at grade level or above by third grade and, most importantly, encourage reading for enjoyment, learning, and the ability to see themselves in the stories.
- Attend schools where visual and performing arts, including learning how to play an instrument, are part of the core curriculum and they participate and excel in these offerings.
- Attend schools with well-organized physical education and sports programming and they participate and excel in these offerings.
- Attend schools with diverse faculty, staff, and administrative teams.
- Attend schools that encourage and welcome parental involvement, participation, and engagement in the education of their children without any cultural and/or language barriers.
- Attend schools that prepare them to take algebra in middle school and provide opportunities to take advanced math courses as part of their high school education.
- Attend schools where students have access to high-quality college preparation programs, including but not limited to honors and Advanced Placement courses and Early College/Dual Enrollment programs, and where they participate and excel in these offerings.
- Be widely represented in honors and Advanced Placement courses and extracurricular activities of their choice like student government, robotics teams, theater groups, etc.
- Have the opportunity to participate in high-quality vocational programs that put them on track for high-paying economic opportunities of their choice, including biotech, engineering, entrepreneurship, and nursing.
- Aspire and are well prepared to attend, apply, and enroll in colleges, universities, and professional training programs of their choice.
- Be able to attend an institution of higher learning for free, regardless of their economic or (im)migration status.
- Be prepared to lead and serve with integrity, stand against discrimination, and hate in all forms and contribute to efforts to improve our Puerto Rican communities, wherever they may be.

One may look at this enumeration and say that there is nothing extraordinary about this vision. But historically speaking, if this vision were to be enacted, it would be remarkable, as it would mean that Puerto Rican children, for the first time in over a hundred years, would have universal access to a high-quality education that could change the lives of generations to come.

Because public education in Massachusetts is largely controlled by local governments, all of the components of the vision would require more in-depth strategic planning and prioritization at the school district level to track how well public school systems are meeting the needs of Boricua students. This type of planning would require that districts develop long-term collaborations with Puerto Rican community members, educators, and activists to ensure that the plans enacted are responsive to the strengths and needs of these communities.

At the state level, three immediate short-term statewide items, merit our attention and study:

From Start to Finish: One approach to vastly improve the schooling experiences and outcomes of Puerto Ricans in Massachusetts is to simply eliminate barriers to accessing educational opportunities. Given its robust knowledge-based economy and its commitment to leading the nation in all aspects of the education enterprise, Massachusetts is uniquely positioned to *in fact lead the nation* through transformative policymaking that fully expands access to education. One starting point that would dramatically impact the lives of Boricuas would be to offer free, high-quality, culturally sustaining early education and care and college for all those who seek it. As it pertains to early education, a robust body of research has consistently found the importance of the first five years of life in all developmental outcomes including learning (See Marta Rosa's testimonio, chapter 10 in this volume). As a state, Massachusetts has invested in improving early education and care; however, in low-income and minoritized communities' quality and affordable early education and care continue to be cost prohibitive. It is imperative that the Commonwealth further expand its free early education and care programs. Because early education programs are often the first formal learning experience of children, and therefore foundational for setting the tone of what schooling is, coupled with expansion there must be a deliberate commitment to culturally sustaining and developmentally appropriate and rigorous pedagogical approaches that will help children and families thrive in their later years.

At the other end of the educational pipeline, the Commonwealth must continue to invest in improving access and opportunities at institutions of higher learning. In the last decade, the Commonwealth has taken steps toward this end. In 2023, the approval of MassReconnect, which funds free community college including costs related to tuition, fees, books, and supplies for adults older than twenty-five who do not yet have a college degree, has expanded learning opportunities to an underserved population. In August of 2024, this policy was expanded so that any Massachusetts resident, regardless of age, could attend any of the state's fifteen community colleges for free. The policy of funding free community college intentionally targets communities that have been historically underrepresented in higher education "connecting students to the knowledge and skills needed to participate and advance in key industries of the Commonwealth's economy."[57] More policies similar to this one that expand educational opportunities and remove barriers to accessing education are necessary.

Ethnic Studies: A robust body of research exists that confirms the benefits of students seeing themselves in the curricula that they experience.[58] Several public school districts, including Boston Public Schools and Holyoke Public Schools, have taken steps to include ethnic studies in their curricular requirements.[59] There are also, of course, a large number of teachers and individual schools that have prioritized this approach to teaching and learning because they see the benefits of culturally sustaining education.

While these individual efforts should be applauded, the Commonwealth has no robust and statewide approach to ethnic studies education. There are examples of more intentional approaches in other states. For instance, in 2021, in response to organizing efforts by students, parents, and educators, Connecticut added African American, Black, Puerto Rican, and Latino studies to the required programs of studies for all public schools. Beginning in 2023, the state has started the process of implementing Connecticut Public Act No. 10–12, *An Act Concerning the Inclusion of Black and Latino Studies in the Public School Curriculum*. It will be important for researchers, educators, and advocates to follow closely how Connecticut conceptualized this policy directive and how it developed and implemented this state education program, particularly as it relates to Massachusetts's efforts to promote a more culturally inclusive curriculum. Special attention, for example, should be given to the Massachusetts State Legislature's proposed Bill H.542/S.288—An Act to Promote Racially Inclusive Curriculum in

Schools. This bill, which was presented by State Senator Adam Gómez, the first Puerto Rican to serve in the state senate, has the potential to expand ethnic studies in K-12 schools statewide. In 2024, the bill was reported favorably by the Joint Committee on Education and was referred to the Committee on Senate Ways and Means.

Collect and Report on Disaggregated Data: To understand where Puerto Rican students are thriving or when they are experiencing the most educational challenges, we need a more robust system of data collection and reporting. This, in part, requires that the MDESE develop the data capacities to report on ethnicity/ancestral background. The state's current demographic data mechanisms treat Latino students as a monolithic group, which contributes to the invisibilities experienced by Boricua communities. Only reporting on Hispanicity is simply not robust enough to let us understand the particular needs, strengths, and schooling contexts of Puerto Rican students. The passing of the Massachusetts Data Equity Bill (August 9, 2023), which mandates the collection of public data on major ethnic groups in the states, presents an important possibility. However, educators, policymakers, and researchers need to ensure that given the particularities of the Puerto Rican community, the appropriate variables are collected and assembled so that who counts as Puerto Rican is as expansive as possible. Variables such as place of birth, national origin, or language spoken all provide a glimpse of the complexities of the Puerto Rican community in the Commonwealth. For example, a student with Puerto Rican heritage who identifies as Puerto Rican but was born in Massachusetts and raised in an English-speaking household is likely to be recorded only as a Latino/Hispanic.

To best capture the Puerto Rican student population in Massachusetts, MDESE would need to partner with school districts that have large Puerto Rican populations and community organizations that work in partnership with the Boricua community to develop appropriate demographic data-gathering protocols on this student population. In sum, this type of disaggregated data is an equity issue for Puerto Rican communities because the data can help us understand opportunity gaps as well as strengths and allow us to use more complex, nuanced, longitudinal, quantitative, and qualitative analysis to evaluate where we are on the implementation of the vision set forth.

Diasporic Schools and Expanded Partnership with Education Systems in Puerto Rico: As previously discussed, it is not unusual for Puerto Rican students to have schooling experiences in both Puerto Rico and the US. This is also tied to the schooling experiences of their parents, which may also be Diasporic. Yet, despite the long histories of Puerto Ricans in the Commonwealth, there are still many families who report losing time, not receiving credits for courses completed, and experiencing discrimination when their children enroll in a new district. The last time this came to bear was in the aftermath of Hurricanes Maria and Irma in 2017 when families who were dealing with the trauma of disasters were further challenged by their transitions to the US schooling system. It is important to emphasize that this is not an issue that impacts only K-12 systems. Puerto Rican college students transferring to US colleges and universities from Puerto Rico have faced similar challenges, as have working professionals whose degrees are at times not recognized and are pushed toward additional training and recertification.[60]

Migration to and from Puerto Rico has never been a one-time event; as such, we can and should prepare for the arrival of future Boricua students from the archipelago and expect circular enrollment patterns. Given the large population of Puerto Rican students in Massachusetts, school districts, colleges, and universities should work to develop stronger articulation agreements with the Puerto Rican Department of Education and selected municipalities that will improve administrative systems so that enrollment, credit transfers, and educational planning can be seamless. These partnerships should also focus on reciprocal learning opportunities. For example, we imagine opportunities for teachers and school leaders from Massachusetts to learn about schooling practices in Puerto Rico and vice versa.

How does this vision and these priority areas that focus on a Puerto Rican education agenda benefit all Latino students? We believe these recommendations will inherently benefit all students in Massachusetts, particularly those who have endured systematic marginalization and exclusion in schools and who are currently facing political and social insecurities. For example, we live in an increasingly global and interconnected world—travel to and from different nations is increasingly becoming the norm, and many industries, especially those based in Massachusetts, have a global reach. In tandem, circular migration patterns and transnationalism across the globe are on the rise; this is in part a response to climate and/or political disasters and globalization writ large. The MDESE is aware of this phenomenon. In 2022, in response to "various global circumstances" that resulted in an increase of new arrivals from Brazil, Haiti, Ukraine, and Central America to Massachusetts public schools, they issued a memorandum to school districts across the Commonwealth outlining the rights of new arrivals and the responsibilities of school districts.[61] The guidance emphasizes that, as was established by the US Supreme Court in Plyler v. Doe, 457 U.S. 202 (1982), all school-aged children and youth are entitled to equal access to a free public education regardless of their (im)migration or residential status and that school districts must enroll these students "as quickly as possible."[62]

A school system that understands the importance of multilingualism, interculturalism, and Diasporic modes of learning is therefore not only helpful for Puerto Rican families; it also prepares all Massachusetts students to understand the economic and social changes that globalization presents us. Similarly, a school that uses disaggregated data and culturally sustaining pedagogies to help improve teaching and learning helps all children, not just Puerto Rican students, as it requires an in-depth analysis of the strengths and needs of various student groups with attention to specific strategies that will improve outcomes and engagement. Toward this end, imagine the long-term implications for children and families who are newly arriving at Massachusetts public schools as they are welcomed by a teaching and education corps that is committed to culturally sustaining and rigorous pedagogies. Imagine the impact on Latino students and the Commonwealth at large if every child, regardless of where they were born or their income, had access to high-quality free early education and care, PK-12, and higher education. Imagine the social and economic impact of Massachusetts children speaking two or more languages. Centering on the needs and strengths of Boricua students will help improve Latino educational outcomes and experiences because bringing the perspectives of those from the margins to the center helps us all get free.[63]

In this chapter, we argue that to understand the Puerto Rican students' educational experience and outcomes in Massachusetts public schools, we need to recognize and understand the unique complexities of the Puerto Rican schooling experience in the US. Experiences with colonialism, linguistic and cultural impositions, circular migration, exclusion, and community activism have played a role in the schooling experiences and outcomes of Puerto Rican students in Massachusetts. We also posit that because Puerto Rican students represent at least 40% of all Latino school-age children in Massachusetts, their specific needs and strengths must be addressed in educational reform efforts that target the Latino community. Central to education reform efforts is critically listening to and learning from the voices of students, teachers, families, and communities who continue to give so much of themselves in the work to make schools more equitable. The work of transforming public education will require that we complicate myths that locate the Latino community as monolithic and require that we purposefully dive into the complexities and myriads of experiences across the diverse Latino communities in the Commonwealth (see, e.g., Araujo Brinkerhoff in chapter 2 in this volume about Brazilian students in Massachusetts) to inform policy and practice decisions. Let us not fear these complexities as it is there the power to transform lies.

Notes

1 Portions of this chapter in appear in Melissa Colón's dissertation, "'We Are Beautiful People:' The Schooling Experiences of Puerto Rican School-Aged Mothers" (PhD diss., Tufts University, Child Study and Human Development, 2019).

2 Vishakha Agarwal and Phillip Granberry, "Diversity Among Latino Groups in Massachusetts: 1980–2019," Gastón Institute Publications 294 (2023), https://scholarworks .umb.edu/gaston_pubs/294; Billie Gastic, Melissa Colón, and Andrew Flannery Aguilar, "The State of Latinos and Education in Massachusetts: 2010," Gastón Institute Publications 160 (2010), http://scholarworks.umb.edu/gaston_pubs/160; Phillip Granberry and Trevor Mattos, "Massachusetts Latino Population: 2010–2035," Gastón Institute Publications 241 (2019), https://scholarworks.umb.edu/gaston_pubs/241/; Ralph Rivera and Sonia Nieto, eds., *The Education of Latino Students in Massachusetts: Issues, Research, and Policy Implications* (University of Massachusetts Press, 1993); Fabián Torres-Ardila and Nyal Fuentes, "The State of Latino Education: 2010–2020," Gastón Institute Publications 292 (2022), https://scholarworks.umb.edu/gaston_pubs /292.

3 Nichole M. Garcia and Oscar J. Mayorga, "The Threat of Unexamined Secondary Data: A Critical Race Transformative Convergent Mixed Methods," *Race Ethnicity and Education* 21, no. 2 (2018): 231–52; Trevor Mattos, Phillip Granberry, and Vishakha Agarwal, "¡Avancemos Ya! Persistent Economic Challenges and Opportunities Facing Latinos in Massachusetts" (Boston Foundation, 2022), https://www .bostonindicators.org/reports/report-detail-pages/avancemos_ya.

4 The MDESE does not yet report data on specific ethnic groups. The presented data on Puerto Rican students are drawn from the American Community Survey. These data were compared to descriptive figures presented by MDESE. We are grateful to Phil Granberry, research associate of the Gastón Institute, for his guidance on how to use these data points to understand the Puerto Rican school-age population in Massachusetts. Steven Ruggles, et al., *IPUMS USA: Version 13.0 [2022 American Community Survey]* IPUMS, 2023).

5 Borikén is the Arawak name for the largest island of the archipelago today known as Puerto Rico. Borikén is a popular word used to describe a person who identifies

as Puerto Rican. In this chapter, we use the terms "Borikén" and "Boricua" inter-changeably with "Puerto Rico" and "Puerto Rican."

6   Jason G. Irizarry, Rosalie Rolón-Dow, and Isar Godreau, "Después Del Huracán: Using a Diaspora Framework to Contextualize and Problematize Educational Responses Post-María," *Centro Journal* 30, no. 3 (2018): 254–78; Jason G. Irizarry and René Antrop-González, "Ricanstruction Sites: Race, Space, and Place in the Education of Diasporican Youth," *Taboo* 13, no. 1 (2013): 77; Rosalie Rolón-Dow, "Taking a Diasporic Stance: Puerto Rican Mothers Educating Children in a Racially Integrated Neighborhood," *Diaspora, Indigenous, and Minority Education* 4, no. 4 (2010): 268–84.

7   Rolón-Dow, "Taking a Diasporic Stance."

8   Angela Valenzuela, *Subtractive Schooling: US-Mexican Youth and the Politics of Caring* (State University of New York Press, 2010).

9   Paulo Freire, *Pedagogy of the Oppressed* (Seabury Press, 1970).

10 Freire, *Pedagogy of the Oppressed.*

11 Antonia Darder, *A Dissident Voice: Essays on Culture, Pedagogy, and Power* (Peter Lang, 2011); Freire, *Pedagogy of the Oppressed*, 125; bell hooks, "Teaching to Transgress: Education as the Practice of Freedom," *Journal of Leisure Research* 28, no. 4 (1996): 316.

12 Billie Gastic, "Don't Believe Them When They Tell You That I Don't Exist," *Centro Journal* 19, no. 2 (2007): 86–93.

13 Gastic, "Don't Believe Them."

14 Sonia Nieto, *Puerto Rican Students in U.S. Schools: Sociocultural, Political, and Historical Studies in Education* (Lawrence Erlbaum Associates; 2000).

15 Virginia Sánchez Korrol, *From Colonia to Community: The History of Puerto Ricans in New York City* (University of California Press, 1994); Nieto, *Puerto Rican Students in U.S. Schools.*

16 Jorge Duany, "Nation on the Move: The Construction of Cultural Identities in Puerto Rico and the Diaspora," *American Ethnologist* 27, no. 1 (2000): 5–30, https://doi.org /10.1525/ae.2000.27.1.5; Joseph Carvalho, "The Puerto Rican Community of Western-Massachusetts, 1898–1960," *Historical Journal of Massachusetts V* 43, no. 2 (2015): 34–63.

17 Carvalho, "The Puerto Rican Community."

18 Carvalho, "The Puerto Rican Community."

19 Deborah Pacini Hernandez, "Quiet Crisis: A Community History of Latinos in Cambridge, Massachusetts," in *Latinos in New England*, ed. Andres Torres, 149–70 (Temple University Press, 2006).

20 Mohamad Moslimani, Luis Noe-Bustamante, and Sono Shah, "Facts on Hispanics of Puerto Rican Origin in the United States, 2021," *Pew Research Center's Hispanic Trends Project* (blog), accessed November 5, 2023, https://www.pewresearch .org/hispanic/fact-sheet/us-hispanics-facts-on-puerto-rican-origin-latinos/.

21 "S0201: Selected Population Profile . . .—Census Bureau Table," accessed November 5, 2023, https://data.census.gov/table/ACSSPP1Y2022.S0201?q=Puerto+Ricans+2022 &g=040XX00US25.

22 Phillip Granberry and Krizia Valentino, "Latinos in Massachusetts: Puerto Ricans," Gastón Institute Publications 249 (2020), https://scholarworks.umb.edu/gaston_pubs /249.

23 Granberry and Valentino, "Latinos in Massachusetts."

24 Nieto, *Puerto Rican Students in U.S. Schools*; Joel Spring, *Deculturalization and the Struggle for Equality: A Brief History of the Education of Dominated Cultures in the United States* (Routledge, 2021).

25 Manuel Alers-Montalvo, *The Puerto Rican Migrants of New York City: A Study of Anomie* (AMS Press, 1985); Spring, *Deculturalization and the Struggle for Equality*.

26 Spring, *Deculturalization and the Struggle for Equality*.

27 Spring, *Deculturalization and the Struggle for Equality*.

28 Carvalho, "The Puerto Rican Community."

29 Duany, "Nation on the Move."

30 Edwin Meléndez and Jennifer Hinojosa, "Estimates of Post-Hurricane Maria Exodus from Puerto Rico," Research Brief Centro RB2017–01, Center for Puerto Rican Studies, 2017, 1–7.

31 Jennifer Hinojosa and Edwin Meléndez, "Puerto Rican Exodus: One Year Since Hurricane Maria," CUNY, Centro: Center for Puerto Rican Studies, 2018, p. 8, https://academicworks.cuny.edu/cpr_pubs/5/.

32 Marixsa Alicea, "Dual Home Bases: A Reconceptualization of Puerto Rican Migration," *Latino Studies Journal* 1, no. 3 (1990): 78–98.

33 Spring, *Deculturalization and the Struggle for Equality*.

34 Gary Orfield, et al., "'Brown' at 62: School Segregation by Race, Poverty and State," Civil Rights Project-Proyecto Derechos Civiles, 2016, http://eric.ed.gov/?id=ED565900.

35 MDESE, "2022–23 Enrollment by Race/Gender Statewide Report (District)," 2023.

36 Colón, "We Are Beautiful People."

37 Manuel Frau-Ramos and Sonia Nieto, "'I Was an Outsider': Dropping Out Among Puerto Rican Youths in Holyoke, Massachusetts," in *The Education of Latino Students in Massachusetts: Issues, Research, and Policy Implications*, ed. Ralph Rivera and Sonia Nieto, 147–69 (University of Massachusetts Press, 1993); Irizarry and Antrop-González, "Ricanstruction Sites"; Anthony De Jesús and Rosalie Rolón-Dow, "Challenges, Dilemmas, and Possibilities," *Centro Journal* 19, no. 2 (2007): 4–11; Philip Kasinitz, et al., *Inheriting the City: The Children of Immigrants Come of Age* (Russell Sage Foundation, 2009); Korrol, *From Colonia to Community*; Nieto, *Puerto Rican Students in U.S. Schools*; Sonia Nieto, "Fact and Fiction: Stories of Puerto Ricans in U.S. Schools," *Harvard Educational Review* 68, no. 2 (1998): 133–63; Catherine E. Walsh, "'Staging Encounters': The Educational Decline of U.S. Puerto Ricans in [Post]-Colonial Perspective," *Harvard Educational Review* 68, no. 2 (1998): 218–43.

38 Richard J. Margolis, *The Losers: A Report on Puerto Ricans and the Public Schools* (Aspira, 1968), http://eric.ed.gov/?id=ED023779.

39 Margolis, *The Losers*, 1.

40 Granberry and Valentino, "Latinos in Massachusetts," 5.

41 Granberry and Valentino, "Latinos in Massachusetts," 5.

42 Granberry and Valentino, "Latinos in Massachusetts."

43 Granberry and Valentino, "Latinos in Massachusetts."

44 Granberry and Valentino, "Latinos in Massachusetts."

45 Granberry and Valentino, "Latinos in Massachusetts."

46 Clara Rodriguez, Irma M. Olmedo, and Mariolga Reyes-Cruz, "Deconstructing and Contextualizing the Historical and Social Science Literature on Puerto Ricans," in *Handbook of Research on Multicultural Education*, ed. James A. Bank and Cherry A. McGee Banks, 288–314 (Jossey-Bass, 2004).

47 Spring, *Deculturalization and the Struggle for Equality*.

48 Colón, "We Are Beautiful People."

49 Xaé Alicia Reyes, "Return Migrant Students: Yankee Go Home?," in *Puerto Rican Students in US Schools*, ed. Sonia Nieto, 39–68 (Routledge, 2000); Tatiana MF Cruz, "'We Took 'Em On': The Latino Movement for Educational Justice in Boston, 1965–1980," *Journal of Urban History* 43, no. 2 (2017): 235–55.

50 Jesús and Rolón-Dow, "Challenges, Dilemmas, and Possibilities."

51 Jesús and Rolón-Dow, "Challenges, Dilemmas, and Possibilities."

52 Rene Antrop-González, *Schools as Radical Sanctuaries: Decolonizing Urban Education Through the Eyes of Youth of Color* (IAP, 2011).

53 Gastic, "Don't Believe Them."

54 Ira Shor and Paulo Freire, "What Is the 'Dialogical Method' of Teaching?," *Journal of Education* 169, no. 3 (1987): 11–31, https://doi.org/10.1177/002205748716900303.

55 These conversations were not part of research study or one-time events. They are part of broader conversations that we continue to engage in with member of our communities that center the future of Puerto Rican children and families.

56 Darder, *A Dissident Voice*.

57 Amelia Marcea, "MassReconnect," accessed November 13, 2023, https://www.mass.gov/doc/fy-2024-budget- recommendation-budget-brief-massreconnect/download.

58 Christine E. Sleeter, "The Academic and Social Value of Ethnic Studies (National Education Association, 2011).

59 Yasmeen Khader, "Reimagining Ethnic Studies in BPS—Exploring the Boston Teachers Union Collection," 2022, https://blogs.umb.edu/btuhistory/2022/03/28/the-rapid-growth-of-ethnic-studies-in-bps/; Joel A. Arce, Olivia McNeill, and Kysa Nygreen, "Holyoke Ethnic Studies Program Report: 2021–2022 School Year" (University of Massachusetts Amherst, 2022), https://doi.org/10.7275/KG6R-GB29.

60 Leslie Shelton and Charles Thompson, "Fostering Resilience for Puerto Rican College Students in Transition After Hurricane Maria," *Journal of College Orientation, Transition, and Retention* 27, no. 1 (2020), https://pubs.lib.umn.edu/index.php/jcotr/article/view/2219; Awilda Rodriguez, et al., "College Choice, Interrupted: Understanding the Choice Processes of Hurricane-Affected Puerto Rican Students in Florida," *Journal of Higher Education* 92, no. 2 (2021): 169–93, https://doi.org/10.1080/00221546.2020.1803035.

61 MDESE, "Resources for Supporting Immigrant and Refugee Students—English Language Learners," 2023, https://www.doe.mass.edu/ele/resources/immigrant-refugee.html.

62 MDESE, "Resources for Supporting Immigrant and Refugee Students."

63 hooks, "Teaching to Transgress."

Chapter Four

¡Adelante! Avante!

Advancing the Education Rights of Multilingual Children with Disabilities

DIANA SANTIAGO

Editor's Note

On June 1, 2023, the *Boston Globe* reported on the systematic exclusion of students with disabilities from bilingual education programs.[1] Tara Garcia Mathewson, the reporter, shared the experiences of two Dominican mothers, María Mejía and Sonia Medina, whose children were denied access to dual-language education programs because they have disabilities. For María, having her autistic child placed in an English-only environment ultimately meant that he lost his ability to communicate with his family in their native language, Spanish. Similarly, Sonia spoke on the damage done to their family when both her children, diagnosed with attention deficit disorder, were assigned to English-only schooling environments. Unfortunately, the struggles of Sonia and Maria are not unique and remind us that the schooling experiences and outcomes of Latine students who also have disabilities in Massachusetts require more attention.

In Massachusetts, 27.18% of enrolled elementary and secondary education students (ages six to twenty-one) were identified as having special education needs under the Individuals with Disabilities Education Act and Massachusetts Special Education Law are Latino.[2] This rate is slightly higher than the proportion of enrolled Latino students, which is 25.1%[3] and is in line with national trends that suggest that Latino students are more likely to be identified as having a disability relative to the overall student population.[4] This is further complicated by the fact that Latino students who have a disability may also be multilingual English learners (ELs). In Massachusetts, 22% of students enrolled in public elementary and secondary schools whose first language is not English are dually identified as students with a disability, with wide variations across school districts.[5] Many leading experts question the accuracy of these figures partly because many school-based and healthcare professionals do not have the language skills to appropriately assess the needs of students who are yet fully English proficient. Currently, there are no widely available data that tell the percentage of Latine students who are dually identified as ELs with a disability.

One of the few reports that focuses on the duality of being both an EL and a student with a disability was published by the Gastón Institute in 2011.[6] Written by Dr. Maria de Lourdes Serpa, a national expert on multilingual learners with disabilities, the report provides a critical overview of civil rights, special education, and language learning laws that protect and guarantee a free and appropriate public education in the least restrictive environment. Unfortunately, despite these protections, school districts struggle to meet the needs of this student population, and Latine families with children with disabilities, particularly those who are immigrants and/or multilingual ELs, are often overwhelmed by the complex political, legal, and educational landscape that they must navigate to ensure their children's rights are being protected.

This is precisely the work of Diana Santiago. A significant part of her role as the legal director with Massachusetts Advocates for Children (MAC) is to direct advocacy focused on advancing the education rights of immigrant and multilingual children. In her role, she oversees education advocacy, support, and training for (im)migrant parents and community groups in Massachusetts and participates in systemic advocacy at the school district, state agency, and legislative levels to remove access barriers to education for immigrant, migrant, and multilingual children. She also leads the Immigrant and Multilingual Children with Disabilities Coalition, a statewide coalition of multilingual and multicultural special education attorneys and advocates.

In this volume, we have chosen to present three testimonios written by educational leaders who have committed to transforming public education in the Commonwealth; Diana's testimonio is our first one. Largely attributed to Indigenous and non-Western oral traditions and knowledge movements, testimonios are used to create knowledge and theory of shared lived experiences by people who have experienced marginalization and are motivated by the urgency to give voice and raise awareness of shared struggle, survival, and resistance in order "to bring to light a wrong."[7] As Delgado

Bernal, Burciaga, and Flores Carmona illuminate, by bearing witness to testimonios, new understandings about how marginalized communities "respond to and resist dominant culture, laws, and policies that perpetuate inequity" are unearthed.[8] In this first testimonio, Diana Santiago's journey to becoming a fierce advocate for the rights of Latine multilingual ELs with disabilities brings to light critical insights and possibilities about how best to serve and advocate for this student population.

MELISSA COLÓN

I am Diana Santiago, an education and disability rights attorney at Massachusetts Advocates for Children (MAC). MAC's model is to advocate for and partner with individual students and families and to create systemic change in collaboration with our coalition partners. Our vision is for all children and youth, particularly those who face the greatest barriers, to have a fair and equitable opportunity to learn, reach their potential, and thrive. MAC was founded in 1969 in response to the widespread exclusion of children from Boston Public Schools, including Spanish-speaking children, many of whom were labeled "unteachable" because of disability-related behavior.[9] My identities as a Latina mother, wife, and daughter are deeply intertwined with my work leading MAC's advocacy, which is focused on advancing the education rights of immigrant and multilingual children. This is my testimonio.

As a Latina born and raised in the United States, I am proud to share my heritage with many of the families and advocates I've met through my work at MAC. I grew up in a bicultural family with mixed traditions. My father always made the best *pernil* on Christmas Eve and made sure that we left food for the *camellos* so that *Los Reyes Magos* would make their way to our home on January 6. Now I do the same with my children. My mother is White and not Latina, but she has a deep connection herself with our Latine traditions through my father and connections in her community. I grew up fortunate to spend several summers on the enchanted island of Puerto Rico with my family. I would spend hours in my *abuelos'* backyard chasing *lagartijos* with a blade of grass looped to catch them around the neck, only to let them go again. Some of my happiest childhood memories are with my cousins on Dorado Beach.

I felt a connection to Puerto Rico through my father and extended family as a young person; however, I grew up in a mostly White town and didn't identify with other Latine youth until later in high school. A friend in college, who was also Puerto Rican, decided to study for a semester at the University of Puerto Rico in Rio Piedras and I joined her on a whim. When I first arrived, I was surprised to experience what I later came to realize was culture shock. Growing up at home, while my father and grandmother always spoke with my sisters and me in Spanish, we would respond in English. I didn't realize how limited my Spanish was until I was immersed with other Spanish-speaking youth.

It turns out that responding to calls like "Dinner is ready!" or questions like "How was your day?" do not prepare you for fast-paced Spanish full of slang on the one hand and college-level vocabulary on the other. For me, especially because I am a Latina, it was a humbling experience. Culturally, I also wasn't ready for the generally slower pace of life or the infrastructure that was less than seamless. I remember waiting in line for close to an hour to open a bank account only to be told I would have to come back in the afternoon after lunch break. In that moment I could have exploded. Two or three months later, once I was better acclimated, my response was only slight frustration at myself for not having planned better. Overall, my year living in Puerto Rico was one of the richest in my life. I think about parallels and differences between my experience and that of my clients and their children who are newly arrived to the United States. Most notably they are without the privileges I had as an English-speaking college student.

My perspectives and work as a special education attorney have become interlinked with my Latine heritage, and my role as a parent. I didn't always know that I wanted to be an education lawyer. I went to law school to become a public interest lawyer focusing on practice and policy in the health field. My position immediately prior to starting at MAC was with the Boston Public Health Commission managing a child health research study and after-school programming for youth with special health care needs. After three years there, however, I missed representing clients. I also had a baby and felt driven to find a job that would allow more flexibility than city government. At this time, MAC was looking to hire a Spanish-speaking special education attorney. This was an area in which I had no practical experience, but my time in Puerto Rico and later more than a year teaching English in Colima, Mexico, had made me fully fluent in Spanish. I will always be grateful to MAC for providing me the opportunity to practice education law and for the mentorship they have given me as I became an expert in a field that is so personally and professionally fulfilling. In my work now I take every opportunity to speak out about the many benefits of multilingualism for individuals and for our society. Sadly, I so often see it characterized in schools as a deficit, which is so directly counter to my experience.

At MAC I provide and oversee education advocacy and training for immigrant and migrant parents and community groups in Massachusetts. Informed by patterns of issues that emerge in our case advocacy and training and in collaboration with community and legal services colleagues, I pursue systemic advocacy at the school district, state agency, and legislative levels.

Something I love about working at MAC is the flexibility we have to respond to emerging changes and crises impacting our communities. When Hurricanes Maria and Irma devastated Puerto Rico in 2017, for example, we shifted our outreach, training, and advocacy efforts to ensure that students relocating from Puerto Rico to Massachusetts had access to appropriate educational services, especially special education for students with disabilities. During the COVID-19 pandemic, MAC's advocacy became laser-focused on addressing language- and disability-related barriers for students and families, supporting them at home with remote learning. The devastating impact of the pandemic on Latine communities and widened education gaps throughout the state sadly linger.

Special education laws are important civil rights laws designed to protect access to education for students with disabilities. Under these laws, school districts are required to identify students whose disability impacts their ability to make progress in school—academically, developmentally, socially, emotionally, or functionally. That determination is made by a team that includes educators, administrators, the parent or caregiver, and, starting at age fourteen, the student. The same team then develops an Individualized Education Program, or IEP, that includes the services and supports the student needs and the setting in which the student needs to receive them. A set of goals individualized to the student, also included in the IEP, is used to measure the student's progress.

Parent participation is fundamental to ensuring that the IEP is effective in meeting the needs of students. Special education law sets forth some important procedural requirements in connection with parental involvement that school districts must follow, including written translations of all documents, the use of a trained interpreter in all school meetings where needed, and informed parental consent during key points throughout the process (such as when the district is going to evaluate the student or is proposing a new IEP). Student evaluations must be conducted in the language that will yield the most accurate assessment of the student's skills in all areas that may be impacted by the student's disability. And where a multilingual EL has a disability that impacts or is interconnected with their English-language development, the student is entitled to English-language education support as part of their IEP. This includes instruction in the student's primary language if the student requires it to make progress. When parents' and students' rights are violated, our system largely relies on parents to recognize the violation and pursue dispute resolution options, which can be daunting, especially for immigrant and multilingual families.

As a parent, I know that raising children can be hard. I am also personally familiar with the unique challenges of raising a child with a disability. We all worry about our children, but parents of children with disabilities—whether autism, a learning disability, an emotional disability, ADHD, a physical disability, or an intellectual disability—have additional sets of worries. Despite strong special education laws, we often find that other people define our kids by how they are different or "challenging" rather than as incredible children who experience and interact with the world in ways others may not always understand. Most parents contend with doubts about what is best for our children, and relatedly, judgment from people who think they know best. When your child has a disability, however, the doubts are magnified, as is the judgment from others, both real and perceived. We are not ashamed of our children but worry about the assumptions that others will make about what they can or can't do if we are open about their disability. I have seen how these assumptions and the stigmatization around disability in the Latine community and elsewhere can be incredibly isolating. When I entered the field of special education law I didn't know that my children and our family would be impacted by disability, but the networks and support systems that I have through my colleagues and the parents with whom I work lift me up when I need it the most.

My legal work is focused on immigrant families, and most of my Latine clients are from the Dominican Republic, Puerto Rico, Guatemala, Honduras, and El Salvador. Their time in the United States varies widely, as do the ages of their children and the learning challenges they are facing. Several of my clients' children speak little or no Spanish. Others who have more recently arrived in the United States or have a disability that impacts their language development require significant supports at school to access instructional content at or close to their grade level. I have only a sense of how much harder it is to parent when your children are surrounded by a different language and the influences of a different culture. Add to that navigating an unfamiliar education system, a global pandemic that disproportionately devastated our community, and the trauma too many immigrant families and children experience prior to or during their entry to the United States. It is painful to hear from parents who have been ignored or left in the dark regarding their child's educational needs because of language barriers when attempting to communicate with school district personnel and others in positions of power. Yet it is all too common. So many families are afraid to speak up about their children's needs due to trauma, the discrimination they experience in their daily lives, and/or fear of retaliation. I am at a total loss when I see adults who are cruelly indifferent to students who have behavioral, mental health, or academic struggles stemming from immigration and other forms of trauma. The actions of these adults, as well as the actions of those who are loving and supportive, shape the way children perceive and navigate their little worlds.

Navigating the special education process on behalf of my own child, my approach is very different from my approach when representing a client. With our own child, my husband and I are always carefully weighing how our actions will impact how our child is perceived or treated in school. This means sometimes picking and choosing our battles in ways that my clients do, even when they have me as a buffer. As an attorney, I am very aware of my rights, and I don't experience the language barriers and trauma that many of my clients do. Having been born and raised in the United States and with children who are not perceived as culturally or racially different, I know that the stakes are even higher for my fellow Latine parents who do not have these privileges.

My experience when I arrived in Puerto Rico as a college student was not the only time I have been reminded of how my experiences differ from the experiences of many other Latines. During one of my first years as a special education attorney, I represented a Central American woman who was deeply concerned about the future of her son, Nelson,[10] due to his autism and learning disability and the inadequate level of support he was receiving from his school district to prepare him for life after high school. Nelson was intelligent but at age eighteen did not yet have the skills that he would need to function away from the confines of a structured special education classroom or his home. A first step in advocating for appropriate special education services is to have an independent evaluation done. There are very few linguistically and culturally diverse evaluators, so the one we used was not Latine and relied on an interpreter to interview Nelson's mother. This evaluator ultimately recommended a residential placement for youth with disabilities to allow Nelson the opportunity to develop skills that he would need to live and work independently. When I relayed this to my client, she dismissed the idea. In her culture and family, young adults did not leave the family home until they were married. Since the residential placement was the crux of the recommendations, the evaluation was essentially useless as we advocated for more appropriate services for Nelson. If the evaluator had been culturally responsive, she would have offered an array of options.

I later came to realize that my client's decision-making went beyond attachment to tradition. A staff member from an agency that supports young adults with disabilities recommended that Nelson get on a waiting list for public housing, as it could take up to ten years for an apartment to become available. His mother shook her head no, with tears in her eyes. Due to Nelson's disability, she thought he would never get married but thought that just as her older children had lived with her until they were married, Nelson would continue living with her until she died and then he would live with one of his siblings.

My client's perspective was not unfamiliar to me. After my *abuelo* died when I was in high school, my *abuela* came to live with us, where she remained for fifteen years until she died. Both my older sister and I went to college in the same town that we had grown up in and where my parents and *abuela* still lived, but we both chose to live on campus at our respective schools. My parents supported that. It was not in my *abuela*'s nature to be unsupportive; however, the idea that we would be so close by but living separate from our parents was completely foreign to her.

A focus of my legal work is the inclusion of students with disabilities in general education settings. Inclusion advocacy is especially challenging because, besides the legal arguments, parents are constantly contending with preconceived ideas and lowered expectations for students with disabilities. I have come to understand that decisions about inclusion tend to be based on discriminatory, stereotyped assumptions about children due to their category of disability (e.g., autism or intellectual impairment) rather than their ability, strengths, or educational needs as the law requires.

It is in the context of inclusion advocacy that I represented and remain connected with a Salvadorian couple, Eduardo and Lucia, who are parents to Andrés, a child with Down syndrome, and a younger son who is nondisabled, Miguel. Lucia is insightful, strategic, and endlessly committed to her children and family. Eduardo is generous, friendly, and practical. It is obvious in every interaction that their children are everything to Eduardo and Lucia. Despite innumerable challenges, they have remained steady in their belief that Andrés can and will always be a contributing member of his school and community and that inclusion with his nondisabled peers is how that will happen. Before I got involved, they were completely ignored by the school district in ways that most White, English-speaking parents will never experience. Once I got involved as their attorney, we would have special education or IEP meetings, often with unqualified interpreters, where it was evident that the school district would only consider a limited set of options that largely omitted inclusion with Andrés's nondisabled peers. We ultimately reached an agreement with the district that has allowed Andrés to be included, but Eduardo and Lucia's experience since then illustrates that their fight is ongoing. While it is exhausting, I don't see them ever giving up. Andrés will no doubt continue to do amazing things and contribute to his community as a result of their efforts.

I have a long wish list when it comes to how schools support and welcome our Latine families and students. For students with disabilities, I wish that our special education laws were carried out the way they were intended in practice for all parents and students regardless of language, culture, parent educational background, or experiences and that they were based on the individual needs of students. I wish that we had stronger state and federal monitoring so that it wouldn't be almost entirely up to parents to enforce the laws. I wish that parent engagement was prioritized more in schools because I see on a daily basis all that parents have to offer. Many Latine parents carry the weight of trauma from having been treated poorly or perceived as "less than" by US institutions, including school systems. Newcomer families may be operating under a completely different set of rules and assumptions in relation to schools and their children's education. I wish that more school staff would respond with empathy in learning from and supporting parents with strong home-school collaboration, instead of becoming defensive or protective of themselves and the White and English-dominant institutions that employ them. I wish that the education field were more welcoming and valued by our society as a career path so that more racially, linguistically, and ethnically diverse individuals would enter and remain. Overall, I wish that more school districts could see the brilliant diversity of language and culture that our Latine children and families bring to our schools and society as a whole.

I truly believe that every child has the potential to do amazing things if given the opportunity. Despite enormous inequities in educational opportunities affecting Latine students and students with disabilities, my work with other Latine families gives me great hope. I see the many ways in which we fight hard to see our children thrive and then give back to our community. Despite the difficulties our communities have faced, we don't give up. It is inspiring to see parents who have struggled to advocate for their own children with disabilities turn around to support other parents newly thrown into the special education process. I feel privileged to be part of the diverse and beautiful cultures and values that tie us together.

Dedication

I dedicate this testimonio to Julia Landau, my mentor, and to Robert LeRoux Hernandez, a fierce advocate for Latine children who will be deeply missed.

Notes

1   Tara García Mathewson, "Students with Disabilities Often Left Out of Popular 'Dual-Language' Programs," *Boston Globe*, May 31, 2023.
2   Office of Special Education Programs, "OSEP Fast Facts: Hispanic and/or Latino Children with Disabilities—IDEA" (US Department of Education, 2020), https://sites.ed.gov/idea/osep-fast-facts-hispanic-latino-children-disabilities-20/.
3   Massachusetts Department of Elementary and Secondary Education, "2023–24 Enrollment by Race/Gender Statewide Report (District)," 2024, https://profiles.doe.mass.edu/statereport/enrollmentbyracegender.aspx.
4   Office of Special Education Programs, "OSEP Fast Facts," 2020.
5   Massachusetts Department of Elementary and Secondary Education, Special Request "Special Education Enrollment by Special Populations," 2023–2024.
6   Maria de Lourdes B. Serpa, "An Imperative for Change: Bridging Special and Language Learning Education to Ensure a Free and Appropriate Education in the Least Restrictive Environment for ELLs with Disabilities in Massachusetts," Gastón Institute Publications 152 (2011), https://scholarworks.umb.edu/gaston_pubs/152.
7   Kathryn Blackmer Reyes and Julia E. Curry Rodríguez, "Testimonio: Origins, Terms, and Resources," *Equity and Excellence in Education*, 45, no. 3 (2012): 525.
8   Dolores Delgado Bernal, Rebeca Burciaga, and Judith Flores Carmona, "Chicana/Latina Testimonios: Mapping the Methodological, Pedagogical, and Political," *Equity and Excellence in Education* 45, no. 3 (2012): 363–72.
9   The Taskforce on Children Out of School, "The Way We Go to School: The Exclusion of Children in Boston" (Taskforce on Children Out of School, 1970), https://files.eric.ed.gov/fulltext/ED046140.pdf.
10 Pseudonyms have been used.

PART II

Reimagining
a New Latino
Education Policy
Praxis

Chapter Five

From Culturally Sustaining Classrooms to Culturally Sustaining Campuses

A Call to Action for Hispanic-Serving Institutions[1]

LIYA ESCALERA

> *Stories move in circles. They don't move in straight lines. So it helps if you listen in circles. There are stories inside stories and stories between stories, and finding your way through them is as easy and as hard as finding your way home.*
>
> —TERRY TAFOYA[2]

This project began and ended with stories, so I will begin by telling you mine. When I started this research, I had been working at a community college in Massachusetts for nearly ten years in a variety of roles focused on teaching, learning, and student development. During that time, I had the great fortune to teach, supervise, and learn from increasing numbers of Latinx students as I watched the enrollment of Latinx[3] students at the institution grow from 15% in 2007 to 26% in 2017 and 30% in 2021.[4] My direct experience mirrored a national trend where the percentage of Latinx college students (undergraduate and graduate) between 2000 and 2020 doubled from 10% to 20%.[5]

While I could see that many institutions were enrolling more Latinx students than ever, I had questions about how well we as educators were prepared to support their success. In my work and in my research, I could see that systems of public education—in this state and across the country—were producing inequitable outcomes for Latinx students. While the largest growing student population in both K-12 and higher education identifies as Latinx nationally and in Massachusetts, significant equity gaps persist for Latinx students compared to their peers when it comes to rates of college enrollment, retention, and program completion.[6] According to Excelencia in Education, in Massachusetts, in 2021–22, there was a 7 percentage point equity gap in college enrollment between Latinx adults ages 18–34 (22% in 2023) and White non-Latinx adults (29%).[7] Moreover, Latinx students who enroll in college complete programs of study at rates that are 11 percentage points lower than their peers at associate's degree–granting institutions and 9 percentage points lower than their peers at baccalaureate institutions.[8] In the community college system in Massachusetts, retention of Latinx students varies by institution, but on average Latinx students are retained at a rate 6 percentage points lower than their White peers, 57% compared with 63%.[9] Equity gaps are even more pronounced for Latinx students when we look at on-time credit accumulation, or the percentage of first-time, degree-seeking students who are completing their expected number of credits in their first year. The percentage of Latinx community college students hitting on-time credit accumulation targets[10] is 23% compared with 34% for their White peers.[11] Given the shifting demographics of the US population, and the growing Latinx population, colleges and universities nationwide and in Massachusetts are likely to see growth in Latinx students continue, but based on the student success equity gaps we currently see for Latinx students, how ready are we to create learning environments where Latinx students can thrive?

With this challenge in mind, I sought to better understand the kinds of learning environments that were more likely to result in Latinx student success. Many studies have demonstrated that classroom spaces grounded in culturally relevant and culturally sustaining pedagogies are more likely to support the success of Latinx students; yet faculty who have developed inclusive and culturally based methods for educating Latinx students are often the exception at Hispanic-serving institutions (HSIs),[12] not the rule. Nationally, the professoriate is unprepared to serve Latinx students through culturally relevant and sustaining pedagogy due to three main barriers: representation, training, and incentive. All faculty of color are underrepresented in higher education, particularly Latinx faculty. According to the National Center for Education Statistics, in 2021, 6% of the full-time professoriate identified as Latinx compared with 73% for White faculty, 6% for Black faculty, and 12% for Asian faculty.[13] Even at HSIs, Vargas, Villa-Palomino, and Davis found that in studying 167 Title V funded[14] institutions, the average ratio of Latinx faculty to Latinx students was 146:1, compared with 10:1 for White faculty to White students.[15] There is a growing body of evidence that the presence of Latinx faculty and administrators on community college campuses not only positively impacts Latinx student success but also positively impacts the success of all minoritized student groups.[16] In Massachusetts community colleges, of the 13 out of 15 who share these data publicly, the percentage of full-time Latinx faculty ranged from 0% to 11% between 2016 and 2022, according to data reported by institutions to the New England Commission of Higher Education (NECHE) as part of the institutional accreditation processes.[17]

Due to this underrepresentation of Latinx faculty, very few faculty members on community college campuses have first-hand knowledge of the culture, educational experiences, and epistemologies of Latinx students, and the ways in which traditional educational structures and methods have failed to support their success. In addition to a lack of firsthand experience with Latinx epistemologies, culturally sustaining pedagogies are often deemphasized or not included in graduate school curricula and faculty development programs, so there is little opportunity for faculty to become knowledgeable and skilled in culturally grounded epistemologies.[18] Thus, faculty must actively, and often voluntarily, seek training and development in culturally sustaining pedagogies and practices; however, addressing the cultural epistemic needs of students of color—including effectively serving Latinx students—is frequently absent or undervalued in tenure and promotion processes, so there may be little incentive or reward to do so.[19]

In the absence of a pervasive focus on culturally sustaining learning environments for Latinx students on most campuses, the discourse on Latinx students in circles of research and practice has been historically deficit based. Scholars of higher education have described this dynamic as an "apartheid of knowledge,"[20] "cultural starvation,"[21] "academic dissonance,"[22] "cultural deprivation,"[23] and a form of "institutional micro-invalidation."[24] This lack of representation sends a powerful negative message to Latinx students about their belonging in higher education and their legitimacy as scholars.

In their 2014 study, Rendón, Nora, and Kanagala offered a counternarrative to a deficit-based view by focusing on the strengths of Latinx college students—in the form of *ventajas y conocimentos* (assets and knowledge)[25]—and the ways in which students and institutions can draw upon these strengths to support Latinx student success. Building upon prior asset-based theories—community cultural wealth,[26] funds of knowledge,[27] mestiza consciousness,[28] pedagogies of the home,[29] validation,[30] and liberatory pedagogy[31]—Rendón, Nora, and Kanagala developed an asset-based theoretical framework that was used to analyze the experiences of Latinx students as captured in focus groups and interviews. Through this analysis, they identify ten common aspects of Latinx cultural wealth. While the first six forms of cultural wealth mirror those identified by Yosso to be shared among students of color and low-income students, the final four (ganas/perseverant wealth; ethnic consciousness wealth; spiritual/faith-based wealth, and pluriversal wealth) are unique to Latinx students. They include the following:

1. Aspirational wealth: Students expressed hope and ambition in discussion of their education and career goals.
2. *Linguistic wealth*: Students valued their multilingualism as an asset that enhanced their communication skills and ability to form relationships.
3. *Familial wealth*: familial support—in the form of *consejos* and role models—motivated students to be successful in their academics. This included a desire to achieve individual success and to contribute to the success of their communities.
4. *Social wealth*: Students drew from diverse friendships and social networks but underscored the importance of relationships with other Latin@ students.
5. *Navigational wealth*: Students noted the experience of navigating between distinct and at times contradictory worlds and identified their ability to traverse multiple contexts as a valuable skill.
6. *Resistant wealth*: Students described culture shock and discrimination on campus and discussed the ways in which they overcame these experiences through resistant capital.
7. *Ganas/perseverant wealth*: Students demonstrated persistence and dedication to their academic goals and willingness to make sacrifices to achieve academic success.
8. *Ethnic consciousness wealth*: Students expressed "ethnic consciousness" related to their Latin@ identity and commitment to contribute to the greater Latin@ community.
9. *Spiritual/faith-based wealth*: Many students identified spirituality and humanitarianism as both motivating and sustaining as they encountered challenges.

10. *Pluriversal wealth*: Students expressed the ability to tolerate ambiguities and contradictions related to their experiences navigating the transition between and among their communities and learning environments.

Rendón, Nora, and Kanagala conclude by stressing the importance of acknowledging Latinx strengths and providing curricular and cocurricular opportunities for development and validation of these strengths.

The framework for Latinx cultural wealth, paired with research on culturally relevant and sustaining learning environments, offers a promising model for understanding how to support the success of Latinx students. Focusing on the strengths of African American learners, Gloria Ladson-Billings describes the development of culturally relevant pedagogy as the exploration of her pedagogical shift from a deficit-based paradigm to an asset-based paradigm, "Instead of asking what was wrong with African American learners, I dared to ask what was right with these students and what happened in the classrooms of teachers who seemed to experience pedagogical success with them."[32] The question led Ladson-Billings to develop a culturally relevant pedagogy,[33] which comprises three goals:

1. *Academic success*: The knowledge, skills, and ways of thinking that students need to participate in democracy.
2. *Cultural competence*: Academic success must not come at the cost of cultural authenticity; instead, cultural knowledge is an asset students can utilize to maximize success.
3. *Sociopolitical consciousness*: Students should be challenged and inspired to "develop a broader sociopolitical consciousness that allows them to critique the cultural norms, values, mores, and institutions that produce and maintain social inequities."[34]

Instead of focusing on the instructional strategies or teaching styles study participants employed in their classrooms, Ladson-Billings's culturally relevant pedagogy framework is informed by three propositions, teachers' *conceptions of self and others* (namely, their identity as an educator must extend beyond employment as a teacher to a deep love of learning and a belief that all students are capable of excellence and must achieve excellence), teacher's *social relationships* (which must position the teacher as a facilitator of communities of learning in the classroom and in the community), and *conceptions of knowledge* (which allow the teacher to move beyond the limitations of state curriculum frameworks and mandated textbooks to allow for a critical analysis of the curriculum. Ladson-Billings describes cultur-ally relevant pedagogy as her attempt to reframe the discourse on African American students from deficit-based to asset-based and offers a model for understanding how educators in Hispanic-serving community colleges can transition from learning *about* Latinx students to learning *from* Latinx students. Building on Ladson-Billings's work, Django Paris acknowledges the impact and inspiration on educators and scholars sparked by culturally relevant pedagogy as a vehicle for responding to the "languages, literacies, and cultural practices of students across categories of difference and (in) equality,"[35] and he offers a *loving critique* of this discourse. He notes that such models operated in service of dominant epistemologies and did little to maintain the cultural heritage of students, as they sought to make students successful in learning environments rooted in Western epistemologies at the expense of sustaining native epistemologies. For these reasons, Paris questions how "relevant" and/or "responsive" the Ladson-Billings framework has actually been in practice.[36]

The phrase "culturally sustaining pedagogy" reflects the work of several scholars, including Paris, Alim, McCarty, Lee, Michener, Sengupta-Irving, Proctor, and Silverman.[37] A set of common values and assertions serve as the cornerstone of this work and challenge the boundaries of culturally sustaining pedagogy. These values and assertions are presented below as a series of epistemic shifts.

From a White Gaze to an Inward and Forward-Thinking Gaze

Paris and Alim assert that current educational policy and practice are designed to silence underrepresented cultures by creating a homogenous culture and language based on a Western epistemology reflected in White middle-class language, norms, and values. Essentially, they argue that asset-based pedagogies have focused on "how to get working-class students of color to speak and write more like middle-class White ones."[38] Students of color and their cultural heritages are valued in these pedagogies only so much as they allow students to perform dominant ways of thinking. Drawing on the work of Gutiérrez, Baquedano-Lopez, and Tejada,[39] Paris argues that culturally sustaining pedagogy must move beyond simply using culture to bridge the domains of students' home cultures and the dominant culture. Rather, education should enable students to gaze inwardly and, in doing so, imagine a third space that can integrate and extend both domains into an imagined future.

From a Fixed Cultural Identity to Plural and Fluid Identities and Cultures

Critical to the transition to this third space is a reconceptualization of culture as continuously shifting and evolving as communities themselves evolve, change, and become increasingly pluralistic. To achieve this pluralistic and fluid aspect of culture, students' home cultures cannot function in service to a dominant culture, and conversely, the dominant culture cannot function merely in service to the home culture. Rather, culturally sustaining pedagogy has the explicit goal of sustaining pluralism by supporting multilingualism and multiculturalism in practice and perspective for students and for teachers."[40]

From a Focus on the Disadvantaged/Subaltern to a Critical Analysis of Oppression and Privilege

Ladson-Billings as well as Paris and Alim argue that the oversimplification of culture outlined above has served to oversimplify the use of culture in a "one-to-one" mapping where teachers seek to sustain African American language for Black students and Spanish for Latina/o students.[41] They cite the use—and misuse—of hip-hop as an example of a cultural practice that has been used primarily in cocurricular spaces or curricular spaces targeted at Black and Brown students. It has been used as a bridge between students' home cultures and the dominant culture, but it has not been integrated into curricular and pedagogical settings more broadly.

From Educational Dependency to Educational Sovereignty

McCarty and Lee draw on the work of Paris and Paris and Alim and apply culturally sustaining pedagogy to the education of Native American communities.[42] They argue that for Native American communities, culturally sustaining pedagogy is not only sustaining but also culturally revitalizing in that it has the potential to impact not only issues of difference such as language, race, ethnicity, and social class, but also tribal sovereignty and the ability of Native Americans to be sovereign, to self-govern, and to self-educate.

Putting Theory into Practice

These bodies of work demand that educators value all that Latinx students bring to our campuses and build on these strengths to imagine a campus environment where the system is designed to truly fulfill the promise of higher education for Latinx students. How exactly educators put this into practice remains the challenge: How can/do faculty integrate such pedagogies into their teaching practice, and how can institutions support them in this endeavor? This shift from theory to practice has been a perennial challenge in American higher education, as Paris and Alim assert, because putting culturally sustaining pedagogy into practice "is difficult, inward-looking, and uncertain work. But, in all honesty, that has always been the case in the struggle for educational justice for people of color."[43]

While working in community college, I had the opportunity to collaborate with talented and committed faculty members, many of whom I had observed to be exceptional in their ability to support the success of Latinx students. Rooted in my experience with these faculty members, some but not all of whom identified as Latinx, I sought to better understand how exceptional faculty across New England valued Latinx students' cultural wealth and enacted culturally sustaining practices, ultimately creating more inclusive and equitable learning environments on their campuses. I designed a study to explore the ways in which five exceptional community college faculty working in HSIs in New England successfully bridge theory and practice to enact culturally sustaining praxis.[44]

In 2017, there were only seven community colleges that were designated as HSIs in New England, four in Connecticut and three in Massachusetts. Identifying exceptionally effective educators in public, Hispanic-serving community colleges is dependent upon defining exactly what constitutes an exceptionally effective educator. I was interested in not only quantitative measures of student success but also in transformational learning as observed by and defined by community college students, faculty, and community members. Initial outreach to participants included letters of invitation sent to faculty at target institutions who were identified through a community nominating process and met one or more of the following criteria:

- *Recognition*: Awards or other professional acknowledgment by peers, the institution, or relevant local or national organizations for excellence in teaching and/or excellence in supporting the success of Latinx students.
- *Research*: Engagement in scholarship and/or sharing practices related to culturally sustaining pedagogies, publications, invited speaking engagements, and/or conference presentations/workshops focused on strategies for effective teaching of Latinx students and/or culturally sustaining praxis.
- *Referrals*: Recommendations from study participants, colleagues, students, or community members that arose through the data collection and analysis process.

Eleven faculty members were invited through the nomination process, and five agreed to participate, resulting in a sample of exceptionally effective educators with a diverse range of attributes including disciplinary expertise; faculty rank; gender; race and ethnicity; and teaching experience in community colleges. Over a period of six months, I reviewed teaching philosophies and curricular materials and conducted classroom observations and semistructured interviews to better understand how culturally sustaining pedagogies were conceptualized and enacted by these faculty.

What Works for Latinx Students?

While all faculty participants integrated high-impact practices in community college teaching and learning into their courses, these varied widely. Some faculty were highly structured; others were organic and flexible. Some implemented project-based learning, civic engagement, and/or service learning; others focused on research and reflection in the development of portfolios; still others embedded cooperative learning and/or emphasis on the integration of digital technologies to support learning. In short, they were specific and vague, group and individual oriented, high-tech, and low-tech, so it was not evident on the surface which core practices or themes united the pedagogies of faculty participants if any at all.

It was not until I met the faculty and interacted with them, listened to how they characterize their work, and watched them in action with their students that the true commonalities across their teaching and the core aspects of their pedagogies became apparent. I noted that high-impact practices alone do not result in an exceptional learning environment for Latinx students; rather it is the use of teaching strategies *in service of* advancing a set of asset-based epistemic values that mattered. These shared values rooted the teaching and learning practices of all five faculty:

1. Teaching as love.
2. Centering Latinx identity and culture.
3. Growth through contemplative practices.
4. Building strength in community.
5. Learning for lifelong fulfillment.
6. Embracing holistic experiences.

TEACHING AS LOVE

> *I love this so much. . . . This is everything to me.*
>
> —ISABEL[45]

All faculty characterized teaching as distinct from other professions. It was clear that to be a professor was not simply a profession, but rather a deeply personal, at times spiritual, practice of morality, virtue, commitment, and ultimately, love. Their love of teaching was evident in the mission-driven framing of their work, asset-based assumptions about their students, and countless acts of validation embedded in their interactions in the classroom, course materials, activities, and assignments. When faculty talked about community college students in general, their statements reflected admiration, respect, reverence, and love.

As bell hooks describes, "The heart of education as a practice of freedom is to promote growth. It's very much an act of love in that sense of love as something that promotes our spiritual and mental growth."[46] Similar to Veloria (2024), who describes the role of *cariño* in supporting Latine students, participants' descriptions of the care they put into their work was connected to a deep commitment to students and their communities. For example, when asked how they became community college educators, participant responses included the following: "For me, teaching is my personal mission"; "I think of it, my time in the classroom, as my moral responsibility"; "I do this because of my commitment to impacting my community in a positive way"; "It makes me feel like, I wouldn't say responsible necessarily, but it's giving me that type of feeling that I'm committed to them. I'm committed to helping them. It's bigger than what we are learning. It's that connection"; "I love this so much. This, teaching, especially in this class, it's everything to me"; "I wouldn't be doing this if I didn't love it. I don't think anyone should do this unless they love their work, and they love their students." For these faculty, the concept of love was not only relevant to teaching, but necessary. Often, love was expressed through both academic and interpersonal validation of students, and the faculty enacted many of the core elements of validation theory.[47] These core elements include initiation of contact with students by faculty; settings that support student's self-worth as learners and community members; validation that supports student development; support for students inside and outside of class; emphasis on validation as a developmental process that occurs over time; and intentionality around integrating validating acts at the beginning of the semester. Validation was found in language in course syllabi, "I welcome the opportunity to assist you in your academic endeavors. I strongly urge you to take advantage of my office hours to address any questions or problems you may encounter throughout the semester. Simply put—I am here to help you succeed."

All five faculty members signaled to students frequently that they valued the prior knowledge, experiences, and cultures of their students: "I want them to know they have what they need already, yes. Like the example today when we saw the vocabulary, I'm always asking, have you seen these words before? Do you remember what the context was? They might have some familiarity with the word, maybe it triggers a memory, or it sounds similar to a word in their language. The vocabulary list at first might be alienating, but I'm like, 'Have you heard that word, or something similar? In your family, on the radio or a TV show, or whatever?' Those things can help them, but they don't always realize that their lives are valuable resources for learning. Most of them have been taught the opposite."

CENTERING LATINX IDENTITIES AND LANGUAGES

> *You can't separate the culture and the language. It's like you're cutting them in half . . . that accent is a gift.*
>
> —GABRIELLA

All faculty participants in my study demonstrated a focus on the cultural identities of Latinx students, and intentionality around integrating Latinx communities, cultures, and languages into teaching and learning. This integration was described as both a strategy for creating a more inclusive and culturally responsive classroom and critical to advancing student attainment of learning outcomes for both Latinx and non-Latinx students. Notable in this finding, and as seen in the examples below, is the function of Latinx cultures and languages in creating an interdisciplinary learning environment, integrating experiential knowledge, challenging hegemonic ideologies, providing a lens for critical analysis of cultural norms, and advancing social justice—the core elements of LatCrit in education as outlined by Delgado Bernal and Villalpando.[48] Faculty did not use Latinx cultures and languages as a one-way bridge for Latinx students to process a Western curriculum; instead, Latinx cultures and languages were integrated in service of deeper learning and critical reflection for all students.

Often, faculty were able to center Latinx identities and languages in the classroom because of their own Latinx identities and/or their engagement with ethnic studies and/or as a result of professional development on culturally sustaining practices. As one faculty participant described, "My teaching has always been anchored in a Latinx tradition. For example, you have the idea of creating a space where the students feel comfortable with sharing and understanding and like bringing from the personal and taking it to be theoretical. For me, that's somewhat important. . . . It's always for me central, and I base it also on activism and community service, which is what we do in an ethnic studies tradition. There is always that focus on community and thinking critically about systems. Latino studies really helped me to see that."

In all of the classes that were observed, there was clear representation of Latinx communities and cultures. For example, visual aids that were used to guide classroom activities featured photos and videos that contained asset-based depictions of Latinx people; Latinx names were prevalent in case studies, problem sets, and instructional examples; and students were encouraged to draw upon their multilingualism to make connections to the course material. As one faculty member explained: "Whenever I put my PowerPoints together, I'm very cognizant of the images I use, very much so. Even the cartoons, I always make sure that it's not only gender, but it's people of color, all colors, but especially the communities here. I make sure that there's diversity in everything that they're viewing. . . . I try to bring in culture as well because I think it's respectful to the population, to all their cultures, because then they feel like they're respected. Like, I'm not invisible.

I'm here, you're noticing this." In addition to the representation of Latinx people and communities, the classes observed also contained material that was directly relevant to the communities surrounding the college. Examples include immigration policy, community relations with law enforcement, and engagement with community-based organizations.

Faculty participants also noted that when other faculty do not take the time to understand the Latinx student population, it often leads to miscommunication with Latinx students and/or misinterpretations about behaviors Latinx students present in the classroom. Three participants noted that this is particularly detrimental if students are recent immigrants or first-generation college students, as they are likely to be operating under the cultural expectations and assumptions of the educational systems of their home countries. These assumptions may be counter to the academic expectations in the United States. Additionally, participants emphasized the importance of not only learning about Latinx culture and identity but also appreciating that Latinx culture is not monolithic.

GROWING THROUGH CONTEMPLATIVE PRACTICES

> *That lesson you saw today—I'm already thinking about how I'm going to change it next time.*
>
> —REBECCA

When discussing their process for designing, implementing, and evaluating their work, all participants underscored the importance of reflection and contemplative practices toward continuous improvement and innovation. The cycle of reflection on student engagement and learning, research on pedagogical approaches to teaching and teaching strategies, and constant revision of curriculum and innovation in methodologies were frequent themes. Faculty participants highlighted the cycle of reflection-research-revision as a critical practice for improving teaching and also an important skill to model to students to support them in becoming independent and self-directed in their learning. As one faculty member described,

> I'm doing this activity, but at the end, I have to reflect. How was it? If there was something good, what was good? If it

was appropriate for the outcomes, was it developmentally appropriate? Did I have all the information that I needed, the materials? Did the students really enjoy it, or just learn it? Do I have to make any changes? That kind of reflection helps me to be more intentional in my teaching. I'm always making some kind of change. It's a big part of my practice. I'm always thinking about the students that I see that come in and how I can make things better, more accessible for them. Also, I don't want to get bored. Some faculty, unfortunately, teach out of books that are out of print because they don't want to change anything. I'm always changing and adapting.

Each faculty participant connected the reflection-research-revision process with direct feedback from students. Four of the five participants noted that the student evaluations mandated by their institutions were not helpful tools in this process, so in response, they implemented alternative methods to assess student experiences. Syllabi and course materials revealed that methods for gathering student feedback varied from one-minute papers at the close of class, to reflective assignments and/or journaling throughout the course, to more formal midterm and final course evaluations created by the faculty member or cocreated by the faculty member and the students. The reflection below emphasizes that feedback from students is crucial to improving teaching practice:

I tell them, you make me become a better professor. You're helping me to learn, and to understand, and to help other students. Midway through the semester, they'll tell me things. They'll say, you know, I wish we had more of this, more group work, or less group work and more projects, or whatever. A lot of the assignments and activities that I do in the classroom come from that feedback.

One faculty member noted the difference in meaningful feedback between her own classroom evaluation process and the mandated course evaluations that students complete in each class. She said, "I should be looking at the formal evaluations, but I don't. [chuckles] They're basically useless to me. . . . I gather my own feedback, and I tell them write the good and bad, it doesn't matter. I want to become a better professional. I want to understand what they need, so I can help more students. They're great about giving feedback, and they're honest."

As this faculty member described, she deeply values student input, but in order to gather meaningful feedback from students to advance her teaching practice, she had to design a process to collect feedback from students outside of the institutional course evaluation process.

STRENGTH IN COMMUNITY

> *In here, I have to be everything. I'm their financial aid officer, their counselor, their advisor, I need to know the resources the community has so I can refer them. . . . It's everything.*
>
> —MIGUEL

All faculty participants described the importance of connecting students with resources and support services on and off campus. In particular, knowledge of admissions, financial aid and enrollment processes, registration and academic advising, and community-based services that focus on basic needs including housing and food insecurity were all frequently cited as essential in supporting student engagement and academic success. Often Latinx students are unable to connect with these resources outside of class because of demanding family or work responsibilities, so faculty integrate resources and support services into the classroom. Accessing support services was framed as especially challenging for Latinx students because of the cultural or language barriers they face when navigating the institution.

In response to the challenge Latinx students face, each faculty participant discussed unofficial networks, characterized by one faculty member as an "underground railroad" of support services that are forged by faculty members to support Latinx student success. These networks are composed of a community of Latinx faculty and staff members at the college and/or Spanish-speaking colleagues and/or spaces on campus that are likely to be knowledgeable and sensitive to the cultural contexts of Latinx students' lives and the resources they need to be successful. These unofficial networks are necessary because of the lack of official networks and intentional pathways that are contextualized to the needs of Latinx students.

All faculty had concerns that their institutions' inability to support the success of Latinx students was counter to the community college mission to provide open access to higher education to students; as one noted, "I was told in conversations that I've had with administrators and other folks that we are giving access to Latinos, but access does not mean opportunity if there is no utilization. If the student comes and they have no support structure, we're not really serving them; that isn't truly access to anything."

LEARNING TOWARD LIFELONG FULFILLMENT

I'm here to move you forward.

—ALEX

Academic excellence was clearly a high priority for all of the faculty. Emphasis on academic achievement and rigorous curricular engagement most frequently appeared within the context of overarching pathways to lifelong learning, developing a sense of purpose, and fulfilling career development. One participant described the connection between being a demanding professor in the context of the course and supporting long-term success. They said: "Well, I am demanding, yes. I expect a lot from them, but that's because they can do it, and I want them to know that they just have to push themselves, because the ability is there. The material we cover, it's tough. Some of it is really challenging, but that's why I'm here, and getting through this problem will also help them at the next level. This struggle and this commitment to figuring it out, and developing that confidence, that is the goal, that is a skill that goes beyond one course or one assignment."

Faculty often described themselves as allies or coaches to students in supporting them inside and outside of the classroom. Course materials contained references to future success and advice about the next steps students needed to take to continue to advance their educational and career goals. These included explanations of advising and registration processes, reflective assignments that required students to describe their goals and develop plans to realize those goals, and references to their past successes and future successes. Often these references were accompanied by statements that the faculty member would continue to be supportive of the student long beyond the current class or semester. As one faculty participant stated in the syllabus, "My goal is for your overall success. However, your motivation, efforts, and dedication will help you succeed within any course. I look forward to our educational journey and I hope it will be filled with knowledge, laughter, and success!" References to long-term achievement were often rooted in the assumption that students can and will be successful, as seen in this statement from a faculty member during class: "Remember, I'm not here to fail you, I'm here to move you forward. . . . My goal is to help you work hard and get that A, and then walk across that stage when you graduate, so if you aren't happy with your midterm grade, don't panic, just come see me."

All faculty remarked that internalized self-doubt and insecurity were common in their work with Latinx students. Further, several faculty members made connections between the ways in which Latinx students underestimate their academic abilities and traditional methods of assessment. Three participants noted that traditional methods of assessment are unlikely to support the success of Latinx students and develop their confidence as learners.

When asked about approaches to assessment of student learning, one participant rooted her response in aligned assessment methods with the strengths that Latinx—and other students of color—bring to the classroom. They said,

> Why do I like to do semester-long projects? Because they're giving the students the opportunity to excel. If I go by tests only, it will be very hard for them . . . especially multiple choice, with the language, it's too difficult, and it doesn't tell me anything about what they know. They become frustrated, and they don't think they can succeed here. . . . In projects, students take the time to do the research, to plan it out and create the project. It's like they have the theory, but they practice it together, and once they come to the classroom they can excel because they have given themselves enough time to create something beautiful.

EMBRACING HOLISTIC EXPERIENCES

> *In most courses, they leave their full self at the door. That's not the ethos of this class. . . . The big thing is, I notice them, and I think that's the key piece for students, especially for Latinx students who feel invisible here.*
>
> —ISABEL

All faculty spoke at length about the importance of forming relationships with students, knowing them holistically, recognizing and valuing the pluralities of their identities, and integrating student's lived experiences into the curriculum. This holistic knowledge of students was connected to community building in the classroom, deeper learning, improved student success outcomes, and a commitment to racial and social justice. Many of the faculty spoke about deficit-based biases campus members often hold about Latinx students. One of the faculty members was very candid about their evolution from deficit-based to asset-based assumptions about Latinx students in community colleges:

> When I first came, I didn't get the student population. This was the first time where I taught students full-time at a community college level. I had to learn where people were, I was like, Oh, they don't. Okay, they don't. All right, they can't. Over time, just reframing, where do I start with them, and remembering each semester that this is what we're going to start with, I get a fresh batch of students, so that means I need to repeat those things again. Who are they, what do they need, what do they bring to the classroom, focus on them as people, and then, after that, teaching them the content, it will not be a problem.

Is This Working for Faculty?

> *We need to talk about this, but wait while I shut the door . . .*
> —GABRIELLA

While my engagement with faculty in Hispanic-serving community colleges demonstrated that culturally sustaining pedagogies served as assets to student-facing work, there was another less positive dimension to this research. When participants shifted from speaking about the ways in which their praxis impacted students to the ways in which it impacted themselves as faculty, the bridges turned to barriers. Faculty described their approach to teaching as more comprehensive than student facing or classroom based. Their praxis was a way of operating on campus and pervaded the ways in which they navigated academic careers. The most common reflections from faculty were not that culturally sustaining praxis benefitted them; in fact, there seemed to be an inverse relationship between teaching practice and a sense of belonging on campus. The further faculty delved into culturally sustaining practice that worked for students, the less they felt supported and welcomed by the institution.

Faculty described this dynamic as experiences of silencing, exclusion, and/or microaggressions; professional isolation; frustration with espoused values that conflict with enacted values; dismissal or misunderstanding of culturally sustaining teaching practices; pressure to fulfill an unreasonable number of roles on campus; and competition among underrepresented groups for administrative support and resources. As one faculty member described:

> Well, this is going to be confidential, but it hasn't been easy to be here. It's difficult because I feel that they don't recognize all the effort that you have to put. You have to translate infor- mation, you have to make sure they get what they need. It's very hard. Sometimes if you hand in a syllabus the way that I do, and there is Spanish, they [administrators] want to know why I have to have it there, because they can't read it. For me it has been extremely difficult to work here. But that is also part of this, you can't talk about all the positive things with students without the struggle, too. Believe me, it's not easy.

Many participants expressed frustration and disappointment because although they worked at HSIs, they did not feel supported in enacting the pedagogies and practices that benefit Latinx students. Reflecting on this, one participant said, "You think, you're in an HSI, so it must be supportive of this population, right? Then it's so disheartening to see that the students, they're not supported at all. That that's not the goal. It looked better on paper, honestly. In reality, it's not a priority, it's not institutionalized, and it's not embedded within the culture."

All faculty participants expressed that while they loved teaching and remained committed to their students and the community college mission, enacting a culturally sustaining practice was challenging work that often came at a significant professional and personal cost.

A Call to Action

Enacting culturally sustaining praxis challenges Hispanic-serving commu- nity colleges to identify and value faculty who create learning environments that support Latinx student success, and to intentionally and proactively work to create campus environments that support faculty belonging and success as well. A culturally sustaining campus environment is one that sustains faculty as they sustain students, which increases the likelihood that culturally sustaining practitioners will shift from the exception to the rule. This work requires action on behalf of institutions to reclaim and redefine the core community college mission of access and equity for Latinx students. The action steps below enable institutions to advance their work in creating culturally sustaining learning environments, while simultaneously mitigating the barriers culturally sustaining practitioners report as common experiences. These steps are not sequential; they are reciprocal and interdependent:

- Recruit, empower, and reward scholar-practitioners of culturally sustaining praxis.
- Partner with Latinx communities on and off campus.
- Integrate contemplative practices with intention.

Institutions must prioritize the recruitment of faculty with effective culturally sustaining practices. Doing so not only increases the likelihood that students will experience learning environments that support their success, but it also addresses the underrepresentation, professional isolation, and lack of affinity-based mentorship expressed by the faculty. This may include redefining faculty hiring criteria to include more than the minimum qualifications for educational credentials and teaching experiences that currently qualify faculty for teaching positions at community colleges.

However, hiring faculty with culturally sustaining teaching practices is not sufficient to support and retain them. Institutions must also shift from espoused values of inclusion to authentic and intentional structures for faculty support. Innovative professional development that seeks to explore the epistemic underpinnings of culturally sustaining learning environments and challenges faculty to create epistemic shifts toward more culturally sustaining practices is vital. Institutions must also find ways to incentivize and reward faculty who demonstrate achievement in connecting with students, deepening their learning, and supporting their success.

Engaging Latinx student communities on and off campus is critical to this work, but community memberships are multiple, complex, and evolving; thus institutional responses will be as varied and nuanced as the communities themselves. The engagement of community includes faculty, staff, and administrator practitioners of culturally sustaining praxis, who are also members of communities on and off campus and whose community-based ways of knowing contribute to learning. Meaningful community partnerships are often time-consuming and challenging to establish, nurture, and sustain within the pace and workload of community colleges. However, when they are rooted in reciprocity between partners and authentic mutual respect, they can enable institutions to connect faculty with engaged pedagogies. Community partnerships also expose students to multiple ways of knowing and demonstrating learning, which can empower Latinx students to recognize their ways of knowing and demonstrating knowledge as valid and valuable.

As described by faculty participants, the development of culturally sustaining pedagogies is not linear or finite. Building *puentes* (bridges) that result in culturally sustaining learning environments is a cyclical and inward-facing exploration that is in constant evolution toward future imagining. It is rooted in and responsive to each group of students and the individual and collective strengths and challenges they bring into the classroom. Therefore, cultivating an effective culturally sustaining practice requires significant reflection and contemplation, and this process is never complete. It is ongoing, as it must evolve and change as the students, faculty members, communities, and the world around them evolve and change. Hence, it is necessary for practitioners of culturally sustaining praxis to engage in meaningful cycles of reflection. To this end, culturally sustaining praxis challenges institutions to make space for contemplation. This may involve refocusing and reprioritizing financial and time-related resources toward reflective practice.

A Few Final Words

A student in one of the classes I observed said, "We're not supposed to be here, education is not intended for us." So many of the deficiencies of our current community college system are captured in this sentence. Unfortunately, despite the espoused values of equity, inclusion, and diversity in higher education, the reality is that we are not living up to these values for our Latinx students, and we need to do better. While culturally sustaining pedagogies are relatively new, this emerging field has the potential to turn the tide. Culturally sustaining praxis, standing on the shoulders of many previous models for teaching and learning that are rooted in asset-based pedagogies, critical perspectives, cultural relevance, and acknowledgment of the many strengths and ways of knowing that Latinx students possess, offers a framework for building *puentes* between where we *are* and where we *need to be* in order to create learning environments where Latinx students cannot only survive our institutions but thrive in them.

Notes

1 Portions of this chapter in appear in the dissertation by the author: Liya Escalera-Kelley, "Culturally Sustaining Learning Environments in Public, Hispanic-Serving Community Colleges: Bridging Cultural Wealth, Epistemic Values, and Pedagogical Stances" (PhD diss., University of Massachusetts Boston, Department of Leadership in Education, 2020).

2 Terry Tafoya, "Finding Harmony: Balancing Traditional Values with Western Science in Therapy," *Canadian Journal of Native Education* 21 (1995): 11.

3 Throughout this chapter, the terms "Latino," "Latinx," "Latina/o," and "Latin@" are used. When referring to the work of others, I use the term the reference author(s) used.

4 Massachusetts Department of Higher Education, "Performance Measurement Reporting System," Massachusetts Department of Higher Education, https://www.mass.edu/datacenter/PMRS/home.asp.

5 National Center for Education Statistics, "Fast Facts: Enrollment," US Department of Education, Institute of Education Sciences, https://nces.ed.gov/fastfacts/display.asp?id=98.

6 Fabián Torres-Ardila and Nyal Fuentes, "The State of Latino Education: 2010–2020," Gastón Institute Publications 292 (2022), https://scholarworks.umb.edu/gaston_pubs/292.

7 Excelencia in Education, *Latino College Completion: Massachusetts—2023* (Excelencia in Education, 2023), https://www.edexcelencia.org/research/latino-college-completion/massachusetts.

8 Excelencia in Education, *Latino College Completion.*

9 Massachusetts Department of Higher Education, "Performance Measurement Reporting System."

10 The target is 24+ credits for full-time students, and 12+ credits for part-time students.

11 Massachusetts Department of Higher Education, "Performance Measurement Reporting System."

12 According to the US Department of Education, an HSI has an enrollment of undergraduate full-time-equivalent students that is at least 25% Hispanic students. US Department of Education, "Hispanic-Serving Institutions (HSIs)," US Department of Education, White House Initiative on Advancing Educational Equity, Excellence, and Economic Opportunity for Hispanics, https://sites.ed.gov/hispanic-initiative/hispanic-serving-institutions-hsis/.

13 National Center for Education Statistics, "Characteristics of Postsecondary Faculty," *Condition of Education* (US Department of Education, Institute of Education Sciences, 2023), https://nces.ed.gov/programs/coe/indicator/csc.

14 The Developing Hispanic-Serving Institutions Program, or "Title V" funds grants that are available to HSIs that enable them to "expand educational opportunities for, and improve the attainment of, Hispanic students. These grants also enable HSIs to expand and enhance their academic offerings, program quality, and institutional stability." Department of Education, "Developing Hispanic Serving Institutions Program—Title V"(US Department of Education), https://www2.ed.gov/programs /idueshsi/index.html, accessed September 9, 2023.

15 Nicholas Vargas, Julio Villa-Palomino, and Erika Davis, "Latinx Faculty Representation and Resource Allocation at Hispanic Serving Institutions," *Race Ethnicity and Education* 23, no. 1 (2020): 39–54.

16 Robert Wassmer, and Meredith Galloway, "Evidence That a Greater Presence of Latinx Faculty or Administrators Raises the Completion Rates of Various Cohorts of Community College Students," *Educational Policy* 37, no. 5 (2022): 1380–419.

17 Author's calculations based on New England Commission on Higher Education, *Berkshire Community College 2019 Self-Study*, New England Commission on Higher Education, 2019; New England Commission on Higher Education, *Bristol Community College Interim Five-Year Report*, New England Commission on Higher Education, 2019; New England Commission on Higher Education, *Bunker Hill Community College 2020 Self-Study*, New England Commission on Higher Education, 2020; New England Commission on Higher Education, *Cape Cod Community College—NEASC 2018 Accreditation Self-Study*, New England Commission on Higher Education, 2018; New England Commission on Higher Education, *Greenfield Community College 2020 Self-Study*, New England Commission on Higher Education, 2020; New England Commission on Higher Education, *Holyoke Community College NECHE 2020 Self-Study*, New England Commission on Higher Education, 2020; New England Commission on Higher Education, *Massasoit Community College— NEASC 2016 Self-Study*, New England Commission on Higher Education, 2016; New England Commission on Higher Education, *Middlesex Community College—2019 NECHE Five-Year Interim Accreditation Report*, New England Commission on Higher Education, 2019; New England Commission on Higher Education, *Mount Washington Community College—NECHE 2022 Decennial Self-Study*, New England Commission on Higher Education, 2022; New England Commission on Higher Education, *North Shore Community College 2019 Self-Study*, New England Commission on Higher Education, 2019; New England Commission on Higher Education, *Northern Essex Community College—NECHE 2020 Accreditation Self-Study*, New England Commission on Higher Education, 2020; New England Commission on Higher Education, *Quinsigamond Community College 2018 Fifth Year Interim Report*, New England Commission on Higher Education, 2018; New England Commission on Higher Education, *Springfield Technical Community College 2021 Accreditation Self-Study*, New England Commission on Higher Education, 2021.

18 Escalera-Kelley, "Culturally Sustaining Learning Environments." Robert A. Ibarra, *Beyond Affirmative Action: Reframing the Context of Higher Education* (University of Wisconsin Press, 2001); Gloria Ladson-Billings, "'Yes, But How Do We Do I?': Practicing Culturally Relevant Pedagogy," in *White Teachers/Diverse Classrooms*, ed. Julie Landsman and Charles W. Lewis, 29–41 (Stylus Publishing, 2006).

19 Sara E. Brownell and Kimberly D. Tanner, "Barriers to Faculty Pedagogical Change: Lack of Training, Time, Incentives, and . . . Tensions with Professional Identity?" *CBE—Life Sciences Education* 11, no. 4 (2012): 339–46; Ibarra, *Beyond Affirmative Action*.

20 Dolores Delgado Bernal and Octavio Villalpando, "An Apartheid of Knowledge in Academia: The Struggle over the "Legitimate" Knowledge of Faculty of Color," *Equity and Excellence in Education* 35, no. 2 (2002): 169.

21 Kenneth P. González, "Campus Culture and the Experiences of Chicano Students in a Predominantly White University," *Urban Education* 37, no. 2 (2002): 218.

22 Ibarra, *Beyond Affirmative Action*, 15.

23 Sally Brown and Mariana Souto-Manning, "'Culture is the Way They Live Here': Young Latin@s and Parents Navigate Linguistic and Cultural Borderlands in US Schools," *Journal of Latinos and Education* 7, no. 1 (2007): 26.

24 Derald Wing Sue, et al., "Racial Microaggressions and the Asian American Experience," *Cultural Diversity and Ethnic Minority Psychology* 13, no. 1 (2007): 274.

25 Laura I. Rendón, Amaury Nora, and Vijay Kanagala, *Ventajas/Assets y Conocimientos/Knowledge: Leveraging Latin@ Assets to Foster Student Success* (Center for Research and Policy in Education, University of Texas at San Antonio, 2014), https://www.utsa.edu/strategicplan/documents/2017_12 percent20Student percent20 Success percent20_Ventajas_Assets_2014.pdf.

26 Tara J. Yosso, "Whose Culture Has Capital? A Critical Race Theory Discussion of Community Cultural Wealth," *Race Ethnicity and Education* 8, no. 1 (2005): 69–91.

27 Luis C. Moll, et al., "Funds of Knowledge for Teaching: Using a Qualitative Approach to Connect Homes and Classrooms," in *Funds of Knowledge: Theorizing Practices in Households, Communities, and Classroom*, ed. Norma Gonzalez, Luis C. Moll, and Cathy Amanti, 71–87 (New York: Routledge, 2006).

28 Gloria Anzaldúa. "La Conciencia de la Mestiza: Towards a New Consciousness," in *Chicana Feminist Thought: The Basic Historical Writings*, ed. Alma M. García, 270–73 (Routledge, 1997).

29 Dolores Delgado Bernal, "Learning and Living Pedagogies of the Home: The Mestiza Consciousness of Chicana Students," *International Journal of Qualitative Studies in Education* 14, no. 5. (2001): 623–39.

30 Laura I. Rendón, "Validating Culturally Diverse Students: Toward a New Model of Learning and Student Development," *Innovative Higher Education* 19 (1994): 33–51.

31 Paulo Freire, *Pedagogy of the Oppressed* (Seabury Press, 1970); bell hooks, *Teaching to Transgress: Education as a Freedom of Practice* (New York: Routledge, 1994); Laura I. Rendón, *Sentipensante (Sensing/Thinking) Pedagogy: Educating for Wholeness, Social Justice, and Liberation* (Stylus Publishing, 2009).

32 Gloria Ladson-Billings, "Culturally Relevant Pedagogy 2.0: Aka the Remix," *Harvard Educational Review* 84, no. 1 (2014): 74.

33 Gloria Ladson-Billings, "But That's Just Good Teaching! The Case for Culturally Relevant Pedagogy," *Theory into Practice* 34, no. 3 (1995): 159–65.

34 Ladson-Billings, "But That's Just Good Teaching!," 162.

35 Django Paris, "Culturally Sustaining Pedagogy: A Needed Change in Stance, Terminology, and Practice," *Educational Researcher* 41, no. 3 (2012): 93.

36 Paris, "Culturally Sustaining Pedagogy."

37 Teresa McCarty and Tiffany Lee, "Critical Culturally Sustaining/Revitalizing Pedagogy and Indigenous Education Sovereignty," *Harvard Educational Review* 84, no. 1 (2014): 101–24; Catherine J. Michener, et al., "Culturally Sustaining Pedagogy Within Monolingual Language Policy: Variability in Instruction," *Language Policy* 14 (2015): 199–220; Django Paris, "Culturally Sustaining Pedagogy"; Django Paris and H. Samy

Alim, "What Are We Seeking to Sustain Through Culturally Sustaining Pedagogy? A Loving Critique Forward," *Harvard Educational Review* 84, no. 1 (2014): 85–100.

38 Paris and Alim, "What Are We Seeking to Sustain," 86.

39 Kris D. Gutiérrez, Patricia Baquedano-López, and Carlos Tejeda, "Rethinking Diversity: Hybridity and Hybrid Language Practices in the Third Space," *Mind, Culture, and Activity* 6, no. 4 (1999): 286–303.

40 Paris and Alim, "What Are We Seeking to Sustain," 88.

41 Ladson-Billings, "Culturally Relevant Pedagogy 2.0"; Paris and Alim, "What Are We Seeking to Sustain."

42 McCarty and Lee, "Critical Culturally Sustaining/Revitalizing Pedagogy"; Paris, "Culturally Sustaining Pedagogy"; Paris and Alim, "What Are We Seeking to Sustain."

43 Paris and Alim, "What Are We Seeking to Sustain," 96.

44 Escalera-Kelley, "Culturally Sustaining Learning Environments."

45 Hence forward all quotes are by study participants. To protect their anonymity, limited information about each participant is provided.

46 hooks, *Teaching to Transgress*, 37.

47 Rendón, "Validating Culturally Diverse Students."

48 Delgado Bernal and Villalpando, "An Apartheid of Knowledge."

Chapter Six

The Consequences of Assessing English Learners in a Restrictive and Subtractive Learning Environment[1]

MICHAEL BERARDINO

Every spring since 1998, Massachusetts public school students have partic-ipated in the Massachusetts Comprehensive Assessment System (MCAS). These statewide standardized tests in English Language Arts (ELA), Math-ematics, and Science/Technology/Engineering (STE) are administered in grades 3 through 10. The MCAS exams are the central component of the state's test-based accountability system and carry serious consequences for poor performance. Students who cannot pass the grade 10 tests will not qualify for a high school diploma,[2] while "low-performing" school districts and individual schools that do not improve test scores are susceptible to state intervention or takeover. Proponents of the MCAS argue that the punitive use of MCAS scores is beneficial for all students—that it maintains high standards, mon-itors districts and schools, and provides critical diagnostic information for educators.[3] According to the Massachusetts Department of Elementary and Secondary Education (MDESE), as a result of this test-based accountability system, "Massachusetts is leading the nation in public education."[4]

While it is true that as a state Massachusetts often has the highest aver-age test scores on tests such as the National Assessment of Educational Progress (NAEP), the ACT, Advanced Placement (AP), and Program for International Student Assessment (PISA),[5] as discussed by Torres Ardila, Fuentes, and Colón (in this volume), these claims gloss over the fact that most traditionally marginalized student groups (e.g., Black, Latinx, students with diagnosed disabilities) continue to face large and persistent gaps in all aspects of education. One student group that faces the most severe disparities are English learners (ELs),[6] students whose first language is not English and who are unable to "perform ordinary classroom work in English."[7]

The MCAS exams, with very few exceptions, are administered solely in English,[8] and all public school students in Massachusetts, regardless of English proficiency, are required to take these tests after their first year in the country. With these participation requirements, it is no surprise that ELs struggle on the MCAS tests relative to their English-proficient peers. As shown in figures 6.1 and 6.2,[9] there have been persistent gaps in pass rates between ELs and non-ELs on the grade 10 ELA and Math MCAS tests from 2003 to 2023. On the 2023 grade 10 ELA tests, only 3% of ELs statewide scored "meeting or exceeding expectations," compared with 64% of non-ELs, a larger gap than when the state began tracking the test results in 2003.[10] On the 2023 grade 10 Math test, the percentage of ELs scoring at "meeting or exceeding expectations" was 4% (down from 9% in 2019), with performance gaps of 50 percentage points relative to non-ELs. On the national NAEP tests, the difference in mean scores between ELs and non-ELs in Massachusetts is consistently among the largest for any state in the country. Massachusetts non-ELs have either the highest or second highest mean scores, while Massachusetts ELs score similar to the national average.[11]

Beyond standardized test scores, ELs in Massachusetts also trail far behind their English-proficient peers in key measures of educational progress. For instance, less than three in five ELs in Massachusetts (57%) pass all their grade 9 courses as compared to four-fifths of non-ELs (82%),[12] and under one-third of ELs in grade 11 or grade 12 (32%) are enrolled in advanced coursework as compared to over two-thirds of non-ELs (69%).[13] The 2023 four-year cohort graduation rate for ELs in Massachusetts was 67%, substantially lower than the graduation rate of 92% for non-ELs; the 2023 four-year cohort dropout rate for ELs was 18%, substantially higher than the dropout rate of 4% for non-ELs.[14] Even among ELs who graduate from high school, college enrollment rates for ELs are much lower than for non-ELs, with around one-third of ELs who graduate from high school (34%) enrolling in college as compared to almost three-quarters (70%) of non-ELs.[15] Equally concerning is that the disparities in these crucial educational outcomes are the same or worse than they were ten years ago, a trend that predates school disruptions from the COVID-19 pandemic.

In this chapter, to understand why ELs continue to struggle in high-performing Massachusetts, I explore how state policies on assessment and instruction, instead of helping ELs and the school districts that serve them, actually create harmful learning environments. Before describing the relevant policies and how they negatively impact ELs, I first describe ELs in Massachusetts and explain why this student population is the focus of this chapter. I then describe how current accountability policies, combined with the remnants of English-only instructional policies, create intensely restrictive settings for ELs that weaken the traditional protective factors for immigrant students. After discussing the design and shortcomings of these policies, I present the rationales that proponents provide for the test-based accountability policy and demonstrate how the rationales and the underlying assumptions are flawed. I conclude by offering policy recommendations that would lead to more inclusive learning environments for ELs.

Who Are ELs in Massachusetts?

ELs make up a substantial proportion of students in Massachusetts. As of 2024, ELs were 13% of all students in Massachusetts public schools and over one-third of students in urban school districts like Chelsea (45%), Lynn (43%), Lawrence (42%), and Boston (34%).[16] The number of ELs in Massachusetts' schools has been rapidly increasing: the number of EL students increased by 48% over the past ten years and 141% over the past twenty years.[17] The majority of the growth in EL enrollment has occurred not in large urban school districts but in midsize urban, suburban, and rural districts. However, there is still a high concentration of ELs in a handful of districts—ten districts serve 50% of all ELs in the state.[18]

There is great diversity within the EL student population in Massachusetts in terms of immigrant status/place of birth, home language, race/ethnicity, grade level, level of English proficiency, and disability status. ELs are categorized by English-language proficiency and not by immigrant status—therefore there is a range of generational status among ELs including students born in Puerto Rico, first generation immigrants, and second and even third generation immigrants. While not an entirely reliable measure,[19] according to MDESE, 68% of ELs are born in the US, including Puerto Rico.[20] ELs in Massachusetts include 121 different language groups—Spanish speakers are the largest group at 52%, followed by Portuguese speakers at 19%, while Haitian Creole speakers comprise 5% and Crioulo and Chinese speakers each account for 3% of ELs.[21] Looking at ethnoracial composition, almost two-thirds (64%) of ELs are identified as Latinx, 13% as Black, 12% as White, and 9% as Asian.[22]

There are ELs across all grade levels, but ELs are primarily concentrated in early grades—61% are in grades pre-K through 5, 16% in grades 6 through 8, and 23% in grades 9 through 12. There is also variance in the length of time an EL has been in Massachusetts schools; 39% have been in Massachusetts schools for five or more years, 34% for three to four years, and 27% for one to two years. And there is a wide range in English proficiency levels among ELs—almost two-fifths (37%) of ELs are at English language development (ELD) levels 1 and 2, indicating very low levels of English proficiency; a similar proportion (36%) is at ELD level 3, indicating moderate English proficiency but still requiring English-language support; and the remaining quarter of ELs are in ELD levels 4 and higher, indicating they are close to reclassifying as former EL and able to receive instruction in English.[23]

One group that is not highlighted in this chapter, but merits special attention are ELs with disabilities (EL-SWDs), who account for 22% of ELs.[24] Several studies have shown how outcomes for EL-SWDs, even when controlling for ELD level, are significantly lower than for ELs without a diagnosed disability.[25] Diana Santiago's testimonio (in this volume), articulates some of the systemic challenges that EL with disabilities face in accessing services.

WHY DISCUSS ELS?

Why focus on ELs in a book about Latinx students in Massachusetts? After all, the vast majority (67%) of Latinx students are not ELs.[26] Demographic trends suggest that Latinx students will increasingly be US born, thereby decreasing the proportion of Latinx students that are ELs.[27]Furthermore, two-thirds of Latinx students who are not ELs (i.e., English-proficient Latinx students) have educational outcomes far worse than White and Asian students in the state and face educational barriers beyond the policies related to ELs described in this chapter.[28] Therefore, it is important to decouple the term "Latinx" from "EL" or "immigrant."

So then why am I focusing on the state policies for ELs? While there is diversity within the Latinx and EL student populations in Massachusetts, there is a great deal of overlap between these two groups, especially in large urban school districts. One-third (33%) of all Latinx students in Massachusetts are ELs, and the proportion is higher in the school districts

Grade 10 ELA Proficiency Rate, 2003-2018 & "Meeting or Exceeding"
Rate, 2019-2023

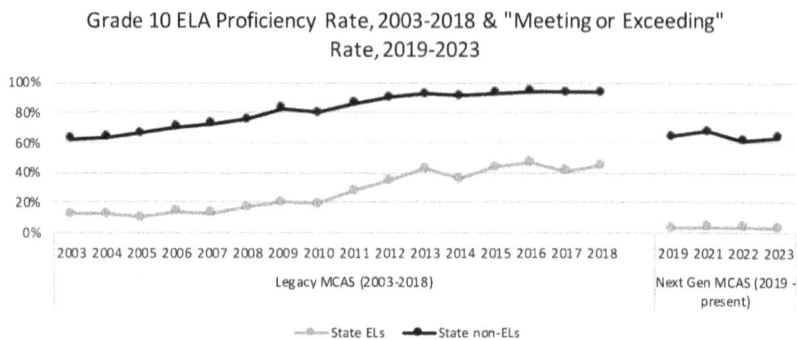

Figure 6.1. Grade 10 ELA Proficiency Rate, 2003–2018 and "Meeting or Exceeding" Rate, 2019–2023.

Grade 10 Math Proficiency Rate, 2003-2018 & "Meeting or Exceeding" Rate, 2019-2023

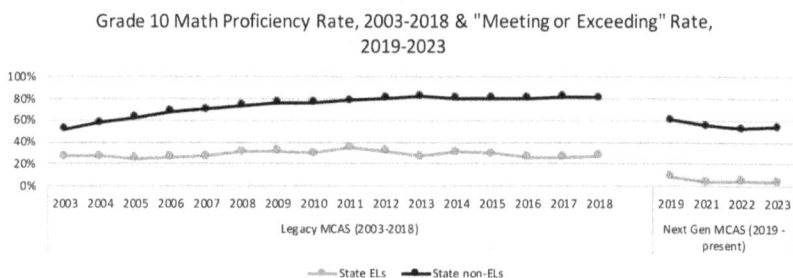

Figure 6.2. Grade 10 Math Proficiency Rate, 2003–2018 and "Meeting or Exceeding" Rate, 2019–2023. Source: MDESE, *2023 Next Generation MCAS*.

with the largest Latinx populations such as Lawrence (44%), Chelsea (46%), Boston (51%), and Lynn (53%). There are also many Latinx students who are former ELs—a designation the state gives to ELs who have acquired adequate English-language proficiency to participate fully in general education classes for a monitoring period of four years. An estimated 14% of Latinx students in Massachusetts are former ELs, meaning approximately 46% of Latinx students are currently an EL or had been designated as an EL over the previous four years.[29] With this sizeable intersection between the EL and Latinx student population, the experiences of Latinx students and ELs are inextricably linked; there is no way to understand the full experiences of Latinx students without also understanding the educational experiences of ELs. Notably, the educational disparities faced by ELs in Massachusetts are so severe that aggregate measures of Latinx student outcomes will always skew lower than for any other ethnoracial groups in the state, creating the potential to entrench a stigma of Latinx students as "underperforming."[30]

Of note—in this chapter I examine the experiences of all ELs, discussing ELs as though they are one uniform group. This is primarily a result of data limitations—MDESE reports on race/ethnicity and EL status as two separate categories and does not provide disaggregation of EL student outcomes by ethnoracial category or language group. With no publicly available data in Massachusetts on Latinx ELs or even Spanish-speaking ELs, current research is limited to addressing ELs as a monolithic group. Unfortunately, this elides many important distinctions within the EL student population and prevents researchers from gaining nuanced understandings of the experiences and outcomes of Latinx EL students.

Massachusetts State Assessment and Instructional Policies

The state policies on standardized testing and instructional approaches for ELs collectively create a highly restrictive environment for ELs—one that places ELs at risk not only for repeated failure on the MCAS but also for academic disengagement leading to larger educational challenges. While there are other state policies that pertain directly and indirectly to ELs (e.g., English-language proficiency assessment, classification and reclassification requirements, and course and credit requirements), the assessment and instructional policies have a major impact for ELs and the school districts that educate them.

RESTRICTIVE ASSESSMENT POLICIES AND TEST-BASED ACCOUNTABILITY

The MCAS tests were created as part of the landmark Massachusetts Education Reform Act (MERA) of 1993, which had the goal of remedying widely documented educational disparities.[31] MERA, part of a national standards-based reform movement, standardized curriculum frameworks and teacher accreditation across Massachusetts and established minimum guaranteed per-pupil funding through state aid to low-income school districts. It also created a statewide assessment system, the MCAS, as a means of evaluating the progress of the expansive reforms found in MERA.[32] The use of the MCAS subsequently expanded in scope. Beginning in 2003, passing the grade 10 MCAS test has been a graduation requirement. As of writing this chapter, Massachusetts, along with Florida, Illinois, Louisiana, New York, Texas, and Wyoming, are currently the eight states in the country with such a graduation requirement.[33] Additionally, MDESE's accountability system is based primarily on MCAS results. While the current accountability rankings are framed in terms of support for struggling school districts and individual schools (e.g., "requiring assistance or intervention"), the system is punitive for districts that have numerous struggling schools. For example, poor accountability outcomes lead to negative coverage in the press, which in turn is likely to impact enrollment and perceptions of school quality.[34] Further underpinning the punitive accountability system is the threat of the state putting a school or district in receivership, which is when a school district loses local control of the school system. In recent years, the state has used persistent poor performance on the MCAS as justification to take control over the Lawrence, Holyoke, and Southbridge public school districts as well as individual schools in Boston and Springfield—all school districts with large Latinx and EL populations.

All students in Massachusetts are required to fully participate in the MCAS after their first year in the country. The tests are administered in English (except for grade 10 Math and Science starting as of 2022), and all scores count toward school-level and district-level accountability measures.[35] The MCAS participation requirements are in direct contradiction to research that shows ELs needing four to seven years to reach academic English proficiency, the type of proficiency necessary to fully participate in classes and tests that are conducted entirely in English.[36] When administered in English only, test results systematically underestimate the academic and cognitive ability of ELs by introducing "construct-irrelevant variance" or score variance that is due to the EL's lack of proficiency in academic English rather than a lack of specific content knowledge.[37]

Federal law permits states to develop accommodations for ELs, defined as changes to a test or the testing environment that are intended to improve access to content without altering the test construct.[38] MDESE allows ELs to use a bilingual word-to-word glossary when taking the MCAS, allows general administration directions read aloud in English or the student's native language (if a native language speaker is available), and (as of 2022) offers a Spanish version of the grade 10 Math as well as the STE test.[39] While there is no consensus on the appropriate form of test accommodations, bilingual word-to-word dictionaries are one of the least beneficial accommodations.[40] Offering subject tests in students' home language is a more beneficial accommodation, but MDESE only offers the grade 10 tests in Spanish, which only benefits the 52% of ELs in Massachusetts schools who speak Spanish as a home language.[41] More helpful accommodations include offering subject tests in other languages in all grades and having a translator record student responses in their native language.[42] The federal Every Student Succeeds Act of 2015 provided states with leeway to develop and use additional measures of school quality beyond standardized tests in their annual accountability measures, but Massachusetts still relies primarily on test-based measures of student learning and school quality.[43]

RESTRICTIVE INSTRUCTIONAL POLICIES

Forcing ELs to participate in English-only standardized testing with limited accommodations helps explain ELs' poor MCAS test scores and some of the lower graduation rates for ELs (as the grade 10 MCAS are a graduation requirement) but does not explain the persistent disparities in other outcomes such as course taking, dropout rates, and college enrollment rates. State EL instructional policies have a direct impact on both MCAS scores and these other educational outcomes. With tests in ELA, Math, and STE, success on the MCAS requires both academic English proficiency and access to grade-level content. Therefore, to prepare students for the state standardized tests, schools have the responsibility to provide instruction that both helps students acquire academic English and teaches grade-level content (e.g., math, science, history, literature).[44] However, acquiring academic English and learning grade-level content are two separate processes and not all EL instructional approaches can provide these simultaneously.[45]

There are currently two primary forms of EL instruction in Massachusetts: Sheltered English Immersion (SEI) and dual-language programs. SEI is a form of instruction where ELs are placed in an isolated classroom, where no less than 90% of instruction is provided in English.[46] This program type is designed to "mainstream" ELs, that is, to place them in general education classes as quickly as possible based on the assumption that students will learn English faster if immersed in English and if they can no longer use their native language as a "crutch."[47] An alternative approach to instructing ELs uses dual-language programs, where all students regardless of native language and English proficiency level receive instruction evenly in two languages, with the focus on teaching both language and content simultaneously. Dual-language programs are open to all students regardless of their native language and aim to produce biliterate/bilingual (or multilingual) students.

In Massachusetts, SEI has been the dominant form of EL instruction since 2002, when the voters of Massachusetts strongly supported a state referendum known as "Question 2," which made Massachusetts one of three states in the country to establish SEI as the default instructional approach for ELs.[48] In 2017, after fifteen years of research and advocacy exposing the limitations of SEI, the state passed the Language Opportunity for Our Kids (LOOK) Act, which allows school districts more flexibility in the instructional approach they offer for ELs.[49] Despite this flexibility, 93% of ELs are still in SEI programs (the same proportion as when the bill was passed) and 3% are in dual-language programs, while 3% of ELs families opted out of specialized instructional programs.[50] Therefore, ELs in Massachusetts are overwhelmingly being instructed in an approach that prioritizes teaching students academic English as opposed to teaching academic content in academic English and the student's native language simultaneously.[51] Furthermore, ELs in the state predominantly receive content instruction in SEI content classes, which are often not as rigorous as mainstream general education classes and where the focus of instruction is on basic skills rather than higher-order thinking.[52] Research also shows that in schools utilizing SEI, once a student reaches an adequate level of English-language proficiency and leaves the SEI program, they are tracked into lower-level courses and therefore excluded from key content areas or placed in classes taught at an English proficiency level above their comprehension.[53] Between participation requirements, limited testing accommodations for ELs, and restrictive English-language instruction policies that deemphasize bilingualism, Massachusetts is one of the most restrictive states in terms of the instruction and testing of ELs.

Beyond limiting access to grade-level content, the current language instructional practices may also serve to reduce academic engagement, a key attribute necessary for sustained academic success.[54] Academic engagement is defined as "the attention, interest, investment, and efforts students extend in the work of learning."[55] English immersion programs, because they marginalize and deemphasize a student's native language and associated culture, can be thought of as a form of "subtractive schooling."[56] Developed by Valenzuela, "subtractive schooling" posits that American schooling devalues the heritage as well as the social and cultural resources of nondominant groups, forcing students of color and language minorities (i.e., individuals who speak a language at home other than English) to assimilate to succeed, thereby placing these students at a disadvantage from the onset of their schooling experience.[57] Teachers in the current educational and language instruction environment, simply by following policy, reinforce racial and cultural differences without "caring" for the students and thereby "betray" students by promoting assimilation and deidentification with the student's native language and culture.[58] As a response to subtractive schooling, many students disengage academically and are more likely to be disruptive in class and violate rules.

Another concern with English immersion policies is that they are built on a narrow conception of literacy. Literacy is treated as an absolute set of rules governing grammar, spelling, and sentence structure, instead of being more properly considered as part of a larger realm of discourse.[59] Gee argues that individuals have a primary discourse that they learn to use at home, and for language minorities this primary discourse is different from the discourse required for academic success.[60] The educational system perceives proficiency as competency with spelling, grammar, vocabulary, and sentence structure but does not consider the larger, more comprehensive discourse an individual needs to have facility with in order to achieve true proficiency with a secondary language. Furthermore, the dominant literacy carries a particular social context with histories of social hierarchy and subjugation of people of color, and language deficiency makes the social context of the larger social discourse more severe and detrimental. In the Massachusetts context, the SEI instruction model and the standardized testing regimes are prime examples of subtractive schooling through a narrow definition of literacy and proficiency. ELs must assimilate as quickly as possible or fall far behind peers from the dominant group.

RESILIENCY AND IMMIGRANT STUDENTS

It should be noted that this critique of the current policies contradicts a large body of research that highlights the protective factors built into immigrant enclaves and the traditional notion of immigrant student "resiliency"— defined as "the capacity for successful adaptation in the face of significant adversity."[61] The general understanding of immigrant student resiliency is that as compared to native-born students of color and despite language deficiencies, immigrant students, and especially those who arrive as young children, maintain high levels of academic engagement.[62] As a result, first- and even second-generation immigrant students are found to be at a lower risk of dropping out than other students of color.[63] Additionally, relative to second and later-generation immigrants, first-generation immigrant students perceive fewer barriers to achieving academic success.[64] This is in part due to immigrant parents placing a high emphasis on academic achievement.[65] Perreira, Harris, and Lee found that immigrant "optimism" helped first-generation youth overcome a lack of cultural and social capital. However, there is no consensus that these generational patterns are true across all immigrant groups and contexts.[66] It is clear that race, class, and location of migration factor into the academic engagement and educational outcomes of immigrant students.[67] For instance, research shows that Latinx students are increasingly being "racialized" with growing negative stereotypes associated with this label disrupting the protective factors of immigrant enclaves.[68] In contrast, some immigrant groups and most notably some Asian groups, such as Chinese and Vietnamese immigrants, develop positive social networks within ethnicities that help foster academic and educational success.[69]

I identify two reasons why the research on immigrant student resiliency may not apply to ELs in the current educational setting. First, by definition, ELs are not all immigrants—there is a range of generational status among ELs including first-generation immigrants, as well as second- and even third-generation immigrants. ELs who are second- or third-generation immigrants are not heterogeneous and may not have the same level of resiliency as first-generation immigrant ELs.

Second, the majority of the research on the resiliency of immigrant students and even the research on the engagement of ELs preceded the passage of the No Child Left Behind Act (NCLB) in 2002. Prior to NCLB, in both Massachusetts and nationally, immigrant students and ELs were given time to learn English and become accustomed to the culture and expectations of US schools, and as a result, the economic and academic consequences of removal from secondary school were less severe.[70] In the current environment all students are required to participate in the tests, their results are included in all composite accountability measures, and ELs are a target subgroup. Therefore, we do not know whether previously identified immigrant student resiliency still applies in this test-based accountability setting; the state's testing and reporting policies may reduce historical protective factors for immigrant students/ELs.

Taken together, ELs in Massachusetts are educated and learn in a system that utilizes narrow assessments (tests administered in English only with limited accommodations) and a narrow language instruction policy for ELs, as SEI favors rapid English acquisition while framing fluency in a native language as a deficiency. The result is a subtractive schooling experience taking place within a system that uses a narrow conception of literacy and language proficiency and fails to consider the social, cultural, and historical context of language. Adding a test-based accountability system exacerbates the problems faced by linguistic minorities, defaulting them to "at-risk" and at a deficit before they even enter the education system. While immigrant groups traditionally have higher levels of engagement than native-born students from marginalized groups, the state's language instruction policies that emphasize SEI over bilingual education and frequent testing may remove the socialization protection that immigrants in previous generations experienced. These factors combine to undermine the stated intention of the educational reforms, creating forces that erode the academic engagement of ELs rather than increasing their engagement and motivation.

Interrogating the Rationales for Test-Based Accountability in Massachusetts

Despite the continued poor MCAS performance, proponents argue that including all students in the test-based accountability system is beneficial for administrators, teachers, parents, community members, and students themselves. In this section, I review the central justifications for the test-based accountability system offered by the state and other proponents and interrogate the assumptions underpinning these rationales in the light of evidence from recent research.

Based on a review of materials from MDESE and other proponents, I have identified three major rationales for the test-based accountability system in Massachusetts:

Rationale 1: Tests with high stakes will improve outcomes for students by giving students, schools, and districts motivation to work harder. Tests that carry consequences will lead to improved educational outcomes because they provide students with extrinsic motivation in the form of punitive consequences if they perform poorly. By linking test scores to high school graduation, low-performing students will be motivated to improve their study habits and ultimately improve their test scores;[71] proponents posit that without stakes, students will underperform on tests, impinging on the validity of the assessments.[72] In addition, through public pressure and the threat of state takeover, the test-based accountability system will provide schools and districts with the motivation to improve instruction and the allocation of resources.[73]

Rationale 2: The state is required to measure student learning, and standardized tests are the most efficient and reliable measures of student learning. Current state policies require a means to evaluate all public school students across the state, and MDESE considers the MCAS as the most efficient and reliable common assessment, allowing for objective and fair comparison of student learning across schools and districts.[74]

Rationale 3: The state tests provide critical diagnostic information for educators. Tests like the MCAS can provide educators with detailed information on where to adjust instruction to serve struggling students, can inform school-wide curricular and instructional design, and can help districts and schools determine how to allocate resources.[75] More recently, this rationale has shifted to a discussion around "learning loss," with proponents of the MCAS arguing that the tests are necessary to measure the amount of learning that was lost during the COVID-19 pandemic.

Common across these rationales for the test-based accountability system are the assumptions that (1) the testing system will lead to improved outcomes; (2) the tests do no harm to students, and (3) the MCAS scores are a useful measure of student learning to inform interventions. There is, however, little evidence to support any of these assumptions. Below, I review these assumptions one at a time.

The Test-Based Accountability System Will Lead to Improved Outcomes

There is limited research that suggests that some students do have positive responses to the punitive extrinsic motivators in high-stakes tests.[76] But these positive reactions to the tests are correlated with prior academic standing and test performance[77] as well as race, gender, and income level.[78]

On the other hand, the experience of almost thirty years of standards-based reforms in Massachusetts shows that apart from improved statewide average test scores, there has been minimal improvement in addressing disparities, especially for ELs. As previously stated, ELs in Massachusetts continue to have outcomes far worse than their English-proficient peers and, in many ways, ELs are further behind their peers than at the outset of the standards-based reforms movement.[79]

The test-based accountability system also does not appear to have any benefit for "low-performing" schools and districts, especially those with large EL (and Latinx) populations. With current participation requirements and accommodations, ELs will always underperform on the MCAS because of a lack of language proficiency and lack of access to grade-level content. Since MCAS results constitute the majority of school accountability measures, the state's accountability system by definition unduly punishes the schools and districts that serve higher proportions of ELs and by extension Latinx students. The punitive nature of the accountability system for EL-serving schools and districts can be seen in the recent accountability status of schools across the state. In 2019, among schools that were in the accountability category "requiring assistance," ELs accounted for 22% of all students on average, compared with only 9% of students in schools "not requiring assistance." Furthermore, in recent years the state has put three school districts with large EL populations in receivership: Lawrence (37%), Holyoke (19%), and Southbridge (20%). In 2022, the Boston Public Schools (30% ELs) had to negotiate a settlement with the state to avoid a state takeover of the school district (2022). These school districts also have some of the largest Latinx student populations—Lawrence (94%); Holyoke (81%); Southbridge (65%), and Boston (44%)—highlighting the critical intersection between Latinx and EL student experiences.

The Tests Do No Harm

Not only is there no consistent evidence that poor performance on the MCAS has any positive impact on ELs and other traditionally marginalized groups; there is evidence that the state tests may actually do harm. Research has shown that test-based accountability systems and the associated negative labeling have had negative impacts on low-income students and students of color, such as lower graduation rates and higher dropout rates.[80] In my research from 2023, I used a regression discontinuity design to look at the impact that failing the tests prior to high school has on students.[81] I found that among all student groups, including ELs, failing the MCAS in middle school had no positive impact on subsequent MCAS scores or academic engagement as measured by attendance, suspension rate, or retention; instead, failing the MCAS was associated with underperformance on subsequent MCAS.[82] In 2020, Acosta et al. conducted a meta-analysis of thirty-seven studies on ELs in high-stakes testing environments, with research sites in multiple states including California, Colorado, New York, and Texas. Through their meta-analysis of these studies, they concluded that high-stakes testing has a direct negative impact on aspects of Els' educational experience.[83] For instance, schools respond to poor performance by ELs on high-stakes tests by limiting EL instruction to basic knowledge and language skills, depriving ELs of instructional practices focused on problem solving and higher-order learning activities that allow students to succeed on tests.[84]

Similarly, there is evidence that test-based accountability systems cause harm to districts and schools and reveal a gross misalignment between the goals of policymakers and the goals of most educators.[85] For instance, research on high schools in Texas with low average test scores found that when facing the state's test-based accountability system, the primary objective for these "low-performing" schools was reduced to improving test scores, to the detriment of addressing the root causes of the inequities.[86] Teachers were incentivized to focus their efforts on improving average test scores and individual student growth on the tests by narrowing curricula to tested materials and focusing instruction only on basic skills,[87] while the students with the low test scores are most in need of a more expansive and pluralistic approach to instruction and assessment.

MCAS as Useful Diagnostic Information

Research shows that MCAS exams have limited utility as a diagnostic tool. Several studies show that standardized test scores such as the MCAS, rather than simply measuring student learning, are influenced by exogenous factors such as previous failure,[88] as well as student demographics including race, EL status, and SWD status.[89] Therefore, student performance on the MCAS is not simply a measure of student knowledge, skills, and ability; it is also impacted by a confluence of external factors outside of a student's control.

From a conceptual perspective, there is a disconnect between the stated goals of test-based accountability systems such as the MCAS and what annual summative state tests are capable of providing for students, educators, and the community. Research has found that state standardized tests do not provide effective information for teachers to provide targeted or personalized support for individual students.[90] This was confirmed by MDESE in a report on twenty years of the MERA and the MCAS, which found that "MCAS has been less useful in informing instruction for individual students."[91] At best, state standardized test scores may help identify students who are on the cusp of passing the exams (referred to as "bubble kids") or reveal student shortcomings,[92] but they do not provide the detail necessary to inform how teachers should respond.[93] The timing of reporting and the format of the reporting reduces any potential diagnostic benefit from the tests, especially for individual students.[94] As a result, interventions stemming from state standardized test scores are typically class-wide or school-wide, most notably increasing instructional time in tested subjects.[95]

Substantial evidence refutes the assumptions underpinning the rationales for the test-based accountability system. The test-based accountability system in Massachusetts was created to ensure that the state was providing an adequate education for all students, particularly traditionally marginalized students. Not only does the system not benefit these students, but the evidence suggests it also likely harms the very students the reforms were intended to help.

Policy Recommendations

Together, the previous two sections have demonstrated how the state assessment and EL instructional policies have not improved outcomes for ELs and are creating restrictive and subtractive environments that may reduce the academic engagement for ELs. This section provides four policy recommendations that would lead to more inclusive and engaging environments for ELs.

MASSACHUSETTS SHOULD MOVE AWAY FROM A HIGH-STAKES TEST-BASED ACCOUNTABILITY SYSTEM

Despite mounting evidence that the test-based accountability system in Massachusetts does not benefit students and is not addressing persistent disparities, the Massachusetts Board of Elementary and Secondary Education (MBESE) is making no discernable effort to move away from this system. At the time of writing, there is a statewide ballot initiative for the November 2024 election that would eliminate the use of the MCAS as a graduation requirement but otherwise keep the MCAS testing structure in place.

As discussed earlier the federal Every Student Succeeds Act of 2015 provided states with leeway to develop and use additional measures of school quality beyond standardized tests in their annual accountability measures, but states, including Massachusetts, have been reluctant to add further measures to state accountability measures.[96] In 2020, the accountability system in Massachusetts was briefly put on pause due to the disruptions from COVID-19, as MCAS were canceled in spring 2020. However, MBESE made the decision to administer the MCAS in 2021, although results were not counted toward graduation requirements for the class of 2021. In 2022, the state administered the MCAS, and once again students were required to pass the tests in order to qualify for a high school diploma. In the summer of 2022, MBESE voted to raise the passing thresholds for the MCAS exams, making it harder for students to qualify for a high school diploma.[97]

Instead of keeping the MCAS and raising the passing threshold, the state should reconsider the use of a test-based accountability system, especially as a graduation requirement. When the state waived the MCAS as a graduation requirement in 2021, these temporary changes served as an indicator of the level to which the MCAS factors into the graduation outcomes of student groups that struggle on the MCAS. For instance, the 2021 graduation rate for all students increased by 1 percentage point compared with the previous year, while the graduation rate for ELs increased by 3 percentage points, with substantially larger increases in several school districts with large EL populations—Fall River (19% ELs) had a 24 point increase in four-year graduation rates, Holyoke (20% ELs) had a 15 point increase, and Revere (25% ELs) had a 14 point increase.[98] In the eighteen school districts with at least one hundred ELs in the four-year high school cohort, all but two had an increase in graduation rates and on average the graduation rate in these school districts increased by 6 percentage points. This increase in graduation rates merits further research, but these increases during the one year that students were exempt from passing the MCAS exams suggest that there were large numbers of ELs in these school districts who had fulfilled all graduation requirements other than the MCAS.

Many states, including the neighboring states Rhode Island and New Hampshire, have created policies that allow students to create graduation portfolios of their work to demonstrate fulfillment of all state standards. This approach is far more equitable for students who struggle on the MCAS and allows these students to engage with deeper learning opportunities instead of remedial courses to ensure they can pass these high-stakes standardized tests.

MASSACHUSETTS SHOULD SEEK OTHER MEASURES OF STUDENT LEARNING AND STUDENT GROWTH

There is now a large body of research highlighting the shortcomings of state standardized tests as a useful measure of student learning. MCAS scores are a complicated measure of student learning, impacted by exogenous factors including failing previous MCAS as well as student demographics such as race, English-language proficiency, and disability status. Therefore, the state should reconsider the MCAS as the basis for accountability decisions and as a tool to inform interventions and instruction. Instead, the state should pursue alternative ways of measuring student learning.

One possible alternative is performance assessments—the real-world application of concepts through authentic assessments that incorporate student choice. There are examples of such performance assessment systems. The Massachusetts Consortium for Innovative Educational Assessment is a consortium of eight school districts in Massachusetts that is building and testing assessment systems based on performance assessments. In New York, thirty-eight schools are part of the NY Performance Standards Consortium, using performance assessment in lieu of standardized tests as a graduation requirement.

MASSACHUSETTS SHOULD DELAY OR WAIVE THE INCLUSION OF ELS IN THE MCAS AND EXPAND ACCOMMODATIONS

Without clear benefits for Els and because of the guaranteed low performance among ELs (as a result of the construct-irrelevant variance of tests administered in English and normed for native English speakers) and an overly punitive accountability system that disproportionately impacts the handful of school districts that serve the vast majority of ELs, the state should consider waiving EL participation in the tests. If the state insists on including ELs in the statewide standardized testing system, the state should delay EL participation until these students can reach an adequate level of English-language proficiency to eliminate the construct-irrelevant variance of the tests.[99] State data show that ELs at the lowest levels of English proficiency face the most severe disparities on the MCAS. For instance, in 2019, across the entire state only sixty-four out of 9,063 ELs at ELD level one or two scored "meeting or exceeding expectations."[100]

If the state wants to include all ELs in the MCAS, the state must continue to expand accommodations. The state added grade 10 MCAS Math and STE tests in Spanish, which is a strong accommodation on the important high-stakes grade 10 test, but this benefits only half of Massachusetts grade 10 ELs who are Spanish speakers. The state should expand this accommodation to other grades and, importantly, to other language groups.

MASSACHUSETTS SHOULD EXPAND EDUCATIONAL APPROACHES THAT SUPPORT THE LEARNING ASSETS OF ELS

There is substantial research demonstrating that English immersion programs are subtractive and when used within a test-based accountability system make it more challenging for ELs to receive rigorous grade-level content.[101] Dual-language programs build on the learning assets of these emergent bilinguals providing ELs with English-language supports while also teaching grade-level and rigorous content in English and in a student's native language.[102]

The Massachusetts LOOK Act of 2017 was intended to create a major change to the ways in which ELs are instructed. The bill was heralded by advocates as a respite from the restrictive nature of the 2002 ballot initiative, which made SEI the default instructional approach. While the LOOK Act allows for more flexibility in program design, there have been few changes in school district approaches to instructing ELs. It is unclear why more school districts have not taken advantage of the increased flexibility in EL program design. Exploring the details of the LOOK Act, we can see that in exchange for more flexibility the state requires school districts to create detailed instructional plans and establish benchmarks for English-language acquisition. This added burden may be too much for school districts with limited central office capacity to develop these plans and benchmarks. Furthermore, while the state provided school districts more flexibility in programming, the state also added metrics related to ELs' "timely" acquisition of English proficiency into the district and school accountability. As a result, the incentives may remain to keep students in SEI programs at the expense of dual-language programs, which may provide more access to grade-level content but may lead to a slower rate of improvement in ELD. Furthermore, after twenty years of SEI, there is a limited pool of certified bilingual teachers to staff dual-language programs. The state has done little to remedy the shortage of bilingual teachers, delegating the responsibility of recruiting and retaining bilingual teachers to individual districts and schools.

It can be argued that the approach to serving ELs in Massachusetts even after the passage of the LOOK Act is still primarily focused on the acquisition of English-language proficiency as soon as possible with the goal of reclassifying students as former ELs so they can learn in monolingual classrooms. Instead, the state should focus on providing programs and resources so that ELs can have access to high-level engaging content. This would require reframing how the state views ELs, shifting away from a deficit view of these students as lacking English proficiency and instead thinking of them as emergent multilinguals in possession of strong educational assets.

The state can also promote practices that promote multilingualism among all students. One current practice that celebrates multilingualism is the state seal of biliteracy, which was created under the LOOK Act. This seal is an insignia on a student's high school diploma that recognizes "high school graduates who attain high functional and academic levels of proficiency in English and one or more other world languages by high school graduation."[103] To determine proficiency in English the state uses the grade 10 MCAS ELA tests. To determine proficiency in world languages, the state provides a list of approved assessments that assess proficiency in eighteen languages including Spanish, Portuguese, and Mandarin, as well as classical Greek and Latin.[104] Notably, there are no approved assessments for Haitian Creole or Crioulo, the third and fourth most common home language for ELs in Massachusetts.

Creating the state seal of biliteracy is a positive step to celebrate multilingualism overall, but it is also at odds with the predominant SEI instructional approach. SEI forces students to shed their native language in favor of acquiring English in order to advance academically. In Massachusetts, there are very few opportunities for ELs or former ELs to maintain proficiency in their home language outside of the limited number of dual-language and heritage language programs in the state. Without aligning instructional practices to the goals of multilingualism, the seal of biliteracy will likely only have limited benefit for native speakers of languages other than English. This trend is seen across the US, where seals of biliteracy are increasingly awarded to native English speakers as opposed to native speakers of other languages.[105]

The seal of biliteracy could be the culmination of policies and practices that promote multilingualism for all students in all grades, elevating multilingualism to being a goal that is equal to reaching proficiency in the subjects tested on the MCAS (i.e., ELA, Math, and Science). To do so, the state can offer subject tests in languages other than English and include assessments of world languages as regular part of student assessment to monitor the development and maintenance of multilingualism. Students in all schools, regardless of their home language, could participate in world language classes beginning in elementary school. To reach these goals, the state should more actively recruit multilingual teachers by providing incentives for multilingual teachers.

Conclusion

The current test-based accountability and instructional policies for ELs in Massachusetts are deserving of scrutiny beyond the rosy picture of aggregate test scores in Massachusetts. The current assessment and EL instruction policies, and even the shortcomings of the LOOK Act, create a restrictive environment that treats their multilingualism as a deficit rather than celebrating and cultivating the multilingualism inherent among ELs, their families, and their communities. While these policies have a deleterious impact on all ELs, the impact primarily falls on Latinx ELs, the largest group of ELs in the state.

Representing one-third of Latinx students, the experiences of ELs and Latinx students are inextricably linked. Even as Latinx students in Massachusetts will increasingly be native-born, families will continue to migrate from Latin American countries and Puerto Rico and there will still be large numbers and proportions of Latinx ELs.[106] The issues facing ELs are felt acutely in the handful of school districts that disproportionately educate large ELs and Latinx populations (e.g., Boston, Lawrence, Holyoke, and Springfield). In a test-based accountability system, these school districts will always struggle relative to districts with small EL populations and as a result, will continue to face the most scrutiny and oversight from the state, which will further restrict instructional approaches. Therefore, improving educational outcomes for Latinx students must consist of addressing the inequitable and restrictive policies for ELs.

Notes

1 Portions of this chapter in appear in Michael Berardino, "Assessing Without Proficiency: The Impact of Standardized Testing on English Learners in Massachusetts" (PhD diss., University of Massachusetts Boston, Public Policy and Public Affairs, 2022). This dissertation research explored the impact that repeatedly failing state standardized tests has on the engagement and academic outcomes of ELs.

2 At the time writing, there is a proposed piece of state legislation (the Thrive Act) and a 2024 statewide ballot question that are both seeking to eliminate the use of the MCAS as a graduation requirement.

3 MDESE, "Parents Guide to the Massachusetts Comprehensive Assessment System (MCAS)," Massachusetts Department of Elementary and Secondary Education, 2022, https://www.doe.mass.edu/odl/e-learning/mcasparentguide/content/index.html#/list/cj4jx65sv00013d65bikexx61?_k=00k2r3.

4 MDESE, "Parents Guide."

5 Thomas Dee and Brian Jacob, *Do High School Exit Exams Influence Educational Attainment or Labor Market Performance? NBER Working Paper No. 12199* (National Bureau of Educational Research, 2006); MDESE, "Parents Guide."

6 For this chapter, I use the term "English learner," which is the official term used by MDESE. However, many researchers and advocates prefer terms such as "emergent bilingual," "emergent multilingual," or "multilingual learner." These terms focus less on deficits and instead reflect the linguistic abilities of these students.

7 MDESE, "Transitional Guidance on Identification, Assessment, Placement, and Reclassification of English Language Learners," MDESE, 2013, http://www.doe.mass.edu/ell/TransitionalGuidance.pdf, 3.

8 As of 2022, the state offers the grade 10 Math and STE tests in Spanish as well as in English.

9 From 2003 to 2018, the state administered the "legacy" MCAS, but beginning in 2019, Massachusetts began administering the "Next Gen" MCAS for grade 10. The scores for the legacy MCAS and the Next Gen are not directly comparable but are shown on the same chart here to demonstrate the consistent gaps despite test design. Note that the state did not administer the MCAS in 2020 due to the COVID-19 pandemic.

10 MDESE, "2022 Next Generation MCAS Results by Subgroup by Grade and Subject," MDESE, 2022, https://profiles.doe.mass.edu/mcas/subgroups2.aspx?linkid=25&orgcode=00000000&fycode=2021&orgtypecode=0&.

11 National Center for Education Statistics, *NAEP 2019 Reading Assessment* (US Department of Education, Institute of Education Sciences, National Center for Education Statistics, NAEP, 2022).

12 MDESE, "Grade Nine Course Passing (2021–22)," MDESE, 2022, https://profiles.doe.mass.edu/profiles/student.aspx?orgcode=00000000&orgtypecode=0&leftNavId=16823&.

13 MDESE, "Advanced Course Completion (2021–22)," MDESE, 2022, https://profiles
.doe.mass.edu/profiles/student.aspx?orgcode=00000000&orgtypecode=0&leftnavId
=16825&.

14 MDESE, "Cohort 2022 Graduation Rates," MDESE, 2022, https://profiles.doe.mass
.edu/grad/grad_report.aspx?orgcode=00000000&orgtypecode=0&.

15 MDESE, "2019–20 Graduates Attending Institutions of Higher Education All Colleges
and Universities," MDESE, 2022, http://profiles.doe.mass.edu/nsc/gradsattending
college_dist.aspx?orgcode=00350000&fycode=2020&orgtypecode=5&.

16 MDESE, "Selected Populations (2022–23)," MDESE, 2022, https://profiles.doe.mass
.edu/profiles/student.aspx?orgcode=00000000&orgtypecode=0&leftNavId=305&.

17 MDESE, "Selected Populations (2022–23)."

18 MDESE, "Selected Populations (2022–23)."

19 Federal support for immigrant students only lasts two years. After two years in the
US, regardless of where a student was born, their country of birth is changed to the
US. Additionally, all students born in Puerto Rico have US as the country of birth.

20 MDESE, "DART for ELLs," MDESE, 2022, http://www.doe.mass.edu/apa/dart/.

21 MDESE, "DART for ELLs."

22 MDESE, "DART for ELLs."

23 MDESE, "DART for ELLs," MDESE, 2022.

24 MDESE, "Special Education Enrollment by Special Populations," Special Request,
2023–24.

25 E.g., Eric Haas, Loan Tran, and Min Huang, *English Learner Students' Readiness for
Academic Success: The Predictive Potential of English Language Proficiency Assess-
ment Scores in Arizona and Nevada*. *REL 2017–172* (US Department of Education,
Institute of Education Sciences, National Center for Education Evaluation and
Regional Assistance, Regional Educational Laboratory West, 2016); Rachel Slama,
et al., *Massachusetts English Language Learners' Profiles and Progress: A Report for
the Massachusetts Department of Elementary and Secondary Education* (American
Institutes for Research, 2015).

26 MDESE, "DART for ELLs."

27 Currently, 37% of all Latinos in Massachusetts (all ages) are foreign-born, and while
the Latinx population is growing in Massachusetts, demographic trends suggest that
the increase will be driven by domestic births rather than by international migration.
Phillip Granberry, Victor Luis Martins, and Michelle Borges, "The Growing Latino
Population of Massachusetts: A Demographic and Economic Portrait," 2023.

28 Fabián Torres-Ardila and Nyal Fuentes, "The State of Latino Education: 2010–2020,"
Gastón Institute Publications 292 (2022), https://scholarworks.umb.edu/gaston_pubs
/292.

29 There are no publicly available data on the ethnoracial profile of former ELs. Using
MDESE, "DART for ELLs," to estimate the number and percentage of Latinx former
ELs, I took the number of former ELs (500,274) and applied the same ethnoracial
proportion as for ELs (64% Latinx). Through this method, I estimate, 14% of Latinx
students are former ELs.

30 Rubén G. Rumbaut, "Pigments of Our Imagination: On the Racialization and Racial
Identities of 'Hispanics' and 'Latinos,'" In *How the US Racializes Latinos: White
Hegemony and Its Consequences*, ed. José A. Cobas, Jorge Duany, and Joe R. Feagin,
15–36 (Routledge, 2009).

31 Kathryn A. McDermott, "Incentives, Capacity, and Implementation: Evidence from Massachusetts Education Reform," *Journal of Public Administration Research and Theory* 16, no. 1 (2006): 45–65.

32 McDermott, "Incentives, Capacity, and Implementation."

33 National Center for Fair and Open Testing (FairTest), "Number of States Requiring Tests for High School Graduation Plunges to EIGHT—Lowest Count Since Mid-1990s," FairTest, January 5, 2023, https://fairtest.org/8093-2/#:~:text=The%20eight %20states%20that%20still,Texas%2C%20Virginia%2C%20and%20Wyoming.

34 Jack Schneider, *Beyond Test Scores: A Better Way to Measure School Quality* (Harvard University Press, 2017).

35 MDESE, "Massachusetts Comprehensive Assessment System: Participation Requirements for Students," MDESE, 2014, http://www.doe.mass.edu/mcas/participation/ ?section=all.

36 Kellie Rolstad, Kate Mahoney, and Gene V. Glass, "The Big Picture: A Meta-Analysis of Program Effectiveness Research on English Language Learners," *Educational Policy* 19, no. 4 (2005): 572–94; Karen D. Thompson, "English Learners' Time to Reclassification: An Analysis," *Educational Policy* 31, no. 3 (2017): 330–63; Ilana M. Umansky and Sean F. Reardon, "Reclassification Patterns Among Latino English Learner Students in Bilingual, Dual Immersion, and English Immersion Classrooms," *American Educational Research Journal* 51, no. 5 (2014): 879–912.

37 Jamal Abedi, "The No Child Left Behind Act and English Language Learners: Assessment and Accountability Issues," *Educational Researcher* 33, no. 1 (2004): 4–14; Sandra Acosta, et al., "The Accountability Culture: A Systematic Review of High-Stakes Testing and English Learners in the United States During No Child Left Behind," *Educational Psychology Review* 32, no. 2 (2020): 327–52; Maria Pennock-Roman and Charlene Rivera, "Mean Effects of Test Accommodations for ELLs and Non-ELLs: A Meta-Analysis of Experimental Studies," *Educational Measurement: Issues and Practice* 30, no. 3 (2011): 10–28.

38 Pennock-Roman and Rivera, "Mean Effects of Test Accommodations."

39 MDESE, "Accessibility and Accommodations Manual for the 2021–2022 MCAS Tests/ Retests," MDESE, 2022, https://www.doe.mass.edu/mcas/accessibility/manual.docx.

40 Michael J. Kieffer, et al., "Accommodations for English Language Learners Taking Large-Scale Assessments: A Meta-Analysis on Effectiveness and Validity," *Review of Educational Research* 79, no. 3 (2009): 1168–201; Pennock-Roman and Rivera, "Mean Effects of Test Accommodations."

41 MDESE, "DART for ELLs."

42 Barbara D. Acosta, Charlene Rivera, and Lynn Shafer Willner, *Best Practices in State Assessment Policies for Accommodating English Language Learners: A Delphi Study* (George Washington University Center for Equity and Excellence in Education, 2008).

43 John Portz, "Beyond Test Scores: 'School Quality or Student Success' in State ESSA Plans," *Teachers College Record* 123, no. 6 (2021): 1–36.

44 Kenji Hakuta, Yuko Goto Butler, and Daria Witt, *How Long Does It Take English Learners to Attain Proficiency?* (University of California Linguistic Minority Research Institute, 2000).

45 Rolstad, Mahoney, and Glass, "The Big Picture."

46 Rolstad, Mahoney, and Glass, "The Big Picture."

47 Keith Baker, "Structured English Immersion Breakthrough in Teaching Limited English Proficient Students," *Phi Delta Kappan* 80, no. 3 (1998): 199–204.

48 There was a provision in this law that families have the ability to opt out of SEI programs and place their children in general education, transitional bilingual education, or a dual-language program if there are sufficient numbers of students and the school offers the program type. MDESE 2013.

49 MDESE, "LOOK Act," MDESE, 2019, https://www.doe.mass.edu/ele/look-act.html.

50 MDESE, "DART for ELLs."

51 Rolstad, Mahoney, and Glass, "The Big Picture."

52 Acosta et al., "The Accountability Culture."

53 Rebecca Callahan, Lindsey Wilkinson, and Chandra Muller, "Academic Achievement and Course Taking Among Language Minority Youth in US Schools: Effects of ESL Placement," *Educational Evaluation and Policy Analysis* 32, no. 1 (2010): 84–117; Peggy Estrada, "English Learner Curricular Streams in Four Middle Schools: Triage in the Trenches," *Urban Review* 46 (2014): 535–73; Ilana M. Umansky, "Leveled and Exclusionary Tracking: English Learners' Access to Academic Content in Middle School," *American Educational Research Journal* 53, no. 6 (2016): 1792–833.

54 Jennifer A. Fredricks, Phyllis C. Blumenfeld, and Alison H. Paris, "School Engagement: Potential of the Concept, State of the Evidence," *Review of Educational Research* 74, no. 1 (2004): 59–109; Helen M. Marks, "Student Engagement in Instructional Activity: Patterns in the Elementary, Middle, and High School Years," *American Educational Research Journal* 37, no. 1 (2000): 153–84.

55 Marks, "Student Engagement in Instructional Activity," 155.

56 Aimee V. Garza and Lindy Crawford, "Hegemonic Multiculturalism: English Immersion, Ideology, and Subtractive Schooling," *Bilingual Research Journal* 29, no. 3 (2005): 599–619; Angela Valenzuela, *Subtractive Schooling: U.S.-Mexican Youth and the Politics of Caring* (State University of New York Press, 1999).

57 Valenzuela, *Subtractive Schooling*.

58 Angela Valenzuela, "Subtractive Schooling and Betrayal," *Teacher Education and Practice* 21, no. 4 (2008): 473–75.

59 James Gee, "Socio-Cultural Approaches to Literacy (Literacies)," *Annual Review of Applied Linguistics* 12 (1991): 31–48; James Gee, "Discourses and Literacies," *Social Linguistics and Literacies: Ideology in Discourses* 2 (1996): 122–48; Colin Lankshear and Michele Knobel, "Do We Have Your Attention? New Literacies, Digital Technologies, and the Education of Adolescents," in *Adolescents and Literacies in a Digital World*, ed. Donna Alvermann, 19–39 (Peter Lang, 2022).

60 Gee, "Socio-Cultural Approaches."

61 For this section, I use the short-hand "immigrant," but this also applies for students born in or whose parents/grandparents are from Puerto Rico. Ann S. Masten and Jelena Obradović, "Competence and Resilience in Development," *Annals of the New York Academy of Sciences* 1094, no. 1 (2006): 13–27.

62 Grace Kao and Marta Tienda, "Optimism and Achievement: The Educational Performance of Immigrant Youth," *Social Science Quarterly* 76, no. 1 (1995): 1–20; Rubén G. Rumbaut, "The Crucible Within: Ethnic Identity, Self-esteem, and Segmented Assimilation Among Children of Immigrants," *International Migration Review* 28 no. 4 (1994): 748–94.

63 Krista M. Perreira, Kathleen Mullan Harris, and Dohoon Lee, "Making It in America: High School Completion by Immigrant and Native Youth," *Demography* 43 (2006): 511–36.

64 Nancy E. Hill, Cynthia Ramírez, and Larry E. Dumka, "Early Adolescents' Career Aspirations: A Qualitative Study of Perceived Barriers and Family Support Among Low-Income, Ethnically Diverse Adolescents," *Journal of Family Issues* 24, no. 7 (2003): 934–59.

65 Kao and Tienda, "Optimism and Achievement."

66 Perreira, Harris, and Lee, "Making It in America."

67 Grace Kao, "Parental Influences on the Educational Outcomes of Immigrant Youth," *International Migration Review* 38, no. 2 (2004): 427–49; Kao and Tienda, "Optimism and Achievement."

68 Rumbaut, "Pigments of Our Imagination."

69 Min Zhou, "Segmented Assimilation: Issues, Controversies, and Recent Research on the New Second Generation," *International Migration Review* 31, no. 4 (1997): 975–1008.

70 Alejandro Portes and Rubén G. Rumbaut, *Legacies: The Story of the Immigrant Second Generation* (University of California Press, 2001).

71 Melissa Roderick, and Mimi Engel, "The Grasshopper and the Ant: Motivational Responses of Low-Achieving Students to High-Stakes Testing," *Educational Evaluation and Policy Analysis* 23, no. 3 (2001): 197–227.

72 Steven L. Wise and Christine E. DeMars, "Low Examinee Effort in Low-Stakes Assessment: Problems and Potential Solutions," *Educational Assessment* 10, no. 1 (2005): 1–17.

73 MDESE, "Testing Matters," MDESE, 2022, https://www.doe.mass.edu/mcas/Testing Matters.html.

74 MDESE. "Parents Guide."

75 MDESE, "Testing Matters"; Roderick and Engel, "The Grasshopper and the Ant"; Brian M. Stecher, "Consequences of Large-Scale, High Stakes Testing on School and Classroom Practice," in *Making Sense of Test-Based Accountability in Education*, ed. Laura S. Hamilton, Brian M. Stecher, and Stephen P. Klein, 79–100 (Rand, 2002); Wise and Christine E. DeMars, "Low Examinee Effort."

76 Roderick and Engel, "The Grasshopper and the Ant"; Claude M. Steele, "A Threat in the Air: How Stereotypes Shape Intellectual Identity and Performance," *American Psychologist* 52, no. 6 (1997): 613–29.

77 Elizabeth Dutro and Makenzie Selland, "'I Like to Read, But I Know I'm Not Good at It': Children's Perspectives on High-Stakes Testing in a High-Poverty School," *Curriculum Inquiry* 42, no. 3 (2012): 340–67; Robert L. Linn, "Performance Assessment: Policy Promises and Technical Measurement Standards," *Educational Researcher* 23, no. 9 (1994): 4–14; George F. Madaus and Marguerite Clarke, "The Adverse Impact of High Stakes Testing on Minority Students: Evidence from 100 Years of Test Data," in *Raising Standards or Raising Barriers? Inequality and High Stakes Testing in Public Education*, ed. Gary Orfield and Mindy Kornhaber (Century Foundation, 2001); William. A. Mehrens, "Consequences of Assessment: What Is the Evidence?" *Education Policy Analysis Archives* 6, no. 13 (1998): 1–30; Cheri Foster Triplett and Mary Alice Barksdale, "Third Through Sixth Graders' Perceptions of High-Stakes Testing," *Journal of Literacy Research* 37, no. 2 (2005): 237–60.

78 Audrey L. Amrein and David C. Berliner, "The Effects of High-Stakes Testing on Student Motivation and Learning," *Educational Leadership* 60, no. 5 (2003): 32–38; Jennifer Jellison Holme, et al., "Assessing the Effects of High School Exit Examinations," *Review of Educational Research* 80, no. 4 (2010): 476–526; Laura-Lee Kearns, "High-Stakes Standardized Testing and Marginalized Youth: An Examination of the Impact on Those Who Fail," *Canadian Journal of Education/Revue Canadienne de L'éducation* 34, no. 2 (2011): 112–30; Douglas S. Massey and Mary J. Fischer, "Stereotype Threat and Academic Performance: New Findings from a Racially Diverse Sample of College Freshmen," *Du Bois Review: Social Science Research on Race* 2, no. 1 (2005): 45–67.

79 The differences in MCAS scoring are even more pronounced on the new version of the grade 10 MCAS, the Next Gen MCAS. In 2021, the statewide percentage of students who scored at the meeting or exceeding expectations level on the ELA test was 68% for non-ELs and only 4% for ELs. On the math test the corresponding figures were 55% for non-ELs and, again, only 4% for ELs.

80 Thomas Dee and Brian Jacob. "The Impact of No Child Left Behind on Student Achievement," *Journal of Policy Analysis and Management* 30, no. 3 (2011): 418–46; Michael W. Firmin, et al., "Learned Helplessness: The Effect of Failure on Test-Taking," *Education* 124, no. 4 (2004): 688; John P. Papay, Richard J. Murnane, and John B. Willett, "The High-Stakes Effects of 'Low-Stakes' Testing," presented at Society for Research on Educational Effectiveness Conference, March, 2011.

81 Berardino, "Assessing Without Proficiency."

82 Berardino, "Assessing Without Proficiency."

83 Acosta et al., "The Accountability Culture."

84 Acosta et al., "The Accountability Culture."

85 Daniel Koretz, "Moving Beyond the Failure of Test-Based Accountability," *American Educator* 41, no. 4 (2018): 22–26.; George Madaus and Michael Russell, "Paradoxes of High-Stakes Testing," *Journal of Education* 190, nos. 1–2 (2010): 21–30.

86 Jennifer J. Holme, "Exit Strategies: How Low-Performing High Schools Respond to High School Exit Examination Requirements," *Teachers College Record* 115, no. 1 (2013): 1–23.

87 E.g., Wayne Au, "High-Stakes Testing and Curricular Control: A Qualitative Meta-synthesis," *Educational Researcher* 36, no. 5 (2007): 258–67; James H. Nehring, Megin Charner-Laird, and Stacy A. Szczesiul, "Redefining Excellence: Teaching in Transition, From Test Performance to 21st Century Skills," *NASSP Bulletin* 103, no. 1 (2019): 5–31.

88 Berardino, "Assessing Without Proficiency."

89 Joshua Angrist, et al., *Race and the Mismeasure of School Quality* (National Bureau of Economic Research, 2022).

90 Marsha Riddle Buly and Sheila W. Valencia, "Below the Bar: Profiles of Students Who Fail State Reading Assessments," *Educational Evaluation and Policy Analysis* 24, no. 3 (2002): 219–39.

91 MDESE, "Building on 20 Years of Massachusetts Education Reform," MDESE, 2014, https://www.doe.mass.edu/commissioner/BuildingOnReform.docx.

92 Jennifer Booher-Jennings, "Below the Bubble: 'Educational Triage' and the Texas Accountability System," *American Educational Research Journal* 42, no. 2 (2005): 231–68.

93   Julie A. Marsh, John F. Pane, and Laura S. Hamilton, *Making Sense of Data-Driven Decision Making in Education: Evidence from Recent RAND Research. Occasional Paper* (Rand, 2006); Jonathan Supovitz, "Can High Stakes Testing Leverage Educational Improvement? Prospects from the Last Decade of Testing and Accountability Reform," *Journal of Educational Change* 10 (2009): 211–27.

94   Dean P. Goodman and Ronald K. Hambleton, "Student Test Score Reports and Interpretive Guides: Review of Current Practices and Suggestions for Future Research," *Applied Measurement in Education* 17, no. 2 (2004): 145–220.

95   Cecilia Elena Rouse, et al., "Feeling the Florida Heat? How Low-Performing Schools Respond to Voucher and Accountability Pressure," *American Economic Journal: Economic Policy* 5, no. 2 (2013): 251–81.

96   John Portz, "Beyond Test Scores: 'School Quality or Student Success' in State ESSA Plans," *Teachers College Record* 123, no. 6 (2021): 1–36.

97   James Vaznis, "Backlash Emerges Over State's Proposal to Soften School Accountability," *Boston Globe*, March 15, 2022.

98   Author's calculations based on MDESE, "Cohort 2022 Graduation Rates."

99   Pennock-Roman and Rivera, "Mean Effects of Test Accommodations."

100 Author's calculations based on MDESE, "DART for ELLs."

101 Acosta et al., "The Accountability Culture"; Garza and Crawford, "Hegemonic Multiculturalism."

102 Rolstad, Mahoney, and Glass, "The Big Picture."

103 MDESE, "Massachusetts State Seal of Biliteracy: Frequently Asked Questions," MDESE, 2021, https://www.doe.mass.edu/scholarships/biliteracy/faq.docx, 2.

104 The state has approved assessments in the following languages: American Sign Language, Arabic (bilingual and monolingual), Classical Greek, French, German, Hebrew, Hindi, Italian, Japanese, Korean, Latin, Mandarin, Polish, Portuguese, Portuguese (Brazilian), Russian, Spanish (bilingual and monolingual), and Tamil (MDESE 2021). MDESE, "Massachusetts State Seal of Biliteracy."

105 Angela Sherman, et al., "Improving Language Equity for the Seals of Biliteracy," *Language Magazine*, May 5, 2022.

106 Granberry, Martins, and Borges, "The Growing Latino Population of Massachusetts."

Chapter Seven

A Chance to Compete in Today's America?

Considerations of Academic Performance, Exclusionary Discipline, and Belonging of Latinx Students in Worcester Public Schools

THOMAS E. CONROY, ALEX BRIESACHER, MARY JO MARION, AND TIMOTHY MURPHY

On June 10, 1972, a Worcester *Evening Gazette* article reported that "about a dozen Latino American and Puerto Rican parents" told the Worcester Public School leadership that they were concerned about "the serious failure of Spanish-speaking students" in the public schools.[1] This occurred at a meeting between the parents and superintendent of schools John J. Connor Jr., and the discussion centered on a series of requests from the parents. Theirs was a lengthy list, and the individual items are noteworthy because they talked about a couple of themes. For one, many requests spoke to belonging: the parents called for "more Latin, Puerto Rican, and Black teachers," "Spanish-speaking counselors, coordinators, and counseling aides," strong connections between the [Spanish] community and the schools (including a Spanish parents' council), a bilingual teaching program, and a "sympathetic and knowledgeable bilingual person" in central administration.[2]

Other requests were specifically about learning, and some were likely born from specific experiences. For example, parents asked for "more flexibility in allowing students to transfer to [a] school where they feel they could learn the most."[3] They were also concerned that Spanish-speaking students were dropping out of school as early as the eighth grade. And more generally, they wanted it uniformly explained to school staff that transferring students "should not be dropped below their previous Grade because of 'language problems alone.'"[4] Their request continued, "and in any case (putting a student in a lower Grade) should be considered a serious decision, possibly disastrous to the child's future, not to be taken without special evaluation and recourse to special tutoring." At stake for the Latino parents and community was nothing less than a desire for equal access to future opportunities. As a spokesman for the parents succinctly put it, "we're trying to get at the problem at an early stage and with the community moving in so rapidly there will be hope for the kids so they will be able to compete in this American society."[5]

While the Latino parents were reportedly satisfied with the meeting outcome at the time, a half-century later, today's parents of Latino students continue to make similar appeals to the Worcester Public Schools (WPS) and the City of Worcester administrations. Their requests are at least as urgent today in large part because the concerns of the 1970s Latino parents went largely unaddressed, and they are even more imperative today because the Latino population of Worcester, the second largest city in New England, has burgeoned in that half-century.

In an effort to dismantle structural racism, school systems across the country have begun to assess the numerous ethnoracial disparities impacting their students. Ongoing assessments reveal numerous inequities including but not limited to geographical segregation impacting students' access to quality education,[6] disciplinary practices disproportionally affecting non-White/nonimmigrant students,[7] and the impacts of low numbers of teachers and administrators reflective of the ethnoracial background of students in their schools.[8] At the same time, these analyses increasingly rely on a body of growing work based on cultural wealth models to explore where communities can excel or fall short within systems based on the value of their cultural currencies within institutions, especially aspirational capital and resistant capital.[9]

Examining disparities of race, inclusion, representation, and belonging in WPS in ways that help define the parameters of Latino cultural currency, this chapter explores recently reported school and district data, academic performance metrics, records of exclusionary discipline, and qualitative data from individual interviews and focus groups that are pertinent to Worcester's Latino students through the COVID-19 pandemic years to consider how much remains to be done since 1972. Framed by the idea of considerations, we explore four main areas that overlap and interlock in significant ways: history, social geography and segregation, school metrics and entropy, and belonging. While we make some of the overlap clear, we invite readers to join us in considering the whole as opposed to one aspect more than another, as well as how the example of Worcester may shed new light on related Latino experiences nationwide.

Latinos in Worcester

The Latino population of Worcester has grown significantly over the last half-century. The *1960 US Census of Population and Housing* for Worcester had not yet begun to report Hispanic or Latino residents in their own category for the city. Instead, official census reports categorized Worcester's 186,587 people into three groups: "White" made up 97.7%, "Negro" made up 1.1%, and "Other Races" made up 0.16% (294 residents) of the city population.[10] But only a decade later, this had changed. The 1970 census noted that the 176,617 residents in Worcester, which was itself an overall decline of nearly 10,000 people since 1960, now included 82 Mexicans, 116 Cubans, 516 people from "other America" (transplants from other states and territories), and 772 "persons of Puerto Rican birth or parentage."[11] That report also listed 1,674 "persons of Spanish language" and 1,304 "persons of Spanish mother tongue." Further, 1970 census takers estimated that 15,214 people were classified as "all other [nationalities] and not reported," a number that likely included some undercounted Latino residents.[12]

Beyond the US Census, which has been criticized for undercounting the Latino population during those years, by the early 1970s the growing Latino population was evident in other ways. The State Census Bilingual Information Center, working out of the Massachusetts Secretary of State's Office, claimed in 1972 that there were 155,800 Spanish-speaking residents in the state and "about 5,000" in Worcester.[13] This number was determined by counts in social centers, service agencies, school listings, churches, and health centers. Schools saw a rise in Latino children, as evidenced by enrollment records and the appeals of parents to the superintendent in 1972. The local press occasionally included items about "Spanish-speaking" people and subjects including stories on Spanish immigrant arrivals. As early as 1964, the *Sunday Telegram* ran an article about "35 or 40 families" headed by "professional men" of means who fled Castro's Cuba and landed in Worcester.[14] By 1968, the *Evening Gazette* claimed "there are nearly 150 Spanish-speaking families living in Worcester today" where "there were fewer than ten families only eight years ago."[15] The article continued, "Most came from Puerto Rico and Cuba" and, when asked about their children going to work or school, nearly 80% claimed that "they felt education was more valuable." Yet, it must be remembered that while noticeable, the "growing Spanish-speaking community in the city" was still comparatively small in the overall population,[16] and Worcester very much remained a predominantly White city. One study a decade and a half later put the entire minority population of the city at 7.7% by 1987.[17] By contrast, in 1980, the minority population of Boston was 32%, while even the US Census put Springfield at 24%.[18]

The tract data from the 1970 US Census also indicate where these newer immigrants settled. The largest proportion of Latinos in the city appears to have been individuals of Puerto Rican descent, and although they did not always live in the same census tracts as the city's Cuban and Mexican populations, they were often nearby. The 1970 census data and tract map indicate that four census tracts out of forty-one housed more than half of the Latino population in 1970: three were in the Main South neighborhood and another a short distance away on Union Hill.[19] All could be considered to be part of or akin to the "East Side," which will become important later in the chapter.

However, as this relatively small but noticeable Latino population was increasing, the overall population of Worcester dwindled markedly. From 1950 to 1980, like many mid-sized Northeast Rust Belt cities, Worcester saw its population plummet: from 203,486 to 161,799, mainly from outmigration due to deindustrialization and White flight.[20] From 1950 to 1980, while Worcester was losing 20.5% of its total population, every surrounding town saw significant increases: Grafton (35.7%), Millbury (41.5%), Leicester (56.7%), Auburn (67.9%), Shrewsbury (114%), Holden (123.2%), West Boylston (141.4%), and Paxton (252.9%). And, as in other Rust Belt metropolitan areas, this increase in surrounding town populations was overwhelmingly White and predominantly middle class—even today, and despite continued migration to them, the towns remain predominantly White.[21]

After 1980, Worcester's overall population reversed course, and as overall numbers began to climb, so too did the number of Latino residents. By 2020, the White population of Worcester was just over half (55.2%) of the city's population, and the city's Latinos composed just under a quarter (24.5%).[22] However, even that statistic misses the bigger picture because it fails to consider the tremendous generational shift currently underway in Worcester. In fact, the city's over-fifty-year-old population is vastly White, while the younger population is more evenly distributed among different racial backgrounds. As time moves forward, the city's racial imbalance is evening out, in part because of natural forces—the older, predominantly White population will diminish while the younger, more diverse population increases—and in part because White Flight continues and remains tied to the schools. As Worcester Mayor Joseph O'Brien noted in 2011, the quest for better schools was the "biggest driver" of White flight to the suburbs,[23] a continuing national trend.[24]

This ethnoracial shift has had a considerable impact on the WPS district, the demography of which is more indicative of Worcester's future demography than almost any other measure in the city. Indeed, the sea change that is underway is clearly observable in WPS enrollment for the last twenty-five years. Figure 7.1 shows that Worcester's school system is experiencing a profound demographic and generational shift: a steady rise in the Latino student population, and an equally steady decline in the White student population.[25] The school district tipping point, the moment when the Latino population surpassed the White population in the schools, came in 2010 when Massachusetts Department of Elementary and Secondary Education (MDESE) data indicated that Latinos had become the largest ethnoracial subgroup in the school district.[26]

Figure 1: Worcester Public Schools by Race/Ethnicity, 1993-2021

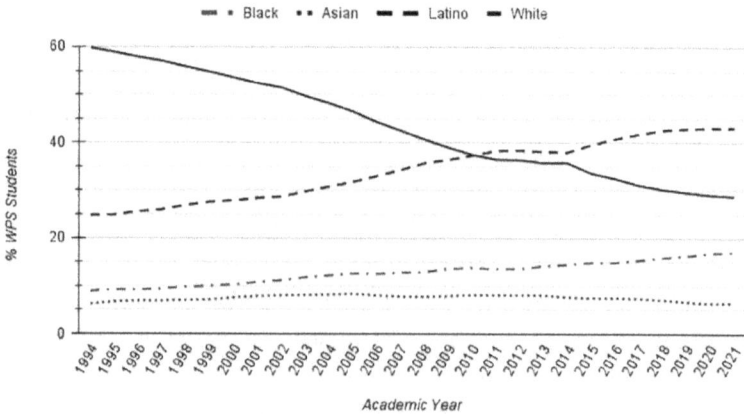

Figure 7.1. Worcester Public Schools by Race/Ethnicity, 1993–2021.

Despite these growing numbers, today's Latino families in Worcester continue to make the same appeals to the WPS administration that they did fifty years ago, because many of the same issues persist. As recently as November 19, 2021, six months short of the fiftieth anniversary of that 1972 meeting with the superintendent, the same newspaper ran a story of a Worcester School Committee presentation that bore this headline: "School District Report Shows Worcester's Latino Students, Disabled Students Lagging Behind Peers."[27] The article went on to say that by many academic measures, Latinos were behind other race-based subgroups, and sometimes by significant margins. As Worcester School Committee member Jack Foley acknowledged in the meeting, "We have major challenges in many areas."[28] Indeed, in addition to academic assessments, there were other indicators that suggested Latino students were having a more difficult time in the schools than other ethnoracial subgroups. Among Latino students, discipline numbers were disproportionately higher, attendance rates were lower, course-taking patterns differed from those of peers, retention rates were higher, graduation rates were lower, and academic metrics were subpar.

Worcester School Committee members and the WPS administration were quick to blame shortfalls of Latino students on the COVID-19 pandemic, which had moved education online for more than a year beginning in March 2020. But community members and many people in the school system knew that these were not new problems solely caused by the switch to remote learning. Although there had been modest improvements in some metrics over time, Latinos, the largest ethnoracial subgroup in the school district, still fell behind their peers in the desirable measures of attendance and academic performance, while taking the lead in the undesirable measure of disciplinary action for years before COVID-19 hit. Ironically, WPS's own attendance data show that school attendance actually increased through the pandemic years for all subgroups, including Latinos, which is something that did not happen in Boston, Springfield, or any of the other nine gateway cities or towns in Massachusetts.[29] Yet, despite such high and anomalous attendance, nearly all students fared worse during the pandemic on most metrics, with both Latino and Black students falling the furthest.

The WPS administration must have known about the performance of all subgroups because the data that are available publicly on the MDESE district profiles website is largely data reported annually by the school districts. People and groups in the city had long known there was a serious city problem in Latino education because it had led to the creation of the first Latino Education Committee in 2010 and its first report in 2011. As shared in the introduction to that report, "an increasing population of Latino students coupled with chronic educational underachievement in this group threatens the socioeconomic and civic fabric of Worcester."[30] But in the decade between then and 2021, the academic improvements were modest at best, and when looked at more closely, were limited to certain schools that were characterized as simply "doing better than others." Importantly, many of these "doing better" schools are clustered in a particular area of the city because of the way that WPS peoples its schools and because the city's social geography is so terribly unbalanced that it creates increasingly segregated schools that, for one reason or another, are dissimilar. Indeed, as Mayor O'Brien noted in 2010, the exclusion of Communities of Color in political, economic, social, and civic arenas was (and remains) a threat to the city and is reinforced in schools that are growing more segregated over time due to the city's social geography and the WPS quadrant system.[31]

Segregated Worcester: Social Geography and the Quadrant System

For most of Worcester's public school students, WPS utilizes a geographically based quadrant system to determine which students go to which school. Each of the quadrants serves a geographic area of the city, with its elementary schools feeding into a single quadrant middle school, which, in turn, passes students to a single quadrant high school. The quadrants are named for the comprehensive high schools in each of them: South Quadrant, North Quadrant, Burncoat Quadrant, and Doherty Quadrant. Although families can petition to go to schools outside their quadrants or opt for school choice outside the district, this is more the exception than the rule because it is not altogether easy for families to manage transportation or obtain permission from the WPS.[32] There are a handful of schools among the district's forty-six schools (in academic year [AY] 2021–22) that operate outside the quadrant structure. Most notable are two magnet schools, a new dual-language school, and the vocational school, Worcester Technical High School. The remaining K-12 schools in the district, which educates approximately 86% of Worcester's youth, are populated by the geographic imperatives of the quadrant system.

Since enrollment in quadrant-system schools is based on where students permanently reside, the social geography of the city affects the student composition of each school profoundly. Like many cities with these systems, the district's enrollment methods often lead to segregated schools. A 2020 report by the Economic Policy Institute (EPI) noted that nationally, segregation still exists and the Black population is largely "paying a price" in that Black students see continued or increased achievement gaps and widening segregation.[33] The EPI report noted that there were four major issues created by such segregation: "it depresses education outcomes for Black students . . . and lowers their standardized test scores"; it "widens performance gaps between White and Black students"; it "reflects and bolsters segregation by economic status, with Black students being more likely than White students to attend high-poverty schools"; and it "means that the promise of integration and equal opportunities for all Black students remains an ideal rather than a reality."[34] But in Worcester, because the city's social geography is so uneven, its schools are unbalanced, and it appears that Latino students pay the price, although Worcester's Black students, the third largest ethnoracial subgroup in WPS, have parallel experiences.[35]

The city's segregated social geography has been well established for decades. The "West Side" refers to a small portion of Worcester that is actually located west-northwest of the city. Less densely populated than other parts of the city, it is the Whitest and wealthiest section and has the highest levels of voter turnout and the highest proportion of college degrees. Zoned mainly for single-family homes with land lots greater than seven thousand and ten thousand square feet, it is home to many of the city's political, municipal, educational, and business leaders. The "East Side," a considerably larger area encompassing much of the city's east and south, is far more diverse, with many pockets of concentrated Latino, Black, and Asian families. Zoning in these areas ranges from industrial and commercial sections to mostly smaller land lots that have both single-family and multifamily houses. The East Side, which could be said to include Main South as it is outside the general boundary, is also where the city's lowest-turnout political precincts are located. This area includes those four census tracts that contained most of the Latino population in 1970 and much of the city's Black population, which has been a discernible part of Worcester since before the first census in 1790.

We can begin to assess the impact of this uneven social geography on Worcester's schools by first determining the level of *multigroup entropy* that exists in each school. In simple terms, multigroup entropy is a measure of balance that can be used to compare levels of diversity and segregation in neighborhoods, quadrants, and the school district. Accordingly,

Worcester's upper-level schools are, relatively speaking, much more diverse than its other schools. Among the middle and high schools in AY 2021–22, only two out of seven high schools—North High School and Claremont Academy—could be considered segregated due to student bodies that were more than 50% Latino, while the other ethnoracial subgroups in the schools comprised less than 25% each.[36] It is important to note that these segregated areas of the city can be traced directly to where people choose or must live based on a variety of factors. It is a de facto segregation based on a geographically determined quadrant system atop a city that is segregated. The schools, then, mirror their communities but are dissimilar from others in the city.

Even though there are important distinctions among them, Worcester's high schools, which sit atop the quadrants, are more diverse because they take students from larger areas. The elementary schools, however, serve smaller, but more homogeneous geographies. Consequently, there is considerably more segregation at the elementary school level. MDESE school profiles show that of the city's thirty-three grammar schools, eighteen had Latino student populations greater than 50% with fewer than 25% in any other category, and three had White student populations greater than 50% with fewer than 25% in any other subgroup.[37] In fact, the list of the most segregated quadrant-based public schools in Worcester is almost entirely composed of elementary schools.

TABLE 7.1. Elementary School Segregation in Worcester Public Schools, AY2022.

Segregation	% White	% Latino	Difference	Quadrant
Most White Segregated				
1. Flagg Street	75.5	11.2	64.3	Doherty
2. Midland Street	54.1	19.9	31.5	Doherty
3. West Tatnuck	50.0	18.5	34.2	Doherty
Most Latino Segregated				
1. Woodland Academy	7.3	72.9	65.6	South
2. Union Hill School	15.7	65.0	49.3	North
3. Chandler Elementary	13.9	61.9	48.0	South

Importantly, all the White-segregated schools are on the West Side, while the three Latino-segregated schools and fifteen others are on the East Side or outside the West Side boundary. The location of the schools is noteworthy as an illustration of how unbalanced the city's social geography is in terms of race, class, and ethnicity and how such segregation can impact school populations. Indeed, the White segregation levels are particularly interesting because White students make up only 27.9% of the WPS student population, whereas Latinos make up 44.7%.[38] In other words, it is more difficult for, say, Flagg Street to have a 75.5% White population than it is for Union Hill School to have a 61.9% Latino population given the proportional starting points of each subgroup (see table 7.1).[39] Or consider the moment in 2010 when Latino students became the largest subgroup in WPS. This change had already occurred at South High Community School in 2005 and North High School in 2007. The shift hit Burncoat High School, a much more northerly school, in 2013, and it has only recently occurred at Doherty High School in 2021, sixteen years after South High. It is important to note that Doherty is the only high school located on the West Side. Such an imbalance in schools is a direct result of Worcester's quadrant system.

Examining school entropy scores over time provides a window into diversity and segregation. In figure 7.2, each dot represents the entropy score of a school stacked vertically with others for any given year. The distance between dots in a column constitutes an entropy spectrum for the corresponding year. Over this thirty-year period, the school district has become more diverse, primarily as a result of an increasing Latino population within the city. Yet over time, the increasing spread of entropy scores in the late 2010s indicates certain schools are being left behind in the diversification of the school district. The chart, in short, indicates that while WPS as a whole is becoming more diverse, individual schools are becoming more segregated. Unless specifically addressed, patterns from around the country suggest this will continue from moderate segregation to more extreme segregation.

If WPS White-segregated and Latino-segregated schools performed similarly, there would be less of a problem, but they do not. As mentioned in the previous section, WPS reports that Latino students attend school less frequently, get into trouble more often, achieve lower scores on standardized tests, and advance and graduate at lower rates, especially when compared to their White counterparts. For decades now, the Latino student population and their families have been singled out as the source of their own

Figure 2: WPS School Entropy 1993-2022

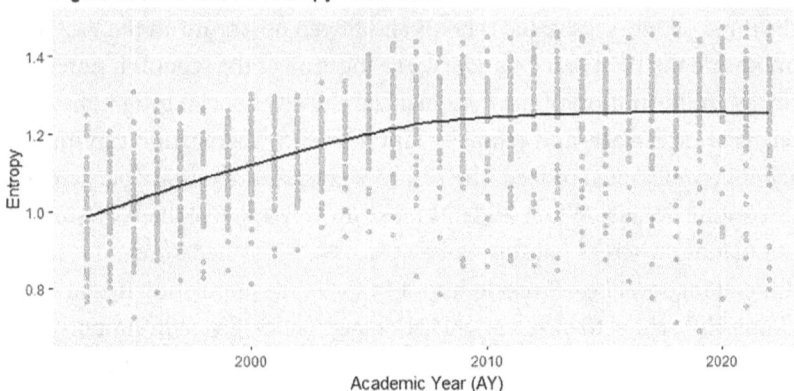

Figure 7.2. WPS Entropy over Time.

problems. Latino students are said to "lag" behind their peers, with language barriers being presented as nearly insurmountable obstacles to education. And sadly, officials associated with the school department have asserted in public forums that they have low expectations of Latino students' ability to succeed in school. Yet, as recently noted in a Mayoral Commission Report on Latino Education, and reflective of current approaches to school inequities that draw on critical race theory, "There is an undeniable equity gap in this segment of our population."[40] But more than an equity gap, Latinos in Worcester experience an opportunity gap, and it needs to be seen as such.

Systemic Inequities of Attendance and Disciplinary Practices

Perhaps the first statistic generated in a student's daily life is attendance. According to the AY2015 Attendance Policy, WPS views daily attendance "as a priority in student achievement and success."[41] The attendance policy further elaborates that "students' academic, social and emotional growth and development depends upon students' daily attendance, classroom participation and exposure to high quality teaching and learning." Moreover, the policy statement concludes that "daily attendance and punctuality habits acquired during schooling are essential skills in the adulthood life."[42] More recently, the Attendance Matters page on the WPS website in early 2022 began, "As a district, we help families build the habit of regular attendance as soon as children start school."[43] Attendance rates from MDESE from AY2018 to AY2021 show that there have been improvements in overall attendance across the school district's largest ethnoracial subgroups and that their rates are higher than many other urban school systems in Massachusetts. Interestingly, AY 2019 and AY 2020, which saw attendance rate improvements in all groups, were the pandemic years when school instruction in much of Massachusetts (including WPS) was done remotely. According to MDESE data, WPS was the only urban school system in the Commonwealth that saw such an upward trend.[44] Nevertheless, before, during, and as the pandemic waned, Latino students had the lowest attendance rates for years, which conversely means they also have the highest absenteeism rate.

School systems submit at least four different metrics of absenteeism to MDESE annually: average number of absences, chronically absent (or the percentage of students who were absent 10% or more of their total number of school days), absent ten or more days, and unexcused more than nine days. School systems are deeply concerned about this because chronic absenteeism is said to negatively affect everyone. According to the WPS website, "If significant numbers of students in a classroom or school are chronically absent, learning for all students is impacted. The pace of instruction slows when teachers spend time reviewing material for those who missed the lessons."[45] In WPS, Latinos lead all the measures of absenteeism including chronically absent, and this has led to friction between the schools and the Latino community.[46] The WPS policy essentially blames Latino students for slowing the "pace of instruction" more than any other ethnoracial subgroup because Latino students have the highest counts and rates of chronic absenteeism.[47] The real story is hidden in the statistics.

What the absenteeism numbers do not tell us is the bigger question: *Why* are Latino students not in school? Local studies have shown numerous underlying causes of chronic absenteeism. Interviews with Latino students, including many from WPS, reveal that in most cases, family, legal, and psychological situations affect student attendance, as well as discipline and academic performance. For example, one Worcester student noted emigrating students often come to Worcester suffering from trauma related to their travels, while others point to difficulties in single-parent households or abusive homes.[48] Of course, such situations are not exclusive to Latino students. Still, urban schools are not always able to help students deal with critical needs relating to a family's socioeconomic status, food or housing security, level of English proficiency, familiarity with local education systems, and so on. As such, WPS singling out Latinos as "the biggest problem" only makes matters worse.

Interviews with Latino students from Worcester and four other Massachusetts urban school systems yielded various examples of common family situations that work against regular attendance, such as the need to work to contribute to household income and the need to care for younger siblings.[49] Students also noted that situations in specific schools themselves often affected their attendance, including a lack of English proficiency, being a victim of bullying, a fear of physical harm at the hands of other students, and a dread of being targeted by teachers and administrators. Relying exclusively on the hard quantitative data in this area and singling out Latino students and their families as the main "offenders" of attendance and rule-breaking misses these situational nuances that feed the problem and thus prevents counteracting it effectively.

When the entropy scores for chronic absenteeism are explored, an even more complex but perhaps obvious situation emerges. The data show Latino students in Latino-segregated schools are more likely to be chronically absent than they are in White-segregated schools. Importantly, if the high chronic absenteeism among the Latino population were based on Latino individuals and/or Latino families, there would be no difference between Latino-segregated and White-segregated schools. But the statistically significant difference points to a more systemic problem: Latino students are treated differently in Latino-segregated schools than in White-segregated schools.

Prior research on WPS has shown that the most effective and stable predictor of chronic absenteeism is a history of disciplinary action.[50] The argument is relatively straightforward: when WPS removes students from school—especially under emergency removals, a discipline category that WPS misused for years—they miss school and are counted as absent. They also miss class time and learning time, presumably impacting all other students' educations. In other words, the more students of a particular ethnoracial subgroup are disciplined, the higher the absenteeism rate for that subgroup and thus the greater the "blame" they receive from the district. Furthermore, when WPS consistently removes students from school, those students often do not want to return, and increasingly miss lessons, drop out, and fail to graduate or even earn a high school equivalency. For the better part of the last decade, discipline in WPS, especially as it is applied to Latino students, has been just as lopsided as attendance and academic measures have been, and to the detriment of the Latino population.

WPS has long been criticized for unfair and discriminatory disciplinary practices, particularly suspensions and emergency removals. A 2013 study from the UCLA Civil Rights Project ranked WPS among the highest-suspending school systems in the US, especially when it came to Latino students and students in elementary schools.[51] That year, researchers working out of the Latino Education Institute at Worcester State University (WSU) released a report showing that the rate of Latino suspension was far greater than their proportional representation in the district's student body.[52] Meanwhile, a 2014 mixed-methods study from WSU's CityLab in the Department of Urban Studies found that Latino students (and parents) felt a high degree of exclusion and prejudice in WPS. Student interviewees for this study spoke of labeling, differential treatment, unreasonable disciplinary actions, and a lack of respect that was especially egregious after they had paid respect to someone.[53] It all came to a head in the 2019 superintendent's contract negotiations during which the Worcester School Committee extracted fourteen pledges from the superintendent that mainly came from long-standing requests of community members. Unfortunately, neither the City Council nor the School Committee nor the mayor, who sits on both bodies, held the superintendent to account for them. Yet throughout this process, the community (especially the Latino community) pushed for better treatment of Latino students. One Worcester parent put a fine point on it in a focus group early on: "That's the truth. . . . Hispanic kids in public schools, they treat them bad."[54]

Since then, researchers have closely followed and charted the continuing disciplinary problems in the district. WPS has recently made attempts to lower suspensions, and they have been successful; relatively speaking, the number of suspensions has been lower since the mid-2010s. In fact, in a 2019 statement issued in the midst of a firestorm about serious and actionable inequities in the schools, Superintendent Maureen Binienda announced that suspensions were way down: "In-house suspensions are down 40.8 percent, out-of-school suspensions 31.4 percent and long-term suspensions are down 18.8 percent from one year ago. I continue to focus on this work as a priority."[55] Yet, regardless of the number of suspended students, the tremendous disparity between White and Latino student discipline that existed in 2013 remained through the 2010s and into the pandemic. From AY2013 to AY2020, Latino students composed between 38% and 44% of the WPS enrollment but accounted for between 55% and 59% of the disciplined students. Over the same time, White students, who composed between 28% and 35% of the district enrollment, accounted for between 19% and 23% of the disciplined students.[56] No matter the year, the Latino population in WPS was *always* disciplined at a notably higher rate, while White students were *always* disciplined at a notably lower rate than their relative presences in the district. Nor did the number of students seem to matter. In AY2013, there were 2,783 students disciplined, and in AY2020 there were only 1,172 disciplined, in part because the schools closed in March, yet the ratio remained constant.[57] Even in AY2021 when WPS schools were remote all year and only thirty-four students were disciplined, 59% were Latino and 9% were White.[58]

What can explain such a continued disparity, especially as WPS says it is actively reducing suspension numbers? Again, employing the entropy scores paints a deeper, more nuanced story. For years, WPS explained that

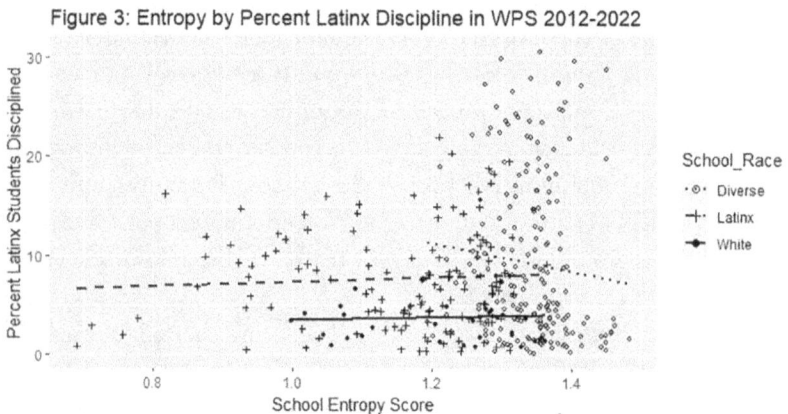

Figure 7.3. Entropy by Percentage of Latinx Discipline in WPS 2012–2023.

the different discipline rates were not systemic. Rather, it was the result of some principals being more zealous about discipline than others. However, looking at entropy and how the students are disciplined at the school level yields interesting results. In figure 7.3, the rate at which Latino students are disciplined by school and the entropy scores of those schools are plotted on a chart over a ten-year period (from AY2012 to AY2021). The symbols distinguish which schools are Latino segregated, White segregated, and diverse. Trendlines indicate the differences among the groups of schools, and they are statistically significant. The chart shows that Latino students in WPS are disciplined at different rates at Latino-segregated, White-segregated, and diverse schools. In other words, as with absenteeism, the issue has less to do with Latino students individually (or their families) and is not explained adequately by a "few strict principals" being scattered around the city. Rather, there are systemic issues at play here because if there were not systemic issues, Latino students would fare the same in all schools and the trendlines would overlap. A particularly important aspect of this, as illustrated on this graph, is that Latino students are more likely to be suspended at White-segregated schools than they are at Latino-segregated schools.

Perhaps more serious still are the personal accounts of students in WPS. By 2016, a mixed-methods study of five urban Massachusetts school systems found continued disparities in Worcester Latino student suspension and heard from students about their experience.[59] Some students related positive experiences in school even when they had been disciplined. They recognized that they had been out of line, and some were thankful that they had been called out on their youthful behavior. But many, even some who had positive experiences, had critical comments about the WPS that are supported by the quantitative data. In a focus group that was discussing racism in the WPS, one Latino student noted, "We need people to be more aware about the problems we are facing. People aren't aware of the problems we have."[60] Participants in other studies and student testimonials in public forums agreed and provided critical assessments of racism in the schools.[61] In 2019, the Youth Civics Union, a self-convened activist group of mostly Latino and Black WPS students, put a fine point on it when they issued a statement to oppose the renewal of the superintendent's contract that claimed, "Your perception of the WPS being a utopia free of racism is flawed, ignorant, and shows how disconnected you are from us as Students of Color."[62]

BELONGING

Over the last decade, qualitative studies have begun to shed more light on problems in public school systems. In Worcester, researchers have found that besides general evidence of bias and prejudice against Latinos in public schools, students told specific stories of bullies who won as well as those who were defeated, of teachers who changed students' lives for both good and ill, and of principals who went out of their way to provide structure and others who were completely disinterested. Despite a mix of experiences in schools, a common refrain among Latino students was clearly born out of feelings of discrimination and exclusion: a desire to feel as if they belong. Indeed, researchers often encountered a sense that Latino students felt they were outsiders in their schools, frequently under surveillance, treated differently than their White peers, regularly disrespected, labeled, and expected to fail. A Worcester Latino student from "a school that has the most kids of color going to it" noted in a 2018 focus group that "as a community, unless we change the way our narrative is about how we talk about our kids in our school, like, we're perpetuating the conversation of 'they're messed up, of course, they're broken, that school needs to do something.' It's like yeah, but is that helping?"[63] Feeling as if one belongs without having to compromise cultural values in a reasonable way in school is critically important for many Latino students in multiple studies. As one Latino young man put it, "'Cause there's no greater feeling than feeling like you belong somewhere."[64] Frequently embedded in this sort of testimony was the idea that adults, teachers, and administrators did not and/or could not understand them. One frequently cited explanation is a simple numerical fact that in this nearly 75% minority-majority district, the faculty and administration are overwhelmingly White.

For the entire existence of WPS going back to its inception in the nineteenth century, the most extreme examples of racial imbalance at WPS are found among the adults in the school department. A century and a half ago it perhaps was more understandable, but to be as homogeneous as WPS is in modern America's urban environments is far more difficult. MDESE data show that while the WPS enrollment is only 28.8% White students, the overall WPS staff is 83.3% White.[65] White teachers comprise 88.2% of the WPS faculty, and White administrators comprise 86.6% of the district leaders. In fact, in no job category is the ethnoracial disparity small. At the school level in AY2021–22, eleven of the city's forty-five schools (24.4%) had 100% White faculties according to MDESE data. All were elementary schools. Moreover, 60% of all schools had faculties that were 90%+ White— twenty-five elementary schools and two high schools. The four middle schools had the smallest percentage of White faculty, but the lowest was 77.1% at East Middle, where only 23.7% of students were White. The larger point is that at WPS, faculty, staff, and administration—the adults who are most representative of a school system and who most regularly touch students' lives—are largely unrepresentative of WPS's student body. This prevents students of color from seeing themselves reflected in school leadership and White students from seeing leadership as arising from communities of color. All the while, this continues against a backdrop in which MDESE has made diversification of school staff a high priority.[66]

There is, of course, no automatic correlation between the teacher's skin color and their teaching skills, but this unbalanced situation has real-world impact because representation matters in students' lives. The effects of ethnoracial segregation on cities have been well-documented for decades as has the impact on public school systems and the diversity of school staff. In short, segregated schools with woefully unbalanced faculties and administrations become disadvantageous learning environments that often end up compromising educational achievement in the short and long term by limiting opportunities for students of color.[67] MDESE recognized as much in pushing for a "diverse and culturally responsive workplace." As noted on the MDESE website, "A growing body of educational research demonstrates the positive impacts of Teachers of Color on short- and long-term academic outcomes of Students of Color. Specifically, the research finds that having a single Teacher of Color can boost academic achievement, high school graduation rates, and college enrollment for Students of Color. In light of the research, recruiting and retaining a diverse and effective educator workforce can be a promising strategy for districts to address educational inequity."[68]

Indeed, plenty of educational, sociological, and psychological research also shows that in systems with an overwhelmingly White faculty/administration, Latino and Black students lack the necessary role models to pattern their own lives after—role models whom they can authentically relate to and who contribute positively to their lives. While this ethnoracial disparity is both a national and state problem, it is particularly acute in Worcester. A recent report by the Rennie Center for Education Research and Policy shows that Black, Indigenous, and other people of color (BIPOC) constitute only 9% of teachers, 12% of principals, and 5% of superintendents across all of Massachusetts, which means thousands of students will never learn from a teacher of color, be at a school with a principal of color, or be able to point to a superintendent of color.[69] Importantly, those numbers are state averages that include many suburban and rural systems. In Worcester in AY2021, the school district located in the second largest city in New England with a student body that was 72% BIPOC, only 11.8% of teachers, 17.2% of principals, and 0% of superintendents were non-White. As a WPS staffer noted in an interview, "Go to high schools in Worcester, what do you see? There's no role models, there's no one there that will fight for their rights. . . . And that's why we need the Worcester Public Schools to say 'hey, we need to hire Men of Color, we need to hire role models for these kids.'"[70] Put simply, for students of color in WPS, and Latino and Black students in particular, teaching and education administration is the realm of White people, a world in which they face many obstacles that their White counterparts do not. Both quantitative and qualitative research bears out this trend as WPS drifts toward more segregated schools with staff that is highly unrepresentative of the student population.

Worcester respondents in qualitative studies that speak about school climate have referred to all sorts of interactions in which bias is active. Many subjects spoke about the difficulty students of color have in obtaining a second chance to reverse reputations once a label—often "bad kid," "troublemaker," or "underachiever"—had been applied to them by teachers or administrators, even if they had intentionally changed their behavior or acknowledged and reconciled their mistakes. Although this sentiment was best summed up by a Latino student from Springfield—"They're always gonna see me as a f**kup, so I might as well just stay in these waters"—WPS students made similar points.[71] Similarly, others spoke of inheriting the labels attached to older siblings without the ability to prove themselves to be different. Stories of bias permeated discussions of "tracking," which students noticed even if schools did not technically use a tracking system. As one Latino student noted, he was the only Latino student in honors classes at his school, and "he felt labeled as a gang-banger and was ostracized despite being in honors."[72] Latino, Black, and White students alike have recognized different treatment in classrooms and have spoken out about it. In April 2019, the Youth Civics Union asserted, "Our voices will be heard. Racism is real, and it is happening in the Worcester Public Schools, and it needs to be addressed."[73]

A 2017 theater exercise conducted by two WSU professors—Tom Conroy and Adam Zahler—with a group of eighth- and ninth-grade students similarly suggested how students perceive differential and prejudicial treatment. The multiday activity asked the thirty girls from different cultural backgrounds to divide into six mixed groups, each of which would write and act in an original scene on a topic of their choosing. Because the girls were from different schools and different parts of the city, most groups wrote skits on school-related topics they had in common but with general enough themes to incorporate experiences from multiple contributors. Accordingly, scenes referred to acts of subtle and overt prejudicial treatment that they witnessed even if the scene subject was not about discrimination: a teacher seemed to favor a White student, someone had trouble pronouncing an ethnic name and did not appear concerned enough to correct it, principals appeared clueless and teachers were unprepared, authoritarian, or scatterbrained. Most were meant satirically and in the spirit of good fun, but they nevertheless contained evidence of differential treatment that was sprinkled into their scenes like common occurrences that were universally experienced.

By far the scene with the most impact was divided into four short vignettes. In the first, five girls (two White, two Black, one Latina) played together on the stage while one actor set the scene. Turning to the audience, the narrator said, "This was us in elementary school." They played, talked, and laughed together. A minute later, they broke into the second vignette, which is when the color line emerged. "This is us in middle school," the narrator said, and they split into two groups, one White and the other with students of color. Divided into two groups, the students still talked across the stage to each other: "Hi," "How are you?" "See ya' later." The third vignette was "This is us in high school." The groups remained apart, but the cross-stage talking stopped. In the final vignette, "This will be us in college," the Latina student walked off the stage. There was a beat or two, a brief moment of absolute silence before the girls from all the other groups applauded enthusiastically. At twelve and thirteen years old, these students, overwhelmingly from WPS, already had an idea of how their lives might go, and it was not especially optimistic, particularly for young Latinas, who, in the end, did not belong. Yet, the story seemed to speak to everyone there. Inequitable biases have informed these students' lives in a profound way.

Conclusion

Today, as fifty years ago, Latino students, parents, and community leaders regularly appeal to the City of Worcester and school leaders to improve the education of the city's Latino youth. Discouragingly, they are necessarily addressing many of the same issues because of the inertia in Worcester's city and school department administrations despite judicial orders, lawsuit settlements, and broken promises made to the community. The repeated questions and concerns of a half-century ago seem to fall on deaf ears in

Worcester's circles of power. Indeed, the power brokers of Worcester failed to hold the superintendent to the list of fourteen promises they extracted from her in her final contract negotiation, many of which spoke to the issues of Latino parents and community members. Unfortunately, for much of the Latino community and communities of color more generally, the Worcester public education system fails their children, and it has been doing so for at least half a century, which is continually evidenced in the WPS data. Even when there have been noteworthy improvements in academic performance, attendance, discipline, and even staffing (when it occurs), the rate at which Latinos achieve and are afforded opportunities to achieve remains far below their White counterparts and is particularly alarming when looking at differences among White-segregated, Latino-segregated, and diverse schools in the same district. As members of the Youth Civics Union put it in a public meeting, "We are all extremely dissatisfied with the superintendent and the school committee, as they have failed to address the larger issues of systemic racism that are plaguing our schools."[74]

Moving forward, it is time to take a deep and rigorously self-critical look at why, for over fifty years, most of these issues continue in Worcester. More qualitative research must be conducted and shared, and it is essential that Latino, Black, and Asian community members and their firsthand experiences inform the discussion and solutions to ethnoracial disparities in public education in Worcester. Further, the segregated nature of Worcester's quadrant system must be acknowledged, critically assessed, and reformed, and ongoing equity assessments of student absences and disciplinary practices are crucial. WPS and the city of Worcester must also begin to take seriously, place value on, and invest in the recruitment of working professionals of color citywide, including teachers and administrators, so that the ethnoracial makeup of the city's public school students mirrors that of people in positions of influence and power, offering students representation, role models, and a sense of belonging in their schools and their city more generally.

The first sentence on the WPS superintendent's webpage is also the first sentence of the 2018–23 WPS Strategic Plan, "Our mission in the Worcester Public Schools is to provide all students the opportunity to advance their scholarship with a rigorous core curriculum and high quality instruction."[75] The strategic plan continues to articulate the vision for 2023: "Worcester Public Schools will be a national leader in education, offering high-quality learning experiences, ensuring that all young people are prepared to thrive, and equipping them to become engaged citizens in their community."[76] WPS will only have a chance at achieving such a status if it is achieved universally so that all WPS students have an equal chance to compete in "this American society."

Notes

1   Richard J. Burrows, "Parents Ask Schools for Bilingual Plans," *Evening Gazette* (Worcester, MA), June 10, 1972.
2   Burrows, "Parents Ask Schools for Bilingual Plans."
3   Burrows, "Parents Ask Schools for Bilingual Plans."
4   Burrows, "Parents Ask Schools for Bilingual Plans."
5   Burrows, "Parents Ask Schools for Bilingual Plans."
6   E.g., John R. Logan, Elisabeta Minca, and Sinem Adar, "The Geography of Inequality: Why Separate Means Unequal in American Public Schools," *Sociology of Education* 85, no. 3 (2012): 287–301; Sean F. Reardon, "School Segregation and Racial Academic Achievement Gaps," *RSF: The Russell Sage Foundation Journal of the Social Sciences* 2, no. 5 (2016): 34–57; Angela Simms and Elizabeth Talbert, "Racial Residential Segregation and School Choice: How a Market-Based Policy for K-12 School Access Creates a 'Parenting Tax' for Black Parents," *Phylon (1960-)* 56, no. 1 (2019): 33–57.
7   E.g., Madeline Campbell, et al., *Suspension in Worcester: Continuing the Conversation* (WSU CityLab, 2014); Edward W. Morris and Brea L. Perry, "The Punishment Gap: School Suspension and Racial Disparities in Achievement," *Social Problems* 63, no. 1 (2016): 68–86.
8   E.g., Hua-Yu Sebastian Cherng and Peter F. Halpin, "The Importance of Minority Teachers: Student Perceptions of Minority Versus White Teachers," *Educational Researcher* 45, no. 7 (2016): 407–20; Constance A. Lindsay and Cassandra M. D. Hart, "Exposure to Same-Race Teachers and Student Disciplinary Outcomes for Black Students in North Carolina," *Educational Evaluation and Policy Analysis* 39, no. 3 (2017): 485–510.
9   Tara J. Yosso, "Whose Culture Has Capital? A Critical Race Theory Discussion of Community Cultural Wealth," *Race Ethnicity and Education* 8, no. 1 (2005): 69–91.
10 US Census Bureau, *1960 Censuses of Population and Housing* (US Census Bureau).
11 US Census Bureau, *1970 Censuses of Population and Housing* (US Census Bureau).
12 US Census Bureau, *1970 Censuses of Population and Housing.*
13 "Unofficial Survey Finds 5,000 in City," *Worcester Telegram*, July 2, 1972.
14 Betty Lilyestrom, "How Are They Doing?" *Sunday Telegram* (Worcester, MA), February 16, 1964.
15 Florence R. Niles, "Latins Are Adjusting to New Life," *Evening Gazette* (Worcester, MA), September 9, 1968.
16 Anthony Simollardes, "Couple Going Home, but Not on Happy Vacation They Planned," *Worcester Telegram*, August 25, 1972.
17 Sandy Conaty, "An Assessment of Urban Neighborhood Dynamics: South Worcester, Worcester, Massachusetts" (Thesis, University of Rhode Island, Community Planning, 1987), 60.
18 Mark Melnik, *Demographic and Socio-economic Trends in Boston* (Boston

Redevelopment Authority, 2011), 9.

19 US Census Bureau, *1970 Censuses.*

20 Authors' calculations based on US Census Bureau, *1980 Censuses of Population and Housing* (US Census Bureau).

21 Ramon Borges-Mendez, Nicole Lavan, and Charles Jones, "Latinos in Massachusetts: Selected Economic Indicators," Gastón Institute Publications 118 (2006), https://scholarworks.umb.edu/gaston_pubs/118; USCensus Bureau, *2020 Demographic Profile*, https://data.census.gov/table/DECENNIALDP2020.DP1?g=160XX00US2582000&d=DEC%20Demographic%20Profile.

22 US Census Bureau, *2020 Demographic Profile* (US Census Bureau).

23 Peter Schworm and Matt Carroll, "Whites Still Fleeing Cities in Mass," *Boston Globe*, March 24, 2011.

24 Jack Schneider, *Beyond Test Scores: A Better Way to Measure School Quality* (Harvard University Press, 2017).

25 MDESE, "Enrollment Data—Worcester," MDESE, 2022, https://profiles.doe.mass.edu/profiles/student.aspx?orgcode=03480000&orgtypecode=5&.

26 MDESE, "Enrollment Data—Worcester."

27 Scott O'Connell, "School District Report Shows Worcester's Latino Students, Disabled Students Lagging Behind Peers," *Worcester Telegram* (Worcester, MA), November 19, 2021.

28 O'Connell, "School District Report."

29 Authors' calculations based on MDESE, "Student Attendance," MDESE, 2022, https://profiles.doe.mass.edu/profiles/student.aspx?orgcode=03480000&orgtypecode=5&leftNavId=16817&.

30 Commission for Latino Educational Excellence, introduction to *Creating the Will: A Community Roadmap to Achieving Educational Excellence for Latino Students in Worcester* (The Commission for Latino Educational Excellence, 2011).

31 Commission for Latino Educational Excellence, *Creating the Will.*

32 Worcester Public Schools, *Student Handbook, 2021–2022* (Worcester Public Schools), 6–7.

33 Emma Garcia, *Schools Are Still Segregated, and Black Children Are Paying a Price* (Economic Policy Institute, 2020).

34 Garcia, *Schools Are Still Segregated.*

35 Dan Scharfenberg, "Massachusetts Public Schools Are Highly Segregated; It's Time We Treated That Like the Crisis It Is," *Boston Globe*, December 11, 2020.

36 MDESE, "Enrollment Data—Worcester."

37 MDESE, "Enrollment Data—Worcester."

38 MDESE, "Enrollment Data—Worcester."

39 MDESE, "Enrollment Data—Worcester."

40 Worcester Mayoral Commission on Latino Education and Advancement, *A Way Forward: Latino Youth and Families in Worcester* (Latino Policy Institute, Worcester State University, 2021), 1–2.

41 Worcester Public Schools, *Attendance Policy 2014–2015* (Worcester Public Schools).

42 Worcester Public Schools, *Attendance Policy.*

43 "Attendance Matters," Worcester Public Schools, accessed February 24, 2022, https://worcesterschools.org/current-families/when-should-i-keep-my-child-home/attendance-matters/.

44 Authors' calculations based on MDESE, "Student Attendance."

45 "Attendance Matters," Worcester Public Schools.

46 MDESE, "Student Attendance."

47 Walter Bird Jr., "Worcester Interfaith: Schools Failing Students of Color; Superintendent Responds," *Worcester Magazine*, April 1, 2019.

48 Campbell et al., *Suspension in Worcester*.

49 Thomas E. Conroy, et al., *In Search of Opportunity: Latino Men's Paths to Post-Secondary Education in Urban Massachusetts* (Boston Foundation and Balfour Foundation, 2016).

50 Alex Briesacher, et al., *State of Our Schools Legislative Breakfast Data Briefing Data* (Worcester State University, 2019).

51 Daniel J. Losen and Tia Elena Martinez, *Out of School and Off Track: The Overuse of Suspensions in American Middle and High Schools* (UCLA Civil Rights Project, 2013).

52 Melissa Colón, "Out of School Suspension Data—Worcester Public Schools" (presentation, Not Present, Not Accounted For: Schools Suspensions in Worcester Conference, Worcester, MA, 2013).

53 Campbell et al., *Suspension in Worcester*.

54 Campbell et al., *Suspension in Worcester*, 11.

55 Bird Jr., "Worcester Interfaith."

56 MDESE, "Student Discipline Data Report—All Offenses," MDESE, 2022, https://profiles.doe.mass.edu/ssdr/default.aspx?orgcode=03480000&orgtypecode=5&=03480000&&fycode=2020.

57 MDESE, "Student Discipline Data."

58 MDESE, "Student Discipline Data."

59 Conroy et al., *In Search of Opportunity*.

60 Timothy E. Murphy, Elliot A. Rivera, and Michael Allevato, *A Deeper Dive into Worcester: A Follow-Up Report on Latino Men and Post-Secondary Education in Worcester, Massachusetts* (WSU CityLab, 2018), 14.

61 Campbell et al., *Suspension in Worcester*.

62 Scott O'Connell, "Student Effort to Oust Worcester Superintendent Grows," *Worcester Telegram* (Worcester, MA), April 15, 2019.

63 Murphy, Rivera, and Allevato, *A Deeper Dive into Worcester*, 19.

64 Conroy et al., *In Search of Opportunity*, 80.

65 MDESE, "Staffing Data by Race, Ethnicity, Gender by Full-Time Equivalents," MDESE, 2022, https://profiles.doe.mass.edu/profiles/teacher.aspx?orgcode=03480000&orgtypecode=5&leftNavId=817&.

66 MDESE, "Diverse and Culturally Responsive Workforce," MDESE, 2022, https://www.doe.mass.edu/csi/diverse-workforce/default.html.

67 Commission for Latino Educational Excellence, *Creating the Will*.

68 MDESE, "Diverse and Culturally Responsive Workforce."

69 Rennie Center for Education Research and Policy, *The Power Gap in Massachusetts K-12 Education: Examining Gender and Racial Disparities Among Leadership* (Eos-Foundation, 2021).

70 Murphy, Rivera, and Allevato, *A Deeper Dive into Worcester*, 14.

71 Conroy et al., *In Search of Opportunity*, 64.

72 Murphy, Rivera, and Allevato, *A Deeper Dive into Worcester*, 21.

73 Bill Shaner, "Student Group Calls for Worcester Superintendent to Go," *Worcester Magazine* (Worcester, MA), April 4, 2019.

74 Shaner, "Student Group Calls."

75 "About the Superintendent," Worcester Public Schools, https://worcesterschools.org/about/superintendent/, accessed March 22, 2022.

76 Worcester Public Schools, *A Strategic Plan for Education in Worcester, 2018–2023* (Worcester Public Schools).

Chapter Eight

"You Are One of Us, Miss"

Autobiographical (Re)calling of Critical Cariño Cuentos, Conocimientos, y Consejos in a College Access Program

CARMEN N. VELORIA

A great deal has been written about notions of care and caring in school contexts, such as caring for and with students, caring for and with fellow educators, and caring about the sociocontext of schooling.[1] So much, in fact, that over the last few decades various conceptualizations of care and/or caring have captured the imagination of many educational practitioners and researchers.[2] For example, some scholars have expanded theories of care/caring to explore how practitioner's race, ethnicity, and class impact curricular and program implementation, while others have offered frameworks grounded on conceptions of "authentic *cariño*" as it relates to working with Latine[3] students in high-need urban contexts.[4]

From a critical orientation, scholars of color have highlighted the need to address the political and ideological dimension of caring, especially when working with increasingly diverse students. Drawing on autobiographical research methods that demand critical reflection, practice thoughtfulness, and have a moral commitment to remembering,[5] this chapter aims to unpack what it means to be positioned as "one of us" and the laden moral, emotional, political, and ideological dimensions of this positioning. I posit that there is a need for the use of cultural, familiar, and gendered notions of *cariño, cuentos, conocimientos y consejos* (care, stories/ways of knowing, and advice) to demonstrate care and to uphold a culture of high expectations and accountability while offering authentic and respectful insights on ways of being and moving about the world that are grounded in lived experience, wisdom, and a desire to help young people thrive in all aspects of their lives.

"Do Work That Matters: Vale la Pena"[6]

In 2000 I arrived at Central Middle School,[7] located in one of Boston's most diverse neighborhoods. I was eager to work on a new college access program called Gaining Early Awareness and Readiness for Undergraduate Programs (GEAR UP) that offered an innovative approach to system-wide change. The goal was to work systemically by supplementing, not supplanting, existing programs in a collaborative manner with partnering institutions: the school district, a college and university, and local community-based organizations and businesses. It focused on fostering a college-going culture and a cohort-model approach to building enduring relationships that would continue at least until high school graduation.

I recall my very first day as if it were yesterday. After a brief conversation with the school principal, I was ushered into a classroom in the basement, a dark space with little ventilation, a desk, a chair, a few pens, and pencils. I reread the grant application in my binder and wandered the halls to get acclimated to the new school. At the end of the day, upon returning to the barren room, I remember thinking: *How am I (literally) going to get this program off the ground?*

In what follows, I recount my experiences working in a college access program and the lessons learned along the way about myself and my practice as well as missed opportunities that have led to deep reflection and growth. The chapter commences with a detailed description of my participation in a federally funded college access program to contextualize deep relationships that continue more than a decade later. Through a revisiting of previously collected data, coupled with current interactions and discussions with former program participants, I recount and retell layered sociolinguistic stories to offer recommendations for working with Latine youth in a manner that capitalizes on educative interactions and the need for critical *cariño*.

A View from the Basement

I knew that I would be working with mostly Latine students and families who lived in the surrounding area. At the time, the student population was over 65% Latine, the majority of Latines were identified as English learners (ELs), and over 75% of the school population was eligible for free or reduced lunch. There was no roadmap for the GEAR UP program as it was new legislation from the Clinton administration. This legislation provided six-year or seven-year grants to states and partnerships to develop GEAR UP programs that provide services at high-poverty middle and high schools. GEAR UP grantees serve an entire cohort of students beginning no later than the seventh grade and follow the cohort through high school. GEAR UP funds are also used to provide college scholarships to low-income students. My program was one of seven programs that were partnered with local middle schools and institutions of higher education. At the time of my arrival, very little programming had taken place, and the school-based staff was not aware of the program, let alone its goals.

While the grant called for a range of academic programming, one thing that quickly became abundantly clear was the need to support practices that would increase test scores. The discursive practices of the school were entrenched in high-stakes testing. No matter whom I asked, everything I did needed to respond to the Massachusetts Comprehensive Assessment System (MCAS).[8] The emphasis placed on this exam was so strong that by the end of my first year at Central, the school principal was ousted. Even though very little was offered in terms of a formal explanation, the talk in the school building hinted at the ill-timed vacation he took while the MCAS exam was being administered in the spring of 2001.[9] Thus, despite disagreement with the district's overwhelming stress on testing and test results, program staff were constrained by what the student had to accomplish to be deemed prepared to attend postsecondary institutions.[10] Therefore, all programmatic activities were planned against the backdrop of the MCAS examinations.

The ousted principal was beloved by the school's mostly Latine population, and many saw his dismissal as a personal attack connected to the highly controversial graduation exit exam. Despite student walkouts, parent complaints, and even picket lines, the district prevailed, and a new principal was hired. He was young, charismatic, and Latine. He was genuinely eager to unify the school, and before long, as the fuss dwindled, he made significant inroads. He was a quick study and truly understood the aim of the program, but more importantly, he recognized the program's potential to help him accomplish some of his goals. Thus, he provided incredible support and access to data that he knew would help him tell much-needed stories of achievement and improvement. Of course, he also needed allies and saw programs like GEAR UP, despite their newness and little to no evaluation data, as instrumental to the success of the school. His support mattered greatly.

Due to the cohort approach and the collaborative nature of the work, I was glad for his support but aimed to strike a balance between meeting the expectations of the grant and aligning my work to his goals. Like him, this meant that I also had to identify allies who would offer connections both inside and outside the school. I would meet my fellow travelers in another section of the basement: the Parent Center. The Parent Center was much brighter, and the furniture was organized to take advantage of a built-in chalkboard. The space was often buzzing with activities and programs for students, parents, and staff, which were made possible by leveraging Title I[11] funds and with the help of outside community-based organizations. It was not long before I settled into the desk across from the part-time parent coordinator, Veronica, a Latina mother of three.

"Parents Just Don't Care"

My program counterparts at other area schools had similar access to data and resources, but it became evident from our monthly check-in meetings where we discussed challenges, shared ideas, and discussed resources, that our sensemaking of our experiences was different. As the only Latina program coordinator, I often felt compelled to speak on behalf of my students and parents to address some of the misconceptions I heard. Research, policy reports, and briefings may document educational conditions that affect students, but they seldom incorporate students' or parents' perspectives on their educational conditions.[12]

The old and worn-out refrain of "Parents just don't care" was often heard from school-based staff. But I simply did not agree with this simplistic notion. I pushed back on my colleagues' assumption, responding, "What does caring look like anyway?" From my corner of the Parent Center, I saw *mamis, tías, abuelitas* who came to school to check on their children. Once they knew about the program and knew me personally, some even gave me permission to *tirar la oreja* (tug or pull at the ear) of their children if I ever saw them misbehaving or not being on task. I got to meet and interact with the parents who attended many of the parent workshops offered by the school and the GEAR UP program. These events were often held in the late afternoon, during which time the staff and I decorated tables with flower-filled vases and offered ethnic food cooked by the mostly Latine cafeteria coworkers. Veronica and I also offered incentives and usually held a raffle. By then, I had hired Veronica on a part-time basis since she was already ingrained in the community. She and I often saw mothers at their wits' end, filled with despair and afraid of losing their children to the streets. We saw mothers who, even after working a night shift, still found time to attend as small English as a Second Language class that was offered at the center, courtesy of Title I funds. Mothers who bared their souls over a hot cup of coffee and *galletitas*.

As I prepared for the after-school program, I often heard their stories and many times saw them shed tears. These moments elicited memories of my mother coming to my school to advocate for me. A vivid memory is when my mother asked my fourth-grade teacher to call me by my given name and not the nickname my teacher had given me. By the time I was working at Central, I was also a mother, and I very much felt their anguish and pain. Therefore, the image some of my colleagues had of parents not caring was simply one I did not share.

It was around this time that I started thinking about notions of care,[13] and the need to explore different conceptualizations of caring.[14] Many researchers have reconceptualized Noddings's theory with findings that demonstrate support for and expand the ethic of care as an instrumental yet complicated construct in educational settings.[15] I was living and working in this complication. What I witnessed in the Parent Center was a different way of caring, one that sounded strangely familiar yet was not often recognized outside places like the Parent Center.

Gendered Programming

Wanda's *abuelita*, Doña Hortencia, was a regular at the Parent Center. Veronica knew her from when she worked at the elementary school. Doña Hortencia was always checking in on Wanda. While Veronica and I enjoyed having her around and listening to her stories of growing up in the Dominican Republic, we were both keenly aware of the strong hand she used in rearing Wanda. We straddled the boundaries of care and support carefully given the potentially negative effects of Doña Hortencia's constant surveillance, rigidity, and pronouncements of an impending pregnancy. We offered parent workshops focused on a deeper understanding of youth development and the need to engage in caring and supportive dialogue with youth. Our strategy relied on trust, intense listening, culturally relevant humor, and the creation of conditions where authentic conversations could emerge without judgment. Veronica was especially adept in engaging parents in these conversations, sometimes alongside a trained facilitator. As a mother of teenagers, Veronica understood their adolescent trials and tribulations and was very affirming with their concerns, which helped to gently guide parents to consider other ways of thinking and acting. We also ran student workshops that focused on healthy construction of self and relationships with mothers. These were mostly attended by girls and their mothers. We attempted to offer specific programming for boys, but it was the girls who consistently showed up and over time became more and more vocal in asking for additional gender-specific programming. As a result, we offered a conversation group for both mothers and daughters facilitated by a psychology doctoral student. There was something about the conversation groups, even the multigenerational ones, that attracted the girls.

Largely influenced by the work of Dr. Jill McLean Taylor, who at the time was the chair of the Gender Studies Department at Simmons College and oversaw GEAR UP for her home institution, we decided to offer single-sex classes in the after-school program. This approach was well aligned with holistic approaches that recognize the important intersection between gendered expectations and culture and how they influence the formation of self-esteem, self-competency, and perceptions of physical, sexual, and social self, particularly in girls.[16] We intentionally separated the students based on research about learning styles, differing inclinations for collaborative approaches in math, and a growing conviction that "single-sex education—especially for girls and low-income families—was essential to remedy for unequal education."[17] This was also based on the notion that in coeducational classrooms, girls are often passive and submissive, whereas males are more assertive, vying for the teacher's attention.[18] Boys also tend to monopolize student-teacher interactions, disrupt lessons, and dominate the physical space.[19] I was also reading and learning from Dr. Taylor's work with others like Dr. Carol Gilligan, from the Harvard Project on Women's Psychology and Girls' Development, who focused on girls' voices, especially when they seemed to blur, fade, or become disruptive in the passage into womanhood.[20] This work really influenced my thinking and practice.

All this led to my interest in learning more about the optimal learning conditions for girls, especially Latina girls. Clara, for example, to this day recalls how I waited by the lockers to make sure she and others made their way to their after-school classroom. "Sometimes we would hear you coming, and we would run to catch the bus," she would later reveal. Of course, I was aware of this, which is why I enlisted the help of their mothers, especially those who constantly visited the Parent Center. Veronica would follow up with phone calls to their home. She also followed up when the boys did not report to the after-school program. She and I even became quite adept at negotiating with parents. When parents lamented that they needed the girls at home to watch over younger children, we asked them to allow them to come at least twice a week. We pleaded for the boys to come as well. We knew some of the boys would accompany their mothers to their office cleaning jobs in the evening. However, it was harder to attract the boys, especially those who felt they needed to work to help support their families. The socioeconomic status of Latine families offers yet another factor that may influence participation in college-going decisions.[21] While most of the girls felt the pull to clean the house or tend to younger siblings, some of the boys felt the need to make money and help their single mothers or families.

"EL CORO GROUP" AT URBAN HIGH SCHOOL

When I first met the students at Central, I told them that I would follow them to "watch them cross the stage." I am not sure how many believed me. However, by the time I moved up to Urban High School, six of the former Central girls were looking for me and found me. Not only did they want additional academic programming, but by then they also needed help navigating the world of dating, a new school, and growing tensions at home. Although I was meeting with them, fielding questions, and offering other types of programming, by their sophomore year, they were looking for a space to "speak their minds."[22] I again enlisted the help of Dr. Taylor along with a social worker who had worked as a counselor with other GEAR UP students. We decided that we would meet after school. The girls named the conversation group "El Coro," to signal the orchestration of discourses that only we were a part of.[23] The four salient themes that emerged from our conversation were:

1. *"For Latinas, the big stereotype is that you'll become pregnant."*—This theme touched on the prevalence of surveillance by the mothers. For example, Wanda, only in her sophomore year of high school at the

time, described, "I can't do anything!" in reference to her grandmother knowing everyone in the neighborhood. It also focused on mothers who struggled with their daughter's sexuality, some getting angry when they wore tank tops and shorts when the mothers' own boyfriends were around. Additionally, most of the girls felt that despite their mother's push for them to continue their education, it would not surprise their mothers one bit if one of them was to become pregnant. Thus, the girls viewed the fact that they had not become pregnant as an accomplishment and a motivator to "prove them wrong."

2. *"This School, Miss . . ."*—This theme dealt with the strong critique the girls had of the school, teachers, and course offerings. They commented on how they had to advocate for themselves, seeking guidance from program staff or having their mothers come to school to complain. They focused on the erasure of Latine experiences in the curriculum, the monolithic view of them, and the politics of skin color; for example, according to Clara, "In our school they think that if you are light skinned you are Puerto Rican and if you are dark skinned you are Dominican . . . that's stupid because I am light skinned, but I am Dominican."

3. *"My Mother's Been Through a Lot, a Lot."*—Although the girls talked about not being able to "have a serious conversation with their mother," most of them acknowledged their mothers' struggles and their resiliency. They critiqued their mothers but also understood their good intentions and all they had to do to survive. They struggled with the dual messages that are sometimes received at home. While mothers espoused the notion of being good and keeping a clean house, they also talked about the need to get an education and not depend on a man.

4. *"You Know What It's Like, Miss."*—In the retelling of stories about growing up in a Latina household, the girls often looked to me for affirmation but also with a sense of solidarity. The discussions ranged from sometimes being hit and yelled at at home while at the same time being told that they should not "put up with nothing" outside the home. Maria nicely captured this contradiction: "But I think that hurts us, because whatever we have to say we are keeping it to ourselves, and if that happens continuously, right, that's more things to keep inside, and that affects your school, that affects how you think, that affects who you are, and how you are going to act."[24]

A long time would pass, well after the girls' graduation in 2006, for me to fully revel in what it meant to be part of the El Coro group. For example, in 2011, I reflected on my positionality as a practitioner. Even back then, Amelia's narratives captivated me the most, *"You know what it's like, Miss," she would say whenever* we crossed over the terrain of schooling experiences to the more fluid flows of mixed messages received from our mothers, the duality of living in two worlds and making sense of what it means to be Latina.[25] Recollecting became a painful process that evoked painful memories and a great deal of questions. *Would it have been beneficial had I shared more about my upbringing and background? Why did I feel the need to keep my distance?*

I recognized then, and even now as I reflect on this, that I worked hard on keeping myself hidden. It would take years before I could critically reflect and unpack. I would later write about what happens when researchers deny emotion, spiritual needs, and nurturance as this leads to physical ailments that manifest when one ignores the signals.[26] I ignored the signals, not only due to my concern with objectivity and simply being a novice researcher but also due to the hustle and bustle of high school and college preparation that did not afford the luxury of time. Yet, practitioner reflexivity is needed. The fact is that their stories vividly resonated with me, and I secretly took pleasure in knowing that I could relate along cultural and gendered lines.[27] I loved being an insider but often felt like I could not show it or talk to anyone about it. *Who would have understood?* The reality is that these girls were onto me, and their actions signaled an emotional connection, and at times, their words chipped away at my masquerade, "Come on, Miss, you know you were raised like that, too."[28] "You are one of us, Miss," they would often say.

In 2021 Clara attended a wedding in Miami, "Miss Veloria, we were remembering and laughing," she said when commenting on the memories of the group with other members of El Coro. To this day, Clara refuses to call me by my first name, "I just can't, you will always be Miss to me." The El Coro meeting time was the only time the girls seemed to slow down. I recall us bonding over laughter and sometimes tears, a healthy mix of both joy and sorrow. I would go on to write about our sensemaking of experiences, the figured worlds we linguistically entered when narrating events, and the multiple selves we all enacted during this time.[29] It has been years, and I am still in touch with most of them, celebrating milestones like graduate school, marriages, new jobs, and motherhood, always offering advice. Some reach out more than others, but I know they all remember. I can only imagine the conversations in Miami that resulted in the eruption of laughter.

A few semesters ago, I invited Rebecca, who is now a social worker, to speak to one of my college classes. As I read her bio, I noticed that she was crying. "It just hit me," she said, "you were there for us all those years." Before long, I was crying too, along with some of the other guests who knew about El Coro because they also attended Urban High School and had been part of the GEAR UP program. I stayed because my work was more than just a job. I cared for the students and my practice centered on helping them become critical of the world so that they could disrupt and navigate systems, not just for themselves, but for those who would come after them. *But was it enough?*

Based on my experiences, critical reflections, and recollections from the field, I am aware of the power of insider stories to potentially rekindle hope that through small local victories achieved through collaborative work, a bigger battle is being won.[30] This is not one of them. While some of El Coro girls would go on to college, and even graduate school, some did not, and others dropped out. Yet, what was it about the group, the dynamics that took place and created the conditions for these relationships to endure? I yearned to be in community with them and enjoyed watching them flourish. A few years later I remember asking one of them, Maria, "Would it have helped if I had revealed aspects of myself?" She simply said, "No, we knew, Miss, we knew." What about the boys? Should I have led a boy's group, too? Did they miss out? Did I?

Expanding on Notions of Authentic *Cariño* and Critical Care

> Necesitamos teoria *(we need theories) that will rewrite history using race, class, gender, and ethnicity as categories of analysis, theories that cross borders, that blur boundaries— new kinds of theories with new theorizing methods.*
>
> —GLORIA E. ANZALDÚA[31]

According to Bartolomé,[32] a great deal has been written about the need for practitioners to care for and identify with minoritized students,[33] but the political and ideological dimensions of caring are seldom addressed.

Valenzuela's notion of "authentic *cariño*" is an asset-based view of low-income, linguistic minority students that considers their native language and focuses on creating psychologically healthy learning contexts, including conversation groups.

In distinguishing between education and *educación*, Valenzuela makes the case for a more expansive view of education.[34] According to her, *educación* is "the family's role of inculcating in children a sense of moral, social, and personal responsibility and serves as the foundation for all other learning. Though inclusive of formal academic training, *educación* additionally refers to competence in the school world, wherein one respects the dignity and individuality of others."[35]

Thus, *educación* is more "values based," rather than human capital based.[36] Often, improving college access, enrollment, and completion is seen as a social value, as graduation is associated with many benefits including higher earnings, better employment, and homeownership.[37] These are all indicators of social mobility and explain the reasons why college access professionals emphasize the need to build social capital related to college access and preparedness.[38] Across the field, this is understood to be a good rationale for focusing on awareness, preparation, and exposure. My thinking, however, is that when working with Latine students, a "folk model" of *educación* is needed that enables them to center their cultural values and attend critically to the pedagogies "*de la casa*" (of the home)[39] or "*el barrio*" (the neighborhood) including gendered and mixed messages, while learning to understand and challenge so-called neutral educational spaces very much like the themes that emerged out of El Coro.

Antrop-González and De Jesús conceptualize critical *cariño* as a type of caring that is undertaken with historical and political consciousness of students' communities and a desire to interrupt inequity.[40] Their analysis of Latine student narratives elucidates the need "to forge a new caring framework that privileges the cultural values and political economy of communities of color as a foundation for education.[41] In practice, frameworks are needed to work with Latine youth in ways that are culturally familiar and that demonstrate critical *cariño* (care) for them to both critique and help build better systems, *conocimientos* (ways of knowing) to build reciprocity and trust while sharing from one's lived experiences, and *consejos* (advice) grounded in an ethical commitment to provide practical ways to navigate and disrupt complex systems, not only as individuals, but as a part of the collective.

I did not have this language back then, but what I did have was a keen awareness of critical *cariño* for students and their families, and the need to raise awareness of the conditions that impacted their lives. I shared many *cuentos y conocimientos* (stories and ways of knowing) based on my own lived experiences navigating systems and my aspirations, fears, and hopes as well as those of others in my community. I also offered an abundance of *consejos* gathered in my journey with fellow travelers, accumulated as I "crossed the bridge on the backs" of many who came before me.[42] These were always offered to promote individual and collective action. In hindsight, my stories liberated me because they were mine to tell, and available for telling.[43] In some small way, this was my way of subverting power and inserting my subjectivities at a time when I thought research neutrality was what mattered most. I now know better.

Practitioners need to braid together theories that explore the complexity of Latine students in various ecosystems. An understanding of developmental psychology is also needed to explore complex identities and promote a strong and stable sense of self across a range of identity dimensions and contexts. However, sociological theories of ethnicity and race are also helpful constructs in exploring systems of inequality especially as youth see themselves in relation to those systems and society. I also advocate for a critical intersectional lens—one that encompasses race, class, gender, sexuality, ability, and age—all the realities that make up a youth's social position.

When it comes to working with Latine youth in urban contexts, practitioners need to leave color-blind college preparatory curricula behind and center the voices and lived realities of students by prioritizing pedagogies *de la casa*, different ways of knowing[44] that center race, ethnicity, gender, and immigration status and a humble disposition to learn from students and families. This also applies to practitioners who may act, look, and come from the same environments as the students. The reality is that we do not know what we do not know. The Latine population is extremely diverse, in terms of race, religion, sexual orientation, political ideologies, immigration status, and so on. Therefore, practitioners must challenge notions that essentialize and position Latines as a static monolithic group.

We all have a need to care and be cared for, but from a critical perspective, as described by education scholar Dr. Curry, caring must focus on "explicit attention to cultures of power with an aim toward helping students master dominant discourses while still valuing and sustaining their home cultures."[45] *Cuentos y conocimientos* humanize us and focus on what we have in common rather than real and perceived differences. It is a way for all of us to make sense of the world. Under most conditions, humans do not fail to make sense when narrativizing experiences. However, "cultural translators"[46] may be needed as the human narrative is expressed differently in diverse cultures.[47] Thus, understanding this important link between culture, gendered language usage, and societal structures should motivate practitioners to be critical of the *consejos* they impart.

Where's Our Group?

From time to time, Jerry would ask, "Where's our group?," meaning that he wanted me to also lead a boy's group. He was one of the boys whom I would chase after school at Central. While active in many aspects of the program, he was often too cool for after school. He always asked about a boy's group with a sly smile, which I often disregarded as him just being Jerry. The fact of the matter is that by high school, most of the young men were preoccupied with sports and after-school jobs. I attempted to capture their attention during the school day by offering in-school tutoring and opportunities for them to get involved in other extracurricular activities. Two White males who worked in the program ran the in-school, drop-in tutoring program. I would often stop by, and was met with friendly arguments about cars or sports teams, before they quickly opened their books, "I know Miss . . ." they would say before "getting down to business." Although most of them had seen me as a mother figure of sorts at Central, by high school they mostly saw me as the lead of the program.

I often question if I should have done more to serve them. *What else could I have done? Should I have spent more time attending to their unique needs? What did I miss in relation to attending to needs of young men?* It was not until senior year when Jerry approached me to tell me that he was upset that I never organized a boy's group. I recall this moment because this time his rebuke felt different. He still said it almost jokingly, but I noticed traces of indignation in his remark. He was still as brilliant, determined, and strong-willed as ever. I was always in awe of his ability to move around the school, demanding respect and excelling in both academics and sports. He was indeed one of the most academically inclined students who had received the highest MCAS scores in the school without really trying. In retrospect, I should have seen that he was bored in school. By senior year, he was disengaged, tired of his surroundings, and looking forward to college simply because he could not be bothered anymore. He had grown into a man, but I will never forget this last exchange and how it would haunt me because of what happened. He has a story to tell. For now, I'll share that because of him, I have always regretted not offering a special conversation group for boys. He asked for one, and I did not offer it and for this, I am profusely sorry.

Jerry and I have remained in contact throughout the years, always skirting the incident, until recently. A few years ago, while having lunch in downtown Boston he looked at me and said, "Miss, it was not your fault." Even though many years had gone by during which he had met me for lunch, introduced me to a girlfriend, and checked in with multiple updates, this was the first time he looked me in the eyes and uttered those words. While I knew that "it was not my fault," I had been carrying tremendous guilt. Not because I could have stopped what happened but because I could have prevented it had I offered him and other boys the same opportunities I had afforded the El Coro girls. As a mother to a daughter and son, I now have a fuller understanding of the unique needs of boys and the possible gender differences in what they ask for and how they need to be cared for. While extant research is almost silent on Latino males and their educational pathways into higher education,[48] I am committed to learning, doing better, and helping to raise awareness for the sake of all Latine students. *What would it look like to have a Latine-centered approach to working with all Latine students?*

Relearning to See Myself

I recently called Jerry to tell him I was thinking about him and to share what I wrote in this piece. After telling him about my recollection of events, I asked him, "Would it have helped had I offered a boy's group?" He started to cry. He is now almost thirty-five years old, solid as a rock, but at that moment he became the seventh grader I used to chase down the hallways of Central. He said, "Miss, you have to remember that back then you were like a second mother to me." Inasmuch as I have always regretted not offering a boy's group, I can honestly say that it was not until that humbling moment that I felt the weight of my inaction and the tremendous impact it had on him and me. He saw it, too. He is now ready to share. "I'm relearning to see myself," he said before asking, "Will you help me tell my story?" Before I could answer he said, "I think you need this, too." He is right, of course. His story can potentially help other youth and practitioners wrestling with how to best offer programming for boys.

Lessons Learned

As a much wiser practitioner who is also relearning to see myself and my practice, I only hope that I can do his story justice because his story matters and *vale la pena* (it's worth) telling it. At a time when degree attainment gaps continue to exist as cited by Rodriguez et al. in this volume, it is important that the reflections of former program participants and practitioners inform school-based and community-based policy to move the educational needle in the right direction and help inform asset-based and culturally sustaining responses to some of the challenges faced by Latine students and families.

Like Jerry, many students excel academically, apply to college, and get in. However, one single action completely derailed his plans. What I did not know at the time was that he was dealing with a complicated father-son relationship that influenced his view of family dynamics, provoked feelings of guilt regarding his immigration status, and impacted his view of manhood. Had I taken the time to provide a boys' group to listen, to help unpack, to offer a space to explore and make sense of what was happening at home and in the neighborhood, perhaps he would have graduated from college.

In chapter 13, Rodriguez et al., the voices of participants elucidate the impact integrated programming has on Latine youth as it relates to the development of both "human" and "technical skills." Becoming "future ready" should involve exploration of self, discussions of career pathways, and connection to community. I remember employing all of these in my approach to programming as well. However, I was not always intentional about explicitly incorporating *critical cariño, cuentos, conocimientos, y consejos*. Yet, in my experience, this is what former participants most recall, "Miss, I remember when you shared," "when you told us about," and so on. At the time these cultural stories seemed nonconsequential, but in hindsight, they bonded, connected, and humanized us along cultural, gender, and familiar lines. *What would it mean to intentionally embed these insights into programming when serving Latine youth?*

Drawing on lessons learned, I have invited others to codevelop a "tool kit" that builds on the insights, critiques, and expansions of caring theory to put forth a framework for working with Latine students focused on conceptualization of "critical cariño" (affection). The aim is to provide a usable framework that is theory and practice focused and student informed and that can be adapted across multiple educational settings.

P-16 and community-based educators can incorporate the framework with existing curricula, when introducing new content, and when making connections beyond the classroom. The framework can inform policymakers in shifting the conversation from "student ready" to "institutional readiness." National organizations like Excelencia predict that by 2031, Latinos will make up 91% of the new workforce. Educational institutions need to cultivate an environment conducive to Latine success that extends beyond academics and serves with intentionality, *con ganas* (with desire) to address inequities, strengthen supports, and better address the holistic needs of Latine students and families. Critical and complex *cuentos* from the field can help in shifting the narrative.

Notes

1   Lilia I. Bartolomé, "Authentic Cariño and Respect in Minority Education: The Political and Ideological Dimensions of Love," *International Journal of Critical Pedagogy* 1, no. 1 (2008): 1–17; Tamara Beauboeuf-Lafontant, "A Womanist Experience of Caring: Understanding the Pedagogy of Exemplary Black Women Teachers," *Urban Review* 34 (2002): 71–86; Corinne McKamey, "Restorying 'Caring' in Education: Students' Narratives of Caring For and About," *Narrative Matters* 1, no. 1 (2011): 78–94; Nel Noddings, *Caring: A Feminine Approach to Ethics and Moral Education* (University of California Press, 1984); Nel Noddings, *The Challenge to Care in Schools: An Alternative Approach to Education* (Teachers College Press, 1992); Angela Valenzuela, *Subtractive Schooling: U.S.-Mexican Youth and the Politics of Caring* (State University of New York Press, 1999).

2   Rene Antrop-González and Anthony De Jesús, "Toward a Theory of Critical Care in Urban Small School Reform: Examining Structures and Pedagogies of Caring in Two Latino Community-Based Schools," *International Journal of Qualitative Studies in Education* 19, no. 4 (2006): 409–33.

3   The term "Latine" is used to refer to individuals of ethnic, racial, national origin and/ or ancestry that stems from Caribbean and Latin America. I acknowledge ongoing debates regarding the appropriate term to use. When citing other scholars, I use the terms used by the authors. The terms "Latine" and "Black" are not necessarily mutually exclusive groups.

4 Bartolomé, "Authentic Cariño."

5 Robert V. Bullough Jr. and Stefinee Pinnegar, "Guidelines for Quality in Autobiographical Forms of Self-Study Research," *Educational Researcher* 30, no. 3 (2001): 13–21.

6 Gloria E. Anzaldúa.

7 Pseudonyms are used throughout the chapter.

8 The Massachusetts Comprehensive Assessment System (MCAS) is Massachusetts's statewide standards-based assessment program that was developed in 1993 in response to the Massachusetts Education Reform Act of the same year.

9 Carmen Veloria, "'You Know What It's Like, Miss' Beyond College Access: A Tale of Multiple 'Selves'" (PhD diss., University of Massachusetts Amherst, Department of Language, Literacy, & Culture, 2011).

10 Jill McLean Taylor, Carmen Veloria, and Martina Verba, "Latina Girls: 'We're Like Sisters—Most Times!,'" in *Urban Girls Revisited: Building Strengths*, ed. Bonnie Leadbetter and Niobe Way (New York University Press, 2005).

11 Title I, Part A (Title I) of the Elementary and Secondary Education Act, as amended by the Every Student Succeeds Act (ESEA), provides financial assistance to local educational agencies (LEAs) and schools with high numbers or high percentages of children from low-income families to help ensure that all children meet challenging state academic standards.

12 Lilia Fernández, "Telling Stories About School: Using Critical Race and Latino Critical Theories to Document Latina/Latino Education and Resistance," *Qualitative Inquiry* 8, no. 1 (2002): 45–65.

13 Noddings, *Caring: A Feminine Approach*; Noddings, *The Challenge to Care in Schools*.

14 McKamey, "Restorying 'Caring'"; Veloria, "You Know What It's Like."

15 Lynn M. Owens and Catherine D. Ennis, "The Ethic of Care in Teaching: An Overview of Supportive Literature," *Quest* 57, no. 4 (2005): 392–425.

16 Janie V. Ward and Carmen Veloria, "Promoting Latina and African American Girls' Self-Construction in Urban Educational Settings," *Race, Ethnicity, and Education: Racial Identity in Education* 9, no. 3 (2006): 39–56.

17 Michael Heise, "Are Single-Sex Schools Inherently Unequal?," *Cornell Law Faculty Publications* 714 (2004), https://scholarship.law.cornell.edu/facpub/714.

18 Teresa A. Hughes, "The Advantages of Single-Sex Education." *Online Submission* 23, no. 2 (2006).

19 Sandra L. Swain and Douglas M. Harvey, "Single-Sex Computer Classes: An Effective Alternative." *TechTrends* 46, no. 6 (2002): 17–20.

20 Jill McLean Taylor, Carol Gilligan, and Amy M. Sullivan, *Between Voice and Silence: Women and Girls, Race and Relationships* (Harvard University Press, 1997).

21 Luis Ponjuán, *Ensuring the Success of Latino Males in Higher Education: A National Imperative*, ed. Victor B. Sáenz, Luis Ponjuán, and Julie López Figueroa (Stylus Publishing, 2016).

22 Jill Denner and Nora Dunbar, "Negotiating Femininity: Power and Strategies of Mexican American Girls," *Sex Roles* 50 (2004): 301–14; Veloria, "You Know What It's Like."

23 Taylor, Veloria, and Verba, "Latina Girls"; Veloria, "You Know What It's Like"; Carmen Veloria, "Dusting Off: Reflections and Recollections from the Field," *Opportunity Matters: Journal of Access and Opportunity in Education* 2, no. 1 (2016): 17–27.

24 Taylor, Veloria, and Verba, "Latina Girls."

25 Veloria, "You Know What It's Like."

26 Aída Hurtado, "Theory in the Flesh: Toward an Endarkened Epistemology," *International Journal of Qualitative Studies in Education* 16, no. 2 (2003): 215–25; Veloria, "You Know What It's Like"; Veloria, "Dusting Off."

27 Veloria, "You Know What It's Like"; Veloria, "Dusting Off."

28 Veloria, "You Know What It's Like"; Veloria, "Dusting Off."

29 Veloria, "You Know What It's Like"; Veloria, "Dusting Off."

30 Dennis Carlson, "Hope Without Illusion: Telling the Story of Democratic Educational Renewal," *International Journal of Qualitative Studies in Education* 18, no. 1 (2005): 21–45.

31 Gloria Anzaldúa, "Haciendo Caras, Una Entrada," in *Making Face, Making Soul/ Haciendo Caras: Creative and Critical Perspective by Feminist of Color*, ed. Gloria Anzaldúa (Aunt Lute Books, 1990), xxv–xxvi.

32 Bartolomé, "Authentic Cariño."

33 E.g., Beauboeuf-Lafontant, "A Womanist Experience"; Noddings, *Caring: A Feminine Approach*; Noddings, *The Challenge to Care in Schools*; Valenzuela, *Subtractive Schooling*.

34 Valenzuela, *Subtractive Schooling*.

35 Valenzuela, *Subtractive Schooling*, 23.

36 Cori Salmerón, Nathaly Batista-Morales, and Angela Valenzuela, "Translanguaging Pedagogy as an Enactment of Authentic Cariño and an Antidote to Subtractive Schooling," *Association of Mexican American Educators Journal* 15, no. 3 (2021): 30–46.

37 Christopher S. Rugaber, "Pay Gap Between College Grads and Everyone Else at a Record," *USA Today*, January 12, 2017.

38 Kayla J. Crawley, et al., "A Proposal for Building Social Capital to Increase College Access for Low-Income Students," *Journal of Educational Leadership and Policy Studies* 3, no. 1 (2019).

39 Luis C. Moll, "Some Key Issues in Teaching Latino Students," *Language Arts* 65, no. 5 (1988): 465–72.

40 Antrop-González and De Jesús, "Toward a Theory of Critical Care."

41 Antrop-González and De Jesús, "Toward a Theory of Critical Care," 413.

42 Gloria Anzaldúa and Cherríe Moraga, eds., *This Bridge Called My Back: Writings by Radical Women of Color* (State University of New York Press, 1981).

43 Patricia Ewick and Susan S. Silbey, "Subversive Stories and Hegemonic Tales: Toward a Sociology of Narrative," *Law and Society Review* 29, no. 2 (1995): 197–226.

44 Belenky, Mary Field, Blythe McVicker Clinchy, Nancy Rule Goldberger, and Jill Mattuck Tarule. *Women's Ways of Knowing: The Development of Self, Voice, and Mind*, 2nd ed. (Basic Books, 1997).

45 Marnie W. Curry, "Will You Stand for Me? Authentic Cariño and Transformative Rites of Passage in an Urban High School," *American Educational Research Journal* 53, no. 4 (2016): 892.

46 Carlson, "Hope Without illusion."

47 James Paul Gee, "Two Styles of Narrative Construction and Their Linguistic and Educational Implications," *Discourse Processes* 12, no. 3 (1989): 287–307.

48 Victor B. Saenz and Luis Ponjuán, "The Vanishing Latino Male in Higher Education," *Journal of Hispanic Higher Education* 8, no. 1 (2009): 54–89.

Chapter Nine

Early Education and Beyond

Centering Latino Children and Families in Policymaking

MARTA T. ROSA

Editor's Note

In this chapter, we learn from the testimonio of Marta Rosa, who grew up in the city of Chelsea, Massachusetts, and who served on the Chelsea City Council and was elected to the School Committee during the city's tumultuous education reform era in the 1990s. According to Marta Rosa: "I ran for School Committee as an opportunity to ensure that Latinos had a voice in the future of Chelsea Public Schools. I also ran because I deeply believe in the power of education, especially early childhood education, and wanted to make sure all education discussions were inclusive. This is what continues to be my life's work and passion."

In the following testimonio, Marta Rosa shares critical insights about the history of Chelsea's Latino politics, especially during the 1990s when Boston University (BU) became the "receiver" of the underperforming Chelsea Public Schools. She recounts how a diverse coalition of Latino residents organized resistance against the BU takeover of the schools. She also reflects upon her leadership roles in the field of early childhood education and laments the fact that the lack of affordable childcare continues to be a serious concern in Massachusetts, where the cost of living is high. Although Massachusetts established the Department of Early Education and Care (EEC) in 2005 and launched its Universal Pre-Kindergarten (UPK) initiative (serving children from age two years, nine months, until kindergarten), there continue to be disparities in the numbers of Latino families that can access UPK. A study by the Education Trust found that Black and Latino children are the least likely to attend a high-quality state-funded preschool in the nation's largest urban areas. Their research on twenty-six states found that none of the states truly provided high-quality and high access for Black and Latino three- and four-year-olds.[1] Rosa discusses these disparities for Latino families and presents an asset-based critique about what constitutes "high-quality" early childhood education and what "high-quality" childcare means for Latino families.

Throughout Rosa's testimonio she stresses the importance of having educators that represent and understand the cultural backgrounds of their students and how this is key for their students' educational and life success. Rosa notes that attracting qualified multilingual teachers for the low-paying early childhood field is a persistent problem both nationally and locally. In 2022, only 14% of the EEC workforce of early childhood educators in Massachusetts were Latina.[2] The American Community Survey showed that nationally the median pay for childcare workers and preschool teachers was $25,000 annually, or a median wage of $15.28 per hour.[3] In Massachusetts, the median yearly income for childcare workers and preschool teachers was $32,000, or a median wage of $21.63 per hour. Indeed, these are not living wages, especially when the average yearly cost for childcare in Massachusetts is estimated to be $17,687.[4] Rosa's testimonio is a powerful call to action for our leaders to increase wages for early childcare educators, to recruit more multilingual and multicultural teachers, and to invest in more quality, affordable childcare for Latino children in Massachusetts and beyond.

LORNA RIVERA

I often watch my busy two-year-old granddaughter, Valentina, while she builds with blocks, talks to her dolls, or throws the ball. It takes such effort. Her face is serious and explosive with excitement when she gets it right. Valentina's best playmate is her mom, my daughter. They sing songs, play with blocks, and dance together. They talk about shapes as they wash the dishes, and count while making dinner. Valentina's great-grandmother, my mom joins the fun. She plays Spanish games or shares a nursery rhyme from Puerto Rico and sometimes I join the games too. Amazing growth happens every moment of every day because children's play is how they learn.

Watching Valentina grow and learn with us is a testament to the love and care our family has for our children. This is the same kind of love that

I have seen over the last thirty years, working in the field of early education with Latino families. Despite the many challenges the Latino community endures, we are very family orientated, treasure our children, and want only the best for them. I have always wondered, what if we could just meet families where they are and build on their innate strengths with respect for their traditions, beliefs, and wants? What if every child in Massachusetts had access to safe, caring, and stimulating environments? What if we could provide high-quality early education and care for all? This has been my life's work, and this is my story.

From Teacher to Policymaking

I was born in Puerto Rico and moved to Chelsea, Massachusetts, in 1968. This was a time when Puerto Ricans were migrating to greater Boston in large numbers, and my family chose to live in Chelsea. When I arrived, there was no bilingual education. The way the school system dealt with children arriving from Puerto Rico was to place us in lower grades because we didn't speak English.

Although I was an excellent student in Puerto Rico and was supposed to be enrolled in the sixth grade, they enrolled me in a fourth-grade classroom, and I lost two years. Many of us did. The fourth-grade teacher noticed that I was a fast learner. She felt bad for me, and she gave me fifth- and sixth-grade material because she knew the curriculum was too easy for me. I quickly became a straight A student, and I remained an honors student until high school graduation. But that was not the case for many of my peers.

Until 1973, Chelsea was predominantly a Jewish community, but there was a huge fire that drove a lot of families out of the city and the Puerto Rican community remained. Within about fifteen years, Chelsea became a predominantly Latino city. First, it was Puerto Ricans, and then came Dominicans, followed by Central Americans. Despite the growing number of Latino students in Chelsea, I was only one of four Puerto Rican students in my fourth-grade class.

There was little effort to support the needs and strengths of Latino students. I remember feeling horrible because I was so much older than my peers. It was an isolating experience, where the schools tried to take away my language and culture. One time when I was in fifth grade a teacher sent me to the office because I was speaking Spanish with the only other Spanish-speaking girl during lunch. Maybe that's where my activism began.

I did not go to the office. Instead, I went home to get my mom. I just knew I had done nothing wrong. Fifty-five years later I still remember the incident and it provokes the same anger. I knew, even then, that the lack of support for English learners, the mistreatment, the isolation, and the "grade back policy" was unfair and detrimental to all of us.

My entry to this field in 1977 was as an early childhood educator at the Kangaroo's Pouch/El Buche del Canguro in Chelsea. The Head Start Act of 1981 rapidly expanded early education in urban areas, including the Greater Boston area, but I soon realized that Latino children were underserved by the early education and care system across the region. Latino families are an extremely diverse constituency. But whether Puerto Rican born in the US or just arriving from the Caribbean or Central or South America, all Latino families need quality, accessible, and affordable early childhood education and care services for their young children. I wanted to make sure that students and their families never had to go through what we did. Bilingual education had passed in Massachusetts in 1971, and children had the right to receive support in their native language. But many families did not know their rights. This was a time when Chelsea Public Schools was in complete disarray. There was a lot of mismanagement and corruption, students were dropping out of high school in high numbers, English language services were limited, and the district did not care to engage Latino families in their children's education. This was around the time when I became an activist.

Back then, I called myself a Chelsea-Rican because I grew up both in Chelsea and Puerto Rico. I knew then that one of the things I needed to learn was about the experience of immigrants who were coming to Chelsea because I am not an immigrant. The immigrant experience is different than mine, and I wanted to better understand it. There are a lot of unspoken feelings among Latinos about the fact that Puerto Ricans are citizens who don't have to worry about immigration status like our peers. But the truth is Puerto Ricans were colonized and colonialism has its impact on our community, one that is not understood, taught, or discussed. To bring our Latino community together in Chelsea, the Chelsea Commission on Hispanic Affairs/*La Comision de Asuntos Hispanos de Chelsea*, a group I cofounded, developed a series of cultural forums. I am a strong believer that to be a good efficient advocate and activist, you need to educate yourself. You need to understand your colleagues' lived experiences; you need to know where your peers are about the work in front of you; and above all you need to identify realistic, intentional ways in which everyone can contribute.

We created cultural forums, where we learned about each other. We explored and learned about the Puerto Rican experience, the Dominican, Salvadorian, and Guatemalan experience, and that of other groups. We learned about the immigrants coming from the Mexican border, and we learned about the hardships, the struggles of each group. We shared our lived experiences, and this brought about a sense of understanding and unity. We did this because unfortunately our history is not taught in the schools. There is a tremendous deficit within our education system; we don't learn our own history. We also learned that despite the challenges we all faced, families cared so deeply about their children, and what happens to their children, that education and the children are a uniting factor. I believe that this work was foundational in what happened next, and what would ultimately change my life.

In 1989, the Chelsea School committee, with the support of state legislation, gave Boston University (BU) control of Chelsea Public Schools. It was shocking because the School Committee, the legislature, and BU made their plans without the Latino community's input at all. The Latino community comprised most of the school district's population. Yet those parents were never informed nor consulted about what was happening with the takeover, even though at that time we were already the majority of public school students. In their negotiations BU was working with the White city and state elected officials, the White-led PTA, and all the White leadership in the community behind the scenes. When the news started reaching the Latino community that decisions were being made without input from the largest group of Chelsea Public Schools stakeholders, Latino students, and families, we began to organize. We mobilized over two hundred Latino parents first to St. Rose Church for a meeting with BU officials and then to city hall not once, but several times, in protest of a contract that had not been discussed with most of the school system families: the Latino community. Working with the teachers' union, attorneys like Roger Rice, and some interested Boston leaders, like Felix Arroyo, and Nelson Merced, we learned what was at stake. I remember one of the first meetings I attended with the BU management team. The way Latinos were ignored and told we were too late to be part of the discussions was deplorable. It was a horrible experience to go to city hall and watch non-Chelsea White folks sitting in the power seats making decisions with no concern for the Latino children. None! Many of us were in tears. It was that night that, with the support of others, I decided to run for School Committee.

What the world needs to understand is that the BU takeover was not about improving the education of Chelsea's kids. It was an experiment that included plans for gentrifying our community. Chelsea was described as "the perfect laboratory"—and the planning discussions included things outside of the scope of public schools including housing, local business, and even research projects that would help BU's rankings. As a point of reference, Chelsea's BU team was being managed by their School of Management, not even their School of Education. Running a campaign is never easy, but we Latinos realized we need each other. We knew that Puerto Ricans have the right to vote and we made sure that we were registering as many voters as possible. But at the same time, Dominican and Central American families who had just arrived needed to be a part of the movement.

We intentionally identified roles for all Latinos. Leafletting, knocking on doors, making phone calls, working at park events, showing up at rallies and holding signs, or volunteering for events did not necessitate citizenship status. It was important that all Latinos in Chelsea felt responsible for inciting change. The betterment of the community was all our business; representation at all levels of city government including boards, commissions, and the elected bodies was our priority. We knew that together we could win to ensure the future of generations to come. On November 7, 1989, our effort led me to having the privilege to serve on the Chelsea School Committee, becoming one of the first three Latino elected public officials in the state of Massachusetts.

BU did take over Chelsea Public Schools. And many might ask, so did the movement fail? The movement did not fail. What the BU takeover did was to mobilize the Latino community in Chelsea. After the election, community activism accelerated, and with the support of Multicultural Education, Training and Advocacy (META), we launched a lawsuit against BU and the elected bodies in Chelsea. We demanded to have the contract changed so that it was more focused on asset building, strengthening bilingual education, and intentionally including the Chelsea community in all decisions, particularly the Latino community. After all, public education is paid for by us, the taxpayers. We fought for the BU management team, which guided the contract, to become more reflective of the community. We lost that lawsuit but not our spirit.

We continued organizing and working with other partners, including other researchers like Maria Brisk, Hubie Jones, Marie Kennedy, and Michael

Stone from the College of Public and Community Service at UMass Boston. They worked with the Latino community to develop plans and trainings that would have helped us get ready for when BU would leave—because we were sure they would. These partnerships were grounded in respect, following the lead of community-based organizations, and we developed new leaders. BU eventually left in 2008, and the value of their experimentation is highly debatable.

What we did in Chelsea, in the 1990s, was historic. During that decade, the Latino community found its voice. And it worked because those of us leading the effort for representation found a place in the campaign for every Latino who lived in Chelsea and wanted to be involved. I am very clear that a leader must know when to leave. In 2001 I decided that after fifteen years of activism and nine years in elected office, it was time for me to take a backseat and let others lead. Today, the children who held signs in my first School Committee election hold elected seats on the School Committee and city council. Inclusion worked then and it works today!

Early Education, Latino Children, and Families: Challenges and Opportunities

I spent over thirty years working in the early childhood education and care field, first as a teacher and later as executive director of the Childcare Resource Center, Inc., where we designed and built family support programs and family childcare systems in the Greater Boston area that were high quality, affordable, and culturally responsive. While I was directing the Childcare Resource Center, Inc., I was also a Chelsea School Committee member and later a city councilor. Almost twenty years ago, I moved from direct work and now lead my own consulting firm. My work there includes partnerships with institutions of higher learning and continuing to advocate to strengthen the field of education beginning with the earliest years to college and beyond. Education is the key to success. Since I began my work in Chelsea in the 1980s, I have never forgotten my roots, my love for Latino children and families, and the importance of the early years in helping children succeed; this shapes my policy and advocacy work in this field.

The early childhood education and care field is extremely diverse and at times very confusing. When thinking about early education and care it may be useful to think about three related concepts and how they impact families:

access, affordability, and quality. In terms of access, there are multiple points of entry for families and children within multiple types of programs. Families who need care for their young children have to consider different options including family childcare homes, private childcare centers, early or head start, nannies or nanny shares, informal care, or even staying at home with their children. The higher the income a family has, the more access they have to different options. Therefore, access and affordability are connected.

For Latinx families, and in particular newer immigrants, many of these options are not possible because they are cost prohibitive. My niece paid $3,000 per month for care when she had two young children in childcare, which is $36,000 per year. When we think about the high number of low-income Latino families in the state, most families simply cannot afford it. While there may be vouchers and programs for very low-income families, there are simply not enough for the families who need them or spots for families that want them. The quality of care a family has access to also depends on how much a parent can afford. Programs with the best paid and trained teachers and a low student-teacher ratio are also the most expensive. And while the government offsets costs by providing categorical funding, vouchers, or free programs, it is simply not enough, leaving families at a loss for how best to care for their youngest children.

Around the 2000s, we were hopeful that this nation would catch up with other nations and seriously invest in early education to improve access, affordability, and access to care. A large body of research emerged that confirmed what we early educators already know. The early years, particularly from ages zero to three, are paramount to a person's lifelong development. In *Neurons to Neighborhoods*, for example, the researchers concluded that during these early years, neurons in the brain connect at their fastest pace, allowing learning to take place faster than at any other period in one's life, that early environments matter, that the needs of young children are not being addressed, and that the nation needs to demand changes to improve early education and care.[5] More importantly, the work highlighted the need for young children to have access to stimulating, structured, safe environments where they can thrive, enjoying learning that propels their future. Those of us in the field thought that the study would shift public opinion and more importantly political support for universal access to early childhood education and care services. But that did not happen.

To address some of these challenges, in 2005 there was a legislative mandate to establish the Massachusetts Department of Early Education and Care

(DEEC). Its mandate was to develop a statewide system to provide childcare and early education services including after-school care to eligible children in the Commonwealth. The department is also responsible for licensing all types of care and ensuring the access, quality, and affordability of programs and services. In addition, DEEC certifies the workforce, providing guidelines for the requirements for all levels of the early childhood education and care workforce. The development of a highly trained workforce is also a challenge that further complicates access and affordability.

For over two decades, there has been a movement to require early childhood teachers to have degrees. Like many states, Massachusetts has provided funding for training and professional development support including scholarship funds. However, people who work in the childcare industry, which is increasingly Black and Latina women, spend long hours with children and have little time left to care for their own families, attend school, and do assignments. In addition, early childhood educators make some of the lowest salaries in the teaching profession. Many early childhood teachers work two jobs, and many times go to food pantries to make ends meet for their own families. Going to school becomes a hardship for many and for their families; although the will and enthusiasm may be high, degree completion takes many years, and the compensation does not increase commensurate with degree attainment. Upon degree attainment, many leave the early childhood field for the public schools or leave the field entirely. Further, low pay deters many people from entering the field, which has led to workforce shortages and fewer options for parents. Across the state, programs have closed classrooms due to a lack of teachers, especially in the infant-toddler age group. In sum, teachers and administrators work long hours with minimal breaks, inadequate pay, and little recognition from society for the invaluable service they provide. This is unjust and has gone unaddressed for decades. The workforce can't afford to live on the salaries paid, and most employers, although they need workers, will not support childcare costs. There is a real disconnect. I believe that better compensation and benefits for the early education and care education workforce is one of the greatest needs in the field.

For Latino families, quality of care is also connected to cultural values. In the Latino community, we want our children to learn about their culture, their language, and their traditions. We are very family oriented and want our children to be cherished and loved. When Latino families are considering early education, they want to know if somebody's going to be attentive and loving to their child. Will someone feed them, cuddle them if they cry, or take care of them when they are hurt? When I was a preschool teacher, I remember a Latina mom asked if someone was going to redo her daughter's hair if it got messy. It was important to her that when she picked up her child, she could walk through her community with her child looking well-kept. This firsthand experience helped me to understand and pay close attention to what parents want for their kids. Another mom worried about the food and whether her child would eat strange foods that did not align with her culture.

Ensuring that a child is loved and that a lot of personal attention is given is a question of quality of care for Latino families, so there are a lot of misgivings within the Latino community about the care of strangers. My grown daughters today would not even think of giving their babies to a childcare center, even though their mother was considered a national expert on early childhood education. They tell me, "Yes but you are not the one in the classroom, right?" They don't trust a stranger; they say, "Maybe at three years old." And families might consider using childcare for a preschooler but not for an infant. My youngest daughter said, "I'm not comfortable with a stranger touching my baby." However, in this country, relative care is not well understood by early education professionals, even though it is what most Latinx families trust and can afford. This creates tremendous conflict. There are ongoing critiques of why Latino children are behind in reading or not up to speed on their literacy skills by kindergarten. Some believe it is because we are the least likely to have been in a structured preschool situation. Others blame families for delays in learning. Few see the potential of kin care, and there is a misconception that children are not learning unless they are in structured licensed childcare centers.

When I watch my granddaughter with her mom and my mom, her *bisabuela*, learning is taking place. The mainstream professionals may not acknowledge the learning that goes on in the relative care space, particularly as it pertains to learning a second language and cultural development. The mainstream fails to recognize the value of children coming in speaking Spanish. It is an asset, not a deficit. Instead, schools, including early education centers, encourage Latino families to wipe Spanish away. Now, if you live in Brookline, Newton, Wellesley, or Weston, and you speak two languages, you are considered cultured. If you can speak two languages by the age of five, you speak French and English, my God you are amazing. But if you come speaking Spanish or learning Spanish from birth that is most likely not celebrated; it is seen as a deficit.

We must shift that deficit narrative, and there are good examples of how we can do this. When I was leading the Childcare Resource Center, Inc., we provided trainings to family childcare providers in Chelsea and Chinatown because we knew these were spaces where immigrant families would most likely have enough trust to send their children. We also developed formalized programs for supporting kin care, acknowledging that for many immigrant families, this was their preferred or only choice. At our family trainings, for example, we helped parents talk about expectations with their kin about how best to take care of their babies and toddlers, as these conversations were not always easy. Let's face it, it's hard to tell your mother how to care for your child. You may not want to give your child cookies, but that grandma is going to give them a cookie. We would also expose caregivers and parents to community resources like libraries, local parks, playgroups, and things they could do at home to promote literacy and language development, as well as support services for caregivers. Our goal is to support early childhood educators and caretakers, wherever they were.

Unfortunately, DEEC does not fully support the work in familial placements, as they see themselves as a licensing and protection entity—and kin care is too complicated for them. One DEEC commissioner even said to me, "That's where abuse happens." Seriously? I could not believe it. My kids stayed with my mother until they were ready for preschool. Most of my professional Latina friends and colleagues preferred to leave their young children with family. In the suburbs, when middle-class women help each other with coordinated informal care we applaud them for building social networks. But when a poor person or an immigrant uses relative care, there's something wrong; it is risky. It is time to change the narrative; respecting cultural preferences does not translate to supporting neglect. This is a reminder that it is important to analyze where the policies come from and who they're made for, especially punitive policies that may impact one group more than others. Think about what our racist structures sometimes perpetuate unintentionally.

My mantra as the leader of Childcare Resource Center, Inc., where I sat at important policy tables, was "if we know the children are there, then it's our responsibility to make sure it's a good quality place for them." Today I feel the same way. I was reminded of this during COVID-19 in 2020 while working on a project with immigrant families. I learned that in Somerville there was an underground network of childcare services that included transportation so that essential low- wage workers could work and take care of their families. Underground networks exist because policymakers are turning a blind eye to the communities' real needs. And communities are resilient and will take care of their own. Unfortunately, we have not fully addressed issues of access, affordability, and high-quality care. Some may believe the challenge has gotten more complex as demand for these services has increased. And discussions on how to improve these systems continue to take place without the voices of Black and Brown families.

The Future

Early childhood education and care is a must have for Latinx and all families in the United States. Not just because it allows working families to be productive at work but more importantly because children deserve the best start in life. I really believe that we in the United States should do what other nations have done and provide this type of education and care, free for families who want it; the US needs universally accessible early childhood education and care services where teachers are well compensated. There is an opportunity for the state of Massachusetts to impact the education of Latino students for the long term by providing learning support and adequate childcare at the earliest age possible. It will, however, take an intentional effort at the DEEC to collect the data, analyze it, and ensure the right people are at the table to develop culturally relevant and appropriate programming.

"Where are the Latino children?" must be a key question. It is negligent to not be able to document the number of Latinx children using services and/or needing services. The state must collect the necessary data and consult Latino educators and families to inform itself about how best to reach, care for, and educate the youngest Latino children who make up a large percentage of the population. The state should no longer close its eyes to the needs of Latino working families and their children. The future of the Commonwealth's economy depends on how well we care for our youngest residents. And right now, the fastest-growing population within our schools and communities is the Latinx population. The state ought to expand funding to include strategic initiatives focused on supporting Latinx early childhood teachers' professional growth.

Local, state, and federal legislatures, governors, Congress, and even the White House pay a lot of lip service to the value of early childhood education and care, yet we still do not have universal access to high-quality care. Some say it is because of a lack of funding, but my thirty years of experience has taught me that funding is not the issue. If we spend even a small percentage of what the government spends on wars, we would have enough to fully fund universal early education and care. The issue is that there is a lack of political will. Most elected officials in Congress are very far removed from the challenges families face in accessing affordable high-quality care because their families do not have this problem. I am hopeful that as more women enter Congress who themselves see the struggles of working families, like Congresswomen Ayanna Presley and Alexandria Ocasio Cortez, we will see change happen. If the needs of children and families guided funding decisions, we would have had universal early education and care for all decades ago. Today, some communities are beginning to explore this option, but we have a long way to go.

To make early childhood education and care a reality, we need more advocacy, particularly at the policy level. Yes, we have Latinas who are leading large organizations in Lawrence, Worcester, Springfield, New Bedford, and even Boston. We have Latina teachers, school leaders, and even professors. But few if any are sitting at the policy and planning decision-making tables, which impact the future of Latino children. Throughout my career, I had the privilege of sitting at the city, state, and national policymaking tables, but unfortunately, I was almost always the only Latina in the room.

Middle-class White women started the field of early education and care, and even today most of the leadership in this field, particularly in Massachusetts, continues to be this demographic, which means that those making policy and program decisions remain predominantly White. In my work, I noticed that there was a savior mentality that permeates discussions, "Oh, let's do this for the Latino kids," without knowing what Latino families want for their children. There is also a reluctance to bring diverse ideas to policy discussions. We have had several commissioners leading DEEC who have not invited Latino leaders to their planning table. One even told me that she had no time to convene any more groups. Representation matters because we need people who have direct experience working and learning from Latino families to influence early education and care policy and practice. If we do not have Latinos at the decision-making table, the needs of

Latino children are not acknowledged, or understood; their assets are also never recognized. The absence of Latinos at the policy-making tables is not because there is a lack of well-prepared Latinx people; it's because diversity of opinion and experience is not valued by those in power.

I have had a wonderful career as a teacher, activist, elected official, senior executive, thought leader, and advocate. Today I see my role more as that of mentor, especially for those who want to run for office. I have seen what we were able to accomplish together in Chelsea and in other parts of the state. I am proud and believe the work continues with a new generation of Latino leaders that we should support. As an advocate for children, youth, and families, I ask people to keep Latino children at the center of their discussions. We need to ensure that children are thriving in environments that provide a healthy, safe, and quality learning experience.

Our children deserve better. An investment in our children is an investment in the future of this nation. Moreover, the Latino population is the fastest growing in this country; not investing in the education of Latinos from cradle to grave is not just myopic but may be the downfall of this nation. A stronger safety net for all children guarantees a stronger family, a stronger community, a better-prepared society, and a thriving economy in the long term! Our future depends on it.

Chapter Nine

1   Gillispie, Carrie, *Young Learners, Missed Opportunities: Ensuring That Black and Latino Children Have Access to High-Quality State-Funded Preschool* (Education Trust, 2019), https://edtrust.org/wp-content/uploads/2014/09/Young-Learners-Missed -Opportunities.pdf.

2   Steven Ruggles, et al., *IPUMS USA: Version 13.0 [2022 American Community Survey]* (IPUMS, 2023).

3   Ruggles et al., *IPUMS USA.*

4   "Living Wage Calculation for Massachusetts" Massachusetts Institute of Technology, 2023, https://livingwage.mit.edu/states/25.

5   Institute of Medicine and National Research Council, *From Neurons to Neighborhoods: The Science of Early Childhood Development*, ed. Jack P. Shonkoff and Deborah A. Phillips (National Academies Press, 2000), https://doi.org/10.17226/9824.

PART III

Culturally
Sustaining
Student-Centered
Practices and
Programs

Chapter Ten

Student Community- Engaged Policy Research for Transformative Educational Success

ASHLEY TORRES CARRASQUILLO, ESTER R. SHAPIRO, AND LORNA RIVERA

This chapter describes findings from a participatory evaluation of the Latino Leadership Opportunity Program (LLOP) at the Mauricio Gastón Institute for Latino Community Development and Public Policy (University of Massachusetts Boston).[1] The LLOP was created in 1986 by the Inter-University Programs on Latino Research (IUPLR), a national consortium of Latinx-focused research centers in the US. The IUPLR established LLOPs so Latinx undergraduate students could gain policy research skills by working with faculty and community leaders, positioning them as future leaders in academia, community-based organizations, and other settings. Today, IUPLR Research Centers are located at over twenty-two colleges and universities across the US, and these centers vary widely in their institutional affiliations, their missions, and the communities that they serve. Some of the original IUPLR Centers that had LLOPs include the Dominican Studies Institute (City University New York), Center for Puerto Rican Studies (Hunter College), Julian Samora Research Institute (Michigan State University), Center for Latino/a and Latin American Studies (Wayne State University), Chicano Studies Center (University of Texas El Paso), Chicano Studies Center (University of California Los Angeles), Center for Mexican American Studies (University of Houston), Cuban Research Institute, (Florida International University), and Gastón Institute (University of Massachusetts Boston).[2]

While LLOP programs varied by the IUPLR sites, common elements across sites included a recruitment process designed to identify and select academically accomplished Latinx students and other students dedicated to working with Latinx communities and an emphasis on mentoring, applied policy research, and leadership development training. Originally the program culminated in a national summer leadership institute in Washington, DC, where LLOP students from across the country presented their research and met with leaders from the Congressional Hispanic Caucus. During the national summer leadership institute, the LLOP students learned about policymaking, community organizing, building solidarity, and how to use research to advocate for social change. Currently, the Gastón Institute's LLOP is the last remaining of the original IUPLR programs. The LLOP continues to emphasize undergraduate training in policy research connected to community activism that offers transformative knowledge, opportunities for sharing culturally affirming "counter stories," working with mentors who share their struggles/successes, and developing new networks that amplify power and promote social change.

The Contexts of the LLOP Evaluation

Programs like the LLOP aim to increase Latinx undergraduate student success, so it is important to highlight a few realities of Latinx communities in Massachusetts. As the introduction to this volume illustrates, Latinx communities in Massachusetts are very diverse, with large numbers from Puerto Rico, the Dominican Republic, and Central and South American nations. As described in Colón and Frau-Ramos (chap. 3), Puerto Rico remains a colony of the US, and consistent migration to Massachusetts from the island has been happening since the 1940s.[3] Latinx migration to Massachusetts has been motivated by political instability: these include immigrants from the Dominican Republic beginning in the 1960s after the fall of the dictator Trujillo, Central Americans during the 1980s, and many US military and covert interventions in regional conflicts and across the Caribbean and Latin America, including Colombia, Brazil, and Venezuela.[4] According to the Gastón Institute (2020), 5% of the state's Latino population identifies as Afro-Latino and the number of Afro-Latinos in Massachusetts has increased by 57% since 2009.[5] The Greater Boston area also has a high number of undocumented/mixed-status families and Latinx subgroups with Indigenous identities.[6] About one in four Massachusetts Latinx live in poverty,[7] and these abysmal socioeconomic outcomes are intertwined with other barriers to educational opportunity described in this volume.

Our lives as scholars, teachers, students, and community members traverse these realities. Before we discuss the findings from our participatory evaluation of the LLOP, we describe how our experiences as first-generation college students inform and inspire our research, teaching, and learning with the LLOP. We seek to demystify and democratize research by using multivoice narrative methods to present our positionality in relation to the LLOP students' *caminos* and to highlight our shared experiences.[8]

ASHLEY'S POSITIONALITY

For this reflection, I, Ashley Torres Carrasquillo, describe the ways in which my experiences influence this and future research projects with Latinx students and other racialized and politicized communities in the US, Latin America, and the Caribbean. I am a queer Black Boricua, with thick lips and roasted caramel skin, in constant resistance to other(ing) due to the social conditions of racialization, gendering, and dis/ability. Born to a Black woman from the urban coast and a *jíbaro*/farmer from the countryside of the archipelago of Puerto Rico, we were poor, growing up in government housing in a *caserío*/the hood, in Santurce, Puerto Rico. There I witnessed the effects of state-sanctioned violence in the form of a militarized police force, disenfranchisement, employment discrimination, health and education disparities, infrastructural neglect, and gender and sexual violence. As a young Black girl, displaced from the archipelago of Puerto Rico due to sociopolitical violence, I had a peculiar experience in educational spaces in Massachusetts. *La bienvenida* to my new middle school was not unusual, I later learned. I was questioned about the ways my hips moved while I walked from my only classroom to the lunchroom by the only Puertorriqueña teacher in the school. As the weeks went by, she insisted that I was exaggerating my walk to draw attention. This is one of my earliest experiences in Massachusetts public schools, and from that moment forward I was often placed in in-school suspension for being distracting to other students due to my gold bracelets bangling or for not following instructions or for skipping class. During this time, I started losing interest in school because for two years I was mainly in one classroom with one teacher and over twenty-five students from mainly Spanish-speaking countries. I spent two years not being academically challenged and being overpoliced, criminalized, and oversexualized by teachers who believed that I was a *negrita pobre de Santurce*.

I am an LLOP alum from the class of 2017 and was later a teaching assistant for the 2019 cohort. My involvement with the Gastón Institute started in 2017, after meeting Dr. Lorna Rivera, who was my first-ever Latina professor in college. In the aftermath of Donald Trump's devastating 2016 election win, I then met Dr. Ester Shapiro at a university-wide gathering that was mobilizing campus activist responses. At that time, I represented the Women's Center, among other student organizations, and Dr. Shapiro encouraged me to join the LLOP class of 2017 that she would be teaching the following semester. Later, I worked at the Gastón Institute as a research intern, at first transcribing research about health disparities; later I became a graduate research assistant and led the LLOP participatory evaluation research team.

The LLOP was a transformative experience for me because it offered me additional language and approaches to critically question and understand our/my own lived experiences[9] as an Afro-Latina. We learned how to be critical of social justice[10] and collaborative[11] ways of doing research with communities.[12] The LLOP readings, class discussions, and experiential learning activities that took place in Holyoke, Massachusetts, radically changed my outlook on academic research, as it meant that there was space for people who are not in the academy to be able to influence and guide research that improves their material reality.

My LLOP experience shaped my leadership as a young community organizer who since high school had been working two jobs and advocating for access to safe housing. While my family deeply believed in the power of education, and I was expected to obtain a bachelor's degree, it was urgent that I had to work and provide additional income to support my family as they struggled to pay for housing. Therefore, being a student was not always a top priority; it took me eight years to graduate with my BA. Then in 2020, I graduated with a master of science in critical ethnic and communities studies at the University of Massachusetts Boston. LLOP helped me cultivate relationships with other racialized students, alumni, graduate student mentors, and faculty mentors (many of whom worked as community organizers and community-based researchers), and these relationships supported my personal and familial goals, as well as some community goals. I was inspired by critical ethnic studies and Black feminist scholars who engaged in community struggles, so the LLOP community helped me clearly identify the various *caminos*/pathways I wanted to set

out, as a community organizer and collaborative researcher. It helped situate me in where I come from, which is the place where I understand the
world—with a poor dis/abled queer Black feminist consciousness and an
urgency to continue to do antiracist and decolonial work with racialized
urban communities in the Caribbean.

ESTER'S POSITIONALITY

I am known as Ester Shapiro, PhD, a White-passing clinical psychologist,
impatient feminist, and enduringly rebellious elder who speaks unaccented
English and loves teaching and learning, even though according to my Cuban
Eastern-European Jewish-American South Florida family, "teaching doesn't
pay." In 1960, I was eight years old and arrived in virulently racist, English-
only nativist, segregated Miami schools. I was placed by a well-meaning third-
grade teacher in a classroom for the "mentally retarded" to learn English,
although that's not all I learned. My family quickly accepted US Jewish
identities as "honorary Whites," building successful family businesses while
maintaining ties to conservative Cuban-American politics.[13] First in my
family to graduate from college, defying the expectation that I would choose
marriage and motherhood in my early twenties, I studied family-centered
resources promoting societal gender equity, and this is still unfinished business. Choosing my life path/camino required financial independence, yet
ignorant about university careers, I trained as a clinical psychologist.

Fortunately, one of my PhD mentors, Castellano Turner, recruited me
in the fall of 1989 to help start the UMass Boston new clinical psychology
PhD program's component of culturally informed community practice
training. That fall I attended the panel opening UMass Boston's Mauricio
Gastón Institute. Director Miren Uriarte introduced Frank Bonilla, founder
of IUPLR and CUNY's Center for Puerto Rican Studies. Bonilla spoke about
a nationwide vision of university centers coproducing activist knowledge
with local communities, increasing political power, and driving policy
change. Within UMass Boston's LLOP, I have taught research methods,
taught the seminar in 2017 and 2019, and mentored undergraduates conducting culturally/developmentally informed, gender-equitable, resource rights
approaches, supporting shared resilience through "wellness as fairness."[14]

In 1993, when the Gastón Institute published the first book on Latino students in Massachusetts, I worked with a team to coauthor *Poverty, Resilience,*

and Academic Achievement among Latino College Students and High School Dropouts.[15] This chapter highlights entanglements of poverty and educational inequalities experienced by Boston Latino youth, rejecting "defectology" and appreciating contextualized decision-making by poor Latino students who dropped out of high school. Using interviews and quantitative measures of personal, familial, and cultural resources that protect student success, we identified meaningful factors consistent with this volume's emphasis on critical race/cultural wealth and culturally affirming environments. At UMass Boston, I teach research as a human right, demystifying "research" by offering students training in community-engaged, systems-minded participatory methods, while cultivating visionary leadership through partnerships mobilizing knowledge for justice.

LORNA'S POSITIONALITY

I am Lorna Rivera, the daughter of Puerto Rican migrants, born and raised in Chicago's Humboldt Park neighborhood and the first person in my family to graduate from college. I started elementary school as a bilingual student, but by second grade I was no longer "limited English proficient." Although I was always an excellent student, I did not have college aspirations because I was on the vocational track at my high school. My older sister dropped out of school, and in my family, we valued working over education. I never participated in after-school programs, summer camps, or sports activities, and I worked every day after school when I was in high school. My father worked as a welder and my mother as a cashier, and they did their best to support our family. College was never discussed in my family; it never seemed like a possibility for me or my sisters. It was my best friend's sister who encouraged me to apply to DePaul University.

College was completely a culture shock for me, but that is another longer story. In my freshman year, I met DePaul University sociologist Felix Padilla, who was researching gangs in my neighborhood. He offered me a work-study job as a research assistant at the Center for Latino Research (an IUPLR center) where he was the director. At the time, I did not fully appreciate how special Dr. Padilla was. He was one of the founders of the field of Latino studies and wrote the groundbreaking books *Puerto Rican Chicago, Latino Ethnic Consciousness: The Case of Mexican Americans and Puerto Ricans in Chicago,* and *The Gang as an American Enterprise.*[16] As an undergraduate research assistant at the Center for Latino Research, I helped with the production and distribution of the *Latino Studies Journal* and had the opportunity to contribute to several research projects led by amazing Latino Studies faculty. The knowledge, mentorship, and loving support I received from the Center for Latino Research's faculty, staff, and students proved to be critical to both my undergraduate and later my graduate school successes.

As a member of the LLOP in the 1990–91 Midwest cohort, I attended summer sessions at UCLA's Chicano Studies Program, where I learned from the nation's leading Chicano studies and Puerto Rican studies scholars. I learned from other Latinx student leaders who represented different universities and the Latinx cultural diaspora from Florida (Cubans and Colombians), Texas (Tejanos), New York (Puerto Ricans and Dominicans), California (Chicanos and Central Americans), and Illinois (Puerto Ricans and Mexicans). I conducted original research as an LLOP student, and this transformed the trajectory of my future.

I had planned to be an elementary school social studies teacher, but when given the opportunity to research the Chicago Public Schools (which I attended) I felt empowered to learn more about how to change public policies and address systemic racial/ethnic inequalities. Dr. Padilla inspired me to pursue a PhD in sociology at Northeastern University in Boston. As a doctoral student, I struggled with feelings of isolation and marginalization and other challenges experienced by many Latinas in graduate school. But I continued to rely upon mentors who guided me and supported me and who were like extended family for me. After finishing my PhD in sociology in 2001, I was hired as a professor at the College of Public and Community Service with a joint appointment at the Gastón Institute at UMass Boston. For over twenty-five years, I have had the privilege of being an LLOP faculty mentor to many Latinx college students who will be our next generation of leaders. It is an honor to share my cultural wealth with my students and to be inspired by their educational journeys.

Methodology

The purpose of our participatory evaluation was to understand LLOP's impact on the undergraduate students who were participants between 1994 and 2020. Consistent with principles and methods of Participatory Action

Research (also see Kruegger-Henney, Dabel, and Ali, in this volume), students from the LLOP cohorts 2017 and 2019 designed the evaluation plan, which included the recruitment of program alumni, conducting interviews, analyzing the collected data, identifying themes, constructing narratives, and reporting findings. In March 2020, when the COVID pandemic required that all our classes and research meetings take place remotely, our research team completed the evaluation described in this chapter.

As the first step, LLOP students learned about cultural wealth frameworks related to Latinx student success (See Escalera, chapter 5, for a description of Latinx Cultural Wealth Frameworks.) The LLOP has been running since 1994, with twenty-four cohorts, so we created a database of all LLOP program participants by cohort years.[17] We used social media outlets (e.g., Facebook, LinkedIn, Google) to locate alumni. Interviews began in May 2019, and they focused on understanding former students' experiences and how the LLOP affected their professional, academic, and life goals. A total of thirty-five interviews were conducted (twenty-six LLOP participants and nine faculty). We interviewed alums from eighteen of the twenty-four cohorts: sixteen in-person and ten by audio/video calls. We transcribed all interviews and used NVivo, a qualitative software program, to explore and identify common themes.

The rest of this chapter will highlight what the LLOP alumni shared in their interviews about their caminos to success. We use caminos (pathways) as both a metaphor and description of critical moments when educators can support positive outcomes for Latinx students and other racialized youth. We explore how the LLOP alumni[18] shared a sense of purpose that built upon a foundation of community cultural wealth. We also describe specific components of the LLOP program including skills building/research training, mentorship, and key turning points in student caminos that expanded networks and supported their leadership development and accomplishments.

Ethnic Consciousness

As Latinx communities include multiple nationalities, immigration statuses, and racialized ethnic origins, students may identify with national origin while also creating their sense of ethnic identity within local *Latinidades*. This consciousness fosters commitments to "give back" to families and communities.[19]

Ethnic consciousness as expressed by our LLOP alumni involves affirmational love of one's culture, traditions, and beliefs and the willingness to be "seen"—for example, wearing clothing associated with the country of origin instead of "blending in." This consciousness also involved an appreciation for solidarity and the collective advancement of the Latinx community. In the following example, an LLOP alum who works as a community organizer described their experience in the seminar, the inspiration gained from mentorship, and the encouragement of the seminar as a group, including students' strength to act:

> LLOP was really the program that sort of started my activism, my social consciousness, my wanting to work with the community. It was Dr. Rivera . . . she's a professor and she's very relatable. Through my LLOP I ended up wanting to become a teacher, to want to help Latinos, inspire them to go on to college. [Professor] Rivera was very instrumental to the relationships I established with other students. They are close friendships that I have still, because of that tight ethnic group. We've gone on vacations together, we communicate all the time, it was an incredible experience. I remember one of the first questions that were asked [in the seminar], who are the Latino leaders, and I think we listed two Latino leaders. But it was powerful because there were very few numbers and that sort of convinced us in our own communities and a lot of us have gone on to do things like that. For me particularly it was transformational, I wanted to do something in my community and ever since then I've been doing it in various different ways.

Another LLOP alum who works at a local community-based organization expressed how LLOP impacted her life and her understanding of her ethnic identity:

> It was definitely an awakening of my dual consciousness as a Mexican American and being able to learn about the struggles. We had also learned about public policy and how it affects Latinas and Latinos in areas that I grew up in and areas that my friends grew up in. [It] was incredible actually. Because

> we see that there's a problem, but you never really understand why there is systematic racism or why folks in our community suffer lower income and are deprived and it was awakening for me. We worked on a project that was focused on transportation and undocumented folks. We focused on trying to see how undocumented folks lived in those areas and how important it was for their livelihood and trying to support folk in using transportation. I find the most passion helping folks in my community.

Another participant who works directly with students of color described how LLOP's seminar supported students and engaged them in hands-on projects using real situations that affected the Latinx community and illuminated ways to make a difference. Ethnic consciousness for this alum then moved beyond just understanding the material effects of being a part of an ethnic group that was invisible in the US Census. During the LLOP seminar the students had the power to change the invisibility narrative by advocating for communities to partake in this national survey, by ensuring that their voices were counted, and by increasing access to resources they urgently needed:

> I will always support LLOP, and I think it is something that every Latino student should take advantage of because it's not just credit or not just a program, it does develop you. . . . The specific campaigns that we were passionate about like the Census. The Census concerned all of us, so we took a big investment into that, and we said we want to have the Latino voice be heard, and we want to make sure that we are recorded and that the Latino population in the state is big and that we matter.

Familismo and the Importance of Family

Family as a motivating factor is a common theme in Latinx Studies and especially in the Latinx-focused higher education literature. Unlike the Anglo/American assumption that "traditional" college students will attend a residential college to break away from family, focus on their individual goals, and develop personal agency, Latinx students draw on family and kinship ties for a sense of heritage and for a sense of giving back to family and community as part of the purpose of education. In the literature on cultural wealth, Yosso and Burciaga use Latinx student cultural capital to describe familial capital as a dimension of cultural wealth: "Familial capital refers to those cultural knowledges nurtured among *familia* (kin) that carry a sense of community history, memory, and cultural intuition."[20]

LLOP alums described how family functions as a primary source of support through college. Students' determination to complete goals is due to familial richness. This richness is evident in the ways in which family plays a main role in encouraging, providing advice, and passing down values. For example, in the following excerpt, an alum described "what keeps him motivated to finish college":

> I think part of it is people just having expectations that I would do well and succeed. Part of it is just wanting to make my family proud, because I'm the first one in the family, and so I want to. So that means a lot to me and that motivates me to do better, to try better, even when it's difficult. . . . I just want to make sure that I keep going. Part of it is proving it to myself, that I can do it, because I, at this point, I'm really sort of committed to finishing school. To complete my degree. And hoping that would bring my success, so that I will be able to make my family proud, and help them out, and build a better life for myself and my family.

Another LLOP alum, who works in the field of public health promoting health equity, explained how she has understood that her values and motivation to succeed are drawn from her parents' experiences:

> My parents are immigrants, I represent low-income, first generation to go to college, in addition to being the first one born here. It's very personal to me and I feel like a sense of my drive is I wanna make sure my parents' immigration experience was not in vain. They never put that pressure on me, but it's a pressure that I feel. Like you guys came here, my grandmother came here. You guys settled in this new country and culture

and language, and I now have an opportunity that you guys never had, so I wanna make the most of it. And because they have been through disadvantages and poverty I see issues differently. I have a different relationship to it and it's not something I read in a textbook. It's something that I lived through, so I had that lived expertise and it drives what I do.

This same participant also described how the process of becoming a leader included connecting to peers at a deeper, more meaningful level of ethnic consciousness through sharing experiences that cultivated new forms of kinship. She identified the importance of a teacher who facilitated those connections. Illustrating caminos, this alum added that her sense of community inspired her to make sure that others believe in their capacities to become leaders who take collective action on behalf of others.

Another LLOP participant described the teachings from his family and how they cultivated a sense of dedication toward bringing about more hopeful futures:

> Some of the greatest contributions have been in terms of moral resources, beliefs about life and the world, values that I hold. The compassion to make decisions with what I think are right and align with my beliefs all came with the experiences that my family did. My grandmother told me at a young age . . . about the world, about service to others, about being a loving person, I learned that from my grandmother and my mom as well. My dad taught me compassion. My mom taught me resilience, and the importance of like persevering and trying hard and [having] a goal or an idea to make a difference. I think I learned that all through really positive models and really positive experiences and also through hardships. At times we had nothing to eat or experiencing things with my mom like homelessness for a short time. Things like that really taught me the value of a human being isn't what you have, it's who you are, and what you do, and how you show up. I learned all of that from them.

In this example, this LLOP alum also speaks to aspirational capital, another dimension of cultural wealth, when he describes how he built on the capacity to hope even amid extreme hardship. His sense of purpose and ability to persevere was inspired by the dedication and strengths cultivated by family and community. His goals, his feelings of aspirations were fostered by his mother, who taught him to maintain hope amidst hardships.

GANAS AND PERSEVERANCE

Our LLOP students were committed to making necessary sacrifices to achieve their goals, and they described strategies to overcome hardships and accomplish their goals. These hardships included navigating undocumented immigration statuses, little to no support from overextended families, and financial difficulties (including having to work full time), among other hardships. Our LLOP students overcame these difficulties, drawing on their inner motivations as well as their family and community commitments. Contrary to the individualistic educational model, *Ganas* is consistent with a more culturally meaningful collective sense of aspirational capital. Aspirational capital in this sense then is the ability to hold on to hope and dreams for a different future than their parents, in this case, that of becoming an educator coming from a family with many barriers to educational success. We see this in contrast to the personality-based ideology of "grit" as an individual characteristic, illustrated in the following LLOP alum's comments, who worked as a high school teacher and now is in higher education:

> I was a homeowner, so I had all these ideas of what success was in my life, marriage, kids, going back to college, and all that. If I didn't finish school, then I would have failed in those things. My parents were huge motivators. They moved back to Puerto Rico in 2006, and they always valued education; they are both high school dropouts, but they were motivating me. Whatever I did I wanted to help people who needed help, or were distressed, socially marginalized. I always wanted to be a teacher, counselor, different things like that. In the past, I always been there to help, so quit(ting) . . . was never an option.

Illnesses also affected the LLOP students, adding to burdens of poverty, associated high levels of stress, and other racial and gender disparities. We usually measure these as public health or population indicators, without appreciating the burdens they create in limiting opportunities and diminishing quality of life. However, our LLOP alums shared their inner strengths to continue pushing toward their goals and advocating for support, even with the high burdens of their health status.

One LLOP alum, who currently works in the health field, shared the following about health concerns and their educational goals during their time as an LLOP student:

> I was going through chemo, so during the semester there was a discussion like of me just stopping the whole year and not graduating. I'm like what I do? Hold off? Or do I go back to school? But I am one of those people that regardless of what is going on when it comes to school, like make sure you get the support, and you'll make it through. I wanted to succeed. I wanted to finish school. I didn't want to wait another year.

An additional theme echoed by this participant's narrative is how LLOP and other programs affirm cultural strengths and values that help students navigate and negotiate hardships they encounter in their social and educational environments in new ways. These students sought out programs and resources that are consistent with their cultural values to fulfill their caminos and accomplish their goals.

Resistance and Aspiration

In our interviews, we learned that LLOP students resisted stereotypes and overcame micro- and macroaggressions in their educational and life journeys.[21] Our LLOP alums were community leaders and activists who challenged inequality and various forms of oppression.[22] In the following example, one of our alums, who is currently a public teacher and who speaks with an accent, recalled a negative experience when a professor at another university had stereotyped them:

> I had a professor, and he was very famous and sometimes in the newspaper and he was teaching science. When I went into his class, I didn't know how to advocate for myself, I didn't have the words, I didn't know how to navigate the school. At one point he was just like giving lectures and lectures and I

couldn't keep up with the writing on the board. It was very difficult for me because of the scientific words. So, I went and I asked him for help. I explained to him that I was having difficulties following his lecture and he just looked at me, and said, "You know what you need to do is stop going to parties and dedicate more time to your school!" At that time, it was tax season and I had three children, I was working full-time, I was going to school full-time, and I was doing the income tax at night. In that specific day I left my kids alone because I had to go to school and that really hurt me. I just told him, I'm Latino but that doesn't mean that I go to parties and that doesn't mean I have a crazy life. So, I left school and I never came back. Then somebody told me about UMass Boston.

This example of the racialized stereotypes imposed on Latinx students, termed "raciolinguistics," adds to burdens of skin color–based racism and predictions of academic failure.[23] Yet this LLOP participant also shared how she built resistant capital in ways that helped her fight back against these violent aggressions. Some use the term "microaggression," focusing on the actor; consistent with this participant narrative, we support emerging work focusing on the person impacted, appreciating these as directly aggressive acts. Amidst the violence experienced at an academic institution, these alumni resisted and finished their studies with the support of a culturally affirming academic community.

Another LLOP alum described the support she received from Latina professors and mentors who helped her overcome challenges when she encountered barriers in professional settings. Drawing on these experiences, she explained how she found her way:

UMB offered me the Latino mentors, especially the Latina women mentors. They were super strong, super supportive. And they were role models to me then and continue to be role models to me. I've had the pleasure to now be working with them as a young professional. It's full circle and I think that's a part of what the LLOP strives to do for us as a Latino community. We want to advance our students to be in a position where like we can collaborate with our mentors. Advance our

> ideas even further because we're now bigger together. Boston has so much segregation and inequality so finding your own path there is a little more challenging because there's not always the mentorship or the leadership that reflect you and the communities you come from. There's more red tape. You put red tape kind of like police yellow tape. If you don't see people in power from your community, it's a barrier. I think that our culture, like any marginalized culture, has a hustle to survive. We have to find work where we can find it. We need to make ends meet. I mean it's super hard but it's that hustle and it's always inside me that pushes me through.

This participant used the term "red tape" as a metaphor for exclusion, the message that you cannot cross this threshold because you don't "belong" here, it is too dangerous to cross. LLOP and Latina women faculty's mentorship offered academic support and "role models that look like me," and this inspired new visions for future possibilities. With these mentors and models, this LLOP alum identified new caminos.

Various alumni described ways that the LLOP seminar supported their dreams and goals while continuously facing real-life barriers.[24] Mentors and seminar facilitators validated their interests and goals, offered role models, and created a community with other students who shared similar values. These narratives emphasized the importance of mentorship as a core component of the LLOP, in which alumni described receiving and later providing *consejos,* and they were able to graduate because the LLOP provided a culturally affirming environment for them, which is a form of resistance in academic space.[25]

Another LLOP alum identified resources provided by the Gastón Institute and LLOP faculty mentorship as key to her successful graduation and fulfilling her goals as an advocate for immigrant workers:

> What was key was the connection, the resources, being integrated with the community, and receiving support from the Gastón Institute. The attention of the mentoring, the support of the student mentors, that each student could achieve their goal of finishing. This is important for you to be able to succeed in this country or have a better life. It doesn't matter what

education you bring from your country; you need to go to another education here. Having a second education here helps you a lot as you can navigate many of the systems. And not to surrender your culture because I am against assimilation. I don't think I've abandoned my culture. I think I can function in both worlds.

This alum provides an important analysis about resisting integration and needed the tools provided by the Gastón Institute and the LLOP to learn how to navigate the US as a migrant without losing or risking her culture, and her values. She ultimately founded a sociopolitical organization that does advocacy work for workers' rights.

Expanding Social Networks

The LLOP students' racial and ethnic backgrounds varied in terms of national origin, recency of migration, documentation status, and class backgrounds. Regardless of these diverse backgrounds, all our interviewees highlighted LLOP's importance as a resource for expanding their social networks. Students described how their friendships changed their trajectories, especially those that were with other Latinx people, which expanded sources of cultural affirmation and validation. For example:

I was on my way to class in the Campus Center and heard Bachata music. I love to dance and saw that there was a Casa Latina event. They were hosting a "Mi Casa Es Su Casa" kind of like an open meet and greet. There was food and dancing, I dropped my book bag and started dancing with somebody, eating food, and then I was like "wait a second, who are you guys? What are you doing, what's going on?" I began to meet other people who happened to be Latino as well and finding that community completely changed my college experience. I went from being like an anonymous student on the campus to actually having a home base on campus. People had begun to feel like friends, like family, and then together we connected one another to more opportunities, especially the LLOP, and eventually set me up for what I'm doing today. What I do now is teach and train leadership to community organizers to folks who are leading campaigns.

This alumni narrative is important because it highlights the interconnected nature between Latinx student groups, where an event led to expanding social networks that later would be used to seek other employment and organizing opportunities across the state.

Another participant described how peer relationships allowed for exchanging knowledge about leadership development:

> One thing I value about LLOP is the peer-to-peer relationships and learning from each other just as much as we're learning from the teacher. Let's say I have advice, or I have something to contribute I can help you on that journey. If I can I want to do that, I want to offer value to you. I want to help you out on whatever you want to accomplish. When you have a safe supportive space where you get to meet people on a deep level and connect with them and you know you have a teacher who facilitates that. We all are on the same boat of using our education and life experiences to create a positive impact on our community I think that contributes to everyone being a leader.

Similar sentiments were expressed by another LLOP alum who is a public health professional. They described the community that was built during the LLOP course and during field trips:

> LLOP was a really good solid community of people to be around. It was probably twelve of us. It was an intimate class with room for discussion and conversation is always going to be productive very interesting. We're not all from the same major or from the same place. There was a wide variety of interests that people brought to the class. And I think that always takes some time to get to know each other. But going to New York brought us together in a way that was pretty unexpected because I feel like all of us went into a class with different expectations but once we had the trip, we kind of like found what we had in common. All of us had different

majors and interests but we all had interest working for the
Latinx community at home and across borders.

An LLOP alum who works in a community-based organization promoting educational equity described how Casa Latina, the Latinx student club
on campus, strengthened his networks and he subsequently built "pipelines"
informing others of opportunities matching their interests and goals:

> We really pipelined members from Casa to go to LLOP. That
> worked in our favor because back then the Gastón had a lot
> of opportunities for us to take advantage of and there were
> a lot of research studies that really meant a lot more for cer-
> tain students than others. And so those students who were
> interested in those projects on the Latino Census and all that,
> and it really triggered a lot of students to say I want to be a
> part of that, and we pipelined them to be part of LLOP and
> it worked out.

This LLOP alum also spoke to the impactful partnership between LLOP
and the Latinx Student Success Initiative, an educational success partnership
between Chelsea High School, Bunker Hill Community College, and UMass
Boston focused on transitions between these institutions, supporting the
multiple caminos that can serve as a first point of contact in reaching out
to Latinx students.

As we have seen in many of the student narratives, our students may be
experiencing significant challenges and responsibilities, but one culturally
meaningful contact can spark a new *entrada* (entrance) to enhance opportunities and possibilities. All the students we interviewed mentioned trusted
mentors who became supportive role models and advisors outside of the
family. One student described how she was inspired by the LLOP seminar
to create supportive networks of students, alums, and professionals:

> I had built a network of other Latino students, Latino ally
> students in the LLOP. Whether it was my cohort, or the cohort
> before or the cohort after, I had this family of what we call
> LLOPianos. When I graduated it was like this friendship group
> that I could still count on and connect with. Every year we

have a retreat that I do with a select subset of LLOP alumni
and it's just great to have that support because we're entering
new spaces and careers and new sectors. You don't know what
you're going to get yourself into. We have a support network
because we had this special experience and because we were
alumni, so just having that network of support I think is the
best thing LLOP gave me.

Another student, who is currently a professor at a higher education
institution, described their LLOP connections and career opportunities
after finishing the seminar, to eventually teaching the course:

I started as a participant in '99 and while I was a participant,
I was selected to take on some leadership roles at the summer
institute like facilitating the whole process and presentation
both in Washington as well as in Boston. A year later after
I had completed the process while I was in grad school, I
was asked to return to co-coordinate the program with the
outreach specialist at the time, which was Giovanna Negretti.
I became sort of her assistant in the coordination of the program, which involved partly recruitment but also supporting
the students. They were able to write their reports and also
present in Washington, DC, and they were able to also go
to a conference where they shared their findings as well and
also present locally. So, I did that for a number of years while
I was in grad school at UMass Boston. So that's been my role
in LLOP, first a participant and then eventually taking a more
active leadership role.

Reflections on Learning: Democratizing Policy Research Toward Leadership Development and Community Transformation

During the process of conducting the evaluation, the LLOP alumni who
were coresearchers would often speak of their takeaways from the LLOP
and how they continue to use what they learned to advance their life goals.
LLOP alums highlighted the importance of having "hands-on" research
practices and participatory research approaches that involved self-reflexivity

to help them think through topics or problems. In the following example, a student described how the skills she learned through LLOP helped her feel part of a community taking impactful action, and how she continues to promote local leadership by understanding the systems they are a part of:

> These types of programs are very important to me because they help you to strengthen your identity, but at the same time they also help you to be part of this society and feel that you too can be part of something else. I have always been replicating leadership programs in local communities. I have a leadership program curriculum that is more focused on grassroots communities to empower women and community members so that they understand that for your power to change in this country you have to participate, you have to be part of social, political, economic life. The LLOP helped me so much that I kept working for all this time in the community.

Another alum, who is currently a professor, described how the seminar served as foundational for their life goals:

> Colleges have all kinds of programs, but the value of programs that focus on specific ethnoracial groups is that it allows us to build our base, it allows us to become more informed about the issues that affect us personally, affect our families, and affect our community at large. Sometimes these spaces are not always available in a university context, and for students to be engaged in these classes in order to develop specific types of skills that have local impact, state impact, regional impact, and even national impact, and sometimes it goes beyond the US, [and] it can even enter into transnational areas as well.

For the following participant, who works on education policy, the LLOP offered a transformed sense of self as a leader, with vision and skills foundational to who they became, skills they still use today:

> If it wasn't for LLOP I wouldn't be who I am now. We really invested our time because that's what we wanted back then

and so because I went in with that mentally I got a lot out of it. It helped me grow in my degree here and personal goals and it really helped spark my leadership development as well. It actually made me be a better leader on campus. It made me take advantage of leadership opportunities during and after LLOP and before I graduated. I think the biggest thing for me was I was able to learn how to public speak and that was something that I could not do. I was always a shy individual until someone would push me and I would be like I would give it a shot, but I wasn't that type of person until I looked at LLOP and maybe this is something that I could do.

In another example, an LLOP alumni, who also works doing policy research, described how the applied research seminar helped them develop a critical understanding of Latino policy issues:

What I noticed was that it went from it being just talking about how the system works, to how it is serving underprivileged and vulnerable populations, such as battered women who have the language cultural barrier, and also the legal status barriers as well. I was like okay; I need to do public policy. I need to definitely give voice to these underrepresented people and that's what I did. LLOP opened up that public policy passion that I have. I didn't know it was in me because I thought it was just law. It prepared me because I was going to go to law school, but then I was like, let me find the gaps that are affecting Latinos, so it helped me focus on like doing more engagement, with the Latino community because I felt like I was kind of not really involved that much with my Latinidad. It got me into my Latinidad, and it allowed me to also to find a passion to represent my Latino people. It also sparked this activist side to me that I didn't know I had. It made me feel like a proud immigrant, so it gave me a space, a safe space to feel like I belong to the immigrant Latinx community.

Another LLOP alum, who works at a social services not-for-profit organization, concurred that the LLOP research could help support Latinx communities and said:

I think the LLOP has been really transformational and having me understand my space and understanding the communities around me and giving me the tools to reflect on. I really loved my cohort coming from a lot of different backgrounds and variances. It wasn't like we were in a group of people who were community organizers. I left feeling like, "Shit, I have to be a community organizer" because look at how passionate these people are. I could see how the work and the research applied to them in different ways. That was really empowering.

We hope by sharing our learning from LLOP alumni reflections that we have demonstrated how LLOP intentionally combined mentorship with collaborative, group-based policy research that also strengthened community cultural wealth. The LLOP curriculum and activities incorporated life experiences, validated students' cultural assets, and centered the role of leadership and public policies for bringing about positive social change for Latinx communities. We hope these narratives inspire readers, educators, policymakers, teachers, and students to expand their own "journeys of inquiry" in order to enhance educational success and equity for Massachusetts Latinx students. Latinx in Massachusetts are among the poorest in the US, compared to the state's White population, in a state where education offers a meaningful opportunity to advance.[26] We need our collective *fuerza*/strength for *la lucha*/our struggle. We exhort you to critically examine the struggles against oppression that our students and communities are facing and to support the work of LLOP and other programs like LLOP that build on cultural wealth and develop caminos for the next generation of transformative leaders.

Notes

1 Hereafter referred to as the Gastón Institute.
2 At that time, IUPLR, as a network of university/community research partnerships, chose the term "Latino" to counter "Hispanic" and highlight both decolonization and the complex cultural encounters cocreating local communities across regions. More recently, the term "Latinx" was introduced to convey gender inclusion, which is the term we use in this chapter.
3 Phillip Granberry and Krizia Valentino, "Latinos in Massachusetts: Puerto Ricans," Gastón Institute Publications 249 (2020), https://scholarworks.umb.edu/gaston_pubs/249.

4 For a useful resource see Boston College's Global Boston website, which traces migration to the Greater Boston area, https://globalboston.bc.edu/index.php/home /ethnic-groups/).

5 Trevor Mattos, Phillip Granberry, and Quito Swan, "Latinos in Massachusetts: Afro-Latinos," Gastón Institute Publications 262 (2020), https://scholarworks.umb .edu/gaston_pubs/262.

6 Rita Kiki Edozie, et al., *Changing Faces of Greater Boston* (Boston Indicators, Boston Foundation, UMass Boston, UMass Donahue Institute, 2019), https://www .bostonindicators.org/-/media/indicators/boston-indicators-reports/report-files /changing-faces-2019/indicators-changing-facesf2web.pdf.

7 Trevor Mattos, Phillip Granberry, and Vishakha Agarwal, "¡AVANCEMOS YA!: Persistent Economic Challenges and Opportunities Facing Latinos in Massachusetts," Gastón Institute Publications 281 (2022), https://scholarworks.umb.edu/gaston_pubs /281.

8 Ester Shapiro and Celeste Atallah-Gutiérrez, "Latina Re-Visionings of Participatory Health Promotion Practice: Cultural and Ecosystemic Perspectives Linking Personal and Social Change," *Women and Therapy* 35, nos. 1–2 (2012): 120–33.

9 Michelle M. Espino, et al., "The Process of Reflexión in Bridging Testimonios Across Lived Experience," *Equity and Excellence in Education* 45, no. 3 (2012): 444–59.

10 Patricia Leavy, *Essentials of Transdisciplinary Research: Using Problem-Centered Methodologies* (Left Coast Press, 2011).

11 Jacques M. Chevalier and Daniel J. Buckles, *Participatory Action Research: Theory and Methods for Engaged Inquiry* (Routledge, 2013): Leonard A. Jason, et al., *Participatory Community Research: Theories and Methods in Action* (American Psychological Association, 2004).

12 Leland Brown, "Ten Commandments of Community-Based Research," in *Community Organizing and Community Building for Health*, ed. Meredith Minkler, 464–65 (Rutgers University Press, 2003).

13 Ester R. Shapiro, Jennifer Jeune, and Nicholas Johnson, "'If You're Brown, Stick Around': Immigrant Anti-Black Pro-White Supremacy Racialization Through 'Honorary Whiteness' Status," in *Racial Inequality, Xenophobia, and Populism: New Forms of Racism in the United States*, ed. Adebowale Akande, 759–84 (Springer, 2022).

14 Ester R. Shapiro, "Transforming Development Through Just Communities: A Life-Long Journey of Inquiry," in *Latina Psychologists: Thriving in the Cultural Borderlands*, ed. Lillian Comas-Diaz and Carmen Inoa Vasquez, 158–75 (Routledge, 2018).

15 Castellano Turner, et al., "Poverty, Resilience, and Academic Achievement Among Latino College Students and High School Dropouts," in *The Education of Latino Students in Massachusetts: Issues, Research, and Policy Implications*, ed. Ralph Rivera and Sonia Nieto, 191–216 (University of Massachusetts Press, 1993).

16 Felix M. Padilla, *Puerto Rican Chicago* (University of Notre Dame Press, 1987); Felix M. Padilla, *Latino Ethnic Consciousness: The Case of Mexican Americans and Puerto Ricans in Chicago* (University of Notre Dame Press, 1985); Felix M. Padilla, *The Gang as an American Enterprise* (Rutgers University Press, 1992).

17 Two years (2000, 2006) did not have an LLOP cohort due to lack of funding.

18 Hereafter, in our description of the findings, we use the terms LLOP students and LLOP alumni to describe the participants of this participatory evaluation.

19 Laura I. Rendón, Amaury Nora, and Vijay Kanagala. "Ventajas/Assets y Conocimientos/Knowledge: Leveraging Latin@ Assets to Foster Student Success," in

Hispanic-Serving Institutions in American Higher Education, 92–118 (Routledge, 2015).

20 Tara J. Yosso and Rebecca Burciago, *Reclaiming Our Histories, Recovering Community Cultural Wealth—Research Brief 5* (Center for Critical Race Studies at UCLA, 2016).

21 Rendón, Nora, and Kanagala, "Ventajas/Assets."

22 Yosso and Burciago, *Reclaiming Our Histories*.

23 José A. Cobas and Joe R. Feagin, "Language Oppression and Resistance: The Case of Middle Class Latinos in the United States," *Ethnic and Racial Studies* 31, no. 2 (2008): 390–410.

24 Yosso and Burciago, *Reclaiming Our Histories*.

25 Ayala Allen, Lakia M. Scott, and Chance W. Lewis, "Racial Microaggressions and African American and Hispanic Students in Urban Schools: A Call for Culturally Affirming Education," *Interdisciplinary Journal of Teaching and Learning* 3, no. 2 (2013): 117–29.

26 Mattos, Granberry, and Agarwal, "¡AVANCEMOS YA!"

Chapter Eleven

Two Is Better Than One

A Dual-Language Approach
for Adult English Learners

LAURIE OCCHIPINTI AND MELISSA SARGENT

Community colleges in the US provide educational opportunities to a very diverse group of students. They are open access, offer programs for all education levels, and are less expensive than most public and private four-year institutions. As such, community colleges are often an attractive option for underserved first-generation college students. At a time when colleges are seeing a major decline in enrollment nationwide, most community colleges in Massachusetts have experienced a proportional increase in Latine students. This is consistent with the research by Excelencia in Education, which suggests that 51% of all Latine college students begin their higher education experiences at a community college.[1]

Since 2011, every single community college in the Commonwealth has experienced growth in its Latine student population.[2] Mount Wachusett Community College (MWCC), which is the focus of this chapter, experienced a six-point growth of Latine students from 2011 to 2020 (from 13% to 19%). While the rate of growth slowed during the COVID-19 pandemic and its aftermath, Latine students continue to be a significant population for the college. In response to this growth, we decided to create a dual-language program, allowing students who may otherwise have been restricted to remedial English language courses to pursue content courses in a bilingual format. This chapter's focus is on the development and implementation of this program as well as policy and program recommendations for meeting the needs of Latine college students who are English learners.

MWCC is a small community college located in North Central Massachusetts and is part of the Massachusetts Community College System. The area that the college serves is largely rural but does include the more urban Fitchburg-Leominster area. The region historically had a local economy based on manufacturing, but much of that industry relocated over the last several decades. The college's main campus is located in Gardner, Massachusetts, with satellite locations in Leominster and Devens and a Fitchburg location for dental programs. Gardner is a small working-class city with a population of 21,287 people of which 78.6% of residents are White (a decrease from 87% in 2010), and 11% are Hispanic/Latino (an increase from 7.1% in 2010). The racial distribution for other races falls under 5%. Leominster has more than twice the population of Gardner at 43,872, of whom 64% are White (a decrease from 75.4% in 2010), 18.9% are Hispanic/Latino (an increase from 14.5% in 2010), and 6.4% are Black/African American (an increase from 4.5% in 2010). The racial distribution for all of the other races falls under 5.5%. Fitchburg, known as Leominster's twin city, has a population of 41,946 (a 4% increase from 2010), of whom 54.6% are White (a decrease from 68.2% in 2010), 30.1% are Hispanic/Latino (an increase from 21.6% in 2010), and 6.1% are Black/African American (an increase from 4.1%). The racial distribution for all other races falls under 5%.[3] The Latino population in the region overwhelmingly traces its origins to Puerto Rico.[4]

As previously stated, MWCC, experienced a six-point growth of Latine students from 2011 to 2020. Like other community college students, Latine students at MWCC start college with a wide range of experiences and backgrounds. They may be part-time students; they may be parents; they may be more or less academically prepared for college learning; they are often first-generation students. At MWCC, over half of the 35% of students who had incomes that were low enough to qualify for Pell grants[5] were Latine students. The age of Latine students is also very diverse, which is similar to the overall age diversity at MWCC. As with the overall MWCC population, women make up the majority of Latine students. Latine students, particularly recent immigrants, have another factor of diversity—their level of fluency in English.

Many Latine students who come to MWCC are long-time residents of central Massachusetts, often in families who have been here for generations. These students may speak Spanish at home but are also native speakers of English. Other students, however, are recent immigrants. MWCC, like many community colleges, offers affordable or even free courses in English for Speakers of Other Languages (ESOL), at both the credit level and in noncredit adult education classes. Some of the college's ESOL students may have completed a local high school with English learning support but need greater fluency to succeed in college. Other students come to the community college as adults, with little or no formal education in English. Some of them may have earned college degrees in another country and are retraining to gain credentials in the US. For these students, their pathway at the college level typically begins with an assessment of their English-language skills, which determines placement: either in college courses, with no ESOL support, or in developmental-level ESOL courses. Those latter courses carry institutional credit, so the students are eligible for financial aid, but the credits do not apply toward a degree or transfer.

At MWCC, then, we decided to build a dual-language program to serve English learning Latine students. This program allows students to take content courses in a bilingual format at the same time that they take ESOL classes. Students who complete the program prepare to move into general English-language college classes, with credits that put them halfway through their associate's degree. A central tenet of our program philosophy is that bilingualism (or multilingualism, for many students) is an asset.[6] The dual-language approach emphasizes this strength as well as the students' intercultural competence. Students are able to engage deeply with content courses in the language in which they are most adept, while at the same time gaining mastery of English.

While there is extensive literature on English learners in the K-12 context (see Berardino's chapter on English learners in this volume), there has been less attention paid to this population at the postsecondary level. The development of our program, at the community college level, drew heavily on research at the K-12 level. As academic deans, the two authors of this chapter were both involved in developing the content for the program, supporting faculty in developing specific courses for the program, and working with stakeholders on campus to build understanding and support for this approach. Laurie is the academic dean who oversees ESOL programs generally and is also a cultural anthropologist whose research has focused on Latin America. Melissa has been a staff member at MWCC for 30 years and became interested in educational barriers while doing research for her master's program in adult and higher education administration.

Dual-Language Approaches

Traditional approaches to ESOL instruction at the community college level have treated those courses as developmental, or courses that are intended to prepare students for college-level work. In this approach, students must take sequenced courses that do not count toward a degree before they are deemed "proficient" enough in English to be able to move into mainstream, English-language college-level courses. This model sees limited English proficiency as a deficit that has to be addressed before the student can move forward with their college education. The underlying assumption has been that language is a skill to be mastered, and the ESOL courses themselves have taken a remedial pedagogical approach.[7] This is largely despite the fact that the skills developed in an ESOL program are not remedial—they are equivalent to a native English speaker learning a foreign language at a relatively high level, which is treated very differently in the credit count at any US college.[8] At the same time, most ESOL students may not even move into college-level courses. A 2019 study of California community colleges, for example, found that only one-third of students who began in an ESOL program successfully completed transfer-level English (i.e., college composition) within six years.[9] While comparable data for Massachusetts are not available, our local experience would not suggest that the outcomes would be better.

Students entering ESOL programs at the community college enter with a wide range of both educational backgrounds and language proficiency in English. This can present a number of challenges and opportunities. Students who have spent much or all of their childhood in the US, for example, often do not see themselves as ESOL students and resist that placement, even though they could benefit from additional formal English instruction.[10] Other students arrived with college degrees or even advanced degrees from their home country, demonstrating excellent academic skills but with low levels of English proficiency. Many students who have arrived recently in the US have fled sociopolitical challenges due to war, poverty, environmental disasters, or other conditions that may have disrupted their education as well as their families and communities. Others may have learning challenges, diagnosed or undiagnosed, or simply not have had access to high-quality secondary education; these students can struggle with college-level learning in ways quite similar to many native English speakers at any community college.

In the design of our program, we drew on two approaches: contextualized ESOL instruction and a dual-language approach. Standard ESOL courses, like foreign language courses, focus on general verbal communication, grammar, and writing. As George Bunch and Amanda Kibler note, "Little evidence exists that building syllabi around traditional ESL grammatical components facilitates students' development of the language and literacy necessary for real-world academic and professional purposes."[11] Rather, Walqui's principles of language instruction for English learner high school students suggests that students "need to learn not only new content, but also the language and discourse associated with the discipline."[12] Bunch's research on the experiences of ESOL instructors and students in California showed that while instructors tended to focus on broadly understood "college skills" such as time management, study skills, and critical thinking, students were often more interested in the ways that their coursework prepared them (or not) for their professional experiences and ongoing academic work in their field.[13]

Our dual-language program is essentially a learning-community model, with students coenrolled in content area and ESOL courses and instructors collaborating on readings and assignments across the courses. This student-focused approach indicates the need for contextualized English instruction for language learners—the kinds of texts that are used in a field or profession, the kinds of writing that students and professionals will need to be able to produce, and the disciplinary conventions in that field. As one example, a study of Latina college students in New Mexico in a bilingual program with contextualized ESOL instruction, similar to our approach, found that the approach did enhance student success.[14] According to Artiaga, the lead researcher, "The primary focus was on learning content, and, depending on the student's level of English proficiency, the instructor modified the language of instruction according to the student's level of understanding. The participants excelled in their academic work first and foremost because they were engaged in learning content that pertained to their area of interest in addition to their L1 [first language] being supported and valued."[15]

Tara Yosso and other educational scholars have rightly critiqued a deficit-based approach in education, arguing that communities and people of color are better understood through models that recognize many forms of cultural capital, including linguistic capital.[16] The dual-language approach is a tool that can fully recognize the cultural wealth and linguistic and other forms of capital of our students. Further, as noted by Escalera (in this volume) an asset-based approach is foundational,[17] as it most effectively serves a range of these populations. This perspective is not just student focused but specifically emphasizes the range of skills and abilities that students have, welcomes and celebrates the diverse cultural and life experiences that they bring, and uses and values their background knowledge.

Expectations are set high and communicated clearly, and at the same time support is offered to assist students in the academic and nonacademic aspects of their college experience. For generation 1.5 students, those who migrated to the US as children or young teens, the emphasis is on bilingualism as a highly valued professional credential, while contextualized ESOL focuses on professional writing and communication skills. For highly educated immigrant students, the accelerated approach ensures that they are able to make much more rapid progress toward a US college credential. And students with a higher level of academic needs as well as a need for support with language learning are able to encounter content in their more familiar language while continuing to develop essential fluency in English. Students are "conceptualized as life-long learners whose linguistic skills develop in response to challenging yet supportive academic environments."[18]

Many students who are learning English burn out from the traditional ESOL pathway. Students who come in with little to no English are required to take several semesters of ESOL before ever stepping into a college-level class. This is frustrating and boring for many who want to learn the content of what interests them. What makes it even more frustrating is that some students have already taken college classes or have even completed a degree in their home country but are unable to transfer in their credits, thereby forcing them to start over in the American college system. Further, while K-12 schools have gradually added dual language to their classrooms, few college programs exist. MWCC decided it was time this changed.

MWCC's dual-language program took several years of planning and is built to support the continued use of a student's native language while learning English. Because Leominster and nearby Fitchburg are the largest urban centers in MWCC's service area, it made sense to locate the program in Leominster, also the site of our traditional ESOL programs. Leominster is closer to Fitchburg than to Gardner (6.1 miles vs. 14.5 miles) and has better options for public transportation than the Gardner Campus. MWCC's internal data show that Leominster also serves a higher percentage of Latine students than the Gardner Campus. Given the demographic profile of our region, it was also not surprising that Spanish was the language most spoken by MWCC's English learning students.

Creating the program was not as simple as determining the location. There were several factors to consider: availability of bilingual faculty and the lack of a Spanish Accuplacer test (a standardized test that is widely used for college-level placement, funding, curriculum, and course format). Even the time of day was a concern. Programs typically run either during the day or in the evenings. For this program, would more students be available during the day or in the evening? Or should it be an online program? As with any program, you must try to choose the options that will meet the needs of most students. The faculty teaching in our program felt that online asynchronous classes were not a great option pedagogically for language learners. However, a new model called hyflex seemed promising. Hyflex rooms are set up with cameras, microphones, and screens that allow the instructor to be in a regular classroom with some students while others participate through live video, offering students the flexibility of coming in person or attending synchronously online. We thought this could promote retention, since students can sometimes be confronted with issues that could prevent them from attending in person. Instead of a student missing class because they had a sick child or a transportation issue, they could log on to the live class from their computer. Little did we know how important this option would become.

During the planning process, a new challenge emerged. The pandemic hit in March 2020, and all MWCC classes and staff pivoted to online remote work. However, by having planned to offer the program as hyflex, we already had a backup plan if classes could not be offered in person, or classes returned to in-person and had to pivot back to remote. With hyflex, a student who contracted COVID-19 but felt well enough to still participate would be able to do so without losing contact time.

For the program to be successful, it needed buy-in from the college community. Presentations were scheduled to share the program idea as well as the data that supported the project. One area we focused on was our need to recruit different populations. For years, the higher education field has been preparing nationwide for an anticipated decrease in the number of incoming eighteen-year-old students due to lower birth rates.[19] With 106 public and private colleges in Massachusetts, recruitment competition is fierce.[20] Add to that the challenge of overcoming the erroneous belief that community colleges are inferior to four-year schools and universities. To stay competitive, it was obvious that MWCC needed not only to look to expand our recruitment efforts but also to become creative with our programs, including offering programs that would target one of the only growing populations in our area. And in a timely move, the Massachusetts Commissioner of Higher Education, Dr. Carlos Santiago, unveiled his Equity Agenda to all Massachusetts colleges, adding strength to our program proposal.[21] This statewide plan puts a great deal of emphasis on the need to serve student populations that are historically underrepresented and underserved by the educational system. One of its specific goals is to significantly increase the percentage of Latine students in the state with an associate's degree or higher.

Feedback during presentations to the college's faculty and our curriculum committee was positive overall. A few faculty raised concerns about courses being equivalent to their English-language counterparts and questioned how a student would learn English. We explained that, in this model, content courses would have a co-requisite ESOL class that uses the same materials and vocabulary words as the content courses, thereby teaching English and content together. Using this contextual ESOL, the goal was for students to have content knowledge in both languages when they completed the certificate program. It also gave them a pathway into the regular business degree program that is taught in English. To demonstrate English proficiency, students would be required to end the program with the standard college writing class. The reason for this was two-fold. It will show that the ESOL classes were successful but would also satisfy the English proficiency required by the New England Commission on Higher Education (NECHE), MWCC's accrediting body. MWCC filed a pilot program application with NECHE to ensure that the program would not be an issue in MWCC's upcoming accreditation. The project was approved by faculty, administration, the board of trustees, and NECHE.

Recruitment

Recruitment was challenging. One glaring issue was the fact that we did not have any bilingual (Spanish/English) admissions counselors, so we felt that adding a position designated as bilingual was important. But there was no budget line for this position. MWCC turned to the Perkins grant for funding. The Perkins grant supports career-based programs, and the business administration certificate program is already identified as a Perkins program. So a senior admissions counselor position was added to the grant application, which was approved. It helped that one of the main special populations that Perkins is meant to serve is English-language learners. Program policy states that full-time positions can be funded for only three years. Therefore, after 2023 MWCC needed to absorb the cost.

But funding the position was only part of the challenge. Finding a qualified Spanish/English bilingual candidate was more difficult than expected. The first search failed, delaying actual recruitment for the program by a full semester. Once the position was filled, the job of actual recruitment began. As expected, there were some students who were interested but either could not take evening courses or were not interested in the business curriculum that we were offering to this first cohort.[22] In the end, there were ten students in the 2021 cohort.

Since many students tested low in math (which is common in our native English speakers as well) it makes sense to offer developmental math and academic Spanish classes. Since the classes are not part of the certificate, Perkins grant money was used to fund the classes. Students thus did not have to use any of their financial aid on these courses. It also funded a non-credit ESOL support course for the math class so that students would have exposure to the English terminology used in math. By taking the courses, students could bypass taking the placement test for math and Spanish.

Some students who did not place into the cohort petitioned the dean to waive the requirements for them. The dean discussed her concerns with the students and told them that they would have to dedicate more time and effort to be successful in their classes. Once they acknowledged this, they were allowed to register. We felt that it was important to give them the same opportunity that we give to general students, who are allowed to register against the advice of their advisor.

Developing a Dual-Language Curriculum

It was important that the program courses use the same course descriptions and the same student learning outcomes as their English counterparts. While the program is different, it must absolutely be equivalent in content and rigor. The certificate program will take students two full years to complete.[23] MWCC ESL chair and associate professor, Otoniel Bolanos-Vargas, has been an integral part of planning the program. Bolanos-Vargas created the new co-requisite ESL courses specifically for this program. The additional time students added to this certificate allows them to focus on their English skills too. Bolanos-Vargas stated, "'Con el tiempo todo se consigue': With time [patience] all is possible. The MWCC Dual Language Program has given us all the opportunity to realize that moving towards our goals is not something done in only one day: It takes time to learn and master the English language, a language that opens doors wide to success both personally and professionally." Jay Villagomez, the ESOL instructor, stated, "The MWCC Dual Language Program is a very practical and opportune way to one, focus on the technical knowledge needed in a future career in business or another field, and two, master the English language, both of which will result in better career prospects and personal fulfillment."

Dual-Language Business Administration Certification (DL-BAC) Students

Of the ten students in the first cohort, nine ranged in age from twenty-six to thirty-eight while one was seventy-nine years of age. The students' birthplaces included Mexico, Puerto Rico, the Dominican Republic, Peru, and Uruguay. The diversity within the program excited the group. Not only were they able to learn in Spanish, but they were able to learn about each other's countries. In the fall of 2021, the program's inaugural year, the college hosted an International Night, with students in the program giving short presentations about their native cultures. They embraced this event, turning up in traditional outfits, bringing handicrafts and decorations, playing music, and even dancing. Attended by students in the program, faculty, and staff, it was covered by the student newspaper.[24] The event was limited in size due to the pandemic, but students expressed hope that it would become a campus-wide event that could also showcase traditional foods. By the spring semester, the students expressed a strong sense of connection with each other. "We are a great team, like a family," one said.

Students in the program note that they appreciate the bilingual format. One student noted, "It is great to know that the professor is bilingual. If you have a question, if you aren't sure about something, you can ask the question and the teacher can reply in Spanish." Another noted, "If English is your second language, this is a huge opportunity to take your first steps" in college. She went on to say that it was great to be able to take business courses at the same time that she was improving her English skills.

Faculty are just as excited about this new community. Math faculty member Eduardo Rivas explained, "It has been a pleasure to be part of this initiative. As an immigrant who had to take ESL classes before starting my college and career journey in this country, I can see this program as the ideal opportunity for any Spanish-speaking student who wants to pursue college in the United States. Providing students the opportunity to receive instruction in their native language makes learning and transitioning to regular English courses smoother. I enjoy talking in my native language in the classroom while helping my Latino community reach their professional goals."

Professor Elmer Eubanks-Archbold, Business Department chair, stated "This has been a very enjoyable journey. Giving students the possibility to keep going to college while learning English will allow students to not have to wait several years to get started on their college degree. Our students have been wonderful to learn from too. Sharing their dreams and aspirations with us and seeing them move ahead towards their goal has also been an inspiration."

Challenges

Despite careful planning, the program still ran into some challenging issues. In the planning phase, it quickly became evident that having fully bilingual, highly qualified instructors for in-person classes was critical to the program. In fact, we launched the program with a business certificate because we had full-time bilingual business faculty. There are currently four faculty members teaching in the program. Two are full-time faculty and two are adjunct faculty members. One of the adjunct faculty members is a full-time faculty member at a sister institution. Three are Spanish native speakers. As the program grows, it will be essential to find additional bilingual faculty to accommodate new cohorts. Other programs planned for launch in the near future have also been identified partly because we are reasonably sure we have faculty available for them.[25] As a side note, it was helpful that Laurie, as the dean overseeing the program, speaks Spanish. This assuaged administrative concerns about course materials and syllabi in Spanish, as well as classroom observations, as she could review all of these aspects of the courses. It provided some unexpected moments of connection with students, as well, who were sometimes surprised as their dean, who is not Latina, addressed the group in Spanish, which they greeted as a sign of solidarity and institutional support.

Developing appropriate placement mechanisms was an additional challenge. We wanted to make sure that students were entering the program with a level of academic preparation and English fluency that would allow them to make progress and succeed. For English proficiency, we were able to use completion of a lower-level ESOL course as a prerequisite, or, for students new to the college, a standard test that we use for ESOL placement in general. We also wanted to make sure that students had a level of academic preparation that would support them for the content courses, which include math. For this, we paid faculty to provide a Spanish-language version of our regular college-level placement exam (no Spanish-language version was commercially available). This was a pretty substantial undertaking; as anyone who has done this kind of professional translation knows, there are interpretive decisions that have to be made to make the test intelligible.

Finally, we wanted to make sure that students' Spanish was at a college-appropriate level (especially for those generation 1.5 students, who may enter with little formal education in Spanish). For this, we devised two options: Students can take either a very short Spanish-language placement test or a Spanish course designed to improve grammar for native speakers. On an individual basis, we also consider a student's prior college-level coursework since many students enter with transfer credits. In reviewing placement and grades from the first completed semester, the placement test seems to be capturing levels accurately.

In the time since the program began, we have been challenged to recruit enough students for subsequent cohorts. There are a number of factors that we believe have contributed to this. Our initial recruiter, a native of Colombia, accepted a new position and has been difficult to replace, leaving us with limited outreach to potential students. Additionally, since we were only offering one degree program option, the program did not appeal to students with other career plans. In 2023, we launched a dual-language program in early childhood education; that program is designed to allow students to attend part time. In addition, we are exploring offering dual-language programs in coordination with area high schools.

Learning a new language, especially at the college level, certainly takes time. This stands in tension with the realization that students who spend a great deal of time in developmental-level coursework often do not complete a degree and the corresponding desire on the part of colleges and universities to reduce the amount of time spent in developmental coursework. Our program model is an attempt to address that situation: allowing students to make progress toward a degree by taking content courses at the same time that they are continuing to gain proficiency in English.

Students in the first cohort responded very positively to the program. "Bilingual education is what we need," said one student. "This is a great opportunity to challenge yourself and see how far you can go. We are happy that we have this as a beginning, and we can go anywhere from here." Her words, focused on students, can be reframed as a powerful call to action for community colleges—bilingual programs are a great opportunity for us to challenge ourselves and see how far we can go.

Notes

1 Excelencia in Education, *Latino College Completion: United States—2023* (Excelencia in Education, 2023).

2 Massachusetts Department of Higher Education, "Data Story: 2020 Enrollment Estimates," Massachusetts Department of Higher Education, 2021, www.mass.edu /datacenter/2020enrollmentestimates.asp.

3 Unless otherwise indicated all data points in this chapter come from MWCC internal data. The authors accessed the data through their roles as deans at MWCC. The data are not publicly available; please contact the authors if you have any questions about the data.

4 Phillip Granberry, Victor Luis Martins, and Michelle Borges, "Latinos in Massachusetts Selected Areas: Fitchburg," Gastón Institute Publications 307 (2023), https:// scholarworks.umb.edu/gaston_pubs/307.

5 Eligibility for Pell grants, an important source of federal funding for college students, is a commonly used metric in higher education to categorize income levels.

6 Tara J. Yosso, "Whose Culture Has Capital? A Critical Race Theory Discussion of Community Cultural Wealth," *Race Ethnicity and Education* 8, no. 1 (2005): 69–91.

7 George C. Bunch, *ESL, Developmental English, and Beyond: Rethinking Pathways for English Learners* (Massachusetts Community Colleges ESL Reform Group, 2020).

8 Olga Rodriguez, et al., *English as a Second Language in California's Community Colleges* (Public Policy Institute of California, 2019).

9 Rodriguez et al., *English as a Second Language.*

10 At MWCC as at many community colleges, students self-identify a need for ESOL support. A student who does not request ESOL classes is generally offered a placement test, in English, which determines entry into college-level writing or developmental-level writing. Students who score low on the placement test are

generally not offered ESOL placement testing unless they request it. As placement has moved toward multiple-measure placement that includes factors like high school GPA, ESOL needs are still only assessed by student request. Anecdotally, many of our students who come to the community college from high school ESOL classes prefer not to be "tracked" as ESOL students, particularly since ESOL courses do not earn college-level credit. George C. Bunch and Amanda K. Kibler, "Integrating Language, Literacy, and Academic Development: Alternatives to Traditional English as a Second Language and Remedial English for Language Minority Students in Community Colleges," *Community College Journal of Research and Practice* 39, no. 1 (2015): 20–33; Amanda K. Kibler, George C. Bunch, and Ann K. Endris, "Community College Practices for U.S.-Educated Language-Minority Students: A Resource-Oriented Framework," *Bilingual Research Journal* 34, no. 2 (2011): 201–22.

11 Bunch and Kibler, "Integrating Language," 20.

12 Aida Walqui, "Scaffolding Instruction for English Learners: A Conceptual Framework," *International Journal of Bilingual Education and Bilingualism* 9, no. 2 (2006): 159–80.

13 Bunch, *ESL, Developmental English, and Beyond.*

14 Maria D. Artiaga, "A Portraiture of Six Hispanic Women's Pursuit in a Community College Setting: A Qualitative Study" (PhD diss., New Mexico State University, 2013).

15 Artiaga, "A Portraiture of Six Hispanic Women's Pursuit," 196.

16 Yosso, "Whose Culture Has Capital?"

17 Maria Veronica Oropeza, Manka M. Varghese, and Yasuko Kanno, "Linguistic Minority Students in Higher Education: Using, Resisting, and Negotiating Multiple Labels," *Equity and Excellence in Education* 43, no. 2 (2010): 216–31; Sonia W. Soltero, "Dual Language Building Blocks: A Framework for Program Equity and Sustainability," presentation, National Association for Bilingual Education Conference, Las Vegas, NV, March, 2019.

18 Kibler, Bunch, and Endris, "Community College Practices," 206.

19 Massachusetts Department of Higher Education, "Equity Agenda," Massachusetts Department of Higher Education, accessed September 20, 2022, https://www.mass.edu/strategic/equity.asp.

20 "Carnegie Classification of Institutes of Higher Education," American Council on Education, accessed September 20, 2022, https://carnegieclassifications.acenet.edu/.

21 Massachusetts Department of Higher Education, "Equity Agenda."

22 Business had been chosen as the first curriculum for the program based on community focus groups. It seemed appealing to a range of older adult students and also can lead directly into an associate's degree and then bachelor's degree program.

23 Course descriptions can be viewed at http://catalog.mwcc.edu/coursedescriptions/.

24 Pamela Day, "International Show 'n' Tell," *Mount Observer* (Gardner, MA), November 3, 2021, 4.

25 We have considered the possibility of dual-language programs in other languages that are common in our region, including Portuguese and Haitian Creole, but finding instructors for those would be a real obstacle.

Chapter Twelve

Seeking Cross-Ethnic and African Diasporic Solidarity Among English-Learning High School Youth

PATRICIA KRUEGER-HENNEY, JUDENIE DABEL, NASTEHO ALI

But now, how do we talk about bringing various social justice struggles together, across national borders?

—ANGELA DAVIS[1]

Introduction

English learning (EL) youth are one of the fastest-growing student populations in Massachusetts public schools.[2] In Boston, they have some of the lowest outcomes in areas of academic success as shown by high school noncompletion rates, low performance on standardized tests, and college enrollment and retention.[3] To respond to the various educational needs of Latinx EL students specifically, Boston Public Schools (BPS) offers a few dual-language or two-way bilingual schools (paralleled Spanish and English instructions in all content areas). These dual-language schools are the Hurley School, Margarita Muñiz Academy, Mario Umana Academy, Sarah Greenwood School, and Rafael Hernández School. It took an enormous amount of cross-community and -constituency collaboration, as well as advocacy and citywide activism, to create these dual-language schools in Boston.[4] While they are not immune to budget cuts and high-stakes education policies and practices (i.e., state-mandated standardized tests, school exit exams, Common Core), the presence of these dual-language schools is encouraging. It suggests that much-needed attention had finally been paid at the school district level for specially bookmarked resources, pedagogies, curriculums, and hiring practices to address the learning needs of EL Latinx students. However, it would be untruthful to make such a celebratory and sweeping statement while other BPS EL students continue to be underserved.

More specifically, less known are the educational needs of EL students from East Africa, and Somalia particularly, many of whom are Muslim and are among the largest new immigrant communities in BPS. Even though they represent only 1.5% of BPS students (numbering 1,116), Somali students are the greatest and longest-standing subgroup among East Africans.[5] In addition, BPS does not offer disaggregated data on any of the education outcomes for Somali EL students. To address this data absence—if not data inequality—affecting Latinx and Somali EL students, co-researching members of the Youth Ubuntu Project (YUP) identified a wide range of social and institutional obstacles that keep both Somali and Latinx EL youth from reaching their education success. YUP is a cross-ethnic and -linguistic solidarity-centered youth participatory action research (YPAR) collective of BPS Latinx and Somali EL high school students in grades 9 through 12. This chapter highlights a selection of some of the collaborative and solidarity-seeking YPAR ethics and processes of this youth research collective that were central to intentionally building cross-ethnic and African Diasporic solidarity among Latinx and Somali BPS EL high school youth.

The goal of the YUP research was to investigate how EL immigrant high school students experience and explain multitiered challenges that impact their academic success and what changes to education policy and schooling practices they believe are necessary to remedy the significant opportunity gaps they face. With BPS as the site of investigation, this activist YPAR project applied a cross-ethnic African Diasporic[6] solidarity-desiring approach to tracing and identifying the ways in which anti-Blackness and xenophobia show up in the EL classroom spaces, pedagogies, and curriculums for Latinx and Somali students. This YPAR project with immigrant youth in Boston rose from the grounds of systemic silencing, erasure, dehumanization, and educational dispossession that English-learning Somali and Latinx immigrant high school students consistently experience while in school. Moreover, marred with histories of colonialism, racism, and racial oppression, BPS is home to Black (this includes Black and Latinx as well as Somali) communities that have historically, as well as presently, refused to allow racism and white supremacy to dampen their fight and desire for recognition, educational equality, and opportunities to live healthy and productive lives.[7]

This EL YPAR study, too, is profoundly held together and guided by the missions and commitments of other vibrant national youth-led social movements and organizations, including Black Lives Matter, the Dreamers, Rethink in New Orleans, Border Angels in San Diego, and the Water Defenders at Standing Rock. Therefore, it is part of a bright constellation of young people's ongoing fierce activism against racial capitalism and the many forms of institutionalized racism and xenophobia that young people encounter while in and outside of their schools.[8] On one hand, the YUP mirrors young people's deep desires to shatter the educational barriers that Somali and Latinx students experience in their EL education and that are compounded by ongoing and underacknowledged forms of racial discrimination.[9] On the other hand, and to fight against the systemic obstacle course young people are asked to clear throughout their EL education, the YUP critically examines how racism, enmeshed with Islamophobia, manifests in EL education. The ethics and research processes of this YPAR fully acknowledge the ways in which Black African, Muslim, and Latinx immigrant youth communities have always struggled for justice in education since colonization.[10]

One specific question drives this chapter: *What distinctive youth-centered and participatory research practices were central to creating cross-ethnic and African Diasporic solidarity among BPS Somali and Latinx EL high school youth to collectively trace and identify forms of racism and xenophobia in their EL education?* This chapter does not foreground the reporting of specific findings of this YPAR study. In this current historical moment of intensified anti-Black racism, Islamophobia, and xenophobia, the authors decided that more attention needed to be directed to illuminating some of the relational processes and values that were critical to the formation and the becoming of this activist group of immigrant youth co-researchers.

Three co-researcher members of the YUP coauthored this chapter.[11] In the sections that follow, the authors present a brief history, the purpose and significance of participatory action research (PAR) and YPAR, the origins that led to forming the YUP, an overview of YUP's scope of activities, and a summary of three specific actionable solidarity-committed research ethics that are fundamental to Black Participatory Research and which are "steeped in freedom to be . . . part of the solidarity of humanity."[12]

Participatory Action Research

PAR is rooted in long-standing global activism legacies that center the lived experiences of socially and economically marginalized communities and individuals with systems of power and issues of social inequalities in their daily lives.[13] Unlike the methods of more traditionally trained researchers who situate economically disinvested people and their communities to be the objects of their studies, PAR methodologies dehierarchize the research process by repositioning "those who have traditionally been the objects" in studies that are led by academically trained researchers.[14] As co-researchers and direct informants for all components and phases of the research process—including the identification of research focus, research design, data collection and analysis, and data dissemination—PAR privileges the expert knowledge of youth, children, women, mothers, LGBTQIA young adults, working-class, Muslim, and immigrant communities, people in prison and foster care, homeless communities, and survivors of state-sanctioned violence. PAR is both a research ethic and a research approach for doing "research with" people. PAR counteracts traditional and top-down power dynamics between researcher and researched, between expert and the so-called "nonexpert." As co-researchers, members of critical PAR collectives intimately steer and guide all research processes and thus reduce the presence of outsiders whose researching gaze interprets and distributes "results with little sense of accountability to or response-ability for the people or communities about whom they are writing."[15]

PAR is also hinging systematic inquiry on instilling more democratic and collaborative relations between co-researchers and the communities they belong to. Processes and procedures for participatory qualitative, quantitative, and mixed-method designs mirror this direct engagement with and inclusion of historically silenced, if not erased, perspectives. To do so, PAR directly connects research with action (the "A" in PAR) throughout its research phases and through a wide array of actions, including media conferences, street theater performances, petitions, co-researcher-facilitated workshops at community and academic conferences, teacher training, social policy, legal reform, and film screenings to advance social change by educating the public, politicians, academics, authorities of educational and legal institutions, and co-authored publications. PAR findings inform the purpose and content of actions with which co-researchers encourage and mobilize people in their own communities (and beyond) to take action against injustice in their lives.

Youth Participatory Action Research

Participatory action research with young people (YPAR) specifically centers the expertise that young people have about their lived lives with and within the spaces of their daily lifeworlds.[16] This includes their perspectives on institutionalized oppressive practices, policies perpetuating converging systems and structures of racism, economic inequality, patriarchy, heterosexism, misogyny, and ableism. All these shape and affect young people's individual and collective journeys in institutional(-ized) spaces of schools, juvenile justice, foster care, housing, recreation, and health care.[17] In YPAR, too, youth co-researchers are both researchers and research participants to directly steer and inform all phases of their research processes.[18] YPAR collectives frequently work in partnership with community organizations and/or individual academic researchers. In addition, YPAR collectives have powerfully ignited youth-led resistance movements against educational injustice.[19] In areas of education research, YPAR collectives have designed a plethora of youth narrative-honoring methods (visual, historical, performance-based) to mobilize other young people toward leading and making changes in schooling practices and education policy.[20]

As co-researchers, between 2017 and 2021, YUP members participated in all stages of this YPAR: engaging in weekly workshop discussions to critically examine the history of public and EL education in US, US international affairs, immigration history and policies, and practices in school finance. They named the sociopolitical contexts that directly shape the daily lived experiences with the structures and practices of their EL programs; identified the research questions that guided their PAR study; learned about different research methods; selected those that best serve their commitment to advocating for EL students' needs; collected quantitative and qualitative data; managed and analyzed the data; and distributed their findings to EL-serving community-based organizations in Boston.

Introducing the Youth Ubuntu Project (YUP)

The Youth Ubuntu Project (or YUP) was launched in 2013 as an immigrant youth leadership project.[21] The project arose from an ongoing partnership between two community-based grassroots organizations that work at the forefront of bringing economic, social, and educational opportunities and literacies to some of Boston's immigrant communities: the Center to Support Immigrant Organizing (CSIO) and the African Community Economic Development of New England (ACEDONE). Adult immigrant leaders from the organizations' collaborative GrassRoots Leadership Network had voiced a desire to create a similar space for Boston's immigrant youth, one where young people could discuss issues that are central to being young, immigrant, and growing up in Boston. CSIO and ACEDONE staff took the lead in creating this space and invited their youth members to join this leadership initiative. In 2015, this emergent youth immigrant leadership program held a Youth Summit as one of its first efforts to bring together Boston-based immigrant teens to discuss issues of cross-ethnic unity. The immigrant teens who participated in this summit were Somali, Latinx, and of various Asian origins. Afterward, both community-based grassroots organizations remained invested in holding this space and facilitated conversations and activities for immigrant teens to examine and understand the histories of African immigrant, Black, and Latinx communities in Boston while building cross-ethnic solidarity and nourishing a collective confidence in their ability to do this work.

However, simply sharing the status of "immigrant Boston youth" did not mechanize a process of becoming a collectivized and unified "we" and "us" among immigrant high school youth. CSIO and ACEDONE staff invited a community activism–raised researcher from the University of Massachusetts Boston to assist with guiding and moving the group through a series of community- and solidarity-building activities in late 2016. Hinged on the community-centered values and ethics of PAR, this youth leadership initiative engaged in a participatory- and youth-centered process of growing into a research collective that engaged in a series of in-depth collective and interactive examinations of issues (through debates, theater-inspired activities, and movement-based exercises) that are vital to their educational desires and everyday realities as immigrant youth leaders. Examined topics during this period included colonialism in the US, racialization of immigrant communities in the US, historical and current forms of state-sanctioned erasures of racialized communities in the US and Boston, immigration policies, and the assimilation purposes of curriculum and schooling processes in public schools. Each weekly meeting began with a whole-group, playful team-building activity that would transition the group into hands-on, experiential, and in-depth critical examinations of one of these topics.

These discussions and activities initiated the PAR process for what would become the YUP because YUP teens discussed with each other their shared struggles as immigrant teens living, learning, and growing up in the city of Boston. Through these exploratory topic conversations and ongoing dialogue, youth co-researchers expressed a deep and collective interest in their English learning (EL) education. Moreover, after many weeks of intensive individual and collective self-reflective conversations, youth co-researchers reached a crucial point of realization from where they worked with their differences. Living in and representing some of Boston's different ethnic and racialized neighborhoods, they listened to each of their individual and families' reasons for migrating to the US and familiarized each other with some of the religious and spiritual traditions they practiced at home and in their communities. Their collective study of EL education in the BPS included examining some of the historical systems and practices of white European settler colonialism and the ongoing economic exploitation and militarization of their home countries by US empire.[22] These discussions were central to co-researchers' collective self-identification as African Diasporic youth. More significant was the collective naming of what co-researchers have in common: all YUP members were immigrant youth who attended a BPS school and were at some point in their educational journeys also EL students. In addition, as members of some of Boston's racialized communities, co-researchers widely experienced racism, xenophobia, and Islamophobia in and out of school.

Throughout their analytical and reflective discussions, this group of immigrant teens always returned to their EL education and the many racist and xenophobic confrontations they endured in their EL classrooms.[23] As current or former EL students, or with siblings and friends as EL students in the BPS, they expressed the ways in which their teachers treated EL students in the classroom, their frustrations with the EL curriculum, the bullying they received from EL teachers and their EL peers, their schools' lack of outreach to their families about progress made in the EL programs, and the emotional isolation they were experiencing due to the Islamophobia and xenophobia that was exercised against them. They were already deeply aware of the low graduation rate (two-thirds) of BPS EL students before they collectively looked up the specific statistics of school noncompletion among EL students in Massachusetts and Boston.[24] They already possessed the lived knowledge and expertise that would fuel what they chose to be their research topic. But they needed guidance and tools to implement their research process around the central questions that framed their YPAR study: What experiences do EL BPS high school students have with their EL education? What do EL students in the BPS need in order to secure their educational success?

In 2017, this youth leadership and immigrant solidarity initiative was named the "Youth Ubuntu Project." Youth leaders wanted to unify the group under a name that they themselves chose. Thus, it had to be a name that would mirror the research collective's prioritization of seeking cross-ethnic and African Diasporic solidarity. When a YUP member from the Margarita Muñiz Academy suggested incorporating "Ubuntu" in the group name, a South African cultural ethos that means "I am because you are," his co-researchers enthusiastically agreed. They felt that "Youth Ubuntu Project" would genuinely represent their wishes to speak openly to and learn about their lived experiences with growing up and going to school in Boston, to participate in bringing about educational justice to increase the academic success of EL students in BPS, and to contribute to their collective goal of building cross-ethnic solidarity.

During weekly research meetings, YUP members co-led with the academic researcher root-cause analyses of some of the social injustices they encountered in their daily lives. They also mapped and annotated their migration stories for each other on poster-sized papers, met with local youth and adult leaders to learn about local and federal immigration and education policies, spoke with BPS administrators and statewide education policymakers, learned about BPS budget priorities, and practiced their skills for immigrant community-based social justice organizing in Boston (i.e., petitioning, media conferencing). CSIO and ACEDONE staff registered YUP with the city's youth employment initiative so that YUP members would receive stipends and biweekly payments for the time and energy spent on cocreating a youth-centered work environment that would also strengthen their financial management skills.

By the end of 2018, after having spent significant time together to create a strong sense of community, alliance, and comradery with and for each other, YUP had grown into a vibrant youth immigrant leadership and grassroots organizing collective with thirty-five immigrant BPS high school students. YUP's co-researching youth were from Somalia, Puerto Rico, the Dominican Republic, Haiti, El Salvador, and Guatemala. They lived in Boston and attended BPS (including some of the aforementioned dual-language schools) and charter schools in grades 9 through 12. The majority of them, or their siblings, were placed in EL education at some point in their K-12 educational journeys. Many of them remained in EL classrooms up until they graduated from high school. A few youth co-researchers returned to YUP throughout their first year in college to dedicate their summers or after-school hours to working with ACEDONE and CSIO and to get to know other immigrant teens better.

Together, they organized and participated in Boston-wide community and neighborhood exchanges and field trips, including to Roxbury, East Boston, and Chinatown, to meet with youth and adult organizers invested in social justice and change in their communities. CSIO and ACEDONE also hired a team of six college-age interns from local colleges and universities who were obtaining undergraduate degrees in areas related to YUP's work (i.e., social work and political science). College interns assisted ACEDONE and CSIO staff with completing administrative tasks and logistics for weekly YUP research meetings, and in return, college interns received credit to count toward their degree completion. The academic researcher assisted with the cofacilitation of weekly topic discussions, guided the group through making decisions towards their final research design, trained youth co-researchers in their chosen research methods, and assisted with data collection, data management, and collective data analysis. Youth co-researchers and staff traveled to the UMass Boston campus to complete the online research ethics training as required by the university's Institutional Review Board. More specifically, from 2017 until the beginning of the COVID-19 pandemic in spring 2020, weekly YUP research meetings took place after school in a community meeting space in Boston's downtown area from where co-researchers put together and executed all components of their mixed-method YPAR project.

This YPAR study wove together various data types: an online survey for BPS EL high school students ($n = 173$), interviews with EL students ($n = 10$), interviews with EL Somali and Latinx parents ($n = 18$; Somali parents, 7; Latinx parents, 11), interviews with EL teachers ($n = 13$), interviews with school administrators ($n = 6$), and interviews with EL education policymakers ($n = 1$).

Also between 2017 and 2020, YUP co-researchers organized and led various research-informed actions to share their findings through their activist work with the different communities they are part of, including open mic sessions in community spaces with and for other immigrant youth and during which co-researchers performed their perspectives on the injustices and harm done to young people in EL education, giving interviews for local newspapers about YUP's work and salient issues in BPS EL, cofacilitating workshops on anti-Muslim racism and Boston's roots of migration with teens from partner organizations, visiting local college and university campuses to present their YPAR work to undergraduate and graduate students, and hosting a virtual exhibit of some of the artwork they created about their immigrant and EL youth identities.

YUP AND COVID-19

In the spring of 2020, when COVID-19 began to rage around the world and produced the massive deadly results that further crystallized the systematic interlacing of racism and disinvested healthcare systems, YUP co-researchers had finished collecting their EL youth surveys but were still conducting their interviews with EL students, parents, teachers, and school administrators. In fact, on the eve of COVID-19-related BPS school closures, YUP co-researchers conducted a series of in-person interviews with EL parents at a Boston public school before and after their evening adult EL classes.

All remaining interviews were held over the phone after March 2020, before the group moved into doing virtual data analysis work via Zoom. The once very large team of co-researchers dwindled down to a group of eight, consisting of college interns, YUP members who were in their final year of high school, one CSIO staff member, the academic researcher, and her graduate research assistant. However, there were serious obstacles that co-researchers had to work around, including the lack of regular access to computers, software technology, and reliable wireless internet connection, as well as little time being available to prioritize YUP meetings over the caretaking of young siblings and elders in their families. The rapidly rising number of COVID-19 infections among immigrants (who primarily work in Boston's service industries as essential workers and who were dominantly represented among YUP co-researchers) made the impact of this deadly global public health pandemic extremely palpable for all YUP members. This already very vulnerable population of BPS EL students would only be further reminded of their educational precarities by way of the racist and economically oppressive realities the COVID-19 virus was linked to.[25] Interview analyses were completed in summer 2022.

It's a Small, Anti-Immigrant and Islamophobic World After All

> In a real sense all life is inter-related. All men are caught in
> an inescapable network of mutuality, tied in a single garment
> of destiny. Whatever affects one directly, affects all indirectly. I
> can never be what I ought to be until you are what you ought to
> be, and you can never be what you ought to be until I am what
> I ought to be. . . . This is the inter-related structure of reality.
>
> —MARTIN LUTHER KING JR.,1963[26]

Cross-ethnic and African Diasporic solidarity among Latinx and Somali
EL high school youth did not happen automatically; inviting EL youth
from different backgrounds to physically work together every week and
colead a YPAR project did not alone cultivate their participation, buy-in,
or enthusiasm. Collectivized trust-building discussions during which youth
co-researchers articulate and practice their stances and opposing positionalities toward real-life and often violent national and international events
and incidents are the most crucial components of growing into a collective
of allied co-researchers and youth activists.

For example, YUP's members were feeling the aftershocks of some of
Donald Trump's anti-immigrant and anti-Muslim statements and executive
orders that he had made two years before in 2015 during his preelection
campaigning. To seek additional global support for his construction of a wall
along the Mexico-US border, he stated that Mexican immigrants are known
for "bringing crime and drugs" to the US and labeled them with "being
rapists."[27] Also at that time, Trump released a series of anti-Muslim and
xenophobic videos on social media to defend and intensify Britain's hateful
stance toward Syrian refugees who were fleeing the civil war raging in their
home country and labeled them to be "real threats" worldwide.[28] In 2017,
when YUP members were putting together their research design, Trump's
racist and Islamophobic hatred led to him signing an executive order "that
banned travel to the United States for 90 days from seven predominantly
Muslim countries."[29] Somalia was one of the countries on this original list,
along with Iran, Iraq, Libya, Sudan, Syria, and Yemen. In addition, Trump
stopped the resettlement of all Syrian refugees in the US and augmented
immigrant detention practices.[30]

Youth co-researchers recalled the immediate consequences these anti-immigrant and anti-Muslim federal decisions in 2015 and discussed their ongoing ripple effects in 2017 or the ways in which their hatred and racist rhetoric and policies added fear, surveillance, and intimidation to their daily lives at school and in public spaces: young Somali women were insulted by their non-Somali and non-Muslim teachers and peers for wearing a hijab at school; Latinx students were racially profiled while grocery shopping by store staff who questioned their documentation status; EL students received hateful stares from their white or non-EL peers while moving through school hallways; and Somali co-researchers spoke to the ongoing Islamophobic remarks they absorb while on their way to their community mosque. The targeting, scrutinization, and criminalization of EL Latinx and Somali student bodies, their beliefs, and behaviors also became "the subject of a very public process of stigmatization" in Boston and in BPS.[31]

Given these global and national contexts, YUP members spent the first four to six months of their time together getting to know each other and collectively familiarizing themselves with the traditions, histories, struggles, and legacies of the communities they self-identified with. These brave and courageous conversations touched upon the following specific points: prior knowledges and experiences that co-researchers had gathered with immigration policies and US public education as a racist system and the many socialized and often internalized racist and xenophobic assumptions they had learned in school as being true about themselves and others.

Solidarity as Actionable Ethic

> *I define solidarity in terms of mutuality, accountability, and the recognition of common interests as the basis for relationships among diverse communities. Rather than assuming an enforced communality of oppression, the practice of solidarity foregrounds communities of people who have chosen to work together.*
>
> —CHANDRA TALPADE MOHANTY[32]

"Knowledging" solidarity (not "acknowledging") signals YUP's intentional delinking or freeing of its participatory knowledge-making processes about the positioning and purposes of solidarity between EL immigrant youth from existing and dominant narratives that tend to exclude their lived experiences with the educational injustices they had been encountering in their BPS EL education. Privileging and believing in Somali and Latinx EL youth's expert knowledges and abilities (thought and action forming a praxis of knowledgeability) to enact solidarity as a prioritized research ethic was central to their collective manifestation of their "right to research."[33]

But how does the coming together of cross-ethnic and cross-linguistic BPS EL high school youth move beyond witnessing their multiculturalism (i.e., showing and sharing out different food, clothing, religious celebrations)[34] into deeper and more critical and youth-centered conversations? Such conversations probe how EL education is rooted in colonial thus racial capitalist histories, state-sanctioned practices of cultural assimilation, and white Eurocentrism that also enforce a heteronormative and profoundly racist (anti-Indigenous and anti-Black) socioeconomic order that thrives on the exploitation of waged workers.[35] How do BPS EL high school youth explain and understand the different experiences they have with how racism and xenophobia collide inside the EL spaces of their BPS? How can cross-ethnic EL youth grow into a solidarity-desiring team of co-researchers who would openly and bravely trace the roots of their different encounters and experiences with racism and xenophobia? In what ways can their discussions guide the processes of their YPAR inquiry to also inform their community organizing work?

Some of the distinctive practices and processes of Black Participatory Research[36] were foundational to finding ways in which solidarity was prioritized, embodied, and enacted as a cross-ethnic and African Diasporic ethic throughout the research processes of the YUP: (1) becoming "bridges over troubled waters," (2) implementing three interconnected layers of critical reflexivity, and (3) nesting YUP in the always-fertile grounds of movement-building work.

BECOMING BRIDGES OVER TROUBLED WATERS

YUP members found their roles and tasks as cross-ethnic and African Diasporic EL co-researchers to be mirroring what Black Participatory Research scholars call "being Black bridges over troubled waters."[37] During the time YUP co-researchers investigated various issues of educational injustice in EL education, the collective identified five specific areas that maintain the running waters between their white-dominated schools and the marginalized communities (i.e., EL peers, EL parents) they belong to as "troubled" or contaminated by white supremacy and racial capitalism. These areas are the lack of properly trained EL teachers (i.e., not certified in EL education), as well as the lack of linguistic and ethnic diversity among EL teachers manifesting in culturally irrelevant EL pedagogies; the consistent absence of direct and personal communication between schools, teachers, and families of EL students about accessing EL services (i.e., translations) and learning opportunities; EL families not understanding the specifics of EL schooling practices (i.e., EL placements) and thus not knowing how to advocate for the learning needs of their EL students; the unequal funding of EL programs across different schools in BPS; and the complete silence around the toll that all of the above has taken on EL students' mental and emotional health.

As "bridges," YUP co-researchers had grown familiar with many scholarly scientific narratives about topics in EL education that they collectively read and reviewed (i.e., peer reviewed journal articles, reports released by research institutes, EL education policies written by the Massachusetts Department of Secondary and Elementary Education, BPS budgets)— narratives that tend to exclude EL student perspectives on injustices and the frustrations and disappointments that EL youth have experienced inside the spaces of their EL education. By also being deeply rooted in and aligned with their communities, YUP co-researchers remained alert to "the power differentials, personal biases, and the racial oppression in academic research" about their lived realities.[38] As bridges running over the treacherous waters of racism, dispossession, and subordination, YUP co-researchers were connecting their own scientific inquiry with dominant views while also readying themselves to demand changes in EL education. That said, YUP co-researchers, too, were running the risks of "reproducing the very forms of oppression that participatory approaches seek to disrupt."[39] YUP co-researchers reflected regularly on "the anxieties that bearing the weight of being a bridge or connector entails."[40]

INTERCONNECTED LAYERS OF CRITICAL REFLEXIVITY

To articulate their precarious position of being simultaneously researchers and community members, during weekly meetings, YUP co-researchers participated in focus group discussions, mapping activities to document individual education journeys, physical movement exercises, role playing, journaling, and debates. The purpose was to become more aware of and acknowledge interpersonal and collective dynamics and the extent to which individual and collective perspectives and knowledges are directly connected to the larger sociopolitical contexts. These activities were co-led by staff and the academic researcher. These relational layers facilitated a reflexivity crucial to evaluating the different spaces of participation "through reflection about collaboration."[41] Black participatory research scholars Elizabeth Drame and Decoteau Irby explain: "This critical reflexivity is a sense-making process that seeks to describe, analyze, and ask questions about critical incidents or events in people's lives. Critical reflexivity processes can be taken up individually, or corporately and can be facilitated through thinking dialoguing, and writing."[42]

In addition, Drame and Irby outline a three-pronged approach to critical reflexivity that specifically consists of (1) self-reflexivity (identification of individual identities, group affiliations, interests, and assumptions that will underpin the collective research design); (2) interpersonal reflexivity (articulations of researchers' positionalities toward each other and consisting of identifying their power relationships and marginalization toward the EL research contexts); and (3) collective reflexivity (involvement of all co-researchers in project design, participation. and evaluation, including project outcomes and impact). Drame and Irby explain that this level of collective reflexivity can be "transformative, affirming, cathartic, or empowering."[43]

For YUP members, engaging with the interconnected layers of critical reflexivity turned the YUP into both a space of sensemaking and an inquiry time where Somali and Latinx EL students openly interrogated and critically engaged with the tensions and contradictions that run between their actual lived experiences with EL education in BPS and how they are perceived by their non-EL peers and teachers. As depicted in the infographic created by YUP members in figure 12.1, the words listed inside the outlined human body reveal that YUP co-researchers identified themselves as being capable, resourceful, human, strong, preserving, adapting, misunderstood, having a range of emotions, reliable, and feeling resentful. Much along contrary lines, co-researchers have listed in the space outside and around the outlined human body words and expressions of what their non-EL peers and teachers have called them, including invisible, fresh off the boat, unsuccessful, rude, helpless, slow, poor, and uneducated.

Figure 12.1. Infographic Created by YUP Members to Illustrate How EL Students' Self-Perceptions Contradict the Ways in Which They Are Perceived and Labeled by Their Non-EL Peers and Teachers.

During critical reflexivity, youth co-researchers individually and collectively traced the origins of these racist and xenophobic verbal assaults, and in their analyses, they voiced their desires to interrupt these daily manifestations of their dehumanization. Youth co-researchers also discussed the ways in which xenophobia and Islamophobia are consequences of racism. According to Muslim educator Alison Kysia, non-Muslim YUP members learned that "American racism is an ideology borne out of white supremacy and of the need to steal land, resources, and labor. Islamophobia, like racism, is used to justify American imperialism or the stealing of land, resources, and labor in Muslim-majority countries."[44] Youth co-researchers made connections between the racist and Islamophobic "circuits of dispossession"[45] they encountered while in school and the ways these school-based incidents are micromanifestations of globalized power systems and structures, particularly of exploitative economic relations under racial capitalism spearheaded by the US government. Somali ACEDONE staff members recalled and shared with youth co-researchers the immediate aftermath of the events on September 11, 2011: after Islamic extremists had flown planes into the World Trade Center towers in New York City, Muslim and Arab youth, including "Muslim- and Arab-looking" youth, were profiled and targeted by adults and students alike and labeled "terrorists." Then and now, schooling practices have actively participated in the policing and surveillance of Muslim-American youth.[46] Somali YUP members, too, spoke openly to how their visible enactments of their Islamic faith (i.e., wearing the hijab, carrying and opening a rug for prayer at sundown, fasting during Ramadan) continue to be targeted by their EL teachers and peers.

While many of the Spanish-speaking, non-Muslim youth co-researchers had not personally experienced discrimination rooted in both racial *and* religious differentiation, many of the dark-skinned Spanish-speaking youth spoke to how anti-Blackness took up a prime space in their everyday lifeworlds. These most often consisted of adults watching and following them while shopping in stores; being racially profiled and stopped by police while hanging out with friends in public spaces; and adults admonishing them for audibly speaking Spanish with their friends in school hallways, in public libraries, and on public transportation. Dominican immigrant youth co-researchers who self-identified as Black and who were racially scrutinized before and throughout COVID-19 openly reflected on how race, ethnicity, and nationality tend to be conflated by adults in schools to signify "Black."

Youth co-researchers agreed that these monolithic constructions of what it is like to be an EL student, or to be a Somali or Latinx immigrant student, are grounded in anti-Black xenophobic and Islamophobic perceptions that adults have of them inside and outside of schools. These include EL classroom spaces. Further, these reflexive conversations ushered YUP members toward naming what they can and must learn from each other about showing up for one another with actionable solidarity: it is through their collective yet distinct experiences with systemic demonization and dehumanization that they move each other toward a shared understanding of the ways in which these experiences can inform and guide their collective fight against the Islamophobia and racism they encounter in school.

Educating Justice Movement Building

The partnering organizations of the YUP, ACEDONE and CSIO, resourced this EL YPAR collective based on a shared commitment to generating EL youth-centered data to push back on BPS's limited insights to BPS's EL student populations and place YUP data at the center of their advocacy for changes EL policy and practices in EL education. Further, both organizations expressed an urgency around positioning EL students' stories as central data points to frame BPS EL students' daily realities. Staff members spoke with youth co-researchers about the need for activist organizations designing and leading their own research projects, and also owning the data with which they steer their education justice work *with* communities—in contrast to university-based academic outsiders who tend to conduct research *on* communities and then leave at the end of the research project along with research findings, thus leaving researched communities without access to their documented knowledges and expertise. Claiming autonomy over knowledge production and knowledge ownership frames, this third approach to cross-ethnic and African Diasporic solidarity is deeply committed to dedicating all decisions and actions to justice movement spaces.

But for solidarity to be transformed into action for social justice movement work, it needs to have a material basis to fuel its purpose, strength, and direction. In this sense, participatory and community-owned data are the material basis for framing and educating social justice movements and helping communities take a collective stance against oppressive and divisive state-sponsored actions.[47] The histories of Black and Indigenous communities remind us that "social movements are not exceptional and not isolated events; they are persistent resistance by ordinary actors with generations of teachers and students before and after them."[48] When research is strategically purposed to not feed the economic self-interests of institutions (i.e., academia, public education, military, health care) and instead dwells in people-led transformative justice movements, research as education for communities across generations has the power to eradicate oppressive assemblages of power.[49]

Figure 12.2 depicts one of the conclusions that youth co-researchers reached about how solidarity is enacted among YUP co-researchers. The photo was taken by a co-researcher showing how she had rearranged differently colored and small-sized pieces of candy from being a pile of mixed colorful candies (on top) to forming single-color rows of adjacently arched lines (on the bottom). According to her, YUP members, too, changed from being a group of diverse EL individuals who agreed to gather weekly while proudly displaying their distinct cultural, ethnic, and linguistic features and discussing their different belief systems and life journeys, into a collective of EL youth activist researchers who are intimate with each other's differences in their raced, gendered, and classed lived realities and thus practice varied ways of showing up for each other with intentional physical, emotional, and intellectual proximity. YUP provided co-researchers with educational guidance for their data-driven and community-wide social actions.

Conclusion: EL Youth Are Fed Up with "Facts"

It is impossible to offer closing remarks on the multiple ways in which BPS EL students continue to encounter and endure racism as expressed through anti-Black, xenophobic, and Islamophobic pedagogies, curriculums, and ongoing verbal, physical, and emotional assaults that are directed against them while they are in school and within the spaces of their EL programs. Since the COVID-19 pandemic outbreak, and since the writing of this chapter, returning and new members of the YUP have co-led pro-COVID-19 vaccination education campaigns through a similar PAR process.[50] In addition, with the support and guidance of CSIO and ACEDONE staff, youth co-researchers continue to be active and collaborate with other community organizations to offer citywide interactive workshops for immigrant youth and adults on issues of people's roots of migration to the United States,

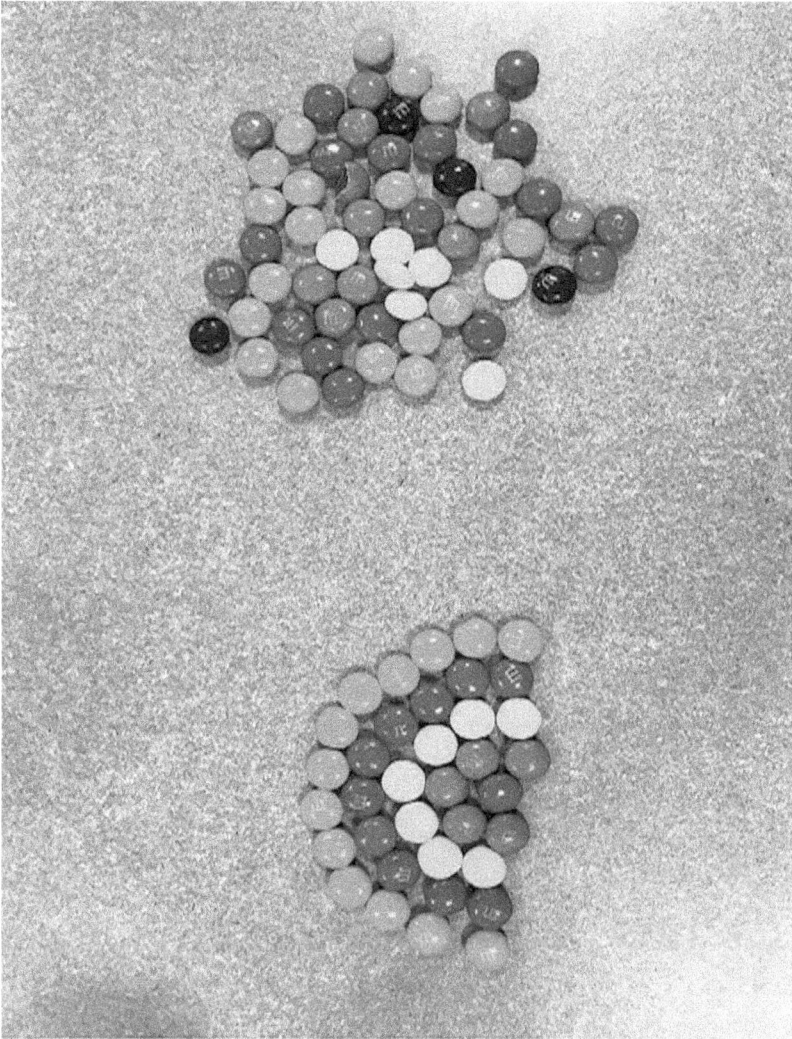

Figure 12.2. YUP's Commitment to Youth Solidarity. Photo of rearranged candies, from mixed-color (top) to arranged-by-color arches (bottom), representing YUPs' commitment to enacting participatory youth solidarity.

colonial history of US public education, and immigration and education policy. Even though membership of the YUP has changed, this solidarity YPAR project between African Diasporic EL immigrant youth binds the two community-based organizations together so that they remain collaborators as they advance and deepen their community mobilizing work around issues of access and distribution of resources in public education.

But with no end of anti-Blackness, xenophobia, and Islamophobia in sight, it is impossible to insert a period when EL students' struggles against the entanglements of racism and xenophobia in EL education remain unresolved in BPS and elsewhere. Instead of listing a few final and content-paraphrasing sentences in this last section, the authors wish to draw attention to a chronically underacknowledged area neighboring EL education that also hosts a despairing amount of ongoing collisions between ableism and racism and where additional cross-ethnic and African Diasporic solidarity-driven action and activism for and with EL students will need to rise.

BPS delights in being the country's oldest public school system and in maintaining a track record of serving diverse student populations. The first page of BPS's annually updated two-page "Boston Public Schools at a Glance" factsheet sprinkles a range of student-, school-, and staff-specific demographic information, including a few details about the superintendent, the district's strategic plan, number of schools, annual budget, teacher salaries, and student enrollment and attendance rates.[51] The second page provides a quick overview of student-specific data, including results of student achievement based on the scores that BPS students obtained on the Massachusetts Comprehensive Assessment System (MCAS), school assignments, average class size, demographic summaries of students in EL and special education programs, students' scores on the Scholastic Aptitude Test (SAT) and Advanced Placement Performance (AP), student graduation rates, and some general BPS administrative contact information. Other than minimally updated statistical values (i.e., the number of languages spoken by EL students), the content of this factsheet has remained unchanged over the years.

YUP co-researchers voiced their frustrations with the content of this factsheet that BPS distributes as a central resource to inform the public about who BPS EL students are. In addition to representing 138 different countries and speaking more than sixty-six languages, YUP members argued that there were other details about EL students worth knowing. Youth co-researchers were probing for more honest glimpses into the structural and procedural arrangements behind the district's diversity- and inclusion-celebrating data performance. For example, YUP members questioned the ways in which punitive schooling practices and more systemic factors stunt EL students' full academic potential. Youth co-researchers wanted to know about school detention and expulsion rates among EL students, and the level of food insecurity, unemployment, and homelessness found among EL youth and their families. BPS's factsheet does not spotlight any of these realities that YUP members were familiar with by having lived through many of them.

YUP's critical examination of BPS's EL student data also drew co-researchers' attention to two structurally and ideologically adjacent education spaces that simultaneously hold and surveille the learning progress of EL students: EL education and special education. Most YUP co-researchers openly spoke to having been placed in both programs at some point during their kindergarten through grade 12 education. Meanwhile, neither they nor their families had been informed about the ableist evaluation and placement processes the school district applies to students with disabilities *and* students for whom English is not spoken at home. In addition, co-researchers were aware of both programs serving disproportionately Black, Indigenous, Latinx, immigrant students as well as students from economically underresourced families.[52] Even though co-researchers traced the ways in which the purposes and outcomes of both programs uphold ableism and a schooling system of race-based discriminatory practices and beliefs that maintain and perpetuate disability oppression,[53] BPS research maintains both education spaces as separate and reports via the factsheet referenced above that 30% of BPS students are EL students and 22% of its students attend special education classrooms.

On behalf of the YUP, the authors flag these mutually constituting ideological collisions between racism and ableism in both EL education and special education as fertile ground from which cross-ethnic and African Diasporic participatory action and educational activism must rise with direct input from students. Cross-ethnic and African Diasporic solidarity-driven transformational changes in education that are envisioned and led by young people are both daunting and awe-inspiring tasks. In the words of Afrocentric education scholar and community activist Joyce Elaine King, "to attack the roots of our miseducation, cultural annihilation, and economic subordination, we must undo the system of thought that has justified our predicament."[54] Paying attention to young people in EL education and other scrutinized and disinvested educational spaces moves a public understanding beyond issues of "diversity and inclusion" to the unequal material conditions that shape the life trajectories of all young people.

Notes

1   Angela Y. Davis, *Freedom Is a Constant Struggle: Ferguson, Palestine, and the Foundations of a Movement* (Haymarket Books, 2016).

2   Phillip Granberry, Victor Luis Martins, and Michelle Borges, "The Growing Latino Population of Massachusetts: A Demographic and Economic Portrait," Gastón Institute Publications 307 (2023), https://scholarworks.umb.edu/gaston_pubs/307.

3   Massachusetts Department of Elementary and Secondary Education, "High School Dropouts 2016–17: Massachusetts Public Schools," Massachusetts Department of Elementary and Secondary Education, 2018, http://www.doe.mass.edu/infoser vices/reports/gradrates/; James Vaznis, "Boston Schools' Language Barriers Persist," *Boston Globe*, March 30, 2015, https://www.bostonglobe.com/metro/2015/03 /29/boston-schools-still-failing-students-learning-english-review-finds/ziqovw PI10eTNQcQTNbh2J/story.html.

4   Jorge Capetillo-Ponce, "The Vote on Bilingual Education and Latino Identity in Massachusetts," Gastón Institute Publications 129 (2003), https://scholarworks.umb .edu/gaston_pubs/129.

5   Boston Planning and Development Agency, Research Division, *Boston by the Numbers 2020* (Boston Planning and Development Agency, 2020), https://www.bostonplans .org/getattachment/51f1c894-4e5f-45e4-aca2-0ec3d0be80d6.

6   With families currently living in and/or originating from the African continent, specifically Somalia, as well as Puerto Rico, the Dominican Republic, Haiti, El Salvador, and Guatemala, YUP members self-identify as representing and participating in the "African diaspora" (not "Black diaspora") as a conceptual term "to appreciate the enormity of the dispersal of those now known as Africans at a moment in European expansion and the tragic and complicated legacy of their brutal dispersal." Rinaldo Walcott, "Diaspora, Transnationalism, and the Decolonial Project," in *Otherwise Worlds: Against Settler Colonialism and Anti-Blackness*, ed. Tiffany Lethabo King, Jenell Navarro, and Andrea Smith (Duke University Press, 2020), 346. YUP members also acknowledge that the dispersal of African people was activated by the genocide and near genocide of the Indigenous populations of the Americas.

7   Matthew F. Delmont, *Why Busing Failed: Race, Media, and the National Resistance to School Desegregation* (University of California Press, 2016); Kandice A. Sumner, "'There's Something About HER': Realities of Black Girlhood in a Settler State," *Girlhood Studies* 12, no. 3 (2019): 18–32.

8   Amanda Hoover, "Internal Review of Boston Latin Found School Officials Did Not Adequately Investigate Racial Remark, Threat," *Boston.com*, February 18, 2016. http:// www.boston.com/news/local/massachusetts/2016/02/18/internal-review percent 20boston-latin-found-school-officials-did-not-adequately-investigate-racial-remark percent20threat/WtslBb09cfkFZ6u7uJM8hJ/story.html.

9   Akinyi Ochieng, "Muslim School Children Bullied by Fellow Students and Teachers," National *Public Radio*, March 29, 2017, https://www.npr.org/sections/codeswitch/2017 /03/29/515451746/muslim-schoolchildren-bullied-by-fellow-students-and-teachers.

10 Alison Kysia, "Rethinking Islamophobia: Combating Bigotry by Raising the Voices of Black Muslims," in *Teaching for Black Lives*, ed. Dyan Watson, Jesse Hagopian, and Wayne Au, 330–39 (Rethinking Schools, 2018).

11 Authors self-identify as Black Somali-American, Black Haitian-American, and Dominican-German women. While participating as coordinators and co-researchers in YUP, Nasteho and Judenie completed their undergraduate degrees (English and social psychology, respectively). Throughout the duration of YUP's research process, Nasteho and Judenie also worked as program coordinators with each of YUP's collaborating community-based organizations, ACEDONE and CSIO, whose staff invited Patricia to join YUP as an academic collaborator and informant to guide their youth co-researchers through PAR ethics and processes. Patricia is a teaching and researching faculty member at the University of Massachusetts Boston. She teaches graduate students about PAR ethics and epistemologies. At the time of writing this chapter, Judenie and Nasteho are pursuing their master's degrees in education and mental health and wellness counseling, respectively.

12 Elizabeth R. Drame and Decoteau J. Irby, eds., *Black Participatory Research: Power, Identity, and the Struggle for Justice in Education* (Palgrave Macmillan, 2016), 3.

13 Arjun Appadurai, "The Right to Research," *Globalisation, Societies and Education* 4, no. 2 (2006): 167–77; Boaventura de Sousa Santos, *Epistemologies of the South: Justice Against Epistemicide* (Routledge, 2014); Orlando Fals Borda and Mohammad A. Rahman, eds., *Action and Knowledge: Breaking the Monopoly with Participatory Action-Research* (Apex Press, 1991); Paulo Freire, *Pedagogy of the Oppressed* (Seabury Press, 1970); Richa Nagar, *Muddying the Waters: Coauthoring Feminisms Across Scholarship and Activism* (University of Illinois Press, 2014); People's Knowledge Editorial Collective, *People's Knowledge and Participatory Action Research: Escaping the White-Walled Labyrinth* (Practical Action Publishing, 2016).

14 Michelle Fine and Maria Elena Torre, *Essentials of Critical Participatory Action Research* (American Psychological Association, 2021).

15 Fine and Torre, *Essentials of Critical Participatory Action Research*, 4.

16 John Horton and Peter Kraft, "Not Just Growing Up, But Going On: Materials, Spacings, Bodies, Situations," *Children's Geographies* 4, no. 3 (2006): 259–76.

17 Michelle Billies, "How Can Psychology Support Low-Income LGBTGNC Liberation?," in *Women's Human Rights: A Social Psychological Perspective on Resistance, Liberation and Justice*, ed. Shelly Grabe, 40–69 (Oxford University Press, 2018); Patricia Krueger-Henney, "Through Space into the Flesh: Mapping Inscriptions of Anti-Black Racist and Ableist Schooling on Young People's Bodies," *Curriculum Inquiry* 49, no. 4 (2019): 426–41; Darla Linville, "Unexpected Bodies and Pleasures: Sexuality and Gender in Schools," *Critical Questions in Education* 8, no. 4 (2017): 377–99; Mayida Zaal, Tahani Salah, and Michelle Fine, "The Weight of the Hyphen: Freedom, Fusion and Responsibility Embodied by Young Muslim-American Women During a Time of Surveillance," *Applied Development Science* 11, no. 3 (2007): 164–77.

18 Julio Cammarota and Michelle Fine, "Youth Participatory Action Research: A Pedagogy for Transformational Resistance," in *Revolutionizing Education: Youth Participatory Action Research in Motion*, ed. Julio Cammarota and Michelle Fine, 9–20 (Routledge, 2010).

19 Django Paris and Maisha T. Winn, "Trust, Feeling, and Change: What We Learn, What We Share, What We Do," in *Humanizing Research: Decolonizing Qualitative Inquiry for Youth and Communities*, ed. Django Paris and Maisha T. Winn, 223–48 (Sage, 2014); Eve Tuck and K. Wayne Yang, eds., *Youth Resistance Research and Theories of Change* (Routledge, 2014).

20 Jennifer Ayala, et al., eds., *PAR EntreMundos: A Pedagogy of the Américas* (Peter Lang, 2018); Caitlin Cahill, "'Why Do They Hate Us?' Reframing Immigration Through Participatory Action Research," *Area* 42, no. 2 (2010): 152–61; Madeline Fox, "Embodied Methodologies, Participation, and the Art of Research," *Social and Personality Psychology Compass* 9, no. 7 (2015): 321–32; Sam Hoyo, "Don't Ignore My Voice: A Call to Action by and for Gender-Expansive Youth" (PhD diss., University of Massachusetts Boston, Urban Education, Leadership, and Policy Studies, 2021), https://www.proquest.com/dissertations-theses/don-t-ignore-my-voice-call-action -gender/docview/2545608770/se-2.

21 "Youth Ubuntu Project," *Center to Support Immigrant Organizing*, https://www .csioboston.org/youth-ubuntu-project/, accessed March 10, 2022.

22 Michael Hardt and Antonio Negri, *Empire* (Harvard University Press, 2001).

23 All group meetings and discussions were held in English. Youth co-researchers never raised attention to having a specific language preference for the facilitation of their research meetings (i.e., Somali, Arabic, Creole, Spanish, English). In hindsight, adult co-researchers could have considered this option but did not. On very few occasions, youth co-researchers from the same ethnic group translated for and among each other from English to the language they speak at home.

24 Massachusetts Department of Elementary and Secondary Education, "High School Dropouts 2016–17."

25 Bianca Vázquez Toness, "To Boston Parents, Treatment of Most Vulnerable Students Underscores District's Poor Planning, Communication," *Boston Globe*, November 12, 2020, https://www.proquest.com/newspapers/boston-parents-treatment-most -vulnerable-students/docview/2459482004/se-2.

26 Martin Luther King Jr., *Letter from Birmingham Jail* (Penguin Classics, 2018).

27 Michelle Ye Hee Lee, "Analysis: Donald Trump's False Comments Connecting Mexican Immigrants and Crime," *Washington Post*, December 7, 2021, https://www .washingtonpost.com/news/fact-checker/wp/2015/07/08/donald-trumps-false-com ments-connecting-mexican-immigrants-and-crime/.

28 Gregory Krieg, "Trump's History of Anti-Muslim Rhetoric Hits Dangerous New Low," cnn.com, November 30, 2017, https://www.cnn.com/2017/11/29/politics/donald -trump-muslim-attacks.

29 "Muslim Travel Ban," Immigration History, https://immigrationhistory.org/item /muslim-travel-ban/, accessed April 20, 2020.

30 Harsha Walia, *Border and Rule: Global Migration, Capitalism, and the Rise of Racist Nationalism* (Haymarket Books, 2021).

31 Jay Timothy Dolmage, *Disabled upon Arrival: Eugenics, Immigration, and the Construction of Race and Disability* (Ohio State University Press, 2018), 3.

32 Chandra Talpade Mohanty, *Feminism Without Borders: Decolonizing Theory, Practicing Solidarity* (Duke University Press, 2003), 7.

33 Appadurai, "The Right to Research."

34 Peter McLaren, *Revolutionary Multiculturalism: Pedagogies of Dissent for the New Millennium* (Routledge, 1997).

35 Jodi Melamed, *Represent and Destroy: Rationalizing Violence in the New Racial Capitalism* (University of Minnesota Press, 2011).

36 Drame and Irby, *Black Participatory Research*.

37 Drame and Irby, *Black Participatory Research*, 1.

38 Drame and Irby *Black Participatory Research.*

39 Drame and Irby, *Black Participatory Research*, 3.

40 Drame and Irby, *Black Participatory Research*, 15.

41 Ruth Nicholls, "Research and Indigenous Participation: Critical Reflexive Methods," *International Journal of Social Research Methodology* 12, no. 2 (2009): 117–26.

42 Drame and Irby, *Black Participatory Research*, 4.

43 Drame and Irby, *Black Participatory Research*, 4–5.

44 Kysia, "Rethinking Islamophobia," 334.

45 Michelle Fine and Jessica Ruglis, "Circuits and Consequences of Dispossession: The Racialized Realignment of the Public Sphere for US Youth," *Transforming Anthropology* 17, no. 1 (2009): 20–33.

46 Zaal, Salah, and Fine, "The Weight of the Hyphen."

47 Drame and Irby, *Black Participatory Research*; M. Brinton Lykes, "Activist Participatory Research and the Arts with Rural Mayan Women: Interculturality and Situated Meaning Making," in *From Subjects to Subjectivities: A Handbook of Interpretive and Participatory Methods*, ed. Deborah. L. Tolman and Mary Brydon-Miller, 183–99 (New York University Press, 2001).

48 Alayna Eagle Shield, et al., eds., *Education in Movement Spaces: Standing Rock to Chicago Freedom Square* (Routledge, 2020), xiii.

49 Mariame Kaba, *We Do This 'til We Free Us: Abolitionist Organizing and Transforming Justice* (Haymarket Books, 2021).

50 Equity Now and Beyond, "Expanding the Health Network: The Role of Immigrant Community Based Organizations in COVID-19 Vaccine Information and Access 2021–2022" (Equity Now and Beyond, 2022), https://www.csioboston.org/equity -now-beyond-report/.

51 Boston Public Schools Communications Office, *Boston Public Schools at a Glance 2021–2022* (Boston Public Schools, 2021), https://www.bostonpublicschools.org/cms /lib/MA01906464/Centricity/Domain/187/BPS percent20at percent20a percent 20Glance percent202021-2022.pdf.

52 Subini Ancy Annamma, David Connor, and Beth Ferri, "Dis/ability Critical Race Studies (DisCrit): Theorizing at the Intersections of Race and Dis/ability," *Race Ethnicity and Education* 16, no. 1 (2013): 1–31; Maria Cioè-Peña, "Disability, Bilingualism and What It Means to Be Normal," *Journal of Bilingual Education Research and Instruction* 19, no. 1 (2017): 138–60; Nirmala Erevelles, "Understanding Curriculum as Normalizing Text: Disability Studies Meet Curriculum Theory," *Journal of Curriculum Studies* 37, no. 4 (2005): 421–39.

53 Sins Invalid, *Skin, Tooth, and Bone—The Basis of Movement Is Our People: A Disability Justice Primer* (CA: Sins Invalid, 2019).

54 As cited in Joyce Elaine King, ed., *Black Education: A Transformative Research and Action Agenda for the New Century* (American Educational Research Association, 2005), xxi.

Chapter Thirteen

Using STEM Learning, STEM Career Development, and Civic Engagement to Support Middle School Latinx Youth Becoming Future Ready

ANGELICA RODRIGUEZ, LUIS ENRIQUE ESQUIVEL,
CHONG MYUNG PARK, DEYJA ENRIQUEZ, JAZMIN RUBI
FLETE GOMEZ, ISAHIAH ERILUS, HEILAM XIE, STEVEN
LUE, ALEXANDRA OLIVER-DAVILA, PAUL TRUNFIO,
CECILIA NARDI, KIMBERLY A. S. HOWARD,
AND V. SCOTT H. SOLBERG

While the diversity of our Massachusetts Latinx population continues to expand, a range of structural inequities contributes to extreme wealth gaps.[1] One of the most important barriers to future income and wealth is gaining access to certifications and/or postsecondary training and education programs that enable access to higher-paying occupations. There is evidence that nationally Latinx youth are making gains with respect to high school graduation rates and postsecondary engagement.[2] In 2023, only about 20% of Massachusetts's entering ninth grade Latinx and English learners (ELs) are expected to successfully complete a two-year or four-year postsecondary training or degree program.[3] Education challenges faced by Latinx youth include language barriers, stigma-related concerns, not understanding the parents' role in engaging with schools, lack of transportation, and schools being unable to support immigrant families in successfully transitioning in and through school.[4]

To address these challenges, Sociedad Latina was established (in 1968) as a community-based organization serving the needs of Boston-area Latinx youth and their families, with a mission to create the next generation of

Latinx leaders who are confident, competent, self-sustaining, and proud of their cultural heritage. Starting with middle school–age youth and their families, Sociedad Latina has a track record of ensuring that Latinx youth graduate from high school with the skills needed to enter and complete a two-year or four-year postsecondary training or degree program. The organization's success is due in part to designing programs and services that increase hope for the future, which is strongly associated with increased postsecondary engagement,[5] especially among Latinx youth.[6] At Sociedad Latina, families learn how to navigate US culture while maintaining their customs and cultures. Sociedad Latina's programs reflect such a complex process by actively celebrating and honoring the cultural values and contributions of Latinx youth and their families, what Blancero et al. refer to as "enculturation."[7] Enculturation is the process of maintaining and reinforcing one's own cultural heritage, values, and practices, which can occur independently or in response to cross-cultural contact, whereas acculturation involves adopting and adapting to new cultural patterns when different cultural groups interact.[8] Sociedad Latina programs build academic self-efficacy, which is associated with Latinx youth recording better grades and selecting into more rigorous courses as well as developing postsecondary aspirations.[9]

This chapter describes the collaborative research effort between Sociedad Latina and Boston University that was designed to help middle school Latinx youth develop STEM skills and STEM-related occupational aspirations. The collaboration through the National Science Foundation grant provided the opportunity to further enhance Sociedad Latina's STEAM (science, technology, engineering, arts, and math) programming with network science and career development lessons. STEAM Team is a year-round after-school and summer middle school program. The STEAM program integrates education and enrichment to boost youth academic achievement, support their students' (STEAM) engagement, build social-emotional skills, and explore a wide range of careers. The majority of the participating youth are ELs who learned about Sociedad Latina's STEAM program in school and/or from their peers, siblings, and community members. During their time at Sociedad Latina, the youth receive academic support and use STEAM to address community issues through service-learning projects. STEAM youth also have the opportunity to celebrate their culture and create positive relationships with their peers and adults.

In implementing the network science and career development lessons, it was clear that the youth made stronger connections between education and themselves when cultural elements were incorporated into the lessons. For instance, the youth identified some of the Latinx leaders in the STEM field, met with Latinx leaders in the community, and visited different landmarks through virtual reality that represent Latinx culture. The youth learned from community leaders with similar backgrounds who value Latinx culture in their lives and could demonstrate how their culture is empowering their Latinx identities.

The overarching framework of this collaborative research is community-based participatory action research (CbPAR), a form of research that takes an equitable approach rooted in a social justice framework.[10] CbPAR begins with a team of stakeholders, which includes community members. Together, youth, family/community members, and researchers collectively engage in decision-making efforts to identify a shared perspective on the problem and then, with this shared perspective, design and implement new data-based practices in ways that promote social transformation for the target population.[11] CbPAR requires multiple strategies, time, and in-depth collaboration to collect and analyze data to better understand the reality of the problem.[12] CbPAR was considered an optimal framework to discuss this project, Collaborative Research: Network Science for All; Positioning Underserved Youth for Success in Pursuing STEM Pathways, and the efforts being piloted collectively to serve the needs of Boston-area Latinx youth and their families.[13] Our efforts are part of a larger national effort to increase the representation of Latinx professionals in STEM fields and advance postsecondary achievement among Latinx populations.[14] While Latinx adults account for 17% of all workers in the US, only 7% are participating in STEM occupations.[15] A focus on STEM is critical as a social issue where more youth can have access to role models in STEM and see STEM occupations as viable career pathways. In addition to encouraging STEM career aspirations, the effort was conducted as an after-school and summer school program designed to provide an array of educational and training opportunities that would increase readiness to participate in postsecondary education and thereby enable access to high-demand, high-wage careers.[16]

The chapter describes the design and implementation of activities associated with (1) network science, (2) STEM career development, (3) a youth-led civic engagement effort, and (4) qualitative evidence for the impact of these experiences including a case study analysis of the experiences for two youth participants. The two participants were selected for case analysis because of their active involvement in all four activities and their focus-group participation at the end of the programming where the youth had the opportunity to provide overall feedback about their experiences (e.g., skills they were able to develop through the program). The four activities listed above incorporate a number of key qualities that increase Latinx youth academic achievement and postsecondary engagement, such as improving peer support, establishing a positive cultural identity, increasing college-going self-efficacy, and providing access to caring and encouraging mentors and role models.[17] Interventions that include cultural identity and self-efficacy are also likely to decrease high-risk behaviors and increase academic success by developing resiliency skills that include creative coping strategies that buffer against barriers that may hinder youth academic success.[18] The availability of role models, for instance, is an important contextual factor that needs to be included in the discussion of identity development.[19] It was also found that participation in the civic engagement effort is associated with the emergence of STEM career identities.[20]

STEAM Program Activities for Middle School Youth

The following section describes the process of engaging with youth and detailed activities by each of the four elements.

NETWORK SCIENCE

One of the innovative aspects of this project is that youth develop STEM skills by exploring real-world problems through the lens of network science.[21] Lessons were designed to help youth understand the network organization associated with "big data" by exploring basic science concepts. By delving into different examples of networks, youth developed an understanding of what a network is, the types of networks that exist in everyday life, and how network maps connect to data. In one lesson, for example, the youth focused on electric circuits to analyze the flow of electrons and think about it in terms of networks and their applications in real life, such as the flow of blood in the human body and the flow of cars in traffic. Another example is the map game lesson, which utilizes Google Maps. The youth explored different forms of transportation (e.g., walking, biking, car) and identified the shortest route from Sociedad Latina to a destination in the community, such as the Museum of Fine Arts, Franklin Park Zoo, or Boston Public Schools. The youth also enjoyed the bucket drumming activity, where they built a network of sound by choosing their own instrument from among recycled materials, bringing a unique beat to the mix and forming a song.

The lessons on water molecules and electric circuits provided foundational knowledge for the youth to apply to real-world issues, such as how to manage the spread of COVID-19. The youth were then introduced to the discussion of disease and epidemiological models and their application to COVID-19. This real-world problem facilitated youth engagement in different network scenarios. An online program called VAX! Activity was used to help youth understand how viruses spread and how to prevent them from spreading. To understand the impact of the virus and vaccines on the community, the youth generated their own network data by thinking about their personal relationships (whom they talk with and are connected to) and entering the information into a spreadsheet and then a graphic visualizer. Gephi software then visualized how the youth are connected to their bigger network. The youth continued to explore different networks in everyday life, such as politics and how politicians are connected to each other and different parties and the ice bucket challenges and how social networks can be used for positive good.

STEM CAREER DEVELOPMENT

Once the network science lessons were completed, the second phase of the project involved youth participating in a number of career development activities. Initial lessons were designed to help youth become aware of the nature and value of the data science skills they were learning from the network science lessons and how these skills transfer to a wide range of STEM and non-STEM occupations. Subsequent lessons helped youth explore self-care strategies that would enable them to focus on remote learning and exploring future life goals related to the impact they hope to have in supporting their community. These activities were part of a statewide initiative referred to as My Career and Academic Plan (MyCAP), which is being supported by the Massachusetts Department of Elementary and Secondary Education and has been adopted by the Boston Public Schools.[22]

MyCAP is a youth-driven process that aims to build their "capacity to aspire."[23] Most Latinx youth are not exposed to STEM career role models. The MyCAP process helps youth consider the nature and value of STEM careers by connecting the skills they are learning to the skills associated with STEM occupations, shows youth the labor market and income projections associated with these occupations, and connects them to caring and encouraging role models who look like them and help them take advantage of learning opportunities in and out of school that will further develop their STEM skills.

Given the negative impact of COVID-19 and challenges related to remote learning,[24] our MyCAP lesson focused on helping youth identify challenges that get in the way of their learning and identify strategies that could assist them in getting the most out of their learning opportunities (Optimizing Your Learning Part One). As a follow-up lesson, the youth participated in an experiment where half of the youth participated in a stressful activity and the other half participated in a mindfulness activity. Then both groups completed an exam, and the youth were asked to consider the strategies discussed previously to perform better in a stressful situation (Optimizing Your Learning Part Two).

As part of the self-exploration and career exploration domains of the MyCAP process, youth were provided with a series of Who Am I lessons. Who Am I Part One focuses on helping youth identify their unique qualities that may relate to future career aspirations. Who Am I Part Two enables youth to find connections between the skills they are currently developing and future job opportunities by exploring the O*NET website. Who Am I Part Three focuses on exploring youth career interests and relevant skills using the CompTIA website,[25] with a worksheet that asks a number of questions they can answer while exploring these websites (e.g., the level of education needed for a particular occupation, its future labor market projections, academic courses that are important in pursuing this occupation, its average salary, and the pros and cons of this occupation).

Other MyCAP lessons like Personal Road Map Part One helped youth identify a life purpose and personal mission. During these discussions, youth participated in an open discussion on the COVID-19 pandemic and how it was impacting their community. They revisited how vaccines work, why they are so important for the community, and what occupations are involved in creating vaccines. The youth had a virtual conversation with a role model from Boston University's National Emerging Infectious Disease Lab (NEIDL), who described tasks associated with biomedical research and biosafety and explored the occupational opportunities available at NEIDL. A Latinx graduate student who had experienced COVID-19 and subsequently became vaccinated was invited to class to speak about their experiences and discuss myths surrounding vaccination.

CIVIC ENGAGEMENT PROJECT

A civic engagement effort was the third phase of the project. In addition to integrating and applying what they learned about network science, civic engagement develops a number of workforce readiness skills. Schuch, Vasquez-Huot, and Mateo-Pascual found that civic engagement projects enable Spanish-speaking residents to develop leadership skills and help youth develop a wide range of "human" and technical skills.[26] The overall aim of creating the opportunity for youth to conduct a civic engagement activity was to enable them to become more strategic and proactive in identifying the learning opportunities they need in order to pursue their emerging and changing career and life goals—what we refer to as becoming "future ready." Within the MyCAP career development model adopted by Boston Public Schools, civic engagement is considered an important example of a work-based learning activity that seeks to develop leadership and public speaking skills while also increasing access to caring and encouraging role models.

The youth decided that in order to have a positive impact on their Boston community, they wanted to design a public service video that applied what they had learned about networks and would showcase to their Latinx community how vaccines can slow down or stop the spread of COVID-19. The design of the public service video was iterative in nature as youth discovered new knowledge about the science of vaccination as well as racial disparities in COVID-related deaths and vaccination rates and the barriers to accessing health care in their local community. From a career and workforce development perspective, we examined how the process of video making contributed to building student talent and added to their skill sets on top of what they had learned in the other STEM and career development activities during the earlier part of the academic year. By helping youth advocate for creating a healthier and safer community, our aim was to show how combining STEM learning and career development efforts can have a short-term impact on developing STEM career identities as well as shape their intentions to continue seeking ways to have a positive impact on their community in the future.

In spring 2021, the Sociedad Latina youth completed a six-week civic engagement project. Previously, the youth learned about the science behind the COVID-19 vaccine, how the virus spreads, and careers related to creating vaccines. Based on this knowledge, the youth collectively decided that the PSA video would discuss the importance of vaccines and thereby increase vaccination rates among members of their Latinx community. The youth were divided into three workgroup committees based on their interests and skills: film, notetaking, and visuals. The Film Committee determined what video details were needed and made a list of interviewers/interviewees. The Notetaking Committee worked to keep track of their efforts and identify important messages they wanted to deliver. They decided that the main message should be "we all should get vaccinated." The Visuals Committee worked to determine how to display different pieces of graphics and short videos (e.g., how people felt after getting vaccinated; why the vaccine benefits us; how we contribute to society by getting vaccinated). After the first round of independent committee meetings, the youth came together to identify what additional materials and information were needed in order to finalize the video and discuss how to put things together to make a story. Culture played an important role in the PSA project as well. The youth spoke with the adults in their community, which provided an opportunity to deepen their knowledge of network science and their understanding of how we are connected to each other and can influence all in a positive way. Youth also shared with us that they were able to convince some of the community members who were hesitant to get COVID-19 vaccines due to myths and misconceptions. As a result, the PSA video was released in May 2021 and is publicly available on YouTube.[27] Through the PSA experience, the youth were able to reinforce their identity as members of the Latinx community.

Evidence of Impact

The impact of the PSA project can be observed through various sources. Youth reported that committee participation helped them develop planning and video-making skills (Film Committee), communication and detail orientation skills (Notetaking Committee), and graphic design and editing skills (Visual Committee). While youth selected into committees that aligned with their current emerging skills, they considered the project an opportunity to build additional skills: "I learned that I have to save often so that I don't lose my work" (Student H., May 6, 2021). Developing positive peer relationships was evident as they learned how to work collaboratively and discovered what others were good at: "H is a good drawer and draws about 100 times better than me" (Student S., May 6, 2021); "L has the talent to be a voice actor and is so positive" (Student H., May 6, 2021). One of the coaches summarized it by saying, "[Sociedad Latina youth] have different talents and when they share their unique skills and work together, they can create a huge impact on the community" (Coach A., May 6, 2021). While each committee focused on different parts of the project, the youth also developed some of the important workplace skills that are transferable across different occupations and industries, such as collaboration, communication, and conflict resolution skills. Research indicates that Latinx youth are likely to be motivated to engage in civic engagement activities.[28] Additionally, our experience suggests that youth developed a better understanding of how civic engagement projects help them develop a range of "human skills" (i.e., social and emotional learning skills) that have been found to increase academic achievement and decrease adverse outcomes.[29] In examining the youth's future plans before and after the sequence of network science, career development, and civic engagement, examination of qualitative pre- and postprogram responses indicated more confidence in their ability to identify their emerging talent and skills and the academic courses needed to pursue future goals. At the outset of the civic engagement project, for example, youth reported that in order to pursue their future goals they should go to "high school," "set [their] goals," and "be a good person." After participating in the network science and MyCAP lessons and completing the PSA project, the youth were much more specific about the content knowledge and skills they needed to develop such as "psychology," "biology," "cosmetology," and "editing and writing." Some youth described their next steps in pursuing their goals such as "joining a health career program" and "learning more about the human body and how it works." Their pattern of responses indicated that the program not only developed their STEM knowledge and workplace skills but also impacted their choice of educational opportunities. Such intended exposure to network science, career development, and civic engagement helped the youth establish long-term goals that could have an impact on the community and identify the next steps they needed to take to enter one of the occupational goals they were pursuing.

By engaging with their peers, families, and the community through interactive STEM and career lessons and a youth-led PSA project, youth developed their ability to identify their strengths, long-term goals, and educational pathways that are aligned with their interests, skills, and goals.[30] Below are some of the examples of what youth said about the program and how it affected their skills and future plans:

> I really enjoyed creating a business because it was fun and it's interesting to think about something I could be doing in the future. My business plan was about a company that helps old and young people with their needs of attention and more. My favorite club was the Network Science Club because I like to develop new networks like how the coronavirus spreads. . . . I learned some skills that I may use in the future if I decide to follow this career. (Student, September 25, 2020)

> This summer my class worked on jobs and careers. I really enjoyed learning the differences between jobs and careers. . . . The job and career that stood out to me the most was market researcher analytic and pharmacist. . . . I learned about the experience STEM professionals had in the past and what skills we need for that job or career, and I learned different types of careers and jobs on O*NET with Mr. Scott from Boston University and teachers that I would study with in the future like technology and other interesting things." (Irene, September 25, 2020)

These testimonials highlight the program's success in engaging youth with career development. Students gained practical knowledge about various professions and recognized the importance of skill development. Importantly, the program broadened students' perspectives on potential career options, sparking interest in diverse fields from entrepreneurship to scientific research. With youth being able to identify skills and potential career pathways, below we provide two case studies that describe (1) youth experiences, (2) skills developed, and based on this information, (3) suggestions for educators and parents on how to engage in career conversations with youth and provide guidance on navigating future educational opportunities.

Case Study One

Santiago[31] joined Sociedad Latina's STEAM program three years ago and is currently in the tenth grade. He had always been interested in science and when he heard about the STEAM program at Sociedad Latina from his friends, he immediately wanted to join its summer program. He described that his love for science was "medium" before the STEAM program and "blew up" as soon as he started the program, and he began loving science even more. Using interactive software, he enjoyed learning how viruses spread and found his experience of learning about careers in STEM "cool."

Santiago was highly involved in the PSA project by using his voice for one of the animation characters they created to talk about the vaccine and volunteering to showcase the video and speak on behalf of the whole team. He was able to identify his talent in filmmaking and build additional planning and video-making skills. He practiced his leadership skills by gathering ideas and strengthened his negotiation and conflict resolution skills when it was difficult to reach an agreement within the group.

Using the skills Santiago was able to develop, it is possible for educators and parents to provide him with guidance on how to navigate future educational opportunities. O*NET, a free access career information system, enables users to identify their transferable skills. The skills search option then provides a list of a wide range of occupations aligned with those skills and detailed information for each occupation (e.g., skills required, typical tasks) that educators and parents can utilize in having career conversations with youth. Based on the skills Santiago identified, the following skills are selected in the skills search: "active learning" for his love for science and joining the STEAM program, "speaking" for volunteering to speak on behalf of the team, "management of material resources" and "operation and control" for recording his own voice to play one of the animation characters in the PSA video, and "coordination" and "negotiation" skills for bringing others together when there is disagreement.

When these skills are selected, the skills search resulted in 293 occupations matching Santiago's skills set. Among the jobs he could enter with an associate's degree, becoming a hydroelectric production manager would provide him a median wage of fifty-two dollars hourly or $108,790 annually. If he chooses this career path, he would need to build his knowledge of the practical application of engineering science and technology, including applying principles, techniques, procedures, and equipment, as well as public safety and security to protect people, data, and property. The skills search provides a list of technology skills and software he should work on building, such as VMware (configuration management software) and SCADA software (supervisory control and data acquisition software). He would need to further develop skills in judgment and decision-making to consider the costs and benefits of potential actions and monitoring of himself and others to assess and make improvements. With a bachelor's degree, Santiago could aim for occupations such as wind energy development manager or biofuels production manager. With a graduate degree, he could enter a pathway to higher-paying occupations, such as general dentist (a median wage of seventy-six dollars hourly or $158,940).

The case study recommendation for Santiago was "Engaging in Meaningful Career Conversation."

Identifying youths' talents and existing skills opens up more opportunities for educators and parents to have a deeper conversation about what they are good at, are interested in, and can use improvement in. They can work to create formal portfolios of their skills and further dive into what courses they need to take and what resources are available in school and the community to support their learning. This process emphasizes the engagement of caring and encouraging adults and meaningful conversations with youth.

Case Study Two

Isabella joined the STEAM program in the eighth grade and is currently attending high school. She contributed immensely to the PSA project by leading the Visual Committee. She identified her skills in creating and editing video clips and showed her coping skills after experiencing a system crash that made her redo the entire work from scratch. From this experience, she also learned to save often, so she does not lose projects in progress. She confessed she had trouble with some of the team members but told us it was an opportunity to learn how to resolve conflicts. One of her classmates shared that Isabella has a strong skill set in drawing, and her skills were appreciated by others throughout the project.

Using the skill set identified by Isabella and her classmates, the following skills are selected in the O*Net Skills Search: "management of material resources" and "operation and control" for creating and editing video clips, "monitoring," "systems analysis," and "operations monitoring" for coping with software difficulties, and "negotiation" and "social perceptiveness" for being aware of conflicts among the team members and trying to reconcile.

The skills search resulted in sixty-one occupations that matched Isabella's skill set. Among the jobs she could enter with an associate's degree, becoming a geothermal production manager would provide her a median wage of fifty-two dollars hourly or $108,790 annually. If she chooses this career path, she would need to build her knowledge of raw materials and quality and public safety and security to protect people, data, and property. Some of the technology and software skills she would need to develop include data logging software and Infostat RIMBase, which is a database user interface and query software. With a bachelor's degree, Isabella could consider becoming a forester, managing public/private forested lands for economic, recreational, and conservation purposes, or a quality control systems manager (median wage of fifty-two dollars hourly or $108,790 annually). With a graduate degree, Isabella could consider becoming a microsystems engineer (median wage of fifty dollars hourly or $103,380) or nurse anesthetist, which has a faster-than-average projected growth until 2030, with a median wage of eighty-eight dollars hourly or $183,580 annually (estimated in 2020).

The case study recommendation for Isabella was "Guidelines for Parents and Educators."

The case studies provide step-by-step guidance for both parents and educators working with youth on how to (1) begin identifying skills and adding them to their formal portfolios, (2) increase their interest in STEM occupations by showing hourly wages (youth often become more interested in high-paying occupations with this process), (3) consider various occupations by exploring transferable skills, and (4) establish concrete future plans together that can be updated regularly. Support should be provided in exploring coursework, work-based learning, and internship opportunities aligned with the occupations of their interest.

Recommendations for Policies and Practices

Culture can play a critical role in advancing success in the STEM field among Latinx youth. With *respeto* and *familia* being identified as two of the most important values within Latinx families,[32] these skills that are critical in many of the pure and applied sciences—such as having respect for authority/supervisors, valuing their opinions, and following protocols—can be identified among Latinx youth and further enhanced through education and training opportunities. Extended family or being part of a group is another important cultural value that, with support, can be developed further as employability skills, such as teamwork and collaboration skills. Most importantly, the youth need to understand that Latinx culture is an asset that allows them to create unique brands for themselves and distinguish themselves from others in the job market. Partnering with community organizations cannot be emphasized enough in this effort. Community organizations have a deep understanding of the culture, values, and beliefs of the community and how they interact with individuals trying to establish their identities and career identities. Collaborating with local experts can only expand opportunities for STEM learning for Latinx youth. Below we have provided policy and practice recommendations at various systems levels.

- At the school and district levels, it is important to provide practical resources to educators and parents who can start meaningful career conversations with youth in a caring and encouraging manner. It is caring and encouraging because the emphasis is not on identifying a job that youth are interested in but on understanding their talent and existing skills and a wide range of occupations that are aligned with their skills, especially the high-demand, high-paying positions. Conversations should be encouraged as early as possible when youth begin establishing their career identities.
- When designing curricula, lessons, and activities, starting from a bigger picture is encouraged as it provides an opportunity to connect different subject matters to the short- and long-term goals of the youth and their career readiness. Connecting STEM, career development, and civic engagement is one example that can increase their motivation, academic achievement, and mental health.
- The school districts with a high number of underserved populations should invest more in working with community organizations that specialize in STEM learning and providing more hands-on experiences that increase youth's interest and desire to pursue STEM-related educational opportunities. National and international research highlights the importance of having meaningful conversations with adults in preparing youth for the future.[33]

- At the state and national levels, policymakers should implement targeted measures to address racial disparities in STEM jobs and enhance career readiness for Latinx youth:
- Increase funding for after-school STEM enrichment programs in districts with high numbers of underserved populations. These programs can provide hands-on experience, mentorship opportunities, and project-based learning that spark interest in STEM career pathways.
- Allocate resources for bilingual STEM education programs that leverage Latinx students' cultural and linguistic assets, helping them see their background as an advantage in the global STEM workforce.
- Implement policies that support and fund culturally responsive STEM curricula and teacher training programs to better engage Latinx students and connect STEM concepts to their lived experiences.

These policy recommendations aim to increase Latinx youth's access to quality STEM education, provide practical experience, and create clear pathways to high-demand, high-wage careers in STEM fields. Continuous collaboration with the research community, school districts, and community organizations is critical to ensure these policies effectively address the needs of Latinx youth and lead to improved outcomes in STEM education and career readiness.

Notes

1 For example, the net median wealth is $0 for Boston-area Dominican households and around $3,000 for Puerto Rican households. Ana Patricia Muñoz, et al., *The Color of Wealth in Boston* (Federal Reserve of Boston, 2015), https://ssrn.com/abstract=2630261.

2 Laura M. Gonzalez, et al., "Latino Adolescent Educational Affiliation Profiles," *Hispanic Journal of Behavioral Sciences* 39, no. 4 (2017): 486–503; Deborah A. Santiago, Emily Calderón Galeano, and Morgan Taylor, *The Condition of Latinos in Education: 2015 Factbook* (Excelencia in Education, 2015).

3 Massachusetts Department of Elementary and Secondary Education, "District Analysis Review Tools (DARTs)," Massachusetts Department of Elementary and Secondary Education, 2023, https://www.doe.mass.edu/dart/.

4 Nancy E. Hill and Kathryn Torres, "Negotiating the American Dream: The Paradox of Aspirations and Achievement Among Latino Students and Engagement Between Their Families and Schools," *Journal of Social Issues* 66, no. 1 (2010): 95–112; Kristin Turney and Grace Kao, "Barriers to School Involvement: Are Immigrant Parents Disadvantaged?," *Journal of Educational Research* 102, no. 4 (2009): 257–71; Grace S. Woodard, et al., "The Effect of Child Gender, Parent School Involvement, and Parent

Language Use on School Functioning Among Trauma-Exposed Latinx Youth," *Hispanic Journal of Behavioral Sciences* 43, no. 3 (2021): 294–310.

5 Catalina Covacevich, et al., *Indicators of Teenage Career Readiness: An Analysis of Longitudinal Data from Eight Countries* (OECD Publishing, 2021).

6 Javier C. Vela, et al., "Using a Positive Psychology and Family Framework to Understand Mexican American Adolescents' College-Going Beliefs," *Hispanic Journal of Behavioral Sciences* 39, no. 1 (2017): 66–81.

7 Donna Maria Blancero, Edwin Mouriño-Ruiz, and Amado M. Padilla, "Latino Millennials—The New Diverse Workforce: Challenges and Opportunities," *Hispanic Journal of Behavioral Sciences* 40, no. 1 (2018): 3–21. See also Stephen M. Quintana and Nicholas C. Scull, "Latino Ethnic Identity," in *Handbook of U.S. Latino Psychology: Developmental and Community-Based Perspectives*, ed. Francisco A. Villarruel, Gustavo Carlo, Josefina M. Grau, Margarita Azmitia, Natasha J. Cabrera, and T. Jaime Chahin, 81–98 (SAGE Publications, 2009).

8 Blancero et al., "Latino Millennials."

9 Harold Manzano-Sanchez, et al., "The Influence of Self-Efficacy Beliefs in the Academic Performance of Latina/o Youth in the United States: A Systematic Literature Review," *Hispanic Journal of Behavioral Sciences* 40, no. 2 (2018): 176–209.

10 Elena Wilson, "Community-Based Participatory Action Research," in *Handbook of Research Methods in Health Social Sciences*, ed. Pranee Liamputtong, 285–98 (Springer Singapore, 2019).

11 V. Scott H. Solberg, Chong Myung Park, and Gloria Marsay, "Designing Quality Programs that Promote Hope, Purpose and Future Readiness Among High Need, High Risk Youth: Recommendations for Shifting Perspective and Practice," *Journal of Career Assessment* 29, no. 2 (2020): 183–204.

12 María Sanz-Remacha, et al., "A Community-Based Participatory Action Research with Women from Disadvantaged Populations: Strengths and Weaknesses of a Multiple Health Behaviour Change Intervention," *International Journal of Environmental Research and Public Health* 19, no. 11 (2022): 6830.

13 Chong Myung Park, Angelica Rodriguez, Jazmin Rubi Flete Gomez, Isahiah Erilus, Hayoung Kim Donnelly, Yanling Dai, Alexandra Oliver-Davila, et al. "Embedding Life Design in Future Readiness Efforts to Promote Collective Impact and Economically Sustainable Communities: Conceptual Frameworks and Case Example," *Sustainability* 13, no. 23 (2021): 13189.

14 Diley Hernandez, et al., "Dismantling Stereotypes About Latinos in STEM," *Hispanic Journal of Behavioral Sciences* 39, no. 4 (2017): 436–51; National Science Foundation, National Center for Science and Engineering Statistics, *Women, Minorities, and Persons with Disabilities in Science and Engineering* (National Science Foundation, 2017).

15 Richard Fry, Brian Kennedy, and Cary Funk, *STEM Jobs See Uneven Progress in Increasing Gender, Racial, and Ethnic Diversity* (Pew Research Center, 2021), https://www.pewresearch.org/science/2021/04/01/stem-jobs-see-uneven-progress-in-increasing-gender-racial-and-ethnic-diversity/.

16 Kassandra Hernández, et al., *Latinas Exiting the Workforce: How the Pandemic Revealed Historic Disadvantages and Heightened Economic Hardship* (UCLA Latino Policy and Politics Initiative, 2021).

17 Blancero et al., "Latino Millennials"; Zachary Giano, et al., "Parental Documentation Status and Educational Aspirations Among Latino Adolescents: Mediating Effects

of School Connectedness and Parental Attitudes Towards Education," *Hispanic Journal of Behavioral Sciences* 40, no. 3 (2018): 279–93; Manzano-Sanchez et al., "The Influence of Self-Efficacy"; Amanda Taggart, "Latina/o Youth in K-12 Schools: A Synthesis of Empirical Research on Factors Influencing Academic Achievement," *Hispanic Journal of Behavioral Sciences* 40, no. 4 (2018): 448–71.

18 Manzano-Sanchez et al., "The Influence of Self-Efficacy."

19 Ruth Sealy and Val Singh, "The Importance of Role Models and Demographic Context for Senior Women's Work Identity Development," *International Journal of Management Reviews* 12, no. 3 (2010): 284–300.

20 Ali Borjian, "Academically Successful Latino Undocumented Youth in College: Resilience and Civic Engagement," *Hispanic Journal of Behavioral Sciences* 40, no. 1 (2018): 22–36.

21 Catherine Cramer, et al., "NetSci High: Bringing Network Science Research to High Schools," in *Complex Networks VI (Studies in Computational Intelligence)*, ed. Giuseppe Mangioni, Filippo Simini, Stephen Miles Uzzo, and Dashun Wang, 209–18 (Springer International Publishing, 2015).

22 Solberg, Park, and Marsay, "Designing Quality Programs."

23 Covacevich et al., *Indicators of Teenage Career Readiness.*

24 Lorna Rivera, et al., "COVID-19 and Latinos in Massachusetts," Gastón Institute Publications 253 (2020), https://scholarworks.umb.edu/gaston_pubs/253.

25 "Interested in Advancing your Career in IT?," CompTIA, https://www.comptia.org/content/it-careers-path-roadmap.

26 Claire J. Schuch, Ligia M. Vasquez-Huot, and Wendy Mateo-Pascual, "Understanding Latinx Civic Engagement in a New Immigrant Gateway," *Hispanic Journal of Behavioral Sciences* 41, no. 4 (2019): 447–63.

27 Boston University Wheelock Center for Future Readiness, "Sociedad Latina STEAM PSA COVID-19 Vaccine Video," https://www.youtube.com/watch?v=h1crVLIjigo.

28 Borjian, "Academically Successful Latino."

29 Joseph A. Durlak, et al., "The Impact of Enhancing Students' Social and Emotional Learning: A Meta-Analysis of School-Based Universal Interventions," *Child Development* 82, no. 1 (2011): 405–32.

30 Richard F. Cantalano, et al., "Positive Youth Development in the United States: Research Findings on Evaluations of Positive Youth Development Programs," *ANNALS of the American Academy of Political and Social Science* 591, no. 1 (2004): 98–124; Amy Lopez, et al., "Development and Validation of a Positive Youth Development Measure," *Research on Social Work Practice* 25, no. 6 (2015): 726–36.

31 Pseudonyms have been used.

32 Esther J. Calzada, Yenny Fernandez, and Dharma E. Cortes, "Incorporating the Cultural Value of *Respeto* into a Framework of Latino Parenting," *Cultural Diversity and Ethnic Minority Psychology* 16, no. 1 (2010): 77–86.

33 Anthony Mann, Vanessa Denis, and Chris Percy, *Career Ready? How Schools Can Better Prepare Young People for Working Life in the Era of COVID-19* (OECD Publishing, 2020).

Chapter Fourteen

My Story and My Why

A Superintendent's Testimonio of Hope

ALMUDENA (ALMI) G. ABEYTA

Editor's Note

Bordering Boston, the City of Chelsea is a vibrant, multicultural urban community that is central to understanding the history of Latines in Massachusetts, and in particular, the tensions and opportunities related to Latine education. With a total area of just 2.46 square miles and approximately 41,000 residents,[1] Chelsea is considered the smallest city and the second most densely populated city in Massachusetts.[2] Historically recognized as a place where different waves of (im)migrant communities settled and have made significant contributions to the development of the Greater Boston area, Latinos started settling in Chelsea in significant numbers in the 1960s. Currently, 67% of residents are Latino; Salvadorans constitute the largest Latino subpopulation in the city, followed by Puerto Ricans, Hondurans, Guatemalans, and Dominicans.[3] Eighty-eight percent of Chelsea Public Schools (CPS) students are Latino, the second highest concentration of Latino students in the state.[4] Chelsea is also the home of many well-established community organizations, businesses, and social institutions that work to improve the lives of the residents. Local officials largely reflect these realities; for example, the majority of current School Committee members are Latinas. But this was not always the case.

Thirty years ago, when the Gastón Institute first published *The Education of Latino Students in Massachusetts* (1993),[5] the City of Chelsea was undergoing massive changes. In the summer of 1989, in a first-of-its-kind agreement, the Chelsea School Committee, with the support of the Massachusetts State Legislature, relinquished its governance power to a private institution to run its public schools: Boston University (BU). This decision was met with both support and outrage. CPS had a long history of not meeting the needs of students, and CPS and the City of Chelsea were accused of mismanagement and corruption.[6] In some circles, this agreement was perceived as an innovative approach to reforming the local public school system. However, as documented by Glenn Jacobs in *Latinos and Education Reform: The Privatization of Chelsea Public Schools* (1993),[7] the process of privatizing CPS was contentious as it failed to authentically engage its large Latino community. In response to the "BU takeover," Latino leaders and organizations across the city began to mobilize to develop accountability measures so that BU would not negate the needs, strengths, and visions of high-quality culturally responsive education for the city's Latino and immigrant children. These leaders and organizations were also organizing to prepare for when BU would leave, which occurred in 2008.

Whether CPS improved under the BU management continues to be a point of debate. At the time of the takeover in 1989, the city and its schools were on the verge of receivership due to mismanagement, including dilapidated school buildings, lack of school supplies and curricula, and low teacher pay. One of the first actions the BU management team took was to raise $116 million primarily sourced from the state for school construction, resulting in the opening of seven new school buildings in 1996. Investments were also made in early childhood education, the arts, and curriculum development. Despite these efforts, the school district continued to be labeled as "low performing" by the state. Consequently, the BU takeover concluded in 2008 with mixed outcomes and limited improvements.

This testimonio, by Chelsea School Superintendent Dr. Almudena (Almi) G. Abeyta, begins in 2020. Dr. Abeyta is the first Latina superintendent of CPS. She started in this role a few months before the COVID-19 pandemic. It is a testimonio grounded in strength, wisdom, and an unwavering belief in children, families, and communities. When she first considered applying for this role, Dr. Abeyta was discouraged by her colleagues, who pointed out the challenges of leading a district with so many achievement and opportunity gaps. But as Dr. Abeyta shared with us, "despite some of the discouraging remarks, I decided to apply for the job because this is a community that I wanted to serve—and that made my heart sing because this community is me."

MELISSA COLÓN

The year was 1956 when my paternal grandparents immigrated to the United States from Mexico. My father vividly remembers the day he came to live in the United States. He told me, "*Jita*, it was seven days before my twelfth birthday when we came to the States on November eleventh." For years, my father's family lived off a migrant worker's pay. In fact, he still has the wooden shoe box he made for shining shoes in Laredo, Texas. Years later, my father pursued education, and he is a beautiful example of using education as a vehicle to succeed in life. My forefathers' dreams and tenacity have instilled in me the essence of hard work and a devotion to education. It is my desire to pass on this legacy and gift to my own child and to the children who are under my care in CPS.

My mission in life is to ensure that my students receive a high-quality education that will give them access to higher education. I will do whatever it takes to fight this uphill battle because I am not that far removed. As a testimony of the work that I do in public schools, my daughter has always been enrolled in the schools that I lead. I strongly believe that if my schools are not good enough for my own child, then they are not good enough for other people's children. It is my hope that by passing on the gift of education, future generations will be impacted one life at a time.

Thus, when I see my students, many of whom are immigrants from Central America, I see my family. And my students see me as their family. For example, recently, I was sitting on stage during the Chelsea High School National Honor Society induction ceremony. Afterward, there was a reception in the school cafeteria. While at the reception, a high school senior came up to me and said, "Excuse me, can I talk to you? I was watching you on stage and you remind me of family. I feel like I can talk to you. I need to talk to you about some concerns I have with my AP statistics class." At that moment, I smiled inside because that was a special moment and truly is my why. This student related to me because I looked like *familia* to her. Representation matters. Our students need to see people who look like them in leadership positions; they need to see mirrors of themselves. Now this student and I have a sweet relationship, and she can reach out to me at any time. After I met with her, she said, "Thank you for listening to me. I feel better." In Chelsea Public Schools, we say, "We will know our students by name, strength, and story." This story is one that represents that to me. This was one of those proud mama superintendent moments I will always cherish.

The Superintendency

Prior to the pandemic, before my arrival at the superintendency, Chelsea Public Schools continued to struggle with student achievement but had begun to gain some traction. The elementary schools had finally pulled out of state monitoring for accountability, and the high school was showing signs of slight improvement. I was excited to get to work and begin crafting a five-year strategic plan to improve our schools. But, after just two months on the job, the COVID-19 pandemic hit the city of Chelsea. The pandemic magnified the harsh realities of achievement and opportunity gaps, food insecurity, student mental health, and gaps in technology access that disproportionately impacted Chelsea. Of all cities in the Commonwealth of Massachusetts, Chelsea was one of the cities hardest hit by the pandemic.

THE CITY OF CHELSEA'S RESPONSE TO COVID-19

I remember being horrified by the thought of calling a snow day when I first took the job of superintendent. But a pandemic? This was beyond what I could ever imagine. It is not as if there were a course in my superintendent training titled Pandemics 101. With just two months and thirteen days on the job under my belt on March 13, 2020, I closed the schools—at first for two weeks and then indefinitely. By March 16, 2020, we had organized to provide our community with meals and later that month distribute Chromebooks for remote learning. Our operations and food services staff efficiently established seven meal distribution sites at schools. This distribution of meals persisted from March 16, 2020, until we resumed full in-person operations in April 2021.

I distinctly recall a conversation in mid-April 2020 with our city manager at that time, Thomas G. Ambrosino, during the peak of the pandemic's impact. During that conversation, I conveyed to him that members of our food service team had tested positive for COVID-19 and some others were expressing reluctance to come to work, fearing exposure to the virus. At that point, several neighboring districts had already suspended their meal services due to staff falling ill with COVID-19. Consequently, I seriously considered closing our meal services as well. However, after discussing the situation with Mr. Ambrosino, he strongly urged me to continue providing meals due to the significant food insecurity prevalent in our city. As a compromise, we decided to reduce the number of meal sites from seven to three and implemented a staff rotation system to keep three sites operational.

Throughout the pandemic, I collaborated closely with our city officials and actively participated in weekly pandemic phone calls, which were sponsored by the City of Chelsea and held every Thursday. These calls brought together various stakeholders, including community partners, nonprofit organizations, city officials, the interfaith community, and the School Department. During these gatherings, we received regular updates on the latest COVID-19 rates in the City of Chelsea, while Mr. Ambrosino provided crucial information on food distribution, vaccinations, and COVID testing. These calls served as a valuable means to stay informed about all aspects of the COVID-19 situation. As a united community, we rallied together during this challenging time to offer support to our fellow Chelsea families and to one another.

In the summer of 2020, the Massachusetts Department of Elementary and Secondary Education required school districts to prepare plans for the reopening of schools. Thus, every superintendent in the State of Massachusetts worked tirelessly over the summer to plan for either fully remote, hybrid, or in-person learning. Not knowing what course the virus would take, we held community forums about school reopening. Many teachers attended the online community forums. They were frustrated, angry, and scared. I held several meetings to go over our school reopening plan and to listen to their concerns and answer questions. I was not prepared for the anger with which I was confronted. It was shocking. Never in my almost twenty-seven years in education had I been met with so much emotion. For example, this is a sample of a mass email we received on August 5, 2020:

> I never thought that I'd need to write to a School Committee member to help save my life and those of my colleagues, students, and their families in the midst of a global pandemic . . . but here we are. To put it simply, we can't go back to school in person yet. We want to, but we can't until it is safe and equitable for ALL. This means that the virus would be managed and tracked accurately within the state and in Chelsea (it's not), schools would be appropriately suited to protect students and staff (they're not), and staff would be part of the

decision-making process to reopen in person (we're not)....
We know Covid travels through air particles, and masks won't
keep us safe . . . The answer is clear: Vote Remote. Encourage the Committee to start thinking about and planning for
remote learning because it's inevitable.

Looking back, I came to understand that people were filled with fear
and uncertainty. But, at the time it was frustrating because we were all
trying to navigate the pandemic. When vaccinations became accessible, I
took the initiative and approached my city manager, requesting assistance
in securing vaccines for our educators. He worked with the East Boston
Neighborhood Health Center, which led to the successful vaccination of
our educators in March 2021. This significant step played a crucial role in
enabling us to resume in-person schooling for our students because we had
to ensure that our students and educators would be safe.

We continued to work with our city to vaccinate students when the
vaccines were available for students. We had lines of families coming to
our schools to get their children vaccinated. Our COVID-19 vaccination
rates for the city and the children in our city were among the highest in the
state. It was a community effort, with our nonprofit organizations offering
vaccinations almost every day from March 2021 until the end of the public
health emergency on May 11, 2023.

While waiting to get vaccinated, I had conversations with several high
school students who expressed their eagerness to be vaccinated. They mentioned having family members who had contracted COVID-19, which
motivated them to get vaccinated to safeguard themselves and protect their
families. It is worth noting that our community is home to many intergenerational families who live together, so our students did not want to spread
COVID-19 to their grandparents or extended families.

Our primary focus throughout the pandemic was the safety and well-being
of our students, families, and educators. I was fully aware that the return to
in-person learning would be a unique experience for our community. Together
with the School Committee, we made decisions with the utmost consideration
for the safety of everyone involved. Taking a cautious approach, we refrained
from rushing into immediate in-person learning. This decision was appreciated by many parents. Even when we resumed in-person classes in April

2021, only half of our families chose to return, as a significant number still harbored concerns about the safety of sending their children back to school.

The process of getting all our students back on campus took until September 2021, demonstrating our commitment to ensuring a safe and gradual return. Moreover, we maintained our mask mandate until January 2023, making us the last district in Massachusetts to lift it. This decision was another testament to our unwavering dedication to prioritizing the health and safety of our students, staff, and community members. The School Committee and I had to do what was best for Chelsea because our community was unique in being the hardest hit.

DUAL PANDEMICS

Shortly after COVID-19 hit our community, the country witnessed the murder of George Floyd on May 25, 2020. Then, superintendents across the country had to navigate "dual pandemics." Seven months later I found myself in an equity training session with my leadership team. The facilitator was really pushing us on issues of equity when I decided to make myself vulnerable with the team. I shared with the team that when we were having community conversations about the reopening of schools, I now realize that the anger toward us was really fear. Educators were fearful of getting COVID-19, spreading it, and bringing it home to loved ones. It was a scary time for all of us.

I wholeheartedly comprehended the situation, and throughout that period, I endeavored to lead my district with empathy, grace, and love. However, despite my efforts, I could not ignore the fact that I experienced complete disrespect at times, which was deeply hurtful. I am human, too. During a vulnerable moment in a professional development session, I could not help but wonder if the treatment I received would have been different had I been a White male superintendent. Would they have yelled at me in the same way? Would they have called me by my first name? I questioned whether part of the disrespect was linked to my name, "Dr. Almudena Guajardo Abeyta," and why do I have to ask myself such questions. It is disheartening to have these doubts and uncertainties.

During a School Committee meeting, educators raised concerns about the lack of retention of teachers of color and put the onus on me to retain teachers of color. Interestingly, despite the majority of educators being White in 2020, they expressed their frustrations toward the mostly Latino School Committee and the newly appointed Latina superintendent (myself). It was undoubtedly a challenging moment, and I had to gather strength to sit there during the public comment period of that School Committee meeting and hold the tears in as I said to myself, "Give me a chance. I just got here." Looking back on this situation three years later, I take pride in saying that Chelsea Public Schools is now leading Massachusetts in terms of educator diversity.[8] For example, as stated in the *Chelsea Record*, on October 1, 2023:

> 23.9 percent of CPS staff identify as people of color, an increase of 13.8 percentage points from its staffing data in 2019, when 10.1 percent of CPS staff members identified as people of color. Two key initiatives have been identified to account for this increase in educators of color: outlining the importance of this work in CPS' Strategic Plan for Improving Teaching and Learning for Every Student, Every Day as well as CPS' participation in DESE's Teacher Diversification Grant.[9]

To increase the diversity of educators we built pipeline programs internally. We now have parent-to-paraprofessional, paraprofessional-to-teacher, and teacher-to-administrator pipelines. We also focused on recruitment of educators of Color and retention through focusing on belonging and providing training in building a culture of belonging in our schools. We are proud of our diverse work, although we still have more work to do.

Although those events originating from the pandemic caused pain, I have chosen to forgive and lead with love. Nevertheless, questions still linger about the treatment and challenges we faced. I have dedicated countless efforts to reach this point in my career, obtaining two master's degrees and a doctorate, which should speak about my expertise and qualifications. However, it often feels as if my expertise is persistently questioned or challenged. These experiences have been disheartening and leave me wondering why I have to endure such struggles despite my twenty-seven years of experience in education and well-earned achievements. But I stay centered on my why––my students. This is legacy work, and I am helping change the trajectory of students' lives.

INCREASED FAMILY ENGAGEMENT AND TRUST DURING THE
COVID-19 PANDEMIC

In the fall of 2020, knowing that our students would be in remote learning, we did our best to connect with families. Since the COVID-19 virus rates were down in the summer of 2020, we decided to conduct what we called "trust visits." Trust visits were held outside on school playgrounds or on the sidewalks in front of homes. Our desire as a district was to connect with families and build relationships in person. During these trust visits, educators often met their students and learned about parents' hopes and dreams for their children. We held trainings in every school about the importance of these trust visits; it was to build relationships with families so that we would have increased engagement with students in virtual learning.

Engaging families was part of our equity work and a pillar in our five-year strategic plan. I believe that as educators we should work alongside our families in educating our children. During the pandemic, we witnessed parent engagement in teaching and learning at a whole new level because teaching happened in living rooms and bedrooms. As such, the steps we took as a district during the pandemic improved our parent and community engagement. We also learned that during the pandemic, parents were very engaged in school events over Zoom; thus, we have continued many of our parent meetings over Zoom because our families are busy. The ability to do this is definitely a silver lining of the pandemic for us!

Family and community engagement is viewed as a crucial lever for advancing equity. We are committed to giving families and schools the chance to build relationships with one another. For instance, the local newspaper, the *Chelsea Record*, captured the essence of our trust visits at the time:

> Open Houses and shaking the new teacher's hand—maybe chatting over coffee in the morning at the school building— have all been hallmarks for back to school in the Chelsea Public Schools to build relationships with parents, but COVID-19 has forced the district to think differently about such things.
>
> Therein was born a new initiative called "Trust Visits," and teachers and administrators all over the district are carrying out these visits this week as the staff and teachers prepare to return to learning remotely on Wednesday, Sept. 16.

"We're calling these trust visits because we're starting off the year remote" said Supt. Almi Abeyta. "It's an opportunity to reach out to our families and introduce ourselves. The teachers will go out in and into the community to meet families, or they will contact them via Zoom, or even on the phone. We wanted to be able to build trust up front."

Many of the teachers this week are conducting the trust visits across the city, and a good deal of them are in-person and socially distanced. Teachers and administrators talk to parents about how students learn, what their interests are, how they did during emergency remote learning, and if they have a ChromeBook/Wi-Fi . . . "Our goal is we'll have more kids plugged into remote learning and we'll be more successful with it," said Abeyta.[10]

Concluding Reflections

As I reflect on the first four years of my superintendency of the Chelsea Public Schools, I feel immense gratitude for the opportunity to lead in this beautiful community. Despite its small size, the Chelsea community displays incredible strength and unity during challenging times. The trials have drawn us closer to each other and made us stronger. I have also learned that creating diversity in our schools starts from the top. We must know our teachers and students by name, strength, and story!

I will forever cherish the Chelsea School Committee of 2019 for selecting me. This predominantly Latino committee recognized my Latina heritage as an asset and placed their trust in me. Their belief in me is something I will always be thankful for. When I was appointed in 2019, I was one of just three Latina superintendents in the state of Massachusetts. Leading in Chelsea, I have been able to be my authentic self, and my being Latina has been embraced and celebrated. As a result of my feeling that I belong, I am able to extend this to our students and their families as we strive to provide the high-quality education that our students deserve.

Notes

1   Phillip Granberry and Vishakha Agarwal, "Latinos in Massachusetts: Chelsea," Gastón Institute Publications 273 (2021), https://scholarworks.umb.edu/gaston_pubs/273.

2 It is important to note that community organizations have reported that there is a substantial population undercount largely due to the fears of undocumented residents with regard to completing the census forms.

3 Granberry and Agarwal, "Latinos in Massachusetts."

4 Massachusetts Department of Elementary and Secondary Education, "Enrollment Data (2022–23)—Chelsea (00570000)," Massachusetts Department of Elementary and Secondary Education, 2023.

5 Ralph Rivera and Sonia Nieto, *The Education of Latino Students in Massachusetts: Issues, Research, and Policy Implications* (University of Massachusetts Press, 1993).

6 Glenn Jacobs, "Latinos and Education Reform: The Privatization of Chelsea Public Schools," in *The Education of Latino Students in Massachusetts: Issues, Research, and Policy Implications*, ed. Ralph Rivera and Sonia Nieto, 88–105 (University of Massachusetts Press, 1993).

7 Glenn Jacobs, "Latinos and Education Reform."

8 "CPS Among State Leaders in Staff Diversity Growth Rate," *Chelsea Record* (Chelsea, MA), October 5, 2023, https://chelsearecord.com/2023/10/05/cps-among-state-leaders-in-staff-diversity-growth-rate/.

9 "CPS Among State Leaders in Staff Diversity Growth Rate."

10 Seth Daniel, "A Distant Welcoming: Back to School Preparation Brings in 'Trust Visits,'" *Chelsea Record* (Chelsea, MA), September 9, 2020, https://chelsearecord.com/2020/09/09/a-distant-welcoming-back-to-school-preparations-brings-in-trust-visits/.

Chapter Fifteen

Conclusion

LORNA RIVERA AND MELISSA COLÓN

*Rather than continuing to blame conditions outside of the
school as the sole or primary reasons for Latino students' failure, we need to create possibilities for their academic success
by focusing on school policies and practices that will improve
educational outcomes.*

—RALPH RIVERA AND SONIA NIETO[1]

In this concluding chapter of *Critical Perspectives on Latino Education in
Massachusetts*, we discuss the connections between the different issues and
research findings about Latinx students that were presented in previous
chapters and their implications for educational policies and practices. Each
of the contributing authors offered important theoretical and empirical evidence about the education of Latinx students while also peppering us with
important questions including, How can educators and practitioners use
this information to inform public policies and shape liberatory schooling
practices? What can be learned about asset-based approaches in education
and strengthening the cultural wealth of Latinx students? And what are
the implications of this work for national conversations about the state of
Latinx education in the US? In this concluding chapter, we also discuss what
further changes in policies, practices, and research are needed.

The chapters in this book make it abundantly clear that the educational
success of Latinx young people is critical to Massachusetts's future workforce
and economic prosperity. Yet the research presented also demonstrates
that Latinx students largely attend schools in districts with long histories
of educational disparities and increasing economic and racial segregation.

A June 2024 article in the *Boston Globe* highlighted the chronic racial/ ethnic segregation of students in Massachusetts public schools. In 2024, about one-fourth of all students in Massachusetts K-12 schools identified as Latinx, and there were twelve school districts where Latinx students make up more than 50% of the student population (Lawrence, Chelsea, Holyoke, Lynn, Springfield, Everett, Greater Lawrence Technical, Southbridge, Revere, Fitchburg, Marlborough, and Methuen). As discussed by Torres-Ardila, Fuentes, and Colón (chapter 1), Lawrence Public Schools, for example, have the highest concentration of Latinx students in the Commonwealth, accounting for 94.5% of all students in the district. Conroy and colleagues' research (chapter 7) further reveal the ongoing and systemically underre-sourced educational realities for Latinx students, especially in segregated school districts. They argue that despite the high Latinx student population, most of the teachers are White: "Both quantitative and qualitative research bears out this trend as WPS drifts toward more segregated schools with staff that is highly unrepresentative of the student population" (p. 158). Indeed, these patterns in Massachusetts mirror national trends showing that Latinx students are more likely to attend segregated public schools with teachers that do not reflect their diversity.[2]

All of the chapters in this book showed the urgency to better under-stand the specific strengths and experiences of different groups of Latinx students and that a nuanced asset-based educational policy and planning approach is necessary for addressing their needs. Our contributing authors have emphasized, for example, that the education challenges and strengths of newcomers are not the same as third- and fourth-generation Latinxs. Araujo Brinkerhoff (chapter 2) and Colón and Frau-Ramos (chapter three), for example, focus on the different experiences and educational outcomes for Brazilian and Puerto Rican students in Massachusetts. Further, the schooling contexts of Latinx students living in large urban centers like Worcester and Boston are different from those of Latinx students living in more rurally situated communities like Southbridge or Pittsfield, and the schooling experiences and contexts of Portuguese-speaking Brazilian students who are living in suburban Framingham are not the same as the Spanish-speaking Dominican students living in urban Lawrence. Indeed, more research is needed about subgroups of second-generation and third-generation Latinx students and the ways the structural factors that families encounter play a significant role in the degree to which they integrate into society. For example, where students' immigrant parents resided before migration, why they migrated, when they migrated, what happened during the migration process, and where they settled all affect the life outcomes for their children.

The Gastón Institute's October 2023 report on second-generation Latinos presents data that are both promising and concerning about the future generations of Latinx students in Massachusetts.[3] Their findings provide some evidence of intergenerational progress and intergenerational mobility between second-generation Latinx and their parents in Massachusetts. For example, with their increased educational attainment, second-generation Latinx experience less occupational segregation than Latinx typically experience in the Massachusetts labor force.

In addition to differences in race, ethnicity, culture, languages spoken, migration histories, generational status, and geographic dispersion of Latinx communities, there is a diversity of perspectives and intersectional identities that also matter for Latinx student success.[4] The chapters by Torres-Carrasquillo, Shapiro, and Rivera (chapter 10) and Krueger-Henney, Ali, and Dabal (chapter 12) discuss the deficit-based schooling practices that negatively affect the overall academic success of Latinx students. Too many Latinx students experience low expectations, discrimination, and hostile learning environments in schools, especially if they are Black, multilingual, low-income, or Muslim, have mental health issues, live with a disability, or identify as LGBTQIA+ youth. Contributing authors argue that having educators who understand Latino culture can make a positive difference for Latinx students. Latinx students benefit from having mentors and educators who look like them, who understand their cultural values, who speak their languages, and who hold high expectations and always encourage them to succeed. Unfortunately, there is a crisis nationally and locally in the recruitment and retention of teachers of color. In the United States, only 10.6% of teachers identify as Latino, and the numbers in Massachusetts are worse, where only 3.9% of teachers identify as Latino. In July 2024, the Educator Diversity Act was adopted by the Massachusetts state legislature with the goal of addressing racial/ethnic inequities in the educator workforce,[5] so these abysmal numbers will hopefully improve. More research will be needed to understand and monitor the impact of this legislation.

Other important educational public policies have been referenced throughout this book, and these new laws and policies are expected to have a positive impact on the quality of education for Latinx students in Massachusetts. For example, the Student Opportunity Act of 2019 overhauled the state's antiquated school funding formula and increased funding to school districts in communities such as Fall River, New Bedford, Brockton, Revere, Haverhill, Holyoke, Springfield, and Chicopee, where there are large Latinx student populations. In chapter 1, Torres-Ardila, Fuentes, and Colón discuss the continued differential access to high-quality education in public school districts where Latinx students are concentrated. As of 2024, the state's "chronically underperforming" districts were all Latinx-majority school districts.[6] Historically, these underperforming school districts received less funding compared to suburban districts and wealthier school districts. The Student Opportunity Act is expected to deliver $1.5 billion in additional annual state aid to local public schools, and hopefully these funds with remedy the many setbacks students suffered during the COVID-19 pandemic.[7]

As Berardino (chapter 6) and Conroy and colleagues (chapter 7) argue, some educational policies are at the root of the inequitable and detrimental educational environment experienced by Latinx students. A prime example is the Massachusetts Comprehensive Assessment System (MCAS) test, which is a graduation requirement for students. Bernardino writes, "Notably, the educational disparities faced by ELs in Massachusetts are so severe that aggregate measures of Latinx student outcomes will always skew lower than for any other ethnoracial groups in the state, creating the potential to entrench a stigma of Latinx students as 'underperforming'" (p. 117).

In November 2024, voters in Massachusetts will determine the fate of the MCAS high-stakes testing graduation requirement for students. The Massachusetts Teacher Association argues that "this ballot question would align Massachusetts with the 42 states that don't use a single, high-stakes test to deny diplomas to high school students. It would require instead that districts certify that students have demonstrated through satisfactory completion of coursework that they have mastered the skills, competencies and knowledge required by the state standards."[8] How the MCAS ballot initiative, if it is approved, will impact Latinx students remains to be seen. We do not know whether Massachusetts leaders will pursue alternative measures of student learning such as performance assessments and graduation portfolios similar to what other states and school districts have been doing. It is hoped that without the MCAS as a barrier to graduation then graduation rates may increase for underserved Latinx students and that their college enrollments may also improve.

Nationally, between 2000 and 2020, the number of Latinx students enrolled in US four-year institutions jumped from 620,000 to 2.4 million, a 287% increase. In the US 20% of students enrolled in higher education institutions were Latinx, but in the state of Massachusetts, only 12.3% of Latinx are enrolled in higher education.[9] Latinx high school graduates who do enroll in college attend community colleges at nearly twice the rate of Massachusetts high school graduates overall (about 40% as compared to 20% for all high school graduates). Therefore, community colleges are an essential incubator for higher education for Latinx students. While the number of Hispanic-serving institutions (HSIs) and emerging HSIs in Massachusetts is growing (23 in 2024), most of them are underresourced community colleges that too often are underprepared to serve Latinx students well, and have unacceptable retention and graduation rates.[10] As noted by Escalera in chapter 5, "Given the shifting demographics of the US population, and the growing Latinx population, colleges and universities nationwide and in Massachusetts are likely to see growth in Latinx students continue, but based on the student success equity gaps we currently see for Latinx students, how ready are we to create learning environments where Latinx students can thrive?" (p. 88).

Latinx immigrant students attending community colleges also face special challenges. Occhipinti and Sargent (chapter 11) discuss how Mount Wachusett Community College faculty and staff collaborated to develop and implement dual-language classes for Latine English learners (ELs). Massachusetts higher education institutions seem to be headed in a positive direction as evidenced by an inaugural conference held in July 2024 at Salem State University, "From Enrolling to Thriving: Transforming Hispanic and Minority Serving Institutions," which drew more than four hundred attendees and twenty-five Massachusetts college presidents who strategized on how to best serve Latinx college students in the Commonwealth.[11]

The Commonwealth of Massachusetts will continue to experience an increase in migrants, refugees, and asylum seekers needing more than just linguistic support; they need housing, legal, and health services as well. We must therefore consider how we address the current academic gaps in education for Latinx and other immigrant students while making space for new students and how we prioritize youth, educators, parents, policymakers, and community members to more effectively advocate for immigrant students' needs and desires. In chapter 2, Araujo Brinkerhoff discusses the strong collaborative efforts of organizations, such as Stories Inspiring Movement (SIM; formerly Student Immigrant Movement), the Brazilian Worker Center, and Centro Presente, to form the Massachusetts Tuition Equity Movement. In July 2023, Massachusetts lawmakers passed the Tuition Equity law that allows in-state tuition for students who have attended Massachusetts high schools for at least three years and earned a Massachusetts diploma. Latinx immigrant youth in Massachusetts will now have greater access to higher education.[12] This was an important victory for immigrant advocates, and to date twenty-five states now allow undocumented students to receive state financial aid.[13] In 2023, the Mass Reconnect program established free community college for all Massachusetts residents ages twenty-five and older.[14] And in 2024, Governor Healey signed a bill to make community college free for any Massachusetts resident without a bachelor's degree (regardless of age).[15] These free community college programs as well as the Tuition Equity Law have great potential to increase educational opportunities and expand college access and college success for Latinx students in the Commonwealth.

To ensure students develop linguistically and emotionally in a language different from the ones spoken at home and in their community spaces, there is a greater need for research to focus on dual and multilanguage programs. Chapters by Berardino (chapter 6) and Occhipinti and Sargent (chapter 11) offer strong evidence for the positive outcomes of dual-language instruction. Berardino (chapter 6) notes that despite much research exposing Sheltered English Immersion's (SEI) limitations as an approach to EL instruction, "93% of ELs are still in SEI programs" instead of dual-language programs which are considered to be more effective than SEI programs in a number of ways (Bernardino, p. 120). He argues that the state should "focus on providing programs and resources so that ELs can have access to high-level engaging content" (p. 131) and the state should implement a state seal of biliteracy as a policy and practice that can "promote multilingualism among all students" (p. 131), which involves strategizing to recruit more multilingual teachers.

The LOOK (Language Opportunity for Our Kids) Act was signed into law on November 22, 2017, and it gives Massachusetts school districts more flexibility to deliver language acquisition programs in addition to SEI such as dual-language and heritage language programs. The LOOK Act mandated the establishment of Parent Advisory Councils and that schools must collect more nuanced data about EL student outcomes.[16] The impact of the LOOK Act is not clear as its implementation has been criticized by immigrant student advocates as problematic and too many schools are still not adequately supporting the linguistic needs of immigrant students. Indeed, services for Massachusetts English learners, the majority of whom are Latinx, have been lacking even in some Latinx-majority school districts such as Boston.[17]

All of this book's chapters demonstrate how research can validate and legitimize the lived experiences of young Latinx students. Chapters by Escalera (chapter 5), Torres-Carrasquillo, Shapiro, and Rivera (chapter 11), Krueger-Henney et al. (chapter 12), and Rodriguez et al. (chapter 13) show the ways educators and practitioners can implement cross-ethnic solidarity-building activities in their classrooms and incorporate critical reflexivity practices in their teaching to amplify the cultural wealth of students. These chapters describe the development of a student-centered curriculum that acknowledges and values Latinx and other students' cultural backgrounds and experiences. As discussed earlier, these chapters also call for more Latinx educators and Latinx leaders in shaping educational policies and practices.

Several contributing authors also emphasize the important role of community-based organizations and community leaders in advancing Latinx student success. In Massachusetts, Latinx leaders and Latinx-serving nonprofits play impactful roles in supporting the education of Latinx students by offering social and academic enrichment in after-school settings and community development through education. For example, Rodriguez and colleagues (chapter 13) contribute to this body of knowledge by describing a community-based participatory action research at Sociedad Latina, a fifty-year-old community-based organization in Boston that provides education, leadership, and arts programs for Latinx youth.[18] Sociedad Latina partnered with Boston University to work with middle-school Latinx youth on developing their STEAM (Science, Technology, Engineering, Arts, and Math) skills and to provide a rich intersection of mentoring, culture and arts activities, STEM education, and career development for Latinx youth.

This book's three testimonios (chapters 4, 9, and 13), as well as chapters by Veloria (chapter 8) and Torres, Shapiro, and Rivera (chapter 10), highlight the role of caring teachers and faculty, practitioners, and leaders in embracing community cultural wealth in Latinx educational settings. Testimonios by Rosa (chapter 9), a former city councilor and School Committee member in Chelsea, Abeyta (chapter 14), a superintendent, and Santiago (chapter 4), an attorney advocate, all provide valuable insights based on their experiences as Latina leaders who center the voices of Latinx communities in education policies and practices.

As several authors have emphasized because of the unique cultures, languages, migration experiences, and differences among over twenty-five Latinx subgroup populations it is critically important to disaggregate the category of "Latino/Hispanic" when crafting education policy or designing pedagogical practice.[19] An "Act ensuring equitable representation in the Commonwealth" known as the Data Equity Bill was signed into law by Massachusetts Governor Maura Healey in August 2023. The Data Equity Law will allow state agencies to collect, organize, and assemble public data on major ethnic groups.[20] This law promises to present more accurate data about the different subgroups of Latinx populations so that we can more effectively address their specific community needs and improve their socio-economic status and quality of life. With more nuanced data we can inform new policies to advance Latinx student success in Massachusetts.

A discussion about the experiences of Latinx students in Massachusetts charter schools is not covered in this book. Understanding Latinx student experiences in charter schools is important because as noted earlier, Latinx students comprise the majority of students in the state's chronically underperforming school districts that include charters. In 2016, Massachusetts voters rejected a ballot initiative, the "Massachusetts Charter School Expansion Initiative, Question 2," that was aimed at lifting the cap on new as well as expanding existing charter schools. The only school districts in the Massachusetts Department of Elementary Secondary Education's history to have been placed under state receivership have been Latinx-majority school districts—Chelsea, Holyoke, Lawrence, and Southbridge. Charter schools in underperforming school districts offer an alternative for Latinx families, especially in the Commonwealth's gateway cities. Massachusetts public charter schools, however, are not serving Latinx ELs or students with disabilities well.[21] Gastón Institute researchers found that 71% of all Latinx students attend school in districts that are eligible for charter school seats and yet charter schools continue to underserve ELs. The EL population at charter schools differs from traditional public schools, with lower proportions of ELs with disabilities and students with higher levels of baseline English proficiency.[22] As suggested by Santiago (chapter 13) more research is needed to understand the experiences and the rights of Latinx multilingual ELs with disabilities and how best to serve this student population.

In addition to an increase in charter schools serving Latinx students, there has also been a dramatic expansion of early college initiatives, so more research will be needed to better understand the outcomes for Latinx students who participate in early college. The Massachusetts Department of Higher Education has developed the Massachusetts Early College Initiative, which targets underserved students, many of whom are Latinx, and as of March 2024, Massachusetts has fifty-three designated early college programs across sixty-one high schools and twenty-eight higher education institutions. Early college is being promoted to increase college readiness and college success for underserved Latinx students in Massachusetts and nationally, but we still do not know enough about the experiences of Latinx high school students who participate in early college programs, or how early college impacts other higher education outcomes.[23]

Finally, several contributing authors suggest we need more research about the negative long-term effects of the COVID-19 pandemic on Latinx schooling and youth mental health. We know that in Massachusetts during the COVID-19 crisis, Latinx students experienced increased responsibilities for childcare due to remote learning; increased caring for sick family members; increased hours as "essential" workers; limited access to computers and internet firewalls in housing developments; food insecurity and social isolation; limited access to health care and COVID-19 testing; and fear of accessing social services due to racist and xenophobic climate. We also know that for many Latinx children and youth, the COVID-19 pandemic is one of many crises that has disrupted their education. Massachusetts is not unique in this challenge as other states are also grappling with the aftermath of the pandemic. Without a doubt, additional research is needed about what schools can do to better support students who are contending with the effects of trauma.

While the focus of this book is on education in Massachusetts, these chapters reveal important contexts, experiences, and outcomes related to Latinx education that are relevant in all US educational systems. This book presents challenges and raises questions about the future of Latinx education beyond Massachusetts. We hope that our next generation of leaders will learn from Latinx students, and that student perspectives and knowledges will be heard, respected, and valued. We hope this book has presented opportunities for educators, practitioners, researchers, policymakers, and community leaders to reflect upon their own spheres of influence, to advocate for important policies affecting Latinx students, to identify new areas for research, to see the multifaceted identities of Latinx students, and to appreciate the complexities of Latinx education in Massachusetts. As the Latinx population continues to grow, the success of our Commonwealth and our country depends on it.

Notes

1 Ralph Rivera and Sonia Nieto, *The Education of Latino Students in Massachusetts: Issues, Research, and Policy Implications* (University of Massachusetts Press, 1993), 244.

2 "'It's heartbreaking': 225,000 Mass. Students Attend Substandard Segregated Schools, New Report Finds," https://www.bostonglobe.com/2024/06/10/metro/massachusetts -segregated-schools-report/; "Boston's Schools Are Becoming Resegregated," *Boston Globe*, August 4, 2018, https://www.bostonglobe.com/metro/2018/08/04/boston -schools-are-becoming-resegregated/brwPhLuupRzkOtSa9Gi6nL/story.html?p1= Article_Inline_Text_Link; Bruce Fuller, Yoonjeon Kim, Claudia Galindo, Shruti Bathia, Margaret Bridges, Greg J. Duncan, and Isabel García Valdivia. "Worsening School Segregation for Latino Children?" *Educational Researcher* 48, no. 7 (2019): 407–20.

3 Phillip Granberry and Mary Jo Marion, "Second-Generation Latino Immigrant Assimilation in Massachusetts," Gastón Institute Publications 310 (2023), https:// scholarworks.umb.edu/gaston_pubs/310.

4 Ivan Lozano, Phillip Granberry, and Trevor Mattos, "The Diversity and Dispersion of Latinos in Massachusetts." Gastón Institute Publications 226 (2017), http://scholar works.umb.edu/gaston_pubs/226.

5 "An Act Relative to Educator Diversity" (H.549/S.366), https://malegislature.gov /Bills/193/HD3621; US Department of Education, "Eliminating Educator Short- ages Through Increasing Educator Diversity and Addressing High-Need Short- age Areas" (US Department of Education, 2023). https://www.ed.gov/raisethebar /Eliminating-Educator-Shortages-through-Increasing-Educator Diversity#:~: text=As%20of%20the%202021%E2%80%932022,percent%20identify%20as%20Asian %2C%201; Madeline Will, "See How Diverse Your State's Education Workforce Is" *Education Week*, December 12, 2023, https://www.edweek.org/teaching-learning /see-how-diverse-your-states-education-workforce-is/2023/12.

6 An Act Relative to the Achievement Gap, signed into Massachusetts law in January 2010, requires districts with schools designated as underperforming (level 4) to begin a process for school turnaround designed to support the accelerated improvement of student achievement and a high-functioning learning environment for students within three years. https://www.doe.mass.edu/turnaround/level4/about.html#:~:text= Statewide%20System%20of%20Support%20(SSoS,Contact%20Us; Massachusetts Department of Elementary and Secondary Education, "Chronically Underperforming School Districts," https://www.doe.mass.edu/level5/districts/faq.html.

7 Massachusetts Department of Elementary and Secondary Education. Student Oppor- tunity Act (2019), https://www.doe.mass.edu/soa/.

8 Massachusetts Teachers Association, "Get the Facts," https://massteacher.org/current -initiatives/high-stakes-testing/ballot-question, Accessed August 12, 2024.

9 Lauren Mora, "Hispanic Enrollment Reaches New High at Four-Year Colleges in the U.S., but Affordability Remains an Obstacle," Pew Research Center (2022), https://www.pewresearch.org/short-reads/2022/10/07/hispanic-enrollment-reaches -new-high-at-four-year-colleges-in-the-u-s-but-affordability-remains-an-obstacle /ft_2022-10-07_hispaniceducation_02-png/.

10 Hispanic Association of Colleges and Universities (HACU), "Emerging Hispanic-Serving Institutions (HSIs) 2022–2023," (2024), https://www.hacu.net/images/hacu/OPAI/2024_EmergingHSILists.pdf.

11 Diane Adame, "Hispanic-Serving Colleges in Mass. Support Latino Students, but Some Schools Fall Short," *GBH News*, May 12, 2022, https://www.wgbh.org/news/education-news/2022-05-12/hispanic-serving-colleges-in-mass-support-latino-students-but-some-schools-fall-short; *Boston Globe*, "How to Champion Latinx College Students in Massachusetts," July 15, 2024, https://www.bostonglobe.com/2024/07/15/opinion/latinx-students-higher-ed-massachusetts/.

12 Massachusetts Department of Higher Education, "Celebrating Tuition Equity for Massachusetts Students," https://www.mass.edu/tuitionequity/home.asp, accessed August 12, 2024.

13 National Immigration Law Center, "Basic Facts About In-State Tuition," June 2024, https://www.nilc.org/issues/education/basic-facts-instate/.

14 Massachusetts Department of Higher Education, "Office of Student Financial Assistance/Massachusetts Department of Higher Education," https://www.mass.edu/osfa/programs/massreconnect.asp, accessed August 12, 2024.

15 Steve LeBlanc, "Massachusetts Governor Signs $58 Billion State Budget Featuring Free Community College Plan," *AP News*," https://apnews.com/article/massachusetts-budget-free-community-college-healey-signed-6719ebc4b9fd8964f214c6f7bc57d0f3, accessed August 12, 2024; Massachusetts Department of Higher Education. "Make Your Dream of Higher Education a Reality with MassReconnect," https://www.mass.edu/osfa/programs/massreconnect.asp.

16 Massachusetts Department of Elementary and Secondary Education, "Look Act Overview," https://www.doe.mass.edu/ele/look-act.html.

17 Deanna Pan. "Eight Members of BPS's English Learners Task Force Resign in Protest of District Inclusion Plan," *Boston Globe*, October 31, 2023, https://www.bostonglobe.com/2023/10/31/metro/bps-inclusion-plan-english-learners-task-force-resign/.

18 Sociedad Latina, "Programs & Impact," https://www.sociedadlatina.org/about, accessed August 12, 2024.

19 Trevor Mattos, Phillip Granberry, and Vishakha Agarwal, "¡AVANCEMOS YA!: Persistent Economic Challenges and Opportunities Facing Latinos in Massachusetts," Gastón Institute Publications 281 (2022), https://scholarworks.umb.edu/gaston_pubs/281.

20 https://malegislature.gov/Bills/192/H3115.

21 Michael Berardino, Lorna Rivera, and Trevor Mattos. "How Do Latino Students Fare in Massachusetts Charter Schools?: An Analysis of Student Outcomes, Enrollment, Teacher Preparation, and Discipline Across 10 Districts," Gastón Institute Publications 240 (2016), https://scholarworks.umb.edu/gaston_pubs/240.

22 Presentation at the Forum on Latino Students and Charter Schools held in Worcester, Massachusetts, on November 11, 2016; Berardino, Rivera, and Mattos, "How Do Latino Students Fare."

23 Massachusetts Department of Higher Education, "Massachusetts Early College Initiative," July 5, 2024, https://www.mass.edu/strategic/ec_home.asp; Benjamin Forman Simone Ngongi-Lukula, "Early College as a Force for Equity in the Post-Pandemic Era," *Mass Inc.*, April 2021, https://massincmain.wpenginepowered.com/wp-content/uploads/2021/04/MassINC-Early-College-as-a-Force-for-Equity-Report-Apr-14.pdf.

About the Contributors

Editors

Lorna Rivera, PhD, is the director of the Mauricio Gastón Institute for Latino Community Development and Public Policy and professor of Latino Studies and Leadership in Education at the University of Massachusetts Boston. Her work focuses on Latino student success, critical literacies, race/gender health inequities, and the role of education in the social determinants of health. She is the author of the award-winning book, *Laboring to Learn: Women's Literacy and Poverty in the Post-Welfare Era* (University of Illinois Press). She is currently a co-principal investigator on the project "Advancing Health Literacy to Enhance Equitable Community Responses to COVID-19," funded by the Office of Minority Health Disparities and the Boston Public Health Commission. Dr. Rivera serves on the Board of Trustees for the Anna B. Stearns Foundation and Fenway High School, Boston Public Schools, and she serves on the national board of directors for the Inter University Programs on Latino Research. She earned a doctorate and master's degree in sociology from Northeastern University and a bachelor of science in elementary education with specialization in social studies and language arts grades K–9 from DePaul University.

Melissa Colón, PhD, is an assistant professor of urban education, leadership, and policy studies at the University of Massachusetts Boston. Her research largely focuses on the educational lives of Black and Latine youth and what their experiences can teach us about how race and gender in the shape of ideologies, policies, and programs are lived in schools. Prior to her current role at UMass Boston, Melissa was an associate professor at Bunker Hill Community College, where she also served as the faculty co-facilitator of the Latinx Students Success Initiative (LSSI). Melissa has served as a public school middle and high school humanities teacher, community organizer, and nonprofit leader, including serving as the executive director of Iniciativa: The Educational Initiative for Latino Students. Melissa holds a bachelor's in secondary education and history from Boston College as well as a master's in public policy and a doctorate in child studies and human development, both from Tufts University.

Contributing Authors

Almudena G. Abeyta, EdD, has spent over twenty-seven years working to improve teaching and learning for students in urban communities. She is currently the superintendent of Chelsea Public Schools. Dr. Abeyta earned a bachelor's degree in communications and journalism from the University of New Mexico-Albuquerque, two master's degrees, and a doctorate from the Harvard Graduate School of Education.

Cristina Araujo Brinkerhoff, PhD, is a researcher and lecturer at Boston University School of Social Work and a member of the board of directors of the Brazilian Workers Center. Dr. Brinkerhoff earned a bachelor's in sociology and a master's in applied sociology from UMass Boston and a doctorate from the School of Social Work at Boston University.

Nasteho Ali is a middle school teacher in Boston Public Schools and a graduate student at Northeastern University. Previously, she was the civic engagement coordinator for a nonprofit called ACEDONE, which works with East African families and refugees in the Greater Boston Area.

Michael Berardino, PhD, is an education policy researcher specializing in equity issues. His work focuses on racial equity, multilingual learn-ers, and the development of more equitable and inclusive assessment and instructional practices. Dr. Berardino holds a BA in government from Georgetown University and both an MS and PhD in public policy from UMass Boston.

Alex Briesacher, PhD, is an associate professor of sociology at Worcester State University specializing in race and ethnicity and social psychology. Dr. Briesacher has a master's in sociology from Southern Illinois University and a doctorate in sociology from Kent State University.

Thomas Conroy, PhD, is a professor of urban studies and the director of CityLab at Worcester State University, a research institute in urban studies dedicated to community-engaged scholarship with interdisciplinary teams of university faculty and students. Dr. Conroy has a master's and a doctorate in history from UMass Amherst.

Judenie Dabel, MA, is a mental health counselor. She was the youth program coordinator for the Center to Support Immigrant Organizing, where she co-coordinated the Youth Ubuntu Project. She has a bachelor's in social psychology, a minor in women, gender, and sexualities studies, and a master's from New York University Steinhardt in counseling for mental health and wellness.

Liya Escalera, PhD, is a lecturer on education at the Harvard Graduate School of Education. Her current work focuses on the design and assessment of asset-based learning environments that value the strengths and ways of knowing diverse students, faculty, staff, and community members. Dr. Escalera holds a master's in English from Simmons College, a master's in higher education from the Harvard Graduate School of Education, and a doctorate in higher education from UMass Boston.

Luis Enrique Esquivel is a doctoral student in the Counseling Psychology and Applied Human Development Department at Wheelock College of Education and Human Development (Boston University), where he specializes in designing strategies in education and sport psychology that optimize positive youth development.

Deyja Enriquez is a doctoral student in the Counseling Psychology and Applied Human Development Department at Wheelock College of Education and Human Development (Boston University), where she specializes in sport and performance psychology.

Isahiah Erilus is a program coordinator at Sociedad Latina in Boston's Mission Hill neighborhood. He has a bachelor's in marketing with a minor in English communication from Massachusetts College of Liberal Arts.

Nyal Fuentes is a college and career readiness coordinator at the Massachusetts Department of Elementary and Secondary Education. He earned an associate's degree from Cape Cod Community College, a bachelor's in history from Framingham State College, a master's in Secondary Education from UMass Boston, and a CAGS from UMass Amherst in educational policy, planning, and administration.

Jazmin Rubi Flete Gomez graduated from the University of Notre Dame with a bachelor's degree in Romance languages and literature. Her passion for education stems from knowing the difference an educational opportunity can make in the life of a child and their community, as it did for herself, the daughter of Caribbean immigrants.

Manuel Frau-Ramos, EdD, is an educational leader, teacher, researcher, and journalist who co-founded *El Sol Latino*, the oldest Latinx owned media in Western Massachusetts. He has a master's in economics from the University of Puerto Rico–Río Piedras and an EdD from UMass Amherst. He was a founding member of the Puerto Rican Studies Association and published extensively on topics related to Latinxs in Western Massachusetts, Puerto Rico, and Puerto Ricans.

Kimberly A. S. Howard, PhD, is an associate professor of counseling psychology and applied human development at Boston University's Wheelock College of Education and Human Development, where she serves as director of training of the counseling psychology doctoral program. She has a master's and doctorate in counseling psychology from Boston College and a bachelor's in psychology from Johns Hopkins University.

Patricia Krueger-Henney, PhD, is an associate professor at UMass Boston in the urban education, leadership, and policy studies doctoral program. She has a doctorate from the City University of New York. Before entering academia, Patricia taught social sciences in high schools and organized with youth communities around issues of injustice. Her research interests respond to the power and wisdom of young people.

Steven Lue is a high school student in the Boston Public Schools.

Mary Jo Marion is the associate vice president for University and Community Engagement for Academic Affairs at Worcester State University (WSU). She oversees the Latino Education Institute, Binienda Center for Civic Engagement, and Office of Multicultural Affairs at WSU. She holds a master's in public policy studies from the University of Chicago and a bachelor's in government and Spanish from Suffolk University.

Timothy E. Murphy, PhD, is an associate professor of urban studies at Worcester State University. He has a doctorate and master's degree in anthropology from the University of California Davis and a bachelor's in French communication and culture from Indiana University Bloomington.

Cecilia Nardi is the director of community relations in the Office of Government and Community Affairs at Boston University. She earned a master's in urban and environmental policy planning from Tufts University and a bachelor's in political science from Fordham University.

Laurie Occhipinti, PhD, is the dean of liberal arts, social sciences, and education at Mount Wachusett Community College. She earned a master's and doctorate in cultural anthropology from McGill University and a bachelor's in anthropology from UMass Amherst.

Alexandra Oliver-Davila has served as the executive director of Sociedad Latina since 1999. Through her grassroots community-based approaches, she has forged cross-sector collaborations with colleges, hospitals, businesses, foundations, and schools to offer youth greater access and opportunities to thrive. She has a master's in public policy from Tufts University and a bachelor's in political science and government from Emmanuel College.

Chong Myung Park, EdD, is a research scientist in counseling psychology and applied human development at Boston University. She earned an EdD in educational leadership policy studies and an MEd in policy, planning, and administration from Boston University. She also received BA and MA degrees from Ewha Woman's University.

Angelica Rodriguez is a program director at Sociedad Latina, where she oversees the implementation of their Pathways to Success programming, supervises management staff, and liaises with partners. She earned a bachelor's in music, with a minor in women's, gender, and sexuality studies, and a master's of education, with a track in learning, teaching, and education transformation from UMass Boston.

Marta T. Rosa is president of MTR Consulting Services. She has served in many leadership positions in government, education, and human services organizations and was the first elected Latina in the Commonwealth of Massachusetts. Most recently she served as the executive vice president and special assistant to the president at Roxbury Community College. She earned a master's in education from Cambridge College.

Diana Santiago is a senior attorney with Massachusetts Advocates for Children. She earned a JD from Northeastern University School of Law, a master's in public health from Tufts University, and a bachelor's in legal studies from UMass Amherst.

Melissa Sargent is the dean of academic affairs at Mount Wachusett Community College, where she has worked for thirty-one years to support new ideas for the students of North Central Massachusetts. She holds a master's in adult and higher education administration from the University of South Dakota.

Ester Shapiro, PhD, is an associate professor of psychology at UMass Boston, a research associate at Gastón Institute, and core faculty in the clinical psychology doctoral program and in the critical ethnic and community studies program. She earned her doctorate from UMass Amherst.

V. Scott H. Solberg, PhD, is a professor at the Boston University Wheelock College of Education and Human Development. He has a doctorate in counseling from the University of California Santa Barbara.

Fabián Torres-Ardila, PhD, is the associate director of the Gastón Institute for Latino Community Development and Public Policy at UMass Boston. He has many years of experience providing professional development to STEM teachers who work with English-language Learners and conducts research on educational policies that impact Latino students and communities in Massachusetts. He has a doctorate in mathematics from Boston University.

Ashley Torres Carrasquillo, MS (pronouns: they/she, elle/ella), is originally from Santurce, Puerto Rico. Ashley is an educator, collaborative researcher, and activist-scholar. They hold a master's degree in critical ethnic and community studies from UMass Boston. Currently, Ashley is an art-based educator and organizer with the Dominicans Love Haitians Movement. They also teach in the Ethnic Studies Department at CU Boulder and coordinate the political-education program at Mijente.

Paul Trunfio is a senior research scientist and director of the Science Education Lab in the Complex Systems Collaborative in the Department of Physics at Boston University. He is a principal in data and network science in the K–20 Education Collaborative.

Carmen N. Veloria, EdD, is an associate vice president for academic affairs at Central Connecticut State University (CCSU). Prior to CCSU, she worked at Suffolk University in Boston, where she was a tenured professor in the Sociology Department and served as chair of the Education Department. She holds a bachelor's degree in political science from CCSU, a master's degree in education from Boston College, and a doctoral degree in language, literacy, and culture from UMass Amherst.

Heilam Xie is a high school student in the Boston Public Schools.

Index